A Short History of the Civil War

Ordeal by Fire

Fletcher Pratt

Maps by Rafael Palacios
New Preface by David Madden

DOVER PUBLICATIONS, INC.
Mineola, New York

Bibliographical Note

This Dover edition, first published in 1997, is an unabridged and slightly corrected republication of the revised second edition as published by William Sloane Associates, Inc., New York, 1948, under the title *Ordeal by Fire*. The work was originally published by Harrison Smith and Robert Haas, Inc., New York, 1935. The new Preface was prepared specially for this edition.

Library of Congress Cataloging-in-Publication Data

Pratt, Fletcher, 1897–1956.
    [Ordeal by fire]
    A short history of the Civil War: ordeal by fire / Fletcher Pratt; maps by Rafael Palacios; new preface by David Madden.
        p.   cm.
    Originally published: Ordeal by fire. Rev. 2nd ed. New York: W. Sloane, 1948.
    Includes index.
    ISBN 0-486-29702-0 (pbk.)
    1. United States—History—Civil War, 1861–1865. I. Title.
E468.P83   1997   97-4264
973.7—DC21   CIP

Manufactured in the United States of America
Dover Publications, Inc., 31 East 2nd Street, Mineola, N.Y. 11501

PREFACE TO THE DOVER EDITION

Although the evolution of the Great Depression may be traced back to the Civil War and the Reconstruction era, especially in the South, the Thirties was not a great decade for nonfiction about the Civil War. Fiction flourished in that decade; even so, Fletcher Pratt's *A Short History of the Civil War*, published as *Ordeal by Fire* in 1935, reached the kind of audience that one year later embraced *Gone With the Wind*, this century's best-selling Civil War novel. When a revised second edition was published in 1948, the great era of Civil War book publishing that began with the onset of the Centennial years had not yet begun. For almost three decades, then, Pratt's short history stood as this nation's most appealing introduction to what happened at the crossroads of its history.

Part of Pratt's appeal was that he rejected the pretentions of more scholarly writers. His original subtitle for the book was "An Informal History of the Civil War." The first edition's "Preface for the Nonmilitary Reader," a lucid explanation of military organization, put all other readers on notice that anyone looking for a footnote would, to mangle Twain, be shot. Pratt's forceful prose style was forged in journalism and general nonfiction projects, always aimed at the man in the street. Readers find in his book no academic apparatus, not even a bibliography. The narrative drive and the muscular style carry the reader along at a rapid pace through relevant facts and trenchant insights.

The absence of traditional academic trappings in *A Short History of the Civil War* is more than made up for by the author's enthusiasm for his subject, an enthusiasm he brought to all his projects. In only two decades Pratt, who called himself a "literary mechanic," published over fifty books on an impressive variety of subjects, from the Napoleonic wars to Japanese card games. Naval history was his forte. His first book, *The Heroic Years*, a history of the Madison administration and the War of 1812, opened his great campaign of providing the American public with popular military histories. *Hail Caesar!* demonstrated his ability to write convincingly of military events in other times, other places. During the Forties his books explained World War II to the American people; in the Fifties he wrote several more Civil War books: *The Monitor and the Merrimac* (1952); *Stanton, Lincoln's Secretary of War* (1953); *The Civil War in Pictures* (1955), one of the first modern picture books of which we now see a multitude; and *Civil War on Western Waters* (1956, the year of his death). He left a finished manuscript that was published in 1957, another attempt to give the average reader a sweeping, dramatic view of a vast subject in a short reading experience: *The Compact History of the United States Navy*. To the end he maintained a style, stance and follow-through technique that suggested his early days as a prize fighter.

Fletcher Pratt was born in Buffalo, New York, on April 25, 1897. He died at Long Branch, New Jersey, June 10, 1956. In the years between he was a college drop-out who managed to become a public and a corporate librarian, a reporter and a free-lance writer for true-crime magazines and for various trade, naval and military journals. In 1926 he married the artist Inga Stephens. In the late Twenties he began writing fiction, helping to pioneer the science-fiction genre. He also translated many books into French and German. Bearded, spouting pipe smoke, for almost twenty years the "Dean of Nonfiction" was a star attraction, along with Robert Frost, Bernard De Voto and Wallace Stegner, as a lecturer at Middlebury College's Bread Loaf Writers' Conference, where he was prone during the early Forties to discuss the war then raging. (One of his students was Isaac Asimov, who was to write over four hundred books.) Pratt made time to become eccentric, collecting and raising monkeys. Bernard De Voto spoke of him affectionately as "half genius, half rodent."

Considering the impressive academic credentials and affiliations of the vast army of Civil War historians who thrived before, during and after his time, the question arises whether one should include Pratt as a member of that tribe. The Civil War was only one of his subjects. Although he was a war correspondent and an advisor on military affairs during World War II for *Time, Fortune* and *The New York Post*, his contribution to Civil War studies had best be put into perspective. "Popularizer" is a somewhat odious term, until one looks closely at its implications. Historians and archivists attribute the recent upsurge of interest in the Civil War (not all of it, by any means, superficial) to the popularity of Burns's controversial documentary of the late Eighties, and especially to the segments that feature Shelby Foote, the author first of a Civil War novel, *Shiloh,* and then of the ultimate popular history of the war, a three-volume work that seems massive when compared with Pratt's 410 pages. The academic and the popular historian each has a place and function, and in each camp the quality and impact varies; I place Pratt at the top of the list of popular historians working in the shorter form. Responding to the appeal of the Civil War, many readers begin with something short; armed, they then step off to march the longer distance.

Pratt's was the first history of the war I ever read. On a plane to Omaha, Nebraska, February 27, 1979, I opened a paperback version and plunged into thirteen years of research on the Civil War for my novel *Sharpshooter,* research that also inspired the concept of the United States Civil War Center. Pratt's book remains one of the most stirring histories I have read. Not a single page of static prose impedes the pace. And reading his short history of the war, I experienced a sense of Pratt's having read *many* histories of the war.

At first I thought that Pratt was very pro-North. On rereading I experienced an evenhandedness. It occurred to me that when we read certain books for the first time, we are reading two simultaneously: the one we expect, and the one the author wrote.

Perhaps I diminished whatever powers of persuasion I may have when I revealed that Pratt's was the first history of the Civil War I ever read. I was indeed impressionable. But since then I have read many histories and many topical books on the war; *A Short History* holds its own against them, and I certainly now have a basis for comparison. But what exactly am I comparing? Research ability, thorough documentation? No, Pratt calls his "An Informal History of the Civil War." What struck me, and perhaps De Voto as well as Pratt's publishers Harrison Smith and William Sloane, was the man's lunging style and pugnacious sensibility, his conceptual power. These are all qualities that De Voto, Sloane, Robert Frost, Theodore Morrison and other writers, editors, fellows and students at Bread Loaf Writers' Conference saw in action over two decades. "Command of word and language, mastery of a proper rhetoric or style. My impression," wrote Theodore Morrison in his history of the first thirty years of Bread Loaf, "is that Fletcher talked more about this topic than any other staff member." For reasons other than my own, then, Fletcher's colleagues, too, were impressionable.

But I offer an even more impressive authority, a young teacher from West Virginia who approached me twelve years ago, after I had given a lecture on hard-boiled novelist James M. Cain, to ask if I had read Fletcher Pratt's *Ordeal by Fire*. My affirmative nod set him off on a thirty-minute ramble through the book as he recited, in fine voice, his favorite passages, introducing each with the command "Listen to this!" I did, with a racing pulse. "[General John C.] Frémont was a character out of a Victorian novel—soulful eyes and waving hair, a universal genius who stunned his contemporaries by learning Hungarian and marrying the fairest heiress of the west, the daughter of that formidable old Roman, Thomas Hart Benton…[he] turned up in St. Louis at the end of July, bareheaded in Arsenal Square with a drawn sword in one hand and an American flag in the other—ineffably poetic, ineffably patriotic."

We, he and I, are not alone in our devout belief. "This," said Bernard De Voto, "is the best one-volume history of the Civil War I've ever read." My words exactly. Had enough people believed that over the past six decades, I wouldn't have to back up that declaration now. Harrison Smith and Robert Haas believed it when they published Pratt's history in 1935, with sixteen illustrations by Merritt Cutler. Readers who kept it alive by word of mouth and made it a collector's item when it fell out of print believed it. William Sloane believed it when he published the revised edition in 1948, with fifty new maps by Rafael Palacios—the text reprinted here. Forget that De Voto and Sloane taught with Pratt at Bread Loaf Writers' Conference during the time he wrote the book. Pocket Books believed it when in 1951 they published a paperback edition of the Sloane version as *A Short History of the Civil War*, with four printings in four years. The editors at Harpers and Bantam believed it when they picked up paperback rights in 1966 and 1968. I will go further now as one who admires several other short histories and declare that this work is the most powerful of all short histories of the Civil War published since the Depression. It is the book I chose to present as a rediscovery in a forthcoming book of essays about neglected nonfiction masterworks.

Pratt's style is the main indication that he was speaking to the public of the Depression years, imagining his readers to be the same as those he'd had as a reporter and popular-magazine writer of both short stories and articles. His style is slam-bang, staccato—as if the James Cagney of *Public Enemy* had taken the reader by the arm and said, "Okay, this is how it's going to be—I talk, you listen—got it?" Pratt's style sounds less like that of Pulitzer Prize-winning historian Douglas Southall Freeman than like the first-person voices of James M. Cain's Frank Chambers, Hammett's Sam Spade or Chandler's Philip Marlowe. It is interesting to note that Pratt's contemporary, the Civil War novelist McKinlay Kantor, wrote one of the first gangster novels, *Diversy* (1928).

Pratt talks tough directly to his reader. He says, "Lesson—never kick a man when he's down," then tells how some Union soldiers, refused food when passing through Jackson as prisoners, returned and burned the town down. "Pay attention," he seems to say, with such lines as "What happened was this—" and "Understand the picture; it was in the darkest hour . . . " He gets his reader's attention with such chapter openers as this: "You shall not imagine, either, that all is abounding grace and united effort within the Confederacy . . . Not even Robert Lee is immune . . . proving, if you will, how war acts on the intelligence like the curved mirrors of a hall of grotesques." Another chapter opens this way: "What to make of Ulysses Grant, behind the black cigar . . . his pockets blistered with the letters he never answered?" He quotes criticisms of Grant, then responds: "Wrong! . . . Also write down this about him; he was never jealous or envious of any man." Sometimes he taunts the characters in his narrative in that hard-boiled tone: "Be content, General Bragg, it was a Confederate victory . . . A victory—that cost the victors 23,000 in killed and wounded, the heaviest butcher's bill of the war." Pratt delighted in paradox.

One could follow the passages on Lincoln, Grant, Lee or any other major figure throughout Pratt's book and accumulate a vivid and memorable portrait of him. Pratt's admiration of Stanton, about whom he later wrote a book, is especially clear: "So Stanton, the terrible Stanton, the man of iron, who solved all problems by rule of mathematics and a violent tongue, became Secretary of War. He feared neither God nor man nor devil, only Abraham Lincoln . . . But he was one of the great war ministers of history . . . On the Confederate side they had only Judah P. Benjamin, who spun endless iridescent cobwebs of theory and argument, brilliant as rainbows."

Pratt gives his reader images charged with emotion: "That night Stuart's horse rode into the rebel camp [at Gettysburg], eager but so fagged after their longest raid that men fell asleep while their horses were crossing a fence." He paints group portraits in lightning strokes: "Beyond the river the young Turks gathered round General Lee—Ewell with his piping krawk, jovial Early booming like a cannon behind a fog of beard, gay Stuart, the heart-breaker, all stars and grace, a song on his lips . . . " When his men cheered Thomas' promotion, "the new general of the Army of the Cumberland pulled his hat down on his nose to hide his school-girl blushes."

All the devices of rhetoric are at Pratt's command. Repetition carries the reader quickly through long paragraphs of analysis to a full grasp of the concept: "Admit freely that Lincoln botched his part in the Peninsular campaign. Admit he twice withheld McDowell's 40,000 when they might have struck to a decision; admit he tried to trip Jackson with an elaborately silly map maneuver which ignored not only time, distance and arithmetic but also the psychological element . . . The onus for the failure, nevertheless, must rest upon the young Napoleon" [General McClellan].

His metaphors enable Pratt to give the reader the facts, make the narrative stroke and convey a feeling about the action: "Sherman dangled at Atlanta, a trapeze performer perilously suspended over nothing at the end of a single wire of railroad. Cut the line, he must perish." Pratt was a master of succinct phrasing: "The Confederate government had been and was not . . . "

Pratt's ability to sustain a narrative pace that keeps the reader engaged is a major factor in the success of this short history of the war: "Grant rode through the press, straightening out the sagging lines, directing artillery here, reorganizing a company there, the calmest man on the field. His horse was killed under him; he got another. A bullet took his hat off; he fought bareheaded; another went through his coat . . . " His style enables him to present a major action with brevity but impact: "A tall officer rode among them, the soul of their stand; some rebel sharpshooter drew a bead on him, and down he went, shot through the head. It was Reynolds . . . " That tall officer was a major loss early at Gettysburg.

The pace of the narrative is quickened by Pratt's effective transitions. Pratt ends the Vicksburg chapter this way: "Lincoln proclaimed exultantly, 'The Father of Waters once more flows unvexed to the sea.'" Following that famous quotation he begins the next chapter with a simple line: "There was a man named Bickley." Another technique ends one chapter with a general narrative set-up: "So Grant went down into Virginia . . . [Sherman] was set free at last" to take Atlanta; he begins the next chapter with a general statement: "What followed was the greatest campaign in American history, one of the greatest in any history." (Readers may enhance their appreciation of Pratt's narrative thrust by comparing his key battle scenes with those in other short histories, written before, during and after his time.)

Pratt knew his readers would enjoy trenchant comparisons and contrast: "Lee's one defect as a leader was that there was something unearthly about the man's best moments . . . Lincoln, on the other hand, would have delighted Machiavelli"; "The North obtained its monarchial singleness of control by combination; the South essayed to obtain it through personality, but it moved too slowly."

Pratt knew just when and how to deploy a brief anecdote: "Curious symbolic note—as Sherman rode through a plantation yard he saw a book lying in the mud and dismounted to rescue it. It was a copy of 'The Constitution of the United States' and on the flyleaf was written 'My Property—Jefferson Davis.'" Another example: "The lament of Van Dorn." Catching his wife in bed with the general, a doctor blew Van Dorn's brains out, "which was too bad for the Confederacy as the brains had been better than most in the Confederate west." He was adroit in the use of quotations, as when he reports that Frémont remarked on the suggestion that Grant be promoted, "I am not sure General Grant has the requisite force of character."

Having carried the reader along at a rapid narrative pace in a hard-boiled style, tough guy Pratt would sometimes do what he must have been told not to do—he judged conduct: "Burnside, the personality expert, raging alternately at the 'thieving poltroons' who composed his army and the 'cowardly scalawags' who led it, was proposing to ride up Marye's Heights alone with his staff. They should have let him. It was not till night that he began to weep." Lee sent supplies to his starving army by train, but the politicians "changed the destination of the train to Richmond, threw the food off and loaded it with their archives. Archives! Lee's men had nothing to eat." Unaffected scorn there and here: "Let Longstreet take his corps on a flying march to Knoxville and capture the force Burnside had there as well, how Napoleonic! Psychology is a wonderful thing, but the two Napoleons erred by the calendar . . . "

In his introduction to this edition, Pratt quotes one of the major German military leaders of the years before World War I, who urged the study of the campaigns of the American Civil War; the German military most likely carried those studies on into World War II. Pratt recognized the importance of studying that history, realizing that "the tactics and even the strategies developed in those campaigns in America controlled all subsequent wars down to the beginning of the atomic age." He was the man to write short histories of both World Wars. Too bad he did not.

Pratt's remains the best short history of the Civil War for beginners, even though an academic may cite mistakes and omissions. This Dover edition enables Pratt to capture such readers; let more academic scholars lead Pratt's readers into deeper territory. For those who have read every book on every aspect of the war, Pratt's value is that he is a source of pure enjoyment as one listens to his commanding voice. "Sit still and listen and let the words carry you along," Pratt's veteran reader will tell you.

Fine sounding words alone can not empower a book as Pratt's history is empowered. Pratt had the kind of conceptual and intellectual imagination that I craved in those early days before I had gathered unto myself 4,000 other books on the war. On a Trailways bus from Jacksonville to Tallahassee I read this passage: "What Lee attacked at Glendale was an armed mob; what he attacked at Second Bull Run was a group of quarrelsome old men; at Chancellorsville, he attacked a man; but at Gettysburg he came into collision with a system." A simple action is stated in such a way as to present a concept of Grant: "The bankrupt tanner left the room military dictator of a territory larger than Europe . . . "

Describing an action of Lee's, Pratt slides into a conception of Grant and Sherman in relation to that general. "General Lee smiled and turned to give orders for the march. An impecunious leather-dealer named Grant sat at that moment in a street-car in St. Louis, gazing vacantly as the procession from Lindell's Meadows led through the hooting streets. The car belonged to a company headed by a retired army officer named Sherman." At one stage of the war, a phrase conceptualizes the entire South. "The South limped toward independence on one leg. How to convince the world of national greatness . . . "

Having spoken briefly for Pratt, I will now step back so that you can listen to his own voice.

David Madden, Director
The United States Civil War Center
August 30, 1996

> Their seed standeth fast, and their
> children for their sakes. Their bodies
> are buried in peace; but their name
> liveth forevermore.
>
> Ecclesiasticus 44

Thanks are especially due to Mr. Robert Bruce, the author of so many of the Civil War biographies in the Dictionary of American Biography, for his assistance in checking through the whole manuscript for accuracy, and for his very valuable suggestions; to Mr. J. Sylvester L. Vigilante, of the New York Public Library's American History department, for his knowledge of original sources and their relative credibility; and to the Kentucky State Geological office for help in clearing up the geographical complications of the Perryville campaign; and to several others who have given valuable assistance of one kind or another, particularly reviewers who have pointed out errors in the original edition.

CONTENTS

LIST OF MAPS

INTRODUCTION

THE BACKGROUND

IT is those campaigns in America that we must study,"
said one of the ablest of German military leaders in the
years before World War I. He was speaking from a narrow
technical point of view and in that sense he was perfectly
right, not so much because it was in the conflict of 1861–65
that such modern devices as automatic firearms, armored
warships, submarines and fields of fire first appeared, as
because the tactics and even the strategies developed in those
campaigns in America controlled all subsequent wars down
to the beginning of the atomic age. Nobody has improved
very much on Lee's methods of deception, Sherman's treatment of logistics or Sheridan's handling of combined arms.

Yet it is not for soldiers alone that the Civil War has a
meaning beyond that of most armed conflicts. During the
period when it became fashionable to believe that war could
be prevented by not discussing it (and while some gentlemen
beyond the Pacific and the Rhine were preparing to give
us the greatest of all wars by examining military problems
very acutely) the battle for the Union came to be regarded
with a certain sense of shame in intellectual circles. With
endless elaboration it was explained to us that the causes of
the Civil War were economic and so were its principal results;
that the outcome was a foregone conclusion from the elements
that went into it; that it was a kind of armed election in
which the use of bullets was a regrettable exhibition of bad
taste and bad temper, which had best be forgotten. I have
met college graduates, majors in history, who had never

heard of Chickamauga and to whom the name of Sheridan represented an English dramatist.

The proponents of the point of view responsible for this ignorance need to reread the Gettysburg Address. But leaving aside for the moment the fact that they would deprive us of some of the highest idealism and human drama in the history of the race, it is just not true. It is possible to say today that the material odds were overwhelmingly on the side of the North; it was by no means possible in 1861. It has been noted that the white population of the Confederacy was 5,600,000 and that of the Union 22,340,000; that the South had 57,000,000 acres under cultivation to 105,000,000 for the Union; that the North had 22,000 miles of railroad forming a closely integrated network and the South 9,000 in rather rambling systems; the North 1,300,000 industrial workers and the South 110,000—and so on endlessly. The statistics are as false as those by which Mark Twain demonstrated that in a measurable number of years the Mississippi would be so short that Minneapolis would be a suburb of New Orleans.

Those population figures, for instance; they omit the Southern Negroes who contributed enormously to the war potential of the Confederacy by performing economic tasks, if not quite with the same efficiency as an equal number of Northern farmers at least to an extent that makes the omission ridiculous. They even contributed directly to the military performance of their section; the fortifications at New Orleans, Charleston, Richmond and Vicksburg were built with Negro slave labor. Moreover, no statistical comparison of population in Union and Confederate states means anything. Kentucky was counted a Union state but it furnished many troops to the South and so did Missouri. The combined populations of California, New Mexico, Kansas, Utah and Oregon make up over 700,000 of the Union total; but these states contributed almost nothing to the war in an economic sense and only 5,000 men in a physical sense, none of whom reached or could reach the decisive theaters of action.

The actual comparison made at the time was between the total populations of the free and slave states, where the figures were 12,340,000 for the South and 19,034,000 for the North, with the far western deductions bringing the latter down to 18,275,000, or a proportion of about two to three. The events which determined that not all the slave states would fight on the side of the slave-holders were themselves part of the war, as were those which in a later age changed Italy from a partner of the Axis to a power throwing at least some weight against it.

With the economic comparison the case is much the same. It would have some validity only if the combatants had been locked in a room like Cossack duelists. Before the war the South was part of an economic complex in which its great staple, cotton, was exchanged for all the other things it needed. It never had to produce, and so great was the confidence of the Southern leaders that this arrangement was as vital to the receivers as to the growers of their cotton that they embargoed the material at the beginning of the war with the intention of swapping it against foreign recognition and loans.

The fact that this policy failed, the things that made it fail, that made the industrial production of the North more important than the agricultural production of the South —these were all part of the contest itself. Put it otherwise; the North's economic strength had much to do with determining the result of the war, but not until events in the war had determined that economic strength would be important. That decision was itself one of the reasons why "It is those campaigns in America that we must study." The Revolution had no such aspect and it is very doubtful whether economic power had more than a secondary importance during the Napoleonic Wars, which were fought out within the compass of quite a different cycle of impulsions and ideas.

Moreover, neither population nor economic strength is the determining cause in war. If they were, Frederick the Great could never have held three-quarters of Europe at bay for seven years and run off with the prize of victory; the classic Greeks would have ended as a satrapy of the Persian Empire, and the French Revolution would have been strangled in its cradle. Of course, wars have economic effects and economics is often part of the explosive mixture that sets them off. But in the actual process war is a business of intelligence, spirit and, above all, emotion. Its decisions are reached on the battlefield, however much peaceably minded people may dislike the fact; and those of the Civil War were reached nowhere else.

The present volume was written to describe, in as brief a space as possible, that process of decision; to follow the main currents of event and emotion through the war and by brevity of treatment to give those main currents an emphasis that they might lose in a more detailed narration; to include practically everything that contributed to the final result and to omit nearly everything else. It was a pity to have to leave out so much—an account of Joseph Orville Shelby, for example, who larded his official reports with quotations from "Marmion," in which the names of Scottish chieftains were replaced with those of his own subordinates—but the answer to any given omission is that the item did not seem to bear on the outcome of the struggle.

Since so many of the events included are military, it is probably worth while to supply the reader with a few notes on the military terminology of the period. The smallest unit encountered in the field was usually a company of infantry, a troop of cavalry, or a battery of artillery, theoretically commanded by a captain, with a couple of lieutenants to assist him. Actually, lieutenants commanded many companies, especially in the Federal army, where there was less rank. A regiment consisted of several companies, troops or batteries, and was commanded by a colonel, with lieutenant-colonels and majors as his assistants. The later years of the war often found lieutenant-colonels and majors in command of regiments. Most of the volunteer regiments elected their officers at the beginning of the conflict, often with absurd results. Battalions and squadrons of cavalry were borne on the books, but in the American Civil War they were theoretical and administrative organizations only.

The regiments of both sides were supposed to contain 1,000 men. Few regiments had their full complement in the beginning and as they lost men they frayed away to almost nothing. Some of Lee's regiments at Five Forks contained only twenty or thirty men, but this condition was exceptional, and the Confederacy normally followed the rational system of using recruits to bring existing formations up to strength. In the Union army regiments were allowed to run down to 150 or 200 men, then broken up. Recruits were formed into entirely new regiments, a convenient arrangement which allowed state governors (into whose hands the practical power of appointment devolved) to nominate more colonels. At the beginning of the war a good many wealthy men obtained colonels' commissions and then raised regiments of their own.

A varying number of regiments made up a brigade, theoretically commanded by a brigadier-general, but in the Union army more often by a colonel. In the field Union brigades were generally smaller than their Confederate counterparts in the proportion of about five to eight, since Confederate brigades had more regiments to begin with and their system of reinforcement kept existing formations up better. From two to five of these brigades formed a division, normally commanded in the Union service by a brigadier-general and in the Confederate by a major-general, the next rank higher. In addition to its infantry brigades a division had several regiments of artillery attached and usually at least one regiment of cavalry, with a wagon-train and some engineers.

A division was thus supposed to be a little army, but here one encounters a source of much confusion with regard to the Civil War. Union divisions were so much smaller than the Confederate that they usually matched the latter's brigades in size. The net result was quite a different type of higher organization. A Confederate brigade of, say, 6,000 men would be all infantry; a Union formation of the same numerical size would be a division, including all arms.

Two or more divisions combined to form an army corps, "corps" for short, commanded in the Federal forces by a major-general, usually a lieutenant-general in the Confederacy. Here again the Union formations were individually smaller. After 1862 the Northern corps had individual badges and bore numbers. Confederate corps were known by the names of their commanders, and so were their divisions and brigades, the formation keeping its original name even when the leader had ceased to be the head of it for one reason or another, so that such oddities resulted as Wilcox's Brigade, commanded by Boyston. The cavalry were also organized into corps in both armies, but in the Army of the Potomac this remained purely theoretical until Sheridan took command in 1864.

In many of these arrangements the American Civil War was aberrant, but the thing that renders it unique was neither such technical details nor the fact that it was the first of the modern wars, nor even the personalities that it brought to the fore. The truly special character of the conflict is that there has seldom been any war and never any civil war so thoroughly decided on an ideological basis. Books have been written on the subsidiary issues, some of them good books; yet they do but darken counsel. At the time only two real questions were asked—secession and slavery—and they were answered in such a manner that they need never be asked again. The men of the time had a perfectly clear sense of this. An old New York State farmer used to tell how the first call for troops produced a debate around the local cracker-barrel which he finished to his own satisfaction with: "Well, boys, it's Massachusetts and South Carolina. I'm a-going to take the train to Boston and enlist."

There were a lot like him.

BOOK I. DARKNESS ON THE DEEP

I

CRY HAVOC

THE date—end of February, 1861. Current meteorological condition—bad, with a sloppy drizzle of rain. The place— the "bridal suite" of a Philadelphia hotel, a room of red plush and antimacassars, whose prevailing odor was composed in equal parts of fustiness and petroleum, since the lamp was smoking. It was night.

Judd, the political hack, a vague man with fat hands, came in, accompanied by a full-bearded gentleman whom he introduced as Pinkerton, the Illinois detective. There were only two chairs; the visitors sat on the bed and Judd chewed tobacco while they discoursed of a plot to assassinate the President-elect on the way through Baltimore, the train to be held up for the purpose by a gang of plug-uglies called "blood-tubs." This tallied with the warning Seward, the Secretary of State-to-be, had sent on from Washington the day before, and with the letter from General Scott; the matter was evidently to be taken seriously. Asked his advice, the detective suggested sending the President through to Washington at once, without warning, on a one-car special he had taken the liberty of ordering—

"I can't go tonight," said Lincoln, decisively. "I have promised to raise the flag over Independence Hall for Washington's Birthday tomorrow morning and to visit the legislature at Harrisburg."

They tried to argue with him. John Nicolay, that unobtrusive but inevitable secretary, broke it up by arriving with a batch of telegrams, the most important of which contained the text of Jefferson Davis' inaugural address. The man had been clever. enough not to mention slavery; it was all noble sentiments and righteous indignation— "elections held under the threat of military power," "despotic sectional majority," "nothing left but to prepare for war." No olive branch—was the man mad enough to think he could carry things through with the high hand? "Irrepressible conflict," quoted someone, Lincoln was drawn into the discussion, and the detective and his plot shunted out of it.

Pinkerton adjourned to the next room with Judd and sent out for Franciscus of the Pennsylvania Railroad and a man from the American Telegraph Company. The four of them cooked up a plan of action, got hold of the pale, efficient Nicolay, and after some difficulty persuaded Lincoln to fall in with it. In the morning, the flag-raising and visit to the legislature passed off on schedule. As soon as the handshaking was over, the President-elect drove to the governor's mansion, where they muffled him in a Scottish shawl and flat hat, then hustled him out the servants' door and by back alleys to a special train for Philadelphia. At the same moment Franciscus' men cut the wires leading out of Harrisburg and stopped railroad traffic; the town was isolated. In Philadelphia the little group stumbled across the tracks in the outer yards and Lincoln boarded the ordinary Washington sleeper. He took the middle section of three that had been reserved under false names, with Pinkerton men in the other two, sitting awake in the dark with revolvers in their laps. Unnecessary; the only halt at Baltimore was when the inspectors came down the line, tapping the wheels, and at six in the morning Lincoln was safe in Willard's Hotel.

Seward called in the afternoon, full of sound and fury. He had some changes to suggest in the inaugural, and was disposed to object to the presence of Salmon P. Chase in the Cabinet. The conservative wing of the party, of which he was the mouthpiece, could never stand that "western wild man." Before the interview was ended there arrived that king of all doughfaces, Mr. Caleb Cushing of Massachusetts who, as manager for the Breckinridge wing of the Democrats, had been in Charleston through December. A Job's comforter—"Sir, they are decidedly in earnest. Vigilance committees have expelled every Northerner in the state, including harmless females of the best disposition. Nothing can withhold them, sir, nothing. The Union is destroyed, *de facto*."

Later, he added privately to Seward that he had not told the worst for fear of upsetting Mr. Lincoln, of whose personal courage he entertained some doubt. There was a secret organization among the Carolinans called the Minute Men, admission to which was gained by paying a dollar and swearing to be in Washington on March 4 with rifle and revolver, ready to prevent the inauguration of the abolitionist President. Seward replied that although Lincoln was a simple Susan he believed him to be a brave man, and capped Cushing's tale with that of the Alabama conspiracy to burn the Capitol and Treasury. The two heads wagged dolefully over it half the night, but without arriving at any remedy; probably neither man trusted the other.

On Monday President Buchanan made his duty call, and the two chief executives exchanged compliments. The retiring head of the state looked aged and somewhat haggard. Over the week-end he had been the victim of a racking discussion with the South Carolina commissioners, in which they pressed him so fiercely about his implied promise to yield up Fort Sumter, which was all the national government held in their state, that he burst out at them, "You don't give me time to consider; you don't give me time to say my prayers. I always say my prayers when required to act on any great state affair," and they gazed at each other, uncomfortable and ashamed. Poor old man, he was breaking up, ungracefully—another month of it would kill him. The world spun too giddily for a President who wished to consult God and then compromise with Mammon, and he could no longer trust his Cabinet. It had become certain that Secretary Floyd of the War Department had been selling the secessionists arms from the Federal arsenals. The Treasury had been left in a terrific jam by another secessionist; the government was effectively bankrupt, no money to pay official salaries. Senator Slidell had to smuggle his trunk out at night, being unable to meet his board bill.

Wednesday came the official receptions with flowers and a good deal of oratory. Senator Douglas, who had come so near being President Douglas, remained behind the rest to make an impassioned plea for conciliation of the South. Lincoln asked him what kind of conciliation he meant; he replied by fetching out a document from the peace conference headed by "that old buffer Tyler, reappeared in the ancient cerements of his forgotten grave," which offered the extension of slavery to the territories and a constitutional amendment forbidding Congress to touch slavery thenceforth. Lincoln said no on the territories, the conscience of the North was up, but he was willing to try the amendment. The next morning it was pushed through both houses with lightning speed by united efforts of the Republicans and Douglas Democrats, but that same afternoon the Louisiana senators resigned and the South Carolina commissioners let Seward know that the least they would accept was peaceful separation. No compromise.

In the evening there was a dinner with General Scott and some of the Republican leaders. The general tone was despair—Merrill of Ohio, who had business connections South, had been writing to call in debts and exhibited two of the replies:

"I promise to pay, five minutes after demand, to any northern Abolitionist, the same coin in which we paid John Brown."

"I cannot return the goods, for they are already sold and the money invested in muskets to shoot you damn Yankees."

Conkling and Kennedy of New York had seen the papers; their city was in a turmoil; stocks selling at fractions, and the council considering a proposal to declare New York a free city, maintaining trade relations with both the old republic and the new. *Harper's Weekly* had a vicious cartoon of the "flight of the President from Harrisburg in a fit of ague"; the *Herald* announced that in Georgia they were taking oaths to wear no clothes produced under the régime of the "third-rate slang-whanging lawyer and his gang of "Black Republicans." Lincoln looked round the table and observed that he would like to see some of the Georgia gentlemen clad in costumes produced in their own state, that is, a shirt-collar and a pair of spurs, and the gloom dissolved in snickers.

Next day there was a warning letter about another plot—twenty-five Texans this time, coming to break up the inaugural parade and poignard the President in his carriage. Washington was outwardly quiet, but filled with whispered alarms. A Delaware member called to say he had overheard his wife's maid telling another nigger she was going to slap her mistress' face on March fourth; he seemed to feel that Lincoln should do something about it. The President-elect got rid of him and sat down to break the seal on a note just arrived from Seward. It was the worst possible; the Secretary-to-be felt slighted, had changed his mind about coming into the Cabinet, did not think he could work harmoniously with so radical a man as Mr. Chase. That called for more conferences and wire-pulling, interrupted by a serenade from an earnest but none too competent assemblage of brass musicians. The Seward business took up most of Saturday as well without reaching an end; Sunday was spent quietly.

The inaugural day dawned cold and melancholy, with low-hung clouds and a fine powder of rain. The procession was neither long nor brilliant; the foreign embassies shaved their attendance to a bare representation, fearing trouble, and the crowds along the sidewalk were somber. Patrols of cavalry were stationed in the cross-streets as the Presidential carriage passed, exhibiting menacing bright weapons. The windows of the Capitol were occupied by sharpshooters, and just visible on the crest of the hill opposite was the muted gleam of a battery of artillery, ready for anything.

Under such auspices, in this atmosphere of passion, ruin and distrust, Abraham Lincoln, sixteenth President of the United States, stood up to pronounce his inaugural address;

"The apprehension seems to exist among the people of the Southern states that by the accession of a Republican administration, their property and their security are to be endangered. There has never been any reasonable cause for such apprehension.

"I hold that in contemplation of universal law and of the Constitution, the union of these states is perpetual. It is safe to assert that no government ever had a provision in its organic law for its termination. No state upon its mere motion can lawfully get out of the Union. I therefore consider that the Union is unbroken and shall take care that the laws of the Union are faithfully executed in all the states.

"Physically speaking, we cannot separate. The different parts of our country must remain face to face, and intercourse, either amicable or hostile, must continue between them. Is it possible to make that intercourse more advantageous after separation than before? Can aliens make treaties easier than friends can make laws?

"But in your hands, my dissatisfied fellow-countrymen, and not in mine is the momentous issue of civil war. The government will not assail you. You can have no conflict without yourselves being the aggressors. You have no oath registered in heaven to destroy this government, while I have the most solemn one to preserve, protect and defend it."

. . . Away down in the Carolinas a rocket traced its comet of fire up the night from the water-battery of Fort Moultrie and burst in a rain of stars. At the sound of the cannon that opened against Fort Sumter the bells of Charleston all pealed forth joyfully and the citizens left their beds to rush into the streets and congratulate each other that the war had begun.

2

THE TWILIGHT ZONE

THE Union was destroyed. An uneasy thrill went through
the North; a thrill of numbed surprise at feeling the
active, murderous malignance of men who only yesterday had
been relatives—"Incredible that they mean *war*," thought
George Ticknor; thrill of grief and resignation—"Let the
erring sisters go," said old Greeley of the *Tribune*; thrill of
formless, passionate anger—"Set a price on every rebel head
and hang them as fast as caught," demanded the *Philadelphia
Gazette*. Washington was all confusion and dismay, full of
men in top-hats, clutching at straws. Seward wanted to re-
unite the Union by declaring war on France and Spain;
Arch Dixon, the blue-grass philosopher, to divide it into three
allied leagues of states, eastern, western, southern; Judge
Campbell to have the English ambassador arbitrate. Too late,
too late—the cannon were muttering in Charleston Harbor,
theirs alone the arbitrament now, and Lincoln was calling
on the states to maintain the honor, dignity and existence of
the United States.

The Union was destroyed. North Carolina refused her
troops, Kentucky hers. Arkansas tumbled into secession at the
call. Missouri's governor would send "no men to furnish or
carry on such an unholy crusade"; John Bell's voice, Bell of
Tennessee, who had stood for the presidency on a platform
of keeping the Union, was "a clarion call—To arms! and
repel the base invaders!" John Tyler, ex-President of the
United States, emerged for the last time from the cerements
of his forgotten grave to lead Virginia out of a nation pinned

together with bayonets. In three weeks the Confederacy's territory doubled. Robert Lee, the best general in the service, walked all night among the roses of Arlington, then chose Virginia as his country and refused the leadership of the national armies. Lincoln could only appoint McDowell, second (or twenty-fifth) best. Down went the Union flag at Fort Sumter; up went the rebel flag at Mount Vernon. The Virginians built a boom at Norfolk harbor and old Commodore McCauley had to send six splendid warships and the nation's best naval station up in flames or see them taken. The army's base at Harpers Ferry followed, blown up, burned down. The capital was like a graveyard; Mr. Chittenden found men piling sandbags at the Treasury windows. General Beauregard was coming north by express-train with 6,000 South Carolinans to take the city, and the Spanish ambassador thought enough of his chances to ask for a safe-conduct. The end of the world.

But in the North, 100,000 marching men clapped their hands on musket-butts and swore it was not so:

> " . . . this teeming and turbulent city;
> At dead of night, at news from the south
> Struck with clenched fist the pavement."

When the war news came to Boston bells tolled the day long; before sunset 3,000 soldiers had mustered. The jury walked from the Milwaukee court to enlist, with the judge for a captain. Ohio sent up twenty-one regiments, though her share was thirteen. The Germans of St. Louis mustered in their Turner Halls and sang songs of the '48. New York exchanges were deserted; the businessmen were with two hundred and fifty thousand others in Union Square, hearing the councilors who had wished the city's secession swear devotion to the old flag; the Seventh marched down Broadway through a tempest of cheering two miles long. "Only those who saw it could understand the enthusiasm of that hour. It was worth a life, that march," thought Theodore Winthrop, who gave no less than a life for it, among the pines of Big Bethel, some thousand hours later. No more of incredulity or resignation; in a moment, for a moment, all differences were dead. Follow the flag or wear petticoats. The North has one heart and one mind for war.

Not less the South—or even more. "You see the glittering bayonet and you hear the tramp of armed men from your capitol to the Rio Grande," boomed giant Robert Toombs of Georgia, making his valedictory to the Senate of the United States before he left to be a member of the "conference of seven independent republics" at Montgomery. "Keep us in the Union by force? Come and do it! Georgia is on the warpath! We are ready to fight now." The sound of drum and bugle floated through the windows of the Greek temple where the conference was met. "Companies of soldiers and graceful Southern women" saluted the delegates with bouquets of flowers as they left the building after electing Major-General Jefferson Davis, graduate of West Point and commander of the army of the sovereign Republic of Mississippi, to be President of the new alliance. The election had been an accident and an error, born of a misunderstanding as ridiculous as that in a Sardou play and the fact that Toombs (who was the destined candidate) got drunk at the wrong moment and drizzled tobacco juice onto his white shirt-front. It satisfied nobody, not even Davis himself, who wanted to ride into the presidency, but only with captured battle-flags borne behind him, as general of the armies, like George Washington.

"He is chatty and tries to be agreeable," reported T. R. R. Cobb, "but obstinate as a mule; not a great man in any sense of the word." Gave dissatisfaction by the manner in which he attacked the task, surely one for greatness, of organizing from the roof down a government that had neither treasury nor services, nor even a fundamental instrument of law. Alexander Stephens helped him much in those days—the strange, sickly, melancholy statesman who looked so childish that on the train he had been hailed with "Sonny, get up and give your seat to the gentleman." He had fought to the last

against secession; now he wrote most of the new constitution and would be Vice-President under it, and would
grow to hate it and Davis with consuming vehemence; but
now the guns had spoken under Sumter, Stephens dragged
his racked body into the open to tell ten thousand people that
all personal opinion receded before duty.

Even Toombs became pro-Davis in those days; Toombs,
still bitter over missing the first prize—Toombs who laughed
when the man beside him wrote of the new Attorney-General:
"A grander rascal than this Jew Benjamin does not exist";
Toombs who had growled his dislike of Davis over the nightly
bottle, and strode into an assembled Cabinet to tell them that
"The firing on that fort will inaugurate a civil war greater
than any the world has seen. It is suicide, it is murder." The
guns had fired now; no more doubts, no more opposition.
Toombs would leave his bottle to toil by candle-light while
bands boomed "La Marseillaise" through the Vieux Carré
of New Orleans and carried every young man who followed
them off to recruiting sergeants. In Memphis a regiment of
gentlemen planters ordered so many uniforms from the best
tailors that they refused all other work. Young Mr. Douglas
came home one night to find his mother sewing on a gray
heavy shirt and without a word left the house to enlist, and
General Pierre Gustave Toutant Beauregard, "the hero of
Fort Sumter," came up into Virginia with 50,000 men behind
him, who should demand the surrender of Washington as
soon as Maryland seceded and the District of Columbia re-
verted to the state.

One heart and one mind—North and South hurrying toward the shock. But between lay a belt of states where
neither hearts nor minds were one—Maryland, Kentucky,
Missouri—crucial states, with a combined territory larger
than Germany's, population enough to give the side they
chose the majority. Jefferson Davis, a dry, logical man,
counted on all three—being slave states, how could they fail
to join the slave Confederacy?—and planned a military line
of defense for his new nation, along Mason and Dixon's sur-

veying marks to the Ohio River, thence to the Mississippi, thence to the Black Hills. A perfect "natural frontier," with forts here, strong-points there, mapped out according to the most correctly Napoleonic principles of Jomini.

But Maryland was not logical; Maryland was tumultuous, passionate, divided, a microcosm of the whole. At night a torchlight procession of half a mile, with the blood-tubs bearing transparencies in the van, tramped through Baltimore, chanting "Dixie." In the morning upward of fifty gentlemen gathered round Governor Hicks' mansion and sang "The Star-Spangled Banner" "in an affecting manner." A rebel flag was burned amid hoots on Calvert Street. Yet two days later, when the first of the Boston 3,000 came to town, Baltimore boiled out to hiss, turned from hissing to stone-throwing, from stone-throwing to revolver shots, till the exasperated soldiers fired a volley, then another, and finally charged through the smoking streets with the bayonet, leaving a hundred dead behind, the first dead of the war. The riot flared beyond their leaving, the blood-tubs got out of hand, fired the railroad stations, broke down the bridges and threw the locomotives into the river. Somebody got off a message asking Jefferson Davis for Confederate troops to preserve the city's liberties.

The town was cut off; so was Washington, with all telegraph lines down, only the single Boston regiment at hand to meet Beauregard's South Carolinans, and Baltimore blazing like a volcano across the path of help. The latest paper was three days old; a volunteer corps of clerks drilled on the White House lawn, and rumor had it that the New York Seventh had been cut to pieces by the blood-tubs. Men fled or became fanatically loyal. Mr. Chittenden's friends, over the coffee-cups, shook hands emotionally in a vow to sell their lives high, and the next morning he met the author of "Private Libraries of New York," incredibly decked in false whiskers, who had heard there was a Southerner suspended from every lamp-post in Boston and feared similar treatment, his birthplace being Georgia. The old heroic frigate *Con-*

stitution left the naval academy for Newport on the end of a tow-line. The Cabinet met daily, Mr. Chase's pocket bulging with a horse-pistol. General Scott had trenches dug around the Capitol and planted artillery at Anacostia. Asked his opinion of affairs, he thought that 300,000 men under good generals might extinguish the rebellion in three years. Lincoln, who had asked 75,000 for three months, was appalled—for the moment, even he doubted.

Had they but known it, their fears were groundless. Beauregard came not; the next day the New York Seventh, the Massachusetts Eighth and a Rhode Island battery, in by water from Annapolis, went swinging up Pennsylvania Avenue. Baltimore was quiet again, the blood-tubs beaten down; Pinkerton's plain-clothes men had marked out the ringleaders and the police had clapped them in the calaboose. The Maryland legislature voted hesitation and sent delegations to both sides, begging them to respect the state's property. Lincoln said yes, by all means, he was only interested in protecting Washington; General Joseph Johnston for the Confederates said by no means, his government would respect no property but its own. The Union men made it a battle-cry; the legislature saluted the stars and stripes in tumultuous, passionate resentment and voted to buy for the defense of the state a railroad steam-gun that would fire four hundred Minié balls a minute from behind a conical shield of iron. Maryland for the North.

Kentucky was all philosophical abstractions and memories of Henry Clay, a state of two million metaphysicians, crying peace in the midst of war—"The government and the administration are separate and distinct; the government has never been hostile to the slave states. Secession would be the most fatal of all issues of this controversy. As for that fourth-rate fool, Lincoln, can he make Kentucky help him kill? No! But how soon he will be dragged down and another and better man raised to his place!" The legislature met, adjourned, met again and split hairs with infinite care, finally voting that the hope of the world consisted in Kentucky "hanging, like the prophet of old, between the living and the dead." Make it so—Governor Magoffin issued a proclamation commanding her citizens to abstain from fighting for either side. Kentucky neutral.

Neutral? The struggle went underground. Circular letters from nobody to nobody—let all free men meet at Frankfort on a given day in primary assembly to vote the state out of the Union. Counter-circulars from same to same—let all honest men meet before the given day to hold necktie-parties for the assemblers. At midnight Governor Magoffin received gentlemen in burnished boots and elaborate coiffures; next day they went sight-seeing along the river in the gubernatorial carriage, especially interested in the sites where Jefferson Davis had planned forts. Next day but one they were returned to Tennessee with compliments and coats of tar and feathers. The secesh faction got hold of the state militia; they drilled along the southern border, and whole companies walked over it on practice marches, never to find their way back. The Union men organized "Home Guards" in opposition. They had no guns, but that was all right, a drummer from the north turned up, selling "Abe Lincoln circular saws," which came in coffin-shaped boxes, f.o.b. Watervliet arsenal.

Lincoln, as a matter of fact, knew all about Kentucky. Perfectly at home in this nightmare atmosphere, he cajoled and intrigued like some amiable villain out of Mark Twain—"I hope I have God on my side, but I must have Kentucky." In the morning he assured a delegation of blue-grass Congressmen that he had neither right, power nor disposition to violate Kentucky's neutrality; in the afternoon, he suggested the kidnaping of Governor Magoffin and ordered another shipment of circular saws. Jefferson Davis, that dry, reasonable man, pillared in his own rectitude, his eyes on the map and his mind on Jomini's principles of war, was no match for this sort of thing. He grew nervous about his line of defense along the Ohio River. Lincoln encouraged the nervousness by assembling regiments at Belmont, across the river from Columbus, where the Confederates planned to build a regular Gibraltar, the Mississippi pillar of their defense line. The Union men joined tickets with the Neutrals for the summer election and cleaned up.

Davis and Magoffin could stand it no longer; Confederate General Polk was ordered up with an army to hold Columbus, General Zollicoffer with another to make sure of Louisville. The Union men and Neutrals yelled bloody murder over this invasion, the legislature passed a bill calling on the Confederate troops to quit the state. Magoffin vetoed it; they passed it over his veto and added a rider calling for a treaty of offensive and defensive alliance with the United States. Lincoln titivated coyly; the legislature abandoned metaphysics, called out the Home Guard and frankly asked the Union government to protect them as citizens. Kentucky for the North.

In Missouri secession was the product of white-pillared porticoes and the romance of Walter Scott, a gay, gracious and knightly maintenance of privilege for the gilded classes. The rebels had Governor Jackson—Claiborne Fox Jackson, an oily, small-minded man, a bitter hater—and the legislature; back in February the latter had called a secession convention, but too many damned immigrants voted and when the convention met it was eighty-nine to one against. The next step was refusing troops on Lincoln's call, but the President would not quarrel. Jackson had to think up another. Magoffin of Kentucky gave him the idea of working through the militia; he purged it of all but sons of the best families and called it to camp at St. Louis early in May. There was a government arsenal there with 60,000 stand of arms. The plan was to get them first and then, bingo! heave Missouri over into secession by executive proclamation.

In St. Louis, however, was Francis Preston Blair, an old Jacksonian politician not overweighted by moral sense, but stoutly Union as only a Jacksonian could be; his brother was in the Cabinet. He got a message through to Lincoln in March; the President sent him a note, secret authority to declare martial law if it came to the pinch, and Captain Nathaniel Lyon, a red-bearded Connecticut Yankee of violent manners. Lyon and Blair hit it off at once; the former gathered nearly a thousand Germans—"but we are only doing our Turner exercises!" to Governor Jackson's protests about drilling—the latter smuggled the 60,000 arms across to Illinois and safety.

Jackson sent to New Orleans for guns. The Confederates forwarded them in boxes marked "Marble" which were carried out to the camp, in Lindell's Meadows on the edge of the city. The camp gates were watched, only the aristocracy could get in, and as they were all loyal Southerners, Blair and Lyon had no legal lever for action. But one afternoon blind old Mrs. Alexander, a society lady resplendent in bombazine and black veil, was driven through the camp in a Jenny Lind carriage. On her return she stopped at Blair's house; when she descended a passer-by noticed that blind old Mrs. Alexander was wearing cavalry boots. The next morning Lyon and his 1,000 marched out to Lindell's Meadows, were met at the camp gate by requests to show authority, answered with the word of Cambronne and planted cannon to sweep the place. The camp surrendered; the prisoners were marched back through the city, crying a rescue. A mob gathered to try it; Lyon's men opened fire and slew thirty.

The struggle was open now; Jackson, the legislature, and what was left of the militia fled up-river to Jefferson City, calling the state to rise in arms, and Confederate General Ben McCulloch threw a force in from Arkansas to help them. Blair called a convention of loyalists; it declared Jackson recreant and organized a rival government. Lyon pushed out a flying column to get between him and McCulloch. Missouri split—and the clash of arms about to begin.

About to begin. Confederacy, say twelve million people; Union, say seventeen million. More important is this—General Robert Edward Lee, commander of the army of the sovereign state of Virginia, drew on his gloves and stood up, symphonic in gray and gold. "And what do you think of their commanders?" he inquired half-idly of R. S. Ewell, general of division.

"Of McDowell not highly. I do not know this McClellan;

he is a younger man. But there is one West Pointer, I think in Missouri, little known, whom I hope the Northern people will not find out. I mean Sam Grant. I should fear him more than any of their leaders I have yet heard of."

General Lee smiled and turned to give orders for the march. An impecunious leather-dealer named Grant sat at that moment in a street-car in St. Louis, gazing vacantly as the procession from Lindell's Meadows led through the hooting streets. The car belonged to a company headed by a retired army officer named Sherman.

3

FIRST INTERLUDE

Recruits at Coon Creek

There were trees along the stream, fairly thick. Through
them, as through a cloister, the slope was visible, with the
luxuriant ripe grasses lying over in the July sunlight. Everybody's feet had got wet crossing the ford; it was impossible
to maintain formation among the trees, and the men bunched
up in little chattering knots. The horses strained with the
guns. Captain Konrad, his honest Dutchy face contorted with
effort, kept tripping over his sword, and the laughter had a
strained unnatural edge. It was very hot.

Colonel Sigel pushed through the press, his big brown
horse prancing at shadows, and spoke to Major Bischoff. The
latter moved out to the left, bellowing orders; Companies K
and B untangled themselves from the rest of the regiment and
went stumbling after him across the tree-roots. A bugle blew
three sharp notes, then halted in a kind of gasp as there was a
sound like a blow on an enormous drum and something heavy
crashed through the leaves overhead. Up the slopes a cotton-
boll of smoke hung motionless.

They were out under the edge of the branches now, and
the bugles sounded again, faint, lost, unstirring, altogether
different than in the drill-hall. "Hrrrp!" called the officers
and the line began to move forward with the grasses dragging
at their feet. Along the edge of the swell, far ahead, number-
less black pinheads appeared against the sky. It was hard
to keep one's eyes from them and the increasing number of

smoke-puffs; hard to remember to hold one's musket at the proper angle. The line swayed, bulging and gapping; there was a consciousness of irregular marching, of bad performance. Overhead, a giant was ripping cloth.

Smaller smoke dots broke out along the crest of the slope, it must be half a mile away; there were a few little plumes of dust among the grass-tufts in front, and a man somewhere down the line screeched piercingly. Almost everyone jumped and looked; in Company C a soldier dropped his musket. The bugles blew again. Halt! The artillery horses were unhitched, and the men, fumbling and uncertain with haste, loaded the pieces. Berroum! Boom! Boom! went the three guns of the section and everybody felt better. Some of the men sat down, a sergeant began to hum "Du, du, liegst mir im Herzen" softly, conversation began in muttered, jerky phrases and half sentences.

The artillerymen toiled, perspiring at their cannon. The color-guard squatted, their flag limp, the other men lay or sat. The heat-haze trembled up the swell where they watched; all around was the zip-zipee of Minié balls which seemed to do not the slightest damage. The water was all gone, there was nothing to do but contemplate the smoke, slowly drifting across the breathless air. Battle?

There was an exclamation and a pointing of fingers toward the right. Colonel Sigel's horse had come to a stand and he was looking in that direction through his glasses. Far enough distant to be just visible a confused mass was moving toward the line of trees upstream; occasionally a horse's head would be silhouetted against the blue. The colonel took down the glasses, shut them with a snap and issued an order. The horse-leaders appeared with the military teams, their harness jingling as they switched flies. Zip—zip—zipee. Bugles—blowing retreat. The men stood up, swung their muskets onto their shoulders and slogged angrily back toward the stream. Under the shelter of the trees three dead men were laid out. One of them had only half a head.

4

THE CHILD OF FORTUNE

LYON made enemies. He called the mayor a swill-tub, suppressed the St. Louis papers and told the clergy to let politics alone and preach about God. Besides he had no seniority. This gave the Lyon-tamers a talking point. They put on more pressure than Lincoln could stand; Lyon was kicked upstairs to brigadier-general in command of the Army of Missouri with General John C. Frémont commanding him as head of the Department of the West.

Frémont was a character out of a Victorian novel—soulful eyes and waving hair, a universal genius who stunned his contemporaries by learning Hungarian and marrying the fairest heiress of the west, the daughter of that formidable old Roman, Thomas Hart Benton. The marriage made him; Benton trumpets blew every time he moved, and he moved like quicksilver; explored the Rockies (with the help of mountain men who had lived there for twenty years); engineered the Bear Paw Revolution in California, dabbled in stock promotion and electrical invention, and emerged as Republican candidate for the presidency in 1856. Returning from a tour of the Alps, he met the news of his appointment in New York, made a whirlwind speaking trip through the Middle West, stopping off at Pittsburgh to recite "The Prisoner of Chillon" from a mountain-top at dawn, and turned up in St. Louis at the end of July, bareheaded in Arsenal Square with a drawn sword in one hand and an American flag in the other—ineffably poetic, ineffably patriotic.

Within a week he had made patriotism fashionable. A bodyguard of a hundred horsemen in blue and gold jingled after him when he rode abroad, its leader an authentic count named Zagonyi. There was a review of armed steamers on the river, amid intense cheering. Half the ladies of the city left cards at his door; the hero of the Mexican War announced that he would lead a triumphal march to New Orleans.

But out beyond railhead the Army of Missouri was in rags and starving. Lyon had only 6,000 men; Jackson and McCulloch concentrated 10,000 against him and began to work raiding parties around his flank toward the state capital. Blair's government there was already a rump, short on prestige; if the city went, most of Missouri would follow and Kansas could hardly be held. Lyon got off daily appeals for help but Frémont was too busy drinking in the odor of his own magnificence and only initialed them in his elegant hand. The case became one of desperation. The rebels had so much cavalry that Lyon dared not risk a retreat; he determined to disengage himself by attack and marched out to fall on their camp at Wilson's Creek on a foggy dawn in August. Brigadier Sigel on the right got his orders jumbled (it was to be a normal occurrence with him) and was driven from the field. Lyon had to lead a last-gasp charge right into the mouths of the cannon to get his army out. It succeeded, but he was killed and 1,300 men went with him. The whole state south of the Missouri River went lost.

That was too much for Francis Blair, who was one of your plain-bluff-man politicians, despising the ornamental Frémont by definition. He went to Washington and denounced the magnifico as an opéra-bouffe idiot. Lincoln was unwilling to remove him, he was very popular. But just at this juncture word came in that Frémont had issued a proclamation—he was going to shoot every rebel found in arms and had declared the slaves of rebel owners liberated. It was no longer a war for the Union, but an anti-slavery jihad.

Lincoln was horrified; the fool had upset his whole policy

and demolished his carefully built-up demonstration that slave-owners and the slave states could have ample justice within the Union. He paced the floor half the night, dictating a telegram an hour to Frémont, asking for the withdrawal of the proclamation.

Frémont refused; Lincoln canceled it by executive order. This moved the general to protest through the mouth of the beautiful Jessie Benton Frémont, who held a stormy midnight interview with the President, at the end of which she flicked her handkerchief across his face and hinted darkly that her husband might declare himself independent Dictator of the West if it came to a pinch. Judge Hoadley wrote from Cincinnati that the man was popular enough to carry five states with him out of the Union and match titles with the President. Lincoln sent Secretary of War Cameron and Colonel Sherman out to investigate on the ground. They arrived to find St. Louis in a turmoil and Francis Blair in jail for conspiring to bring Frémont's authority into contempt of the government. There was a double line of guards around the dictator's mansion to head off any messenger who might bring an order of recall, but Sherman was so grim with them that the visitors got as far as the anteroom of the Presence, where an inner door was opened and a face peered cautiously around the edge. It belonged to Isaiah Woods, the California boodler.

The Secretary and the colonel looked at each other wordlessly and returned to Washington. A week later the Dictator of the West was summarily removed. Afterward it was discovered that his bodyguard had lined their pockets with five million dollars' worth of contracts. Incident closed.

. . . Governor Dennison of Ohio heard that Captain McClellan, the officer who had written such interesting reports on the Crimean War without ever having seen the fighting, was available, and summoned him by wire to discuss taking command of the state troops. He turned up late in April, a young man under middle height, brusque, ardent, intelligent. Dennison was pleased with him; wrote out his commission as general then and there, after which they went over to inspect the stock of arms at the arsenal, a mausoleum-like structure which proved to contain nothing but several boxes of Mexican War muskets, a pile of mildewed harness and large numbers of rats. The governor was mortified, but McClellan passed it off with a laugh and asked whether there was a printing office in town which could turn out two thousand copies of Hardee's *Tactics* in a month.

Recruits began coming in the next morning. They drilled in fathomless mud with wooden guns under officers of their own election, who employed words of command invented for the occasion—sometimes with distressing results, as when the 10th and 13th Regiments met on a road. Neither colonel knew how to turn his men aside and there was a lovely fist-fight till McClellan rode in with upraised hand:

"Soldiers! Spare your blows for the enemies of your country!" It touched the spot. The fight dissolved in emotion, which McClellan capitalized by brigading the two regiments together as "The Iron Band." He hustled about everywhere, pursued by a staff of officers like himself young, chattering like magpies, busy as chipmunks. After the first week everybody got enough to eat, and the Zouaves paraded in their red pants piped with blue. Lumberjacks from the Western Reserve corduroyed the roads and built a rustic arbor where the general could listen to the band at retreat. Holiday.

Across the river in western Virginia there was plenty trouble. The mountain valleys had sent "loyalist" delegates to the secession convention in Richmond. The convention threatened to crack their heads if they wouldn't make the vote for secession unanimous and Campbell Tarr of Wheeling was egged through the streets. He came home fighting mad, to call a meeting of hill-billy supervisors who seceded their counties from Virginia as the state had from the Union. A governor was elected and McClellan was asked for military support, but as he was enjoying a controversy with the War Department—subject, Why I have no artillery—he refused to budge.

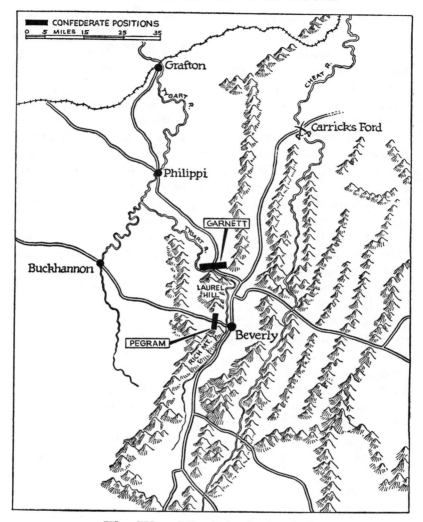

The West Virginia Operation

Meanwhile the state proclaimed the mountain counties contumacious; Robert Lee was to suppress them, but he was doing staff-work for the main Confederate army north of Richmond, so he sent his second, General Garnett, an undistinguished man, with 8,000 men. They could have turned the Alleghanies through the valley of the North Branch, but that would have meant crossing Maryland territory; Lee was immensely high-minded about violating "foreign" soil in those days, and sent Garnett through the passes by the one good road, to Beverly. He established a base there and pushed out a Colonel Porterfield with an advance guard of 1,500 men to Philippi. Supplies were slow in coming through.

At the end of May McClellan heard that Porterfield was raiding farms and breaking down railroad bridges along the Baltimore & Ohio Railroad near Grafton. By this time his recruits could pull triggers without shutting their eyes; when some Indiana batteries joined him, the Union commander sent them on to Grafton forthwith, following with 10,000 men. The Indianians planned a night surprise of Porterfield's force. McClellan arrived before it came off and altered the plan to a concentric attack by two separate columns from different directions—a move that veteran troops might well have hesitated to make or Napoleon Bonaparte to order. To complete the confusion, it was pitch dark with a drenching rain; the artillery horses lay down, panting, and the men had to pull the cannon by hand, but, marvelous to relate, both columns arrived simultaneously. Porterfield's men were all tucked in for the night; the first news of trouble they had was when the guns sent the houses tumbling about their ears. They ran away with great speed, all but the fifteen who were killed. In the South this piddling affair was called "the Philippi races," but McClellan wrote an expansive report on it and by time the news got to New York it was a greater victory than Austerlitz.

There were only two gaps in the western buttress of the mountains. If McClellan were at Philippi, the Confederates thought, he must be coming in against the northern one, Laurel Hill. Garnett dug an extensive trench system there, installing 6,000 men and most of his guns; his second, Colonel Pegram, was posted at Rich Mountain, the southern pass, with the remaining 2,000. McClellan sent a lieutenant to keep the Laurel Hill force amused and adroitly swung his main body across country to Buckhannon, then straight in against Pegram. The rebels, outnumbered seven to one, took to their heels; McClellan followed hard and was in Beverly before news of the attack reached Garnett. When it did, that general had to retreat clear north around Cheat Mountain, with McClellan's big battalions after him. He abandoned his trains, then his artillery, but the pursuit was so hot he had to make a stand at Carrick's Ford. There was a brief fight; Garnett was killed and his force broke up.

Pegram, also divorced from the only supply-line, whirled south with Union Colonel Rosecrans and four regiments dogging him. The Confederates rambled miserably among the hills for a week, trying to find a way out and getting nothing to eat. Then Pegram came in to surrender his whole command. New state of West Virginia for the North.

McClellan telegraphed home that he had "annihilated two armies, commanded by educated and experienced soldiers, intrenched in fastnesses fortified at their leisure." They believed him in the North; the papers called him "the young Napoleon" and sent photographers to take his likeness with one hand thrust into his coat, just like Bonaparte. He was too good-natured to be a success with the frown, but when the correspondents called they found him dictating to three secretaries at once. Unfortunately the letters had to be rewritten afterward.

At Springfield, Illinois, a new colonel named Grant rode into the camp of the 21st Regiment, to which he had been appointed through the kindness of a friend of an uncle's friend. It was a kind of joke: both the commander and the regiment were hopeless, they insubordinate and he a dipsomaniac. He could not afford a uniform; his worldly possessions consisted of a handful of Missouri stogies and an old white horse named Methusalem. The sentry saluted him breezily—"Howdy, Colonel!" The adjutant was very drunk and the sergeants of Company B were playing auction pitch in the mess tent.

5

DISASTER IN THE SCRUB

WINFIELD SCOTT, the fighting leader of 1812, had become a padded octogenarian, but there was nothing wrong with his head. Run a cordon of fortified posts down the Mississippi, station a cruiser off every Southern port and strangle the rebellion in the coils of the Navy, said he; no military advance till we have troops drilled to steadiness. This was too slow for the North, where they wanted the Confederacy eaten up before breakfast. Seven western governors met in Cleveland to telegraph Lincoln tautologically for "action—crushing, irresistible, overwhelming"; Mr. Greeley made up a standing head for the *Tribune*—FORWARD TO RICHMOND! FORWARD TO RICHMOND! and other papers became hilarious over a cartoon of old Scott as a sideshow snake-charmer. "Scott's Anaconda," ha, ha.

Lincoln summoned a council of war. The sense of the gathering was in favor of advance. The troops were green, but no more so than the rebels'; there was a strong stiffening of regulars; the three-month volunteers had only a few weeks more to serve and the worst repercussions would follow if they went home without striking a blow. General McDowell will prepare a plan of attack; a great victory is desired for the Fourth of July.

General McDowell, a formal soldier in the completest sense of that phrase, was at his wits' end. He had not even organized the raw regiments into brigades, there was no cavalry, and he was visited daily by a soviet of elected colonels, all demanding they be made generals of division, but he pulled out a map and went to work.

Across Virginia slantwise runs the Blue Ridge range, shutting the eastern plain in against the sea. Between it and the main crests of the Alleghanies lies a long corridor of a valley, the Shenandoah, immensely fertile, the garden-spot of Virginia, its northern end issuing behind Washington at the pass of the Potomac called Harpers Ferry, its southern outlet through another gap on the rear of Richmond. Midway, the Blue Ridge wall is pierced by Manassas Gap; through it come the roads of stone and steel to meet the main lines from Richmond north at Manassas Junction. Take the junction, you have possession of the gap and can hurry through it to catch any Confederate force in the valley.

There was a Confederate force in the valley; General Joe Johnston, a man who "could trace his family history to the earliest sources" and was considered remarkable for the wooden Indian stolidity he exhibited on all occasions, with 15,000 men. Beauregard, the flamboyant Creole, had 23,000 more along the line of Bull Run River, in front of Manassas. McDowell could bring 28,000 against Beauregard's 23,000, beat him in a battle, dash through the gap and gather in Johnston's force. But what if Johnston joins Beauregard? asked McDowell. Don't worry about that, General, Lincoln assured him; there are 22,000 men under General Patterson of the Pennsylvania militia to hold him tight.

The plan of march was for the 9th; on the 16th, the army got almost ready and sauntered fuzzily toward Manassas—"the only thing the march demonstrated was the total lack of discipline." It was infernally hot; carrying ammunition was too much trouble, so many of the men emptied their cartridge-boxes in the ditch. At every halt the Congressmen who had come along to see the fun got a regiment or two out of line and treated them to a few flowers of oratory. The newspaper correspondents came, too, and on the 17th the Washington papers printed the plan of campaign with

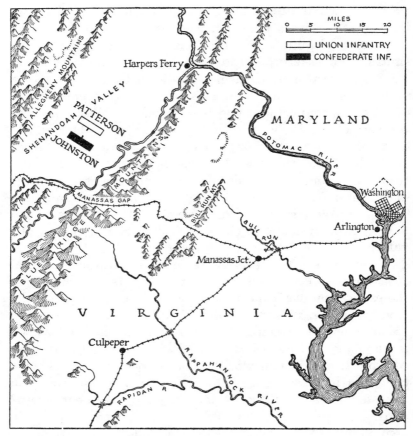

The Bull Run Campaign

maps, which were passed on to Richmond and received with much gratitude. On the 18th, McDowell's advance guard had a brush with the rebel pickets along Bull Run and Joe Johnston was marching double-quick to join Beauregard.

Back in the Shenandoah Valley he left some cavalry and a few outposts which made a good deal of noise every time they saw a Yankee. Patterson was an amiable antique of sixty-nine who had been a dashing lieutenant in the War of 1812 and a subordinate commander in Mexico; his real qualification for command was that he had a lively interest in politics and more money than anyone in Philadelphia. Nobody knows where he got his information about Johnston's strength; certainly not by scouting, for in the easy fashion of the only military service he had seen, he never did any. But as early as the middle of June he began answering Scott's orders to attack with requests for reinforcements and wails that he was outnumbered. Scott sent him a brigade and then another. No use. "My position is most hazardous," wired Patterson, and on the same 18th that saw Johnston marching for Manassas the Union army of the Valley was going as fast as it could in the opposite direction, back toward the Potomac.

There are three feasible fords and a stone bridge across Bull Run—their names, Red House, the bridge, Ball's and Blackburn's. McDowell found them strongly held, with the main body of the Confederates posted behind on some low hills covered with scrub forest. He reconnoitered for two days; then his engineers discovered an unmapped ford at the north of the position, and he determined to use the knowledge to throw an overpowering concentration on Beauregard's left wing. Tyler's division was to feint against the bridge; Hunter's and Heintzelman's to make a circuit through the woods to the unmapped ford and roll up the whole Southern line. The attack was for daybreak Sunday; at two o'clock the men were turned out of their blankets and began to move silently through the woodland roads in the dark.

On the other side Beauregard was also anxious for battle. The first division of Johnston's men had already arrived; with this reinforcement he thought to force Blackburn's Ford on his right and smash the Federal left wing under a concentration formed there during the night. On his own left were only the brigades of Bee, Bartow and Evans, watching Red House Ford and the bridge from the eminence; in the center, Jackson's division, on a high plateau, high only in comparison with the low surrounding land. The attack was for ten o'clock, but before it could get in motion there was a cannon shot, then a whole chorus of them, and half the

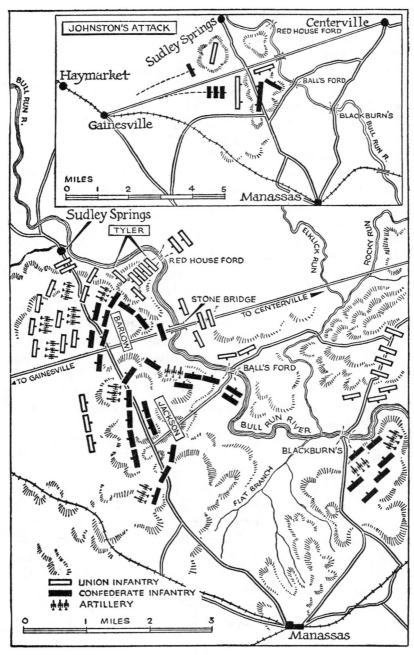

JOHNSTON'S ATTACK

Centerville
RED HOUSE FORD
Sudley Springs
Haymarket
BALL'S FORD
Gainesville
BLACKBURN'S
BULL RUN R.

MILES
0   1   2   4   5

Manassas

Sudley Springs
TYLER
BULL RUN R.
ELKLICK RUN
ROCKY RUN
RED HOUSE FORD
STONE BRIDGE
TO CENTERVILLE
BARLOW
BALL'S FORD
TO GAINESVILLE
JACKSON
BULL RUN RIVER
BLACKBURN'S
FLAT BRANCH

☐ UNION INFANTRY
■ CONFEDERATE INFANTRY
⚔ ARTILLERY

0   1   MILES   2   3

Manassas

Bull Run

Federal army came pouring out of the woods on Evans' flank and rear, while Tyler struck for the bridge.

Evans' men broke at once. Bartow faced about cheerfully, got a couple of batteries into position and held his post briefly, but, as more and more of the Union striking force came against his new front, the pressure grew intolerable, he was forced to draw the guards from Red House Ford. McDowell, riding with Tyler's van, perceived the soft spot, and flung that division against it. The ford was carried, the bridge could not be held either; Bartow's new position was taken from the rear and the entire Confederate left wing encircled and crushed. His and Bee's formations lost all traces of discipline and went streaming in on the center. The Federal tide washed round the foot of the plateau on three sides. McDowell sent off an engineer to telegraph a victory to Washington.

But the attack had been a fumbling, sloppy piece of execution by dead green troops. The men had been up since two in the morning, struggling through dust, heat and tenacious scrub; it was noon, canteens and cartridge-boxes were empty. Formations had mingled, even company officers did not know where their men were, field officers had lost control completely. There was a brief halt at the foot of the plateau, and in it the wrecked Sothorons began to rally. Wounded Bee rode down their line, swinging his hat— "Look!" he cried, melodramatic and glorious, "There stands Jackson like a stone wall!" and then fell dead. The first tentative assault was repulsed.

Now McDowell lost his head and sent in regiments all along the line in piecemeal, disjointed attacks, riding with them like a sergeant. They shattered against the stone wall; the confusion spread, and in the middle of it, down the road onto the new Union rear came the rest of Joe Johnston's troops at the run, headed by the Louisiana Tigers. Helplessly caught, the whole Federal army collapsed; men and officers threw down their arms and ran for their lives. McDowell tried to save the day with some of the sound regiments from his left wing, but they only caught the contagion. The trains, the artillery, the wounded, and even two Congressmen were abandoned, and the mass of terror-haunted fugitives never stopped till they reached the Potomac River bridges.

Lincoln had gone out for his Sunday drive after receiving McDowell's wire; when he came back, he found Seward, white-faced and trembling, with news of the disaster. Not a muscle of the President's face moved. He convoked an extraordinary session of the Cabinet immediately; they sat through the night discussing the salvation or abandonment of the capital. Salvation carried by a narrow margin; Colonel Sickles was summoned from New York with new regiments and Governor Curtin was asked to put the population of Pennsylvania under arms and forward as many men as possible. Before morning they also got off a telegram to Mc-Clellan—send the victorious West Virginia army through the Potomac Valley to hold the outlets of the Shenandoah and hurry on himself by train.

Monday morning brought rain; under the gray clouds the runaways began to drift into Washington. The hotels and barrooms filled up with drunken officers, the whole town dripped heat, moisture and despair, a state of affairs not alleviated by the arrival of a telegram from the governor of Massachusetts asking to have "the martyrs who died in the late battle tenderly preserved in ice and sent forward." Mr. Stanton the lawyer wrote to his old chief, Buchanan, that the imbecility of the administration had reached a satisfactory climax and the low, cunning clown in the White House could not last much longer. The theaters were dark, the London correspondents noted how men looked over their shoulders at the horizon to catch the shine of Beauregard's bayonets.

But it was not Beauregard who arrived; it was little McClellan, his cap over one ear, aureoled in Napoleonic phrases and junior officers. He rode round the Arlington lines, drew out the two steady regiments of regulars and used them to clear the streets. Scouts felt along the Virginia roads, discovered no trace of an advancing enemy and returned to find business almost normal again.

In the North few were the words spoken about the disaster, and those without anger. The cheering stopped, but recruiting doubled, and no three-month volunteers but men who set down their names to fight till the end of the war, should it last a century. Mr. Greeley's standing head came off the *Tribune*; the New York Sabbath Committee pointed out that defeat was the only possible result of a battle engaged on Sunday, and the North settled down to the business of learning how to fight. The South, obviously, had not so much to learn; they had met "the roundhead bullies" and conquered them. "What else could one expect from a clash between the gamecock and the dunghill?" inquired the *Richmond Whig*.

6

PORTRAIT IN FOUR TONES OF RED

THROUGH the long dusty days of summer the troops marched and countermarched at drill among the sands of the Potomac bottom. Fresh regiments arrived daily, parading behind their bands, bayonets and standards all ashine with newness; at night trainloads of freshly cast cannon rumbled through the mountains. McClellan rode among the tents, alert and gallant, his keen eye missing nothing either for praise or blame. On a horizon hilltop a rebel flag was visible, waving over a far-pushed outpost. It could be ignored; when the well-drilled regiments advanced, it would go down with all the crazy structure of secession that supported it.

He found life sweet those days, young Captain McClellan who had resigned from the army to improve his prospects in the railroad business, five years before. "The President, the Cabinet, General Scott, all defer to me; by some strange magic I seem to have become the power of the land." All day the gray-haired captains made obeisance before this power; in the evening there would be a conference with some mysterious and slightly raffish operative of the Pinkerton service, back from a secret mission within the enemy's lines.

They brought in disquieting reports, big with the menace of armies. Beauregard was out, eliminated as a talkative popinjay, and huge forces were being concentrated under Johnston, his successor. There were 200,000 men within the Richmond lines; at any moment they might strike north.

McClellan's brow purled at the thought—and the worst of the situation was that old Scott, still officially commander of the armies of the Union, pooh-poohed the warning. The man must be in his dotage, reliving the days of 1812, when 2,000 soldiers made an army. The President supported the old driveler blindly. The new general was bitter as he explained to his wife how he alone understood the danger.

August brought torrents of rain; for a week the Potomac was impassable. General McClellan breathed a trifle easier; the condition of the roads was undoubtedly the only thing that had saved the capital. More regiments poured in; under the blazing trees of autumn, 190,000 men, the mightiest army the world had seen, now complete with cavalry, artillery and engineers, wheeled to the orders of the young Napoleon.

"Marching along," they sang to the first of those magnificent march-tunes, unequaled in history,

"—we are marching along;
For God and our country we are marching along;
McClellan's our leader, he's gallant and strong—"

The general believed he could defend Washington with such an army—but old Scott refused to credit the Pinkerton reports, snuffled goutily about an advance, and the President and Cabinet were silly enough to take his side. They badgered the dashing general about it at a meeting from which he emerged to write disconsolately that he was disgusted with the administration—"there are some of the greatest geese in the Cabinet I have ever seen."

That brought matters to a head; in spite of his respect for the old Commander-in-Chief, the young Napoleon faced the necessity of insulting him into resignation and sending him home to die. After the disagreeable task was over General McClellan felt as though tons had been lifted from his shoulders, but within a week the weight was back. Lincoln had caught the "We must advance" disease now. While the troops drilled through the dead leaves of November and the bugle-calls from across the river floated through the window, the general argued against it, "sick at heart with the poor beings who control the destinies of this country." They could not be made to understand that Confederate Johnston had at least 250,000 men and was only waiting the opportunity to push in and bring down the whole crazy structure of the Union.

Coming home from a hard day's drill one evening, his orderly informed the general that the President had already been waiting an hour. McClellan saw the chance to get rid of this incubus as he had of Scott; he sent down word he was busy at the moment and went to bed. Lincoln waited another hour and then left; one would have thought the rebuff sufficiently pointed, but Old Abe's intelligence was evidently too opaque to take a plain hint. He merely remarked that he would hold General McClellan's horse for him if he would only win victories.

On other evenings, the young general, Commander-in-Chief himself now, sought asylum from the persecutions of his enemy, the President, at the home of a new-found friend named Stanton. He was the famous advocate and old court opponent of Lincoln, "a frisky little Yankee in a spike-tailed coat," with a grim jaw, who had been the backbone of Buchanan's administration during its last year. The best hater in America, he had a gift of expression that enabled him to put their common opinion of Lincoln into phrases of delicious pungency. They passed charming hours together laughing over the perspiration-splotch, like a map of Africa, that disfigured the presidential shirt; he was "the man from Mars," "the original gorilla"—why had Du Chaillu sought the missing link on the Congo with such a specimen in Washington? On Thanksgiving Day there was a grand review; a quarter of a million voices filled the air with cheers for the gay young leader of the Army of the Potomac. Colonel Baker, Lincoln's dearest friend, was killed in an affair of outposts; the troops drilled, the bugles rang, the rebel flag floated on the skyline, Julia Ward Howe saw the camps by night and there would be a movement in the spring.

In December Congress, which up to that time had taken no part in the conversation, began to grow restive. Simon Cameron, Secretary of War, was the cause, the first and greatest of the long dynasty of political barons who ruled monarchial Pennsylvania, the man who raised graft to the realm of exact science. Lincoln did not like him well, but a Cabinet post had been his price for the vote of the Pennsylvania delegation in the nominating convention. The aroma of speculation that accompanied his movements might have been borne in the interests of efficiency, since there is little purity in a democracy at war, but Cameron was a hog—only his personal friends could get the fat contracts. A House investigating committee reported frankly that he was either a fool or a rascal.

Cameron, frightened off balance, since he had tested Lincoln's integrity, was ill-enough advised to try a snide political trick in the effort to hold his position. The December War Department report was just due; he put into it a strong appeal for arming the Southern blacks and starting a servile insurrection in the Confederate rear; had the report secretly printed as a pamphlet and sent to postmasters all over the country for issuance on a day. When it appeared, he would be leader of the antislavery interest, hence of the Republican Party, and too strong to be dismissed.

Poor idea; Lincoln got wind of the pamphlet, suppressed it by telegraph, and informed Cameron in a curt note that he had been appointed to the embassy of St. Petersburg, the Siberia of American politics.

The night the news got onto the streets McClellan dropped in on his friend Stanton to do a little gloating over the new difficulties of the administration. He found the stocky little man pacing the floor in perfervid excitement, a document in his hand. McClellan glanced at it; it was an official appointment, signed by the original gorilla, and it named Edwin M. Stanton Secretary of War. The general's jaw dropped.

"What are you going to do?"

"I am going to make Abe Lincoln President of the United States."

The young Napoleon staggered out, overwhelmed by this betrayal. Neither of them doubted that the fierce little lawyer would be able to model the yielding putty of the presidential character into something approaching manhood.

They were not the first to hold such an opinion of Lincoln. William H. Seward had felt that way about it once, for instance—a high man, one of the highest. He had been the real founder of the Republican party; a clear, strong intelligence in the Athenian tradition of the Adamses, cool as a mountain peak, wide as the sea. He would have been the natural nominee of the party for the presidency, but round him had gathered the clouds of petty enmities that any man of principle attracts in politics, and had been thrust aside for the unobjectional because little-known Illinois demagogue. But it was understood that he would hold the seals of the new administration and in that intent he had been given the Department of State.

In the early days Washington called him "the Premier"; the Congressional whips consulted him after hours, and he remarked blandly that he was assuming "a sort of dictatorship for the national defense" over the head of the fainéant Lincoln. And then came the affair of the English note—that fatal English note, when Her Majesty's government recognized the belligerent rights of the Confederates. Seward saw crystal-clear that this was only half a stride from recognizing the new government as a government, which meant a British loan and a British fleet to see it was collectible. It could not be permitted; he had prepared a withdraw-or-fight letter to be dispatched to London, sending it round to the White House as a matter of courtesy before mailing it. It came back full of erasures and interlineations that reduced it from a fighting protest to a mere acknowledgment of information.

The worried Secretary prepared a minute on the matter in which he demonstrated with irrefragable logic how wrong

Lincoln's view was and how the safety of the country depended upon the President allowing him to rule. For a week there was silence, relieved only by a note from the President to say he thought the changes best. Then a friend of a friend told Seward one evening how Lincoln had clutched his minute crumplingly with the remark, "I may not rule, myself, but certainly Seward shall not. The only ruler I have is my conscience and these men will have to learn that yet." The English note went as Lincoln had written it; there was no war and Seward was struck dumb. But he was too intelligent to miss the lesson and in another week he was telling an astonished visitor that "The President is the best of us. There is only one vote in the Cabinet and it belongs to him. Executive ability and vigor are rare qualities, but he has them both."

But even so, he could hardly stomach the appointment of Stanton. "Why, Mr. President, no man in American history has treated another so brutally as he has treated you."

Lincoln smiled. "There is a Methodist minister I know out in the West. He gets worked up to so high a pitch of excitement in his exhortations that they have to put bricks in his pockets to keep him down. We may be obliged to serve Stanton in the same way, but I guess we'll let him jump a while first."

The brick came sooner than might have been expected, over some minor order, in which Lincoln himself had transgressed regulations. Stanton bustled into a roomful of people with it in his hand.

"Mr. President, this order cannot be signed. I refuse to sign it."

"Mr. Stanton, I guess that order will have to be signed."

Conversation suddenly died in the room; the wills clashed with the ring of swords, and Stanton's broke. With every eye on him he signed the order.

So Stanton, the terrible Stanton, the man of iron, who solved all problems by rule of mathematics and a violent tongue, became Secretary of War. He feared neither God nor man nor devil, only Abraham Lincoln. He worked like a madman, white-hot with passion every moment; when he was offered a bad contract, he tore it to pieces and flung them in the face of the millionaire contractor; when a Congressman protested the arrest of a Copperhead, he cried in strangling rage:

"This is war, and war is violence! If I tap that little bell, I can send *you* to a place where you will never hear the dogs bark, and by Heaven! I'll do it if you say another word!"

But he was one of the great war ministers of history; greater than Carnot, great as Moltke. Nothing he touched was left undone, and nothing was badly done; a vast flood of energy emanated from him like an electric fluid, animating everyone it touched into inhuman exertion and achievement. For all the rest of that long war no Union soldier wanted for food or ammunition or clothes by his fault, no Union general wanted for soldiers, no army wanted for the best general who could be found, regardless of age or influence. On the Confederate side they had only Judah P. Benjamin, who spun endless iridescent cobwebs of theory and argument, brilliant as rainbows.

7

SCOTT'S ANACONDA

ABRAHAM LINCOLN had seen too much of the Illinois backwoods to retain any of that confidence in guileless self-righteousness which is the curse of liberalism in office. "Statesmanship is the art of exploiting individual meannesses for the general good," he said once; and being now engaged in an unwanted war, he fought in his shirt-sleeves. Many good Northern Democrats supported him because of the erroneous belief that the Southern people were fundamentally loyalists who had been dragooned into secession by a tooth-gnashing minority and who would join the old flag as soon as it appeared. It is improbable that Lincoln did not know better, but he did nothing to explode the myth. This might, in some quarters, be considered deception by suppression of fact; he took the larger view that he was withholding no essential fact from the constituencies and could not afford to be squeamish about minor details. He was not yet ready to accept the military services of Negroes for reasons connected with holding the still-precarious border slave states, but he would have accepted the services of a regiment of pickpockets, or one of trained baboons, if he had any use for them. This was not recklessness with regard to the means employed, but careful decision on the highest grounds as to where the ethical balance lay, each case being decided solely in the light of its own circumstances.

Thus he was in a position to consider Scott's Anaconda in an atmosphere uncontaminated by newspaper cartoons, and the more he looked at that sea-serpent, the better he liked it. When the Confederacy advertised for privateers to prey on Northern commerce, Lincoln's answer was to proclaim the entire coastline of the seceded states under blockade.

A development that pleased Jefferson Davis very much. That bloodless pedant never worried over anything but defective reasoning. Lincoln's mental processes seemed to him hopelessly confused and untidy; they had now led the abolitionist monster into the kind of mess that might have been expected, for the proclamation was an absurd, trumped-up farrago, an announcement of the most transparent of tissue-paper blockades. No one knew better than a former member of the U. S. Senate's Naval Committee that the American Navy consisted of 90 ships, of which a third were unseaworthy crocks that would go to the bottom if they stirred from their piers, while two-thirds of the remainder were scattered from Stamboul to the Moluccas. Blockade!—Old Abe didn't have enough vessels to blockade the North Carolina inlets. What was more, the proclamation constituted a major diplomatic error. England is always sensitive to violations of maritime law unless she is doing the violating, and this blockade, besides being illegal, was a stab at the heart of Britain's precious textile trade. Cotton was king, a logical God would defend the right and two commissioners took ship to lay a protest before the Court of St. James's.

. . . November morning in the Old Bahama Channel, all blue and gold. Picking her way along the coral shoals the Royal Mail Steam Packet *Trent*, Havana to Southampton, with Messrs. Mason and Slidell, Confederate ambassadors before the Queen's Majesty of England and the Emperor of France, on board. Northward away a big steam frigate bore down under a cloud of smoke and canvas, swung out an American ensign at her gaff and fired a shot across *Trent's* bow. Captain Williams put up the privileged blue peter of the English mail service and held his course. The persistent Yankee fired another shot, then came down with the muzzles of his broadside all agape; *Trent* hooted a protest and came to rest. Under the guns a boat discharged a lieutenant and a guard of marines on her deck.

"I have orders to arrest Messrs. Mason and Slidell, traitors to the United States."

"Sir! This is a British ship."

The lieutenant shrugged and pointed to his cannon; the captain bowed and summoned the commissioners, and a week later they were in the bilboes.

Question—is Captain Wilkes of the frigate a hero? Yes, cried the North, Mason and Slidell were the worst of the secesh lot—and for a solid fortnight it rained gold-mounted swords and invitations to dinner around the captain. Yes, thought the Cabinet in exultant meeting, and voted him thanks and promotion. But No! answered Charles Francis Adams from London, it was for this very thing that we fought England in 1812, it is wrong, wrong, wrong, it means certain, desperate, and disastrous war—what a shame that American democracy should end its existence on a note of blunder.

He was disturbed, poor ambassadorial gentleman, not without reason, for England was wild with fury, the Channel Fleet had been placed in commission and 8,000 troops ordered to Canada. The Duke of Newcastle recalled that Mr. Seward told him once over the whisky decanter that he meant to twist the lion's tail when he had the chance, and the London *Times* thundered that the marks of the American character were swagger and ferocity built upon a foundation of vulgarity and cowardice.

Evening of a racking day brought John Bright to the embassy with the inside news. Lord Russell was for war without further parleys; most of the Cabinet and all high life stood with him. Only Palmerston, the premier, had held out against it through a violent session, and he might not be able to stand the pressure of another. Mr. Adams, glad of the opportunity to do something, went around to Palmerston's at once, where he told his lordship that Captain Wilkes had doubtless acted without orders and would be disavowed. His lordship, bucked up by this assurance, began to recover his faculties; war would be a good deal of trouble, and there was just a chance that by taking the opposite side he might score off Lord Russell, who was inclined to look upon himself as the brains of the government and needed a check-rein.

The Queen was in London, but she would do nothing without Prince Albert, who was down at Cambridge, reprimanding Wales for skylarking. Palmerston went round to Downing Street for a look at the precedents pending his return. He found two documents waiting; one the fighting ultimatum Russell proposed to dispatch to the Americans, the other a letter from Napoleon III, offering to help England resent the insult to her flag. Palmerston's heart leaped; anybody could tell what would happen when the Prince saw England being dragged into war on the tail of the Imperial French kite. He got off a note to Paris telling the Emperor that England was exceedingly grateful for his support (as he expected, Napoleon took this as acquiescence and sent an ultimatum to Washington by the next boat); then sent Russell's draft around to the palace with the Imperial letter and a memo urging peace.

In the morning the Prince Consort was back. He was a sick man, but roused himself at seven to tear the ultimatum to bits; when he got through it was a request for the delivery of the prisoners, as innocuous as a Christmas card. Two days later he died, while Princess Alice played gavottes on the piano in the next room, but the revision was on its way to America.

The Cabinet met to consider it on Christmas Day in the morning. Mr. Chase couldn't "bear the thought of giving Mason and Slidell up, it was gall and wormwood" to him, and Lincoln, always close to the popular mind, feared the reaction that would be produced if the government backed down into admitting the justice of the British claim. He had the rest of them all against him, even Stanton, but as they debated, a messenger knocked at the door with an urgent diplomatic document. It was the French protest, couched in a tone of threat. Every face at the table cleared as Seward read it; the way out was obvious. A note was prepared at once, agreeing to turn Mason and Slidell over to the English when and wherever they wanted them, and another one to the French, telling them to mind their own business. Both went to the press together, with the French note thrown up in sharp focus as salve for the national dignity, and there was no reaction.

With a final touch of ingenious irony the Secretary of State offered England the use of Portland, Maine, as an entrepôt for the Canadian army; it was winter and so much more convenient than sending them up the ice-bound St. Lawrence.

In England nobody but the country party had really wanted war, and the Prince's death deprived them of their moorings. The manager of the Drury Lane came out before the curtain to announce the arrival of Seward's note; when he got as far as "The Americans have thought better of it—" the audience rose *en masse* and cheered their heads off. In the general relief, everybody clean forgot the illegality of Lincoln's blockade. When Mason and Slidell arrived with their protest, they could interest nobody in the Cause but "Tiny" Roebuck, a pint-sized M. P. whose very appearance was a source of merriment to his associates. Even the pro-Confederacy *Times* pronounced the commissioners "the most worthless booty it was possible to extract from the jaws of the American lion." Mason wrote home that there was nothing to be done, and Jefferson Davis had heart-burnings over the illogicality of human affairs.

Meanwhile the blockade. Off the coast of North Carolina the sea-islands fence in sounds wide enough to float the navies of the world, and stormy Hatteras makes keeping station outside impossible. The rebels had set forts along the gaps in the island chain; commerce raiders began to come out and war munitions in to make a major problem for Lincoln.

Perhaps it was his sense of humor that led him to combine it with his other major problem, to see whether the two would not cancel out. Benjamin F. Butler, a problem on two legs—necessary to introduce him, he will be met again—a classic example of the bartender politician, with one eye and that usually bleary, two left feet and a genius for getting them into every plate, but a wonderful genius at stuffing ballot boxes, voting dead men, controlling ward-heelers and handling every other device of machine politics. Like most machine politicians his frogship longed for wider puddles; he persuaded Andrew of Massachusetts, the tenderly-preserved-in-ice governor, to make him a general, and turned up in Washington among the first arrivals. Lincoln put him in military command of Baltimore; he removed the mayor and the police chief, jailed half a dozen big-wigs, set the city screaming with rage and came back, wagging his tail. Packed off to Fortress Monroe, he initiated an "attack on Richmond" that cost two hundred lives. Now he was sent to the sounds, where he would certainly do little harm, for the situation was already as bad as possible.

A man who attacks stone forts with wooden ships is a fool; Lord Nelson said so. Ben Butler, who knew nothing of Lord Nelson or of naval strategy, ordered Flag-officer Stringham in against Fort Hatteras, while he started landing men through the surf outside. When three hundred got ashore the sea rose and the surfboats stove in; the troops were marooned, with all their ammunition wet, no water and no food but some of the wild sheep of the dunes which were hacked to pieces with officers' swords and toasted at piratical bonfires on the ends of bayonets. The Confederates in the fort had only to come out and gather them in.

But the Confederates in the fort were otherwise occupied. Stringham kept his ships moving so fast the rebel guns could hit nothing, and deluged the works with twenty-eight shells a minute. The gunners were driven to refuge in the bomb-proof. A shell came through the ventilator and drove them out again; another caved in the roof of the magazine, the next would blow it and them up, so they took down the flag. The fleet hurried past Hatteras into Pamlico Sound, took the fort on Beacon Island in reverse and captured that, too. Fort Macon and Beaufort at the southern end lasted only a week longer.

The Southerners still had the Albemarle Sound. They fortified Roanoke Island and blocked Croatan Inlet with piles behind which a squadron of shallow-draft gunboats was organized. Flag-officer Goldsborough, who had replaced Stringham, saw that the heavy Union frigates could never get through—too much mud and obstruction. But an energetic purchasing agent named Morgan in New York had been buying up all sorts of crazy tugs and river-boats, arming them with any guns Brooklyn Navy Yard had available, and sending them south to join the blockade. With a squadron of these makeshift warships Goldsborough attacked. A strange amphibian grapple raged across the complex of mud and pools through murk midnight, lit by lightning-flashes. The rebels were outnumbered in a blind struggle where numbers meant everything. One of their forts blew up, the Union ships charged through the piles, sank one gunboat by ramming, carried another hand-to-hand, and chased the rest all the way up the sound to Elizabeth City, where they stormed and burned them at the quays. The whole system of sounds went lost and Fort Hatteras became a base for the Union blockaders.

Blockaders who had by this time stiffened their tissue-paper structure into something with metal in it. Every kind of craft that would float and carry a gun—liner, fisherman, yacht, ferry-boat, tug—had been bought indiscriminately, and rushed out under a junior lieutenant to stand off a Southern port. By August a group of "ninety-day gunboats," built in that amount of time from green wood, began to come in; before the end of the year a succession of incredible "double-enders," with paddle-wheels that could work in either direction so they would not have to turn around in rivers. The most unwarlike of warships, the most unseaworthy of sea-going craft, they capsized, they ran aground or burst their boilers daily. Their seamen lived on salt-horse within smelling distance of frying chickens on shore, or searched the cays for turtles' eggs at night. The seas hammered them; they clashed with rebels in the passes; concealed batteries bushwacked them from the shore—all in a service of inglorious accident and unrecorded death which only youth redeemed from misery.

But they sealed the ports. In the fall of '61 there were already no luxuries in the Confederacy, the newspapers had cut their sheets to half-size, and from every pier, where the piled cotton mildewed, a Union cruiser could be seen tossing against the blue. Scott's Anaconda.

8

ALLEGRO MARZIALE

TRUMPETER, sound! The flags are up along the rivers of the West.

Albert Sidney Johnston was leader supreme there for the Confederacy; chivalrous, tall, noble in body and mind, all that Frémont was or hoped to be, with a resplendent record of twenty years of victory in the old army, "the best commander in the South." He came late to the field, by express from California, but, once arrived, struck hard, throwing forward 20,000 men of Leonidas Polk's command to take the Mississippi precipices at Columbus and shatter the absurd fiction of Kentucky's neutrality. The place was fortified; the next Confederate move would obviously be to Cairo in Illinois, and Frémont called a council of war to choose a general for the defense before the Ohio River should be cut.

The wheels of destiny spin. General Justus McKinstry of the staff, hurrying in late, saw a stocky man in civilian clothes smoking a cigar on a bench in the dark entry, recognized Ulysses Grant, whom he had known in Mexico, and stopped to shake hands. Upstairs it was like a Negro lodgenight. Generals were a dime a dozen; Lincoln had just made twenty-one new ones, including Grant, who had offered a surprising protest against his own promotion on the ground he had not earned it. Eight of the new generals were at the meeting and they all wanted the Kentucky command. "Oh, give it to Grant downstairs there," said McKinstry, wearying of their babble. There was a silence. Frémont cleared his throat.

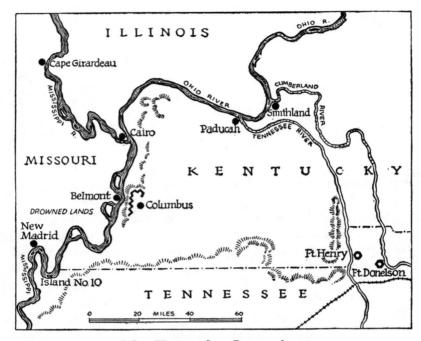

The Kentucky Campaign

"I am not sure General Grant has the requisite force of character. He has been asked to report to headquarters to explain the depredations of his troops upon the citizens of Missouri."

The staff all burst out at that with tales of the brigadier's drinking, but they could agree on no one. Frémont flew into a pet, sent an orderly down for Grant, told him he was appointed to the district of Western Kentucky and raked him over the coals for his troops' bad behavior. Grant took the wigging silently, standing at parade rest, awkward and shabby among the gold-braided staff officers. When Frémont had finished he said "all right," and walked out.

General Grant to Cairo. It was November and the rivers high; there were few troops and those badly drilled, but Grant, commander by annoyance, had to do something to hold his job. He loaded 3,000 men aboard river steamers and went down to Belmont, Missouri, where the rebels had a strong outpost across the Mississippi from their Columbus fortress. The men disbarked and moved through a muddy cornfield toward the Southern position, all firing at once with an infinitude of smoke and banging. Grant was scared and wanted to think. "Stop that infernal noise!" he shouted crossly. The smoke cleared and he made a discovery not without its importance—namely, that the rebels, more afraid of him than he of them, were running away. He cut up their retreat and the Union forces went whooping in to loot the camp, singing "We'll hang Jeff Davis on a sour apple tree."

Confederate Polk could see what was going on from across the river. He put over 10,000 troops below Belmont and came rolling down on Grant's little force. The Union general had to fire the camp to round up his looters; a few shells from the Columbus batteries helped chase them, and he managed to reach the boats before Polk's army struck them.

In the South they counted this a victory—had not the Union army retreated?—but they missed the point. With Missouri in the Union it would be possible to outflank the Columbus position from across the stream lower down; and Johnston read Grant's Belmont thrust as a reconnaissance in force precedent to such a drive. He hurriedly called in his outposts along the Ohio and set every man he could gather to fortifying the weak spot—Island No. 10, where the Mississippi swings a lazy S at the Tennessee-Kentucky border. Grant, still oppressed by the itch to do, hurried off in the other direction; the next news Johnston had of him was that he had seized Paducah and Smithland and was digging in. The two towns hold the outlets of the great rivers Cumberland and Tennessee which ran right through all the Confederate east-west lines. The Southern commander was thunderstruck, he could not imagine that stupid Grant had meant it that way, it could only be an accident, but the covenanted defense-line along the Ohio was broken, and his advance toward Louisville outflanked and compromised.

He had an alternative. Close to the Tennessee border runs

a front of highland, a fortress built by nature, with the roads so bad and few that an army may not mount the glacis save at certain favored points. This highland Johnston made his new defense-line, Columbus its anchor at the western flank, Mill Spring its buttress on the east. In the center are two passes only; one Johnston covered by a fort at Bowling Green, the other, where the two rivers pierce the highland, with a pair of works, Forts Henry and Donelson. Through the winter, then, he made his position secure, while McClellan moaned for reinforcements in the east and Grant tried to control the pillaging tendency of his men.

Riding abroad from Paducah, the general met a woman who complained of a young lieutenant:

GENERAL ORDER, ARMY OF THE TENNESSEE
(Read at dress parade with all troops present)

Lieutenant Wickfield of the Fourth Indiana having this day eaten everything in Mrs. Selvidge's house but one pumpkin pie, he is hereby ordered to return with an escort of one hundred cavalry and eat that pie.

U. S. GRANT, *General Commanding*

And the looting died of ridicule, but Grant had other troubles now, chief among them being General Halleck.

Halleck was Frémont's successor. Henry Wager Halleck, "Old Brains," with pop-eyes and an immense lofty forehead, stuffed with the oddest assortment of erudition ever assembled by a commanding general. Degrees in engineering, law and military science, knew enough to lecture at Harvard on all three subjects, and dabbled in heraldry on the side; had helped write the constitution of California; built lighthouses and ran a quicksilver mine, all with intense success. A man of order and method; the world spins its circuit through the skies by clockwork laws, men should do the same. Grant wanted to storm in against Henry and Donelson before they became impregnable, Halleck said "Tut-tut." Like most book soldiers he found the actual procedure of war disorderly and inefficient; did not want the machine to move till the last rivet was in place and a flag flying from the walking-beam.

Unexpected support for the Grant, or lawless, method turned up from the U. S. Navy. Last fall a crazy contractor named Eads had gone to St. Louis on the understanding that the government would buy seven gunboats if he built them in ninety days. He did it; they looked like square turtles, were plated with iron forward and around the engines and would run on a heavy dew—just the trick for working among the shifting sandbars of the western streams. Flag-officer Foote was their commander; he knew he would have to deal with Henry and Donelson sooner or later, and protested to Washington about giving the rebels time to strengthen them. Welles of the Navy Department took up the matter; he got Stanton interested, and peremptory orders flashed over the wires to let Grant go in.

The brigadier started up the Tennessee River on the sixth of February with 15,000 men and complete ignorance of the enemy's positions, except that they were strong. The men landed eight miles above Fort Henry and immediately became involved in a complex of swamp and felled trees; the gunboats pushed straight upstream and opened fire. Half an hour later a shell from the fort burst through *Essex'* armor, blew up her boiler and scalded half the men aboard to death, but that was the last flicker from the fort. One of its big batteries was already dismounted, the gunboats rapidly got the rest under, and when Grant's men pounded up they found a white flag floating over Fort Henry.

It was a skeleton; most of the Confederates had already departed to make the big stand at Donelson. Grant telegraphed Halleck he was attacking that place immediately, then cut the wires to keep out an order forbidding (which Halleck sent, of course). The gunboats went round to come up the Cumberland River, on which Donelson faced; the troops struck straight cross-country.

The place was three times as strong as Henry, mounted

on a bluff a hundred feet high, with 21,000 men inside, but they were commanded by Floyd, the sneaky Secretary of War from Buchanan's Cabinet. Grant knew him and knew he was a weakling; he pushed boldly in to invest the place, and there were skirmishes between the pickets the night of his arrival. He had three divisions in line opposite the works: C. F. Smith, Lew Wallace, McClernand, reading from north to south. It had come on warm during the march across, the way was toilsome and the Union soldiers threw away their blankets. Now it turned zero-cold with a bitter storm of sleet; Grant's men slept under the stars without coverings and during the night the wounded froze to death between the lines, while the defenders had warm beds.

In the morning Union artillery began to arrive and then the gunboats; the ships attacked at once, but the plunging fire from the heights was too hot for them; gunboat *Louisville*'s tiller was shot away, she fouled another and both drifted downstream. The rest could not keep it up, the admiral was wounded, and the fleet pulled out of action, hard hit. In the night Foote sent for Grant. Conference on board —would it be best to give up? No, said Grant, the army will do it alone, outnumbered though it be. As he was riding back, there came an ominous rumble from southward, then a pale aide, spurring his horse, with the news that the rebels were making a sortie and the Union army was beat.

Floyd had flung 8,000 men in solid column against Mc-Clernand's division at the river-edge and smashed it, then turned in against the open flank to roll up the Union line, but Lew Wallace had put in a reserve brigade and the rebel advance was brought to a stand for the time being around a little eminence. As Grant rode up, a couple of prisoners were being led past; he noted their haversacks bulged, and, calling for one of them, opened it up. It contained nearly a side of fried bacon and a big supply of hardtack. Grant looked round.

"These men are trying to escape," he said. "They have rations for a long march, not a fight. All the strength must

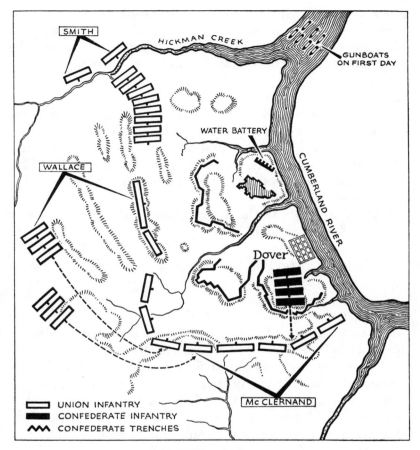

Fort Donelson

be on this side. Tell General Smith to attack the fort on his front at once."

It was up a precipitous hill and through a tangle of abatis and trenches, but Grant had been right; Floyd had drawn out most of his right wing to escape by the left. Smith led the charge in person, an old man with a long white moustachio that flowed over his shoulder, and the drive went right through; the whole line of fortifications on his front was taken, and the pressure on McClernand and Wallace eased as Floyd recalled his advance-guard to keep from being thrown into the river. Night ended the fighting with McClernand solidly across the way of egress again and the fort half-won. In the morning Grant would have artillery on the height Smith had gained; could shell the place to bits, and everyone knew it.

Floyd was afraid they would hang him if he were captured; he turned the command over to Pillow, his second, and got across the Cumberland on a river-boat; Pillow, also afraid of a necktie party, turned it over to Buckner, the third in command, and got away in a hand-skiff. Buckner wrote to Grant asking terms.

At three o'clock in the morning the Union general wrote out a brief note by torchlight:

"No terms except an unconditional surrender can be accepted. I propose to move immediately upon your works."

Buckner was strapped; he wrote an angry little note about Grant's lack of chivalry, then surrendered the whole army, 17,000 men, sixty-five guns and the fort.

The campaign was ended in a clap of thunder. Foote's gunboats went cruising up both rivers clear into Alabama, where they captured a big unfinished ironclad, and Johnston's whole defense-line, built with such elaborate skill, was wrecked. Bowling Green could not be held, Mill Spring went, the great stronghold of Columbus had to be abandoned. Alarm-bells rang from the Nashville steeples and the people tumbled out to see the backs of the Confederate soldiers as the ironclads came bellowing up the river. All Kentucky, all central Tennessee, fell into the hands of the Federals.

Albert Sidney Johnston, the best general in the South, still could not believe there was anything behind the frozen face his opponent exhibited to the world. His information service told him that Grant was a man to rush furiously onward, careless of outposts and scouting, a slam-bang swashbuckler; his intellect told him that the way to deal with such a wild bull was to catch him in a bad position, concentrate quickly and lance him with overpowering numbers in a surprise attack. Fortunately the problem was simplified by the fact that the Union general must advance up the rivers, leaning on his steamers for supplies, since the railroads were inadequate. Somewhere near the Alabama bend of the Tennessee would be the place for the knockout. Secretly, secretly, he began calling in troops all the way from Florida and western Texas for the stroke.

9

EXPERIMENT IN TAUROMACHY

G ENERAL HALLOCK controlled three armies—of Missouri,
under John Pope; of the Tennessee, under Grant; of the
Cumberland, under Don Carlos Buell. Pope, like Grant, was
an energetic unknown; had done well in cleaning out night-
riders and holding off Confederate raids along the Indian
frontier. Don Carlos was a martinet; a perfect drillmaster,
who kept his troops doing the manual of arms a whole year
while the rest were fighting.

Old Brains was no fool at war by the book, and any
oaf could see how Grant's riverain operation had put Albert
Sidney Johnston's back to a wall. The front of the Tennessee
uplands was broken. Behind it lay the railroad from Memphis
to Chattanooga, thence through the mountains, vital to the
Confederacy, an irreplaceable avrone or nerve-cable, the only
way of circling the vast tangle of cypress and frog-swamp in
central Mississippi, the only good line of communication between the supply-lands of the west and the armies of the east.
Swing Pope and the navy against Memphis as a diversion,
concentrate Grant and Buell up the Tennessee River, and
with their united forces slash the rebel nerve-cable where
it most nearly approached the river at the Corinth ganglion—
this was Halleck's plan, sound, but as obvious as a ham sand-
wich, like everything he did.

The outpost of Island No. 10 prevented execution. In
the rebels' hands it could be supplied by water and attacked
from nowhere, backed up against the drowned lands of lower
Missouri, a hundred-mile morass, and the Kentucky side as
bad. Pope went in against it in the early days of March, down

the highlands of the Missouri shore, with Foote's gunboats to help him. At the drowned lands the army wheeled to a stand; the batteries were too heavy for Foote's lightly plated fleet. He brought up fourteen bombing-vessels, one single mortar each on a huge block of wood, and began throwing shells into the place from a distance. The shells squashed in the mud and the rebels laughed at him.

It was spring; the muddy river brimmed the levees, giving Foote an idea—why not cut a canal through the neck of the S to New Madrid, send troops through it to the high ground of the Missouri side and cut the fort off from below? Try it, said Pope, and army and navy fell to frantic effort to finish the canal while the floods lasted, hewing, digging, fighting off fevers by sunlight and torchlight, while rebel sharpshooters sniped at them from trees. "I need one hundred men ten feet tall to work in mud eight feet deep," requisitioned one despairing engineer officer; another lost half a company, twenty men, sucked down by quicksands. In spite of everything the canal was done, it worked; Pope and the army floated through rejoicing to New Madrid.

Second check—the canal was too shallow for the ironclads; the Confederates had set up light batteries all down the Kentucky shore and Pope's men could not cross. The campaign was halted. But Commander Walke of the ironclad *Carondelet*, a young man who had just faced a court-martial for lack of bravery, and, though acquitted, felt a stain on his name—Walke persuaded Pope and Foote to let him try taking his ship down through the teeth of the fortress. He made the attempt on a murk March midnight with a storm raging —as dauntless a stroke as any in the war. The little ironclad foamed through the black water with thunder pealing overhead, the shore outlined by a fitful glare of the rebel artillery in a fair approximation of hell, where a single flick of the steering wheel would put her on a sandbar at the price of every life abroad, a single cannon-shot would tear her entrails out. She made it, by heaven! and next morning moved along the shore below New Madrid, a triumphal parade of one.

After that there was nothing to it; *Carondelet* started at

the bottom of the line of light batteries and worked upstream, knocking them out as she went; behind her Pope's men crossed in swarms. The gunboat choked off relief from downstream and Island No. 10 surrendered at discretion with 7,000 men and three generals.

Out on the other flank of the advance Grant had chosen a camp-site at Pittsburg Landing, where Lick and Snake creeks box a rough parallelogram of interwoven forest. He had been heavily reinforced; there were 35,000 men on the ground, in not much order; the divisions of Sherman and Prentiss farthest south, behind them other divisions around the landing under McClernand, Hurlbut, and Smith (succeeded by W. H. L. Wallace). Wallace, with 7,000 of his sixth division, was upstream at Crump's Landing, wandering vaguely around for no reason at all—perhaps their general was gathering material for the military passages of "The Prince of India." On Saturday night Buell, a day's march distant, sent in an orderly to find out when Grant would make room for his troops to cross the river. "Monday or Tuesday will do," answered Grant. "There will be no fighting here."

He was mistaken; Albert Sidney Johnston was just outside his picket-line with 50,000 men.

General Prentiss woke with the early light to hear an unwonted crackling in the depths along his front. He let the bugle be blown and turned out the troops; before they reached position the forest rang with the rebel yell and the whole Confederate army stormed in on him. The Union soldiers were half in their beds, wholly taken by surprise. Sherman's division collapsed around Shiloh Church; McClernand's front was beaten in and the wreckage of these last two divisions streamed away through the trees, disorganized and weaponless, to take refuge under the bluff at the landing. Prentiss lost a regiment, then a brigade, but he had a moment more warning than the others, and brought the attack to a temporary stand in a grove that crowned a little elevation known as the Hornet's Nest. Hurlbut and W. H. L. Wallace, saved by the time the rebels lost in breaking Sherman, got their men into line and hurried up to make good the defense along

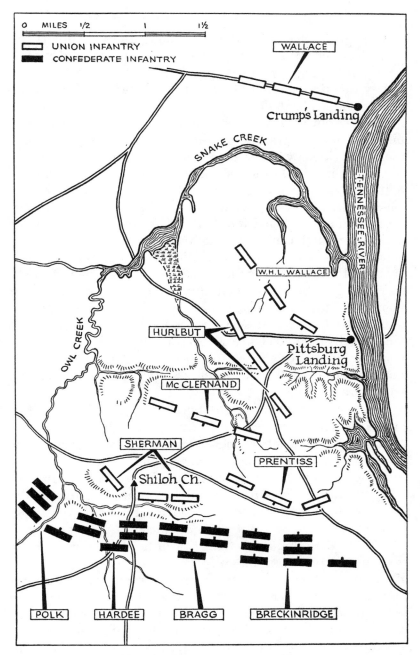

Shiloh—Sunday Morning

a deep gully that split the battlefield midway. Johnston's men, instinct with victory, flowed past Prentiss and pressed on against the gully in sweeping wave-like charges.

By this time Grant, who had breakfasted in the rear, was on the field. He understood at once; Johnston had put his main strength against Prentiss and the left wing, in hope of taking the landing and crowding the Union army back into the sack formed by Snake Creek, there to capture it. Sherman's break on the right, Prentiss' stand on the left, had swung the battle in the other direction, but the situation was one of deadly peril. He was heavily outnumbered, half his formations had dissolved, and if either wing gave only a little more nothing on earth could save the Army of the Tennessee.

Grant, slow Grant, did a million things at once; messengers went off hell-for-leather to summon Wallace and Buell; a wig-wag battalion flashed frantic signals down-river for Foote and the gunboats; a battery of siege-guns intended to hammer the forts of Cornith was handspiked into position where gully met river just in front of the landing; Sherman and McClernand were dispatched to bring some of the skulkers from under the bluff and put them in anyhow, anywhere.

On the Confederate right Breckinridge and Bragg had pushed Prentiss back to the river through the Hornet's Nest and cut him off; by noon he was enfiladed from three directions and forced to surrender what men he had left. But this held up the advance against the landing once more; when it came on again, early in the afternoon, two of the gunboats were on hand to shell it from the flank, the siege-guns blazed into it from straight ahead, and it slowed to a halt. On the other flank there was a hard see-saw grapple, back and forth across the gully, with Hurlbut and W. H. L. Wallace aided by a crazy patchwork of fragments from Sherman's, in which generals fought like privates and privates led regiments. Grant rode through the press, straightening out the sagging lines, directing artillery here, reorganizing a company of infantry there, the calmest man on the field.

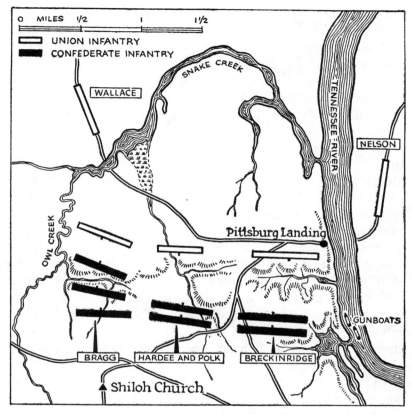

Shiloh—Sunday Night

His horse was killed under him; he got another. A bullet took his hat off; he fought bareheaded; another went through his coat between arm and side, another tore the insignia from his shoulder; the 41st Illinois cheered him when he shook still another from his pocket. Sherman saw trees whose leaves were utterly stripped by balls, the gully ran with blood, you could cross from one side to the other on the piled bodies, but Grant held the frayed lines firm.

Three o'clock; the attack was dying down. Johnston rode to the front—"Once more and we have them!" and went forward, riding with the advance of a deep column headed at the Union center. A bullet hit him in the thigh; he rode on, cheering his men, then swayed from the saddle and fell among the mottled shadows of the glade. Beauregard took command for the Confederates; pulled Bragg out from the right, where he could not close with the siege-guns, and sent him in against W. H. L. Wallace's weakening flank. The Union general was killed, it gave, it gave—and then twilight stopped the advance just short of victory.

All night the men lay on their arms in driving rain while the pickets flashed muskets at each other among the trees; all night the siege-guns boomed on the Union left. At midnight Lew Wallace and his 7,000 came quick-stepping in to stay Grant's weakened right; at two in the morning "Bull" Nelson, a huge man, all head and shoulders, reported with the first division of Buell's well-drilled troops—"Here we are; if stupidity and hard fighting are what you want, we're the men"—at half-past the hour Crittenden, a thin, staring man with insane eyes and hair that hung to his collar, arrived in river-boats with another division of Buell; at three McCook followed Nelson in with a third division. At four Grant had them all in line, at five he swung from defense to attack, Wallace leading.

The Confederates were worn with a day's fighting, their leader was dead, they were oppressed by a sense of failure. Hardee wavered on their right, Bragg on the left. Sherman rode forward, yelling "Give them hell!" in a voice gone cracked, followed by an incredible swarm of men in blue; the rebels could not stand it, the whole army gave way at once, and they were driven from the field in prone rout not to halt till their disorganized army was behind the ramparts of Corinth.

Over 10,000 loss on either side in Shiloh battle; the most terrific combat yet fought in America and one of the greatest victories, but Halleck's orderly soul was revolted. Grant had broken every rule of scientific warfare, failed to scout his enemy, got himself surprised, and when surprised, instead of retreating according to book, had had the temerity to

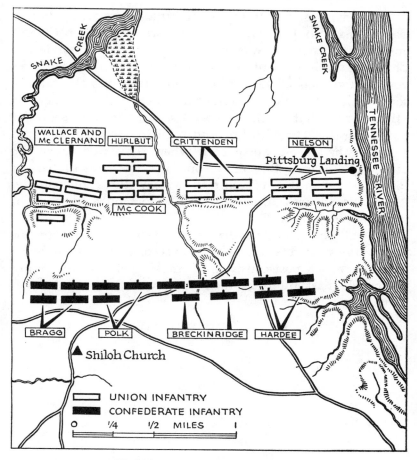

Shiloh—Monday Morning

make a stand-up fight against superior numbers and with men thrown in all hodge-podge; finally he had not pursued the beaten foe. Besides, Grant was a rotten paper soldier—"I have had no communication from him for a week. I can get no returns, no reports, no proper receipts from him"—and Halleck fussed down to Pittsburg Landing to take command in person, firing off a pyrotechnic of requests to Washington for the removal of the crude general.

It arrived at about the same time as a delegation of tissies, male and female, with a complaint that Grant's addiction to whisky was unbecoming the commander of Christian soldiers. Stanton heard them out, then, "Read that, you damned fools!" he snarled, and slid across the table a copy of Grant's "unconditional surrender" letter to Buckner. "If he wrote that when he wasn't sober, I'll issue an order punishing sobriety with fine and imprisonment."

They had even worse luck when they went over the Secretary's head to Lincoln. "You don't say!" ejaculated the President, when they told him their story; then, interestedly, "What brand does he drink? I'd like to send a barrel of it to the other generals."

But all the same Old Brains was leader of the army in the field now, and Grant reduced to second in command, the duties of which post consisted of smoking cigars and giving advice when asked for it, which was never.

I O

VARANUS SALVATOR

MR. MALLORY, naval secretary of the C. S. A., came on to Richmond by water through the sounds, as befitting the Poseidon of the new Olympus. It made him seasick; he came ashore at Norfolk and was propped up in a chair, somewhat greenish about the gills, while an inventive young officer named Brooke, who had been laying for a chance to bring his Big Idea before authority, waved in one hand a model that resembled a cooking pot and descanted on the virtues of an iron-plated floating battery. In that moment of exaltation which comes to a seasick man who has just set his foot on terra firma, Mr. Mallory told him to build the thing. Young Brooke disappeared; next morning Mr. Mallory found he had already ordered 700 tons of iron from the Tredegar Works, and, as it was too late to cancel, made a pet of the project. The craft was jerry-built to seven degrees, makeshift piled on makeshift. The only iron was railroad iron, Southern gentlemen would not soil their hands by laboring as mechanics, so they had to use a second-hand set of engines dredged up with the burned bulk of the frigate *Merrimac*. Brooke greased them till they would run after a fashion and built his floating battery on the hulk—a rectangular citadel of metal sloping back from the edges, pierced from ends and sides to allow ten cannon, the hull part under water, with a big iron dog-tooth fixed at the bow to puncture enemies' ribs on contact. She was christened *Virginia*.

There were five Union frigates in Hampton Roads at the mouth of the estuary on which Norfolk stands—*Cumberland,*

Congress, St. Lawrence, Roanoke, Minnesota. The morning of March 8 was wash-day; the ships swung at anchor with their rigging full of drying garments. At nine *Cumberland*'s lookout noted a column of smoke over the woods toward Norfolk. The picket-boat *Zouave* ran down. She saw the roof of a barn moving slowly into the channel, belching smoke from a chimney, and fired her 32-pounder Parrott at it six times without provoking the slightest attention.

Cumberland and *Congress*, the two nearest frigates, cleared for action and bore up to engage; *Minnesota* rang for steam, *St. Lawrence* spread her sails. *Cumberland* opened the ball with a shell from her pivot-gun. It broke to pieces on the steely sides and on came the unknown, crocodile, dinosaur, ports tight closed, ponderous and disdainful. *Cumberland* swung square across her path, the gunners changed to solid shot and let go a whole broadside. To their horror the shot bounded up and away from the sloping flanks like metal hail; there was a snort of smoke as the monster put on extra speed, and then, with a tearing shock, she struck *Cumberland* square amidship, and at the same moment her port flew open, her guns poked out and a terrible storm of shells deluged the frigate's decks.

Cumberland reeled away from the blow, dripping men from her mastheads, then came shuddering back with a hole in her side. Her decimated crew fired again and again, aiming for the gun-ports, the waterline, anything that might give. Futility—the shot skipped away from the metallic sides to plash in the water and for every shot the frigate gave she took two. Her fire died down, the flag was shot from the gaff. A head appeared at the ironclad's port. "Surrender?" it asked.

"Never!" cried Lieutenant Morris of the frigate. "I'll sink alongside first."

He did. *Virginia* moved off to a little distance and settled down to pound the wooden ship to pieces. On *Cumberland* the mounting water drowned the engines, then the magazines. The cockpit was swamped; the wounded were moved to the upper deck, to be wounded again on their stretchers.

The frigate's sides ran blood, she was afire, the sparks were tumbling around the decks. One by one her crew fell beside their useless guns, but she endured in vain, suicidal gallantry for two whole hours of murder, till a long wave lapped across the gundeck and took her down into the shallows, where only the stars and stripes on her mainmast stood above the tide.

Virginia turned from the whirlpool of her sinking, where a few black specks still fought for life, to seek another prey. *Congress'* captain had put her aground under protection of some shore batteries. Out of range? No, for the ironclad giant found a position a hundred yards from her stern where she could not make a pretense of defense and began firing red-hot shot, one a minute, deliberate and certain. It was *Cumberland* over again; half the crew were down in the shambles of the main-deck, the masts came tearing into the clamor, she was irretrievably ablaze from figurehead to taffrail, the survivors were leaping overboard to die by water rather than fire when *Virginia's* tired crew gave the rest of the United States Navy remand for a night and took their monster home. What did they care for time? Today or tomorrow all the great ships with their proud sails were doomed, for the law of physics were unphysick't, wood sank and metal floated, and Lieutenant Brooke's iron pot was mistress of the world.

The news came to Washington at three in the morning, over the military telegraph. At six the Cabinet met, pale with sleeplessness, taking the blow according to their several temperatures. Seward was motherly, consoling, vague, Chase querulous and whining, Lincoln all eager curiosity—how many guns had she, what was her thickness of plate, could we build one like her? Only Stanton understood; he paced the floor, shouting at the rest—"Nothing can prevent her destroying *seriatim* every naval vessel, laying Washington in ashes and then placing the seaport cities under contribution. I have notified the governors to protect their cities; we can do nothing for them. Why, sir, it is not unlikely that we will have from one of her guns a cannon-ball in this room before we leave it."

There was a silence; then they burst out with quick-thought plans—sink the Potomac full of stone barges, trip the monster in a gigantic net, send spies to blow her up, move the capital to Pittsburgh or elsewhere inland. Stanton sneered at them—halt the revolution of the zones with a charge of buckshot if you will, but not this leviathan with such desperate devices. "The war is lost. Nothing can save us but a miracle"—and, it being Sunday, they adjourned to church to pray for one.

"Before they call upon me, will I answer them."

Unknown to them, the miracle was already at hand. In the red night of Hampton Roads, where blazing *Congress* threw her glare across the ripples, an iron raft with a round iron house atop moved slowly in to take station by the side of *Minnesota*. It was the Ericsson "device for aquatic attack" *Monitor*, forgotten by everyone but the Swedish engineer who had dreamed her long ago as he sat among the beeches of Eskilstuna. He took the idea to France, but the Imperial Lords in Admiralty were pigheaded, so he crossed the Atlantic to offer it to Lincoln. The President had sat on a box, whittling a stick, while he explained, remarked "There seems to be something in this, as the girl said when she put her leg in the stocking," and, the cost not being excessive, said build it as one of the three experimental ironclads. She was finished on Inauguration Day; that same night she started for the Roads. Off Sandy Hook a storm came up; the hatches leaked water, the waves broke over the funnel and filled her with coal gas, a freak of pressure caused awful groans and shrieks, as of dying men, to issue from her anchor well and for four days long the crew were confined in an iron box under water with artificial light and ventilation (the light and ventilation of 1862!) while the escort boats ran away to report her foundered. Yet by a miracle she rode through the storm, by a miracle she came sliding through the red glare of defeat that very night.

The morning mists curled back to show *Minnesota* where *Virginia* had left her the night before, aground. Alongside was a peculiar structure—a floating water-tank, thought some of the rebel crew. But as the ironclad approached, the water-tank cast off, ran up a flag on a pole astern and headed straight for the giant, puffing smoke from a narrow pipe. On *Virginia* they laughed—one shot ought to do, but as the impudent tot drew near, they gave her a full broadside. Most missed; the rest danced up and away in a shower of sparks. Then the iron house spun like a teetotum, two heavy guns struck out their snouts and two thunderbolts struck *Virginia*'s casement a blow so violent that every man on that side of the ship was dashed to the deck with blood running from nose and ears. The plating held, but the bolts were started, the wooden boxing shattered, and the next shot at that point would come in. The officers in *Virginia*'s box exchanged glances and sharp comment: the Ericsson battery.

The big ironclad swung round majestically, firing her bow-gun; *Monitor* one-stepped away, her turret whirling, and fired again on the turn. *Virginia*'s citadel was full of powder-smoke, shivered wood and noise as the one-two of the smaller ship's shot beat it like a drum. "Aim for her gun-ports!" cried Lieutenant Jones, but "Her turret turns too fast," answered Eggleston, the division officer. They aimed for her turret-base, her deck, her pilot house. No result—the turret spun, the ugly gun-muzzles spouted flame again and again. *Virginia* tried to run the turret-ship down, but the dog-tooth glanced harmlessly off a heavily plated deck; tried to escape the diminutive antagonist to get the wooden frigate, but *Monitor* was right across her path, hammering the weakened plates. *Virginia*'s funnel went, her speed dropped off; a shot hit one of her gun-muzzles, tore it away and sent long iron slivers shivering through the casemate, another started a leak at the waterline, the next blow there would sink the ship.

Two hours—"Why are you no longer firing, Mr. Eggleston?" "I can do her as much damage by snapping my fingers every two minutes." A gray haze of defeat mingled with the powder-smoke in *Virginia*'s casemate; she swam silent under the ceaseless doubled blow, every man in her at a peak of angry melancholy, waiting for the shot that would burst the plates and kill them all—and when *Monitor* turned aside for a moment to change helmsmen (gallant Captain Worden blinded by a powder-burst at the window of his pilot-house) the wounded giant turned tail and fled back to her wharf at Norfolk. A month later they blew her up.

So Lieutenant Brooke had his twenty-four hours of glory, and Mr. Stanton had his miracle—Scott's Anaconda drew a long breath and tightened its coils.

That summer was bad in the Confederacy; there was malaria and no quinine.

Note for genealogists—there were two naval officers named Buchanan, brothers. One commanded *Virginia*; the other had remained with the old flag and died in the flames when *Congress* went.

I I

BLACK WEEK

MCCLELLAN spent Christmas Day in bed, feeling sorry for himself. The wolves were after him, even old friend Stanton growing nasty about his lassitude in making war, and when Stanton wanted to be nasty, his remarks left blisters. January was spent in wrangling; on the last day of the month the President lost patience and issued a general order to attack the Confederates at Manassas. McClellan's hand was forced—he had to execute the order or offer a plan of his own. To mark the difference between military genius and amateur ignorance, it was as Napoleon as possible—a feint toward Manassas, then the whole army to the lower Chesapeake by boat and a march straight up the Peninsula of Virginia on Richmond. The Laurel Hill maneuver over again, not unintelligently conceived—wave one fist in the enemy's face, then punch him quickly with the other.

Lincoln couldn't agree; it would leave the capital naked to the shock of the rebel armies. There was a thirty-day argument, in which General McClellan greatly distinguished himself. He won the support of the other army men and the President finally yielded, "on condition that you leave not less than 40,000 men to cover the Washington forts." That will not be difficult, said McClellan in an ably written minute; we have 200,000 men, five army corps—McDowell, Sumner, Heintzelman, Keyes and Banks. The last will guard the tube-end of the Shenandoah; with one whole corps left behind, there still will be 150,000 against Confederate Johnston's 120,000; the navy will support our flanks from the

Virginia rivers and we can go whirling across his line of retreat and into Richmond before he returns overland from
Manassas, where he now lies. Plan approved, then—the command is forward, the troops will march at dawn.

. . . Swing back the curtain that has hidden the Virginia
flatlands these eight months, where Pinkerton's spies have
been counting the dragon-seed of Cadmus. Surprise! Instead
of the hundred thousand, two hundred thousand, quarter-
million, they reported, there has never been but 58,000
rebels, mostly anxious to go home—we proved at Bull Run
that the North can never conquer us, why fight further? The
Washington newspapers had full accounts of the Lincoln-
McClellan debates; Joe Johnston followed them with interest.
It seemed incredible that any commander could be such an
ass as thus publicly to announce that he was going to surprise
his enemy, with date and place, but McClellan might be
playing the double-bluff. To prepare for emergencies, Johnston called up reinforcements and retired to a position along
the Rappahannock. When the Army of the Potomac came
tramping down the roads to the scene of its last year's defeat
(in McClellan's "feint") it found only "the smoking débris of
storehouses, imparting a lugubrious and sinister aspect to the
celebrated plateau."

McClellan's men took to their boats; on April 4 the de-
barkation at Fortress Monroe began, with Heintzelman's
Corps leading toward Yorktown, Keyes coming up on his left.
Heintzelman found Yorktown fortified according to expecta-
tion and was received with hearty salvos of artillery. He
halted till Keyes, who was Irish and eupeptic, should work
around behind. But a little river, the Warwick, reaches right
across the Peninsula here, not even noted on the Union
maps. Keyes found the rebels had dammed it to a marsh,
with redoubts on the far side; McClellan, riding up, said
not to waste men or munitions on an attack, for McDowell
with his corps was to go up the York River on the other bank
and take Yorktown in reverse. Keyes marked time; Sumner
moved his corps into position beside him. That night Mc-

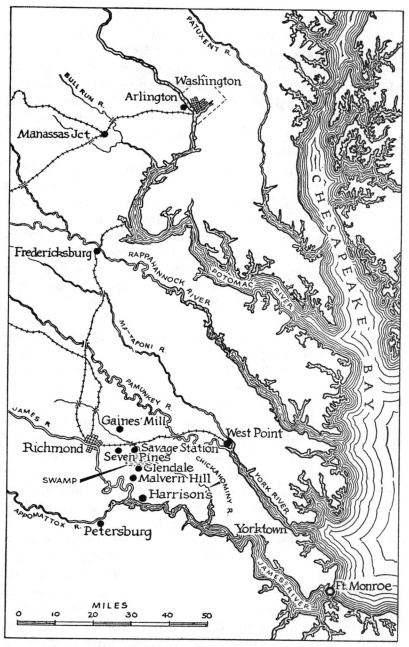

The Peninsular Campaign

Clellan got a telegram from Washington, the most awful shock of his life—Lincoln said that he had not kept his promise to leave 40,000 men for the defense of the capital, McDowell's whole corps was being retained for the purpose.

Whose fault? Probably McClellan's; the ably written minute was ambiguous; it should have said, but did not, that he considered Banks' Corps, out in the Shenandoah, as the shield of Washington.

Because he had been deprived of his flanking column, McClellan sat down sulkily to make a scientific siege of the Yorktown lines, with parallels and approaches all correct. It was a joke; the defense system was nothing but papier-mâché. Confederate Magruder had only 13,000 men (against 90,000) and most of his heavy artillery was painted wood, mounted there to hoodwink the Paul Prys of the Pinkerton agency. On the third day of the ridiculous siege Brigadier Hancock of Keyes' Corps, developing an affair of outposts, put a Vermont regiment in with the bayonet; they actually got through, but McClellan recalled them, considering advance too risky. So Yorktown held out for a month, while Johnston marched down from the Rappahannock to Richmond and made ready to receive the Yankees in style. On May 5 Magruder evacuated before the siege-lines got tight enough to pinch; McClellan went swinging up the Peninsula behind him, established a base of supplies at West Point on the York and thrust his pickets to Seven Pines, five miles out of Richmond. He had reached the anticipated position and was cheerful over it to the correspondents, quite neglecting the fact that the rebels were before him and full of fight instead of making a desperate march from Manassas.

Reinforcements came in by water and the army stood astride the river Chickahominy, in a half-circle, with Heintzelman and Keyes south of it at Gaines' Mill. Johnston was now 80,000 strong; he saw in the arrangement an opportunity for a piece of business. On the night of the 30th May there was a regular tropical hurricane; at dawn on the 31st, three-quarters of the rebel army came sloshing through the new mud against the divisions of Couch and Casey which formed Keyes' left flank. Huger's Confederate Fifth Division was to have worked round and attacked the Yankees in the rear while the rest hit their front. He was late; Couch and Casey, surprised and outnumbered, put up so stout a defense against the frontal attack that it was nearly noon when their commands broke up, partly killed, partly dispersed, partly captured. McClellan rode to the front with the sound of the first guns, saw through Johnston's plan at once, ordered Sumner's Corps to the south bank and summoned the whole artillery reserve of the army.

There was a lull in the early afternoon, then the Confederates came on again, Longstreet against Heintzelman, Huger, arrived at last, against Keyes' shattered flank. It gave; the Union army began to swing like a door, its back to the river, its lines of communication—those invisible wires by which the machine lives—being cut across, but then Sumner's big fresh regiments began to flood in and the magnificently handled Union artillery took all the fire out of the rebel advance. Johnston was wounded; Longstreet, who succeeded, ordered a retirement just as Brigadier Phil Kearney, with a patchwork of dismounted cavalry and floating companies from the rout of the morning, went forward in a stirring charge that carried everything before it. The whole position down to Seven Pines was recovered.

The worst loss of the battle was McClellan's sense of balance; he set up a wall that was outnumbered and asked for McDowell's men. The danger to Washington had faded; Lincoln approved, called in part of Banks' force to hold the forts and ordered McDowell southward overland. McClellan planned to bring him in on his right flank, slashing across the north railroad of Richmond and into the Confederate capital, while his main army held the rebels pinned from the east.

The new Confederate general, vice wounded Johnston, was Robert E. Lee, whose silent modesty made more impression on the Richmond authorities than Longstreet's outspoken contempt for the politicians who told how they would repel the invasion from the safe floor of the Confederate Congress. Lee got news of McDowell's movement; unless he could effect diversion the jig was up. McClellan's stroke was obvious but deadly; he had no sure reply.

There was a means of diversion at hand; the small army westaway in the Shenandoah Valley under Jackson, that same Jackson whom Bee saw standing like a stone wall on the plateau of Manassas, a character worth noting. In his younger days the perfect Virginian, rode like a jockey, gambled like Coaloil Johnny, "ate dinners prepared with Parisian art and participated in the wild delights of the dance"; then "got religion" and a credo not less stern than Cotton Mather's— God ordained slavery as the portion of the Negro race; let the world be sown with corpses, sobeit His will be done. Before the war he was professor of Natural and Experimental Philosophy and Artillery Tactics at Virginia Military Institute, where noted for interrupting classes with *ex parte* prayer. Characteristic remarks—"I hope and pray to Heaven that I shall never again have to fight a battle on the Lord's Day"; "Kill them all, I do not wish them to be brave in the devil's service."

Lee sent him Ewell's division and instructions to make the diversion. With the new troops Jackson had nearly 20,000 men. He was at Swift Run Gap, surrounded by foes—Union Milroy, working slowly through the Alleghanies toward Staunton and the southern end of the Valley with the advance-guard of 15,000 of the West Virginia army; Banks with most of a corps at New Market, McDowell with 40,000 at Fredericksburg, and 30,000 in the defenses of Washington. When Ewell came in Jackson posted him at Harrisonburg to hold Banks, then set off at a wonderful pace across the Valley, fifty miles in three days, and caught Milroy encamped in the neck of a rocky gorge. Milroy had only 4,000 men at hand; they woke in the morning to find Jackson's guns grinning at them from the cliffs, made a gallant, futile attempt to storm them, and were hurled back into the hills, disorganized and beaten.

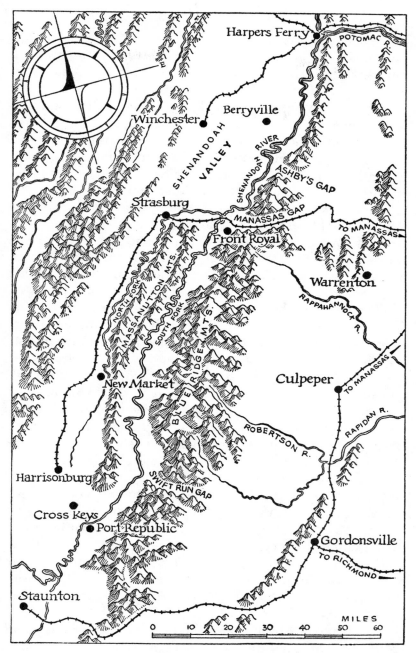

Jackson in the Valley

When the President called in troops to replace McDowell's corps in the Washington defenses, Banks was left out in the Shenandoah with 13,000. Jackson had struck Milroy back among the hills; therefore he was west of the Massanutton Mountains, which divide the Valley down its center. Banks retreated slowly to Strasburg, where he fortified the outlet of the west Valley for a stand. He played square into Jackson's hands; with Milroy broke, the rebel general whirled sharp round on his heel, covered sixty miles in another three days of incredible marching, picked up Ewell and went off up the east Valley like a comet. While Banks thought him still at Harrisonburg, his vanguard was circling round Front Royal; that same night he wiped out the detachment of 900 men the Union general had left there and started for Winchester, the head of Banks' only railroad of escape.

The news reached Strasburg at two in the morning; the Union soldiers tumbled out of their beds and began a desperate race for Winchester. They reached it after an exhausting eighteen-hour march, to find Jackson's men already on hand. There was a fight; Banks' fagged men lost, of course, and streamed north through the town in the twilight, with the inhabitants firing at them from the windows, leaving trains and artillery behind. Jackson followed hard, flung the wreckage of Banks across the Potomac, fired a few shells into Harpers Ferry and then turned south again.

The whole North blazed with anger; in Washington there was tension and fear. Lincoln conceived the plan of trapping the audacious raider's retreat, rushed reinforcements with instructions to follow the enemy, recalled McDowell from Fredericksburg to defend the capital. The forces under General Shields went through Ashby's Gap on Front Royal to close the east Valley; Frémont, ex-dictator of the West, was summoned to swing in from West Virginia and shut the west Valley.

It was not a brilliant plan; Jackson was nearer the point of escape than all three Union columns, bigger than any alone and moving faster. He was at Strasburg when Shields reached Front Royal and the two armies raced each other along opposite sides of the Massanuttons. Jackson's whole force thundered into Port Republic just as Shields' first regiments arrived. The Confederate commander dealt the Union head of column a heavy blow, then fortified his bridge across the river there and turned to face Frémont, who had reached Cross Keys. The rebel caught the West Virginians coming on in route-march column, slashed into them with his cavalry, killed or captured most of the van and routed the rest. That same night he was back at Port Republic. Two brigades only of Shields had come up, but finding the place lightly held, they ventured an attack in the morning. Jackson's whole army was there by that time; the attackers ran into a cross-fire and were simply riddled. Neither Frémont nor Shields would be war-worthy without extensive refitting; Banks was far behind. Having thus eliminated 100,000 troops from the Union campaign before Richmond, Jackson, with a final wave of the hand, went back to join Lee.

McClellan, still the prey of delusions of Confederate grandeur, heard with dismay that he was not to have McDowell's 40,000 after all, and melancholically intrenched before Richmond, expecting disaster. She is a mistress who need not be twice wooed. While the Valley was echoing with the clamor of Jackson's blows, Lee shook loose his cavalry under a new general, a knightly, courteous man out of Alexandre Dumas, bearded Henry Quatre, named J. E. B. Stuart. The horsemen rode north, then east, turned and came down behind the National army in a sweeping circle, too fast for pursuit, cutting across the railroad to West Point, destroying $7,000,000 worth of stores; returned to Richmond without losing a man, and with a map that showed the location of every soldier in McClellan's army, which was a hundred times as much as the Little Napoleon knew about Lee. Porter's Corps was north of Chickahominy, the rest south, the bridges between few and weakened by torrential freshets. It was an invitation to attack.

Lee fortified his front at Seven Pines and posted two divisions, 30,000 men, to hold it against a counterstroke from the mass of the Union army; then, behind the screen of Stuart's horse, concentrated all the rest against Porter's lone corps. Longstreet was to lead the assault; Jackson, already on the march from the Valley, would swing wide in on Porter's flank and rear, destroying the corps and cutting the railroad life-line to West Point for good. The whole Federal army would be bottled in the triangle between the Chickahominy and the big swamp south of it, cut off from supplies and forced to surrender.

On the morning of June 27 Lee had a chit from Jackson; he was in position. Three cannon uttered their voices in signal, and Longstreet's men came storming out of the forest against Porter's left flank around Gaines' Mill. It held; the position was on a crest, the Federal artillery wonderfully accurate. A. P. Hill fell in beside Longstreet, then the other Hill; Porter's line bent back in a crescent that became a horseshoe under the pressure of overwhelming numbers on its right flank, and it had all happened so fast that McClellan only just heard the news when Porter was at the last extremity. If Jackson struck now the Army of the Potomac was gone.

But Jackson did not strike. The soldiers of his corps were sitting on the ground, smoking and talking within five miles of the battle, while their commander stood on a hilltop, having a prayer for himself. When his officers asked for orders, he regarded them with a cold, fish-like eye and answered nothing. He stayed there all through the afternoon, while Longstreet and the Hills strove to break Porter's sturdy line.

McClellan, quite in his element when things were going badly, saw that the north bank and the West Point railroad could not be held. He ordered Porter to stand it as long as possible; meanwhile the south bank was lined with his powerful artillery, wheel to wheel, the magazines of stores were put to the torch, the railroad trains run into the river, and all preparations made for a change of base to Harrison's Landing, on the James, with the navy notified to protect the latter point. Just as a wild twilight of smoke and fury was shutting down, Jackson finished his session of prayer and came up on the run. The arch of Porter's horseshoe caved in under the new assault; two regiments were captured and he lost some guns, but through the night he made good his retreat across the tottering bridges, wounded and beaten but not destroyed, while the Federal cannon, flaming across the dark, prohibited pursuit.

That was a weird night in the Union lines, urgent with thunder as the vast munitions dumps gathered for the siege of Richmond were blown up, and the marching columns poured along the causeways of the swamp under the smoke of millions of tons of burning stores. Sumner had the rear-guard with his own and Franklin's newly organized VI Corps. They got twenty-four hours' respite while Lee flung Stuart's cavalry out toward West Point under the impression that McClellan must retreat that way; then the Confederate scouts discovered what direction the Federals had taken.

Lee made a quick new plan to catch the enemy army; hurled Magruder's and Huger's corps against Sumner's wing at Savage Station to make him face toward Richmond. Jackson was to cross the Chickahominy at its angle with the swamp, make a delayed attack in the rear and pinch Sumner and Franklin between hammer and anvil; same battle-plan as Gaines' Mill. It failed again and for the same reason—viz., Jackson withdrew within himself for another session of public prayer and delayed his movements too long. When he came into line, the omnipresent Union artillery had already shot Magruder's attack into the ground, Sumner had gained the causeways through the swamp and Franklin held the inlets so heavily that Jackson's storm died still-born.

Lee's next effort was to cut the long Union column in two at Glendale, hurl back its rear into the swamp and destroy it. At dawn on the morning after Savage Station, Longstreet and A. P. Hill debouched from the Richmond roads; Jackson and D. H. Hill were to swing a circuit through the swamp and strike Glendale from the east. Longstreet ran into McCall's Pennsylvania division, the best in the Union service —the brigade commanders were Reynolds, Meade and Ord, who were all to command armies. There was a terrific fire fight, with charge and countercharge through wood and field; McCall, outnumbered two to one, gave so good an account of himself that it was night before Longstreet pierced his line, and then Brigadier Kearney brought the New Jersey volunteers in on the flank of the attacking column to break it up. Once more Jackson did not appear; he "was in a very peculiar mood, looking around suspiciously and muttering to himself."

The crisis of the seven days was over. While Kearney was leading the last fierce charges at Glendale, Keyes' Corps was already selecting artillery positions at Malvern Hill on the James, a huge plateau upthrust from the river marshes. All night long the tired troops of the rear-guard filed through the lines to take position, while the outpost muskets flickered around the horizon from east to west in an endless circle of burning dots.

At dawn Lee had his whole army up and united around the plateau. He could see the Federal artillery ranked tier on tier up the slopes as he made the circuit, but imagining McClellan demoralized by six days of retreat and almost-disaster, ordered a general assault, beginning with Armistead of Huger's, who should give the signal by a rebel yell as he advanced. It was the worst failure of all; the Union guns deluged Armistead's line with such a concentration of fire that he never got started. On his left Sumner's batteries smashed D. H. Hill's artillery and played so much havoc that Brigadier Sedgwick of the Union center dared a bayonet charge against the rebel lines. The Massachusetts regiment in the lead went shouting into action; the rest of the Confederates mistook the cry for their own rebel yell and left cover for a brave but frightfully costly attempt to storm those unshakable Federal cannon. Lee drew off into the dark with 7,000 men lost.

So McClellan saved his army thanks to three several miracles, the crotchets of Stonewall Jackson and the cannon built and manned by a race of mechanics; and under the black night around their campfires the men of the 11th Massachusetts were singing to a dead slow beat the words of a song some had found in the February *Atlantic:*

"Mine eyes have seen the glory of the coming of the Lord;
He is trampling out the vintage where the grapes of wrath
are stored—"

In the South they were bitter and disgusted: "We had much praying at various Headquarters and large reliance on special providence, but none was vouchsafed, by pillar of cloud or fire. The campaign was nothing but a series of blunders, one after another and all huge." But in the North they could not forget $7,000,000 worth of lost stores and 20,000 dead men, or that the Little Napoleon had been there, not to save an army but to take one: Thank you for nothing, General McClellan, in your Camp Misery at Harrison's Landing, writing letters to the papers to prove that Lincoln wanted you to fail, the better to make himself despot.

I 2

THE IRONCLAD CARONDELET

USELESS sieges were all the fashion that spring. While Mc-Clellan was doggedly digging toward the wooden artillery of Yorktown, General Halleck called in Pope from the Missouri country and prepared to beleaguer Corinth. For three weeks he paused beneath the trees, in uffish thought like the hunter of the Jabberwock; then as he had 100,000 men and Confederate Beauregard something under 55,000, began closing in on the rebel stronghold with elaborate caution, an inch a century. In thirty-one days the powerful Union army, which included more talent to the square inch than any other the United States has ever seen, managed to crawl twenty miles. Parallels were opened and everything prepared for a lovely siege when Beauregard inconsiderately evacuated and retired into an inexpugnable position among the Mississippi swamps.

General Halleck spent another three weeks thinking over this astounding development, and reached the conclusion that Memphis should be the next objective. It was well defended on the land side and, though provisions were short ("The Provost-Marshal orders that you take that mutton-chop out of the window or we shall have a riot presently"), would probably stand a long siege unless the supply lines by water could be severed.

The rebels had improvised a fleet on the river to prevent that—eight ships under a Commodore Montgomery, who had been a steamboat pilot, a mossback out of "Life on the Mississippi." Names—*Little Rebel*, *Bragg*, *Price*, *Sumter*,

Van Dorn, Jeff Thompson, Beauregard and *Lovell;* armored with cotton bales and heavy planking; armed with light guns and heavy rams; light, fast vessels to strike their blow and then run. Flag-officer Foote had gone home with his wound and his Bible; Flag-officer Davis commanded the seven ironclads the Union had in the river and had formed the habit of sending down a mortar-boat under escort of a fighting ship to shell the Confederate navy by high-angle across an ox-bow loop during the night. On the morning of May 10, *Cincinnati,* the duty ship, saw the rebel fleet coming up. She signaled for help, but there was no wind, the signal flags hung limp, and, before she could get going, *Bragg* was upon her, ramming on the starboard quarter. *Cincinnati's* side was gashed open and the water flowed in, but as she staggered from the shock, she gave *Bragg* a broadside that shattered the rebel's paddle-wheel and sent her drifting downstream. The crash woke the other ironclads; they got up steam but, before they arrived, *Price* and *Sumter* had finished off *Cincinnati.* Down she went in eleven feet of water, with her commander and most of her crew. *Van Dorn* charged into the advancing Union ships, rammed *Mound City* and sent her aground in sinking condition; then Walke brought *Carondelet* thundering into the battle and the honeymoon was over. One flashing broadside ranged across *Price's* decks, knocking her out; a shot burst *Sumter's* steam-chest and filled her with scalding vapor. The Confederates ran away to achieve safety under the Memphis batteries.

It was a month before Davis got *Cincinnati* and *Mound City* raised and repaired; meanwhile an army officer named Ellet had equipped three fast rams—*Queen of the West, Monarch* and *Switzerland*—for the Union side. The whole fleet came downstream on June 6th to find half Memphis' population on the bluffs outside town to cheer on the rebel fleet, which advanced line abreast for a regular naval battle. The fight was short and vicious. The Union ironclads parted; through their line dashed *Queen of the West* to meet the rebel flagship *Lovell,* prow to prow. At the last minute

Lovell tried to veer from the shock. She was too slow; the *Queen* struck her square amidships and cut her in two in a whirlpool of shivered timbers. *Monarch* followed the *Queen* in; *Beauregard* and *Price* tried to ram her from opposite sides, but the Union vessel was too fast; she escaped their blow, they clashed under her stern and *Price* was disabled. The next minute the whole river was a melee of charging ships and flaming artillery with the slender Confederate vessels taking it hard as the strong ironclads closed. *Monarch* swept round in a great circle to countercharge *Beauregard*; before she delivered her blow, the ironclad *Benton* sank the rebel ship with a close-range broadside. *Little Rebel* went aground with a shot in her steam-chest and her men leaping overboard; *Carondelet* got alongside *Jeff Thompson* and blew her up; *Bragg* and *Sumter*, their guns dismounted, their engines crippled, hauled down their flags and the two rebels left fled down the river with *Monarch* and *Switzerland* in hot pursuit. They caught one; the claque on the bluffs went home in tears and Memphis surrendered the next day.

. . . Jefferson Davis judged Beauregard had failed. Braxton Bragg ("A little more grape, Captain Bragg") was commander in Beauregard's room; a tall impatient, clever man, he divined Halleck's character to a nicety, and prepared a lightning riposte against that sluggish pedagogue. Halleck's big army was too strong to be attacked directly; Bragg retreated slowly as it came on into morass and jungle, keeping out a strong front. It was nothing but a façade; the main strength was being drained out behind to Mobile, then switched rapidly northeast along the railroad to Chattanooga, from which he meant a thrust into Kentucky to recover the fruits of lost Shiloh. The first news Halleck had of it was when clouds of partizan cavalry under Morgan and Forrest went rocketing around his flanks, across Tennessee and Kentucky, captured half a dozen detached posts, raided magazines and cut railroads all the way up to Louisville.

To give Old Brains due credit, he had recognized the

importance of Chattanooga. It was the heart of the hills, the great gate of armies for the central west. While the Union commander reached for Memphis with one hand, he had started Buell and 40,000 for Chattanooga with the other, but the march was impossibly scientific. The Army of the Cumberland (it was given that name) was to build lateral railroad as it went and draw supplies along the two sides of a triangle, from St. Louis through Memphis and Corinth. The result was that Buell inched toward Chattanooga; as the railroad line grew longer, it became more sensitive to raids, and Halleck dribbled out half his force to protect it. Buell protested, but that did no good, Halleck insisted on the railroad-building, Bragg got to Chattanooga first with 40,000 men—and just then Lincoln called Halleck east to make him Chief of Staff of the United States armies with the object of introducing scientific coordination into the conduct of the war.

Halleck took General Pope with him, as the most deserving of the western men. Unfortunately, he could not take the ironclad *Carondelet*.

I3

UNDER TWO STANDARDS

ADMIT freely that Lincoln botched his part in the Peninsular campaign. Admit he twice withheld McDowell's 40,000 when they might have struck to a decision; admit he tried to trip Jackson with an elaborately silly map maneuver which ignored not only time, distance and arithmetic but also the psychological element—with which the President should have been familiar. The onus for the failure, nevertheless, must rest upon the young Napoleon. The question of Lincoln's part should never have arisen; without a single man of McDowell's the Army of the Potomac was adequate to its purpose. If the campaign had been launched in February, with a surging drive up the Peninsula, instead of being made the subject of a nice little essay, it is difficult to see what valid defense Johnston had.

McClellan claimed afterward that the delay was founded in Lincoln's resistance to the plan. This is nonsense; it was founded in an interior mental resistance of his own; he felt his force insufficient. Little Mac was one of those commanders foredoomed to failure, who would still have felt too weak with the Golden Horde of Tamerlane at his back. At the time he was freely accused of lacking military skill, and it has since become the fashion to blame his want of moral courage, but neither explanation satisfies. It took moral courage of no mean order to admit the campaign was a failure after Porter had been attacked at Gaines' Mill, abandon the hard-won position before Richmond and burn the magazines. As for his skill it was only necessary to remark that Robert

E. Lee, a not-unqualified judge, said after the war that Mc-Clellan was the ablest military technician he ever faced.

No, the defect lay deeper, in something that only can be realized in the sound of the cheers with which the Army of the Potomac invariably greeted the commander who led it from defeat to galling defeat. The high private in the rear ranks has a curiously infallible instinct. He may not be able to recognize military ability, but he can always recognize a general who loves the men serving under him. McClellan did love the army; he loved every detail of military service, from the minutiæ of officers' returns to the sunset parade with the banners waving and 2,000 regiments waiting on his next word. No one could discuss tactics so interestingly or draw a more intelligent plan for the movement of a quarter of a million men. That army had claimed him from the humdrum duties of a railroad office and had made him "the power of the land." The rise had been so vertiginous, the contrast with the plodding existence he led before the war was so marked, that ambition was sated. He had attained Nirvana, the world was perfect—and, by a thoroughly comprehensible process, he came to regard the army he commanded as a kind of First Estate, to which other activities of the government and the country were subsidiary.

Thus he could fight all the devils of hell when anything threatened to take this blessed state from him, no matter from what direction the menace came. The languid and unenterprising leader who dawdled before defenses he could have brushed aside with a wave of the hand turned overnight into the crisp tactician of Savage Station and Malvern Hill when Lee attacked him. It seems to have been some vaguely adumbrated fear at the back of his brain that an advance on the enemy might mean the end of his career as Commander-in-Chief, either through failure or through too-rapid success that would end the war—it seems to have been some such fear that made him resist with such fury every effort Lincoln and Stanton made to persuade him to attack.

Other Union generals showed the same emotional reaction in the first year of the war; Frémont flamboyantly, as witness the guards around his house to keep out the message of recall; Halleck tortuously, as witness his strictures on successful subordinates. The emotion was an almost inevitable by-product of a great war descending suddenly on a nation that had fought only one minor conflict in half a century—and that under the leadership of politicians in uniform and the warmed-over grandfathers of 1812. "The officers of the army," remarked Sherman, "knew everything about handling fifty dragoons on the Indian frontier and nothing at all about anything else." These fifty-dragoon captains suddenly found themselves lords of the world. It was only natural that they should view their elevation with incredulous delight, not unmixed with a fear that the dream would prove impermanent.

Beside this fear, which in McClellan's case came to overshadow everything he thought or did—the word "removal" beats a threnody through his letters after Malvern Hill—Lincoln's own timorousness about the defense of the capital was insignificant. Moreover, Lincoln was profoundly right as McClellan was profoundly wrong. The business of the President was to preserve—the capital and whatever else was entrusted to his charge; the business of the army was to strike, it was engaged in a war of conquest. Reducing the matter to the least common denominator, McClellan identified himself with the Army of the Potomac and regarded its maintenance in a state of perfection as the essential factor, while Lincoln identified himself with the nation and looked upon the Army of the Potomac as ammunition expendable for the preservation of the country.

Lincoln's blunders were mistakes only in a military sense; as movements in the political field he personally controlled they were quite without flaw. The military strategy of the attempt to catch Jackson was bad; but the North demanded some step against the impudent raider, and nobody could offer Lincoln a better plan. In a military sense there was nothing wrong with the idea of letting McClellan's big army sit still in front of Washington and wait till Scott's Anaconda had crushed the Confederacy into submission. But Lincoln knew it would not do, politically; the North wanted "action—crushing, irresistible, overwhelming." For lack of it Chase was already having difficulty placing his loans.

In 1862 Abraham Lincoln was only the spokesman of an angry people, and no one realized more clearly than he that he did not have *carte blanche* from the nation—a fact which has been obscured by the halo that has since surrounded his name. To the majority he was at that time still the low, cunning clown, the President by hazard, and Chase, Stanton or Seward (according to whether one lived in the West, the Atlantic states or New England) the frequently thwarted brain of the administration. It must be remembered that the arrangement was then the normal one in American politics; the last seven Presidents had all been Merovingians ruled by some Mayor of the Palace. Lincoln's shambling gait, awkward movements and low jokes made him appear as the most inept of all the presidential ventriloquist's dummies. Beside him Zachary Taylor looked like a drawing-room fop and Franklin Pierce like a courtier. When he leaned over and patted the leg of a Congressman who was urging some unfeasible scheme and threw him off balance with the remark "My, my, what big calves you do have," the discomfited legislator could see nothing in it but a piece of *gaucherie*. Even the skill with which the President charmed Kentucky, Maryland and Missouri out of the rebels' lap made no impression. His part in the intrigues was largely secret and both Southerners and Northerners regarded the series of events as fortuitous. The surprising thing in the North was not that the border states remained in the Union but that so many of the others left it.

Which, indeed, still demands explanation today, in spite of the fact that we are contemplating it down the telescope of time. Why did men who possessed the political skill necessary to turn out that very able document, the Confederate States Constitution, deliberately submit their states, their homes and everything they held dear to the hazard of a war that was bound to be long and desperate and might very easily be ruinous? The slave-holding states had always been tenderly handled within the Union. They had received more than justice. The successive "compromises" on the slave question, from the three-fifths vote in the Constitution down through the Missouri, the 1850, the Kansas-Nebraska bills and the Dred Scott decision, had been so many surrenders by the North, accompanied by Southern promises that no more would be asked. The slave-holders and their Northern allies had a clean majority in the Congress elected with Lincoln. The prevailing opinion was that the abolitionist President was a man without special force of character.

Mainly, this was just because the Northern attitude had been yielding. Except in South Carolina, where the genuine fire-eaters were in control, the South does not seem to have believed there would be any war. Secession was a typically Southern and "romantic" gesture of resentment over the election of Lincoln, intended to accomplish something vaguely satisfying—if not the resignation of the new executive, at least the assurance that no more abolitionists would be elected. The South was threatening to pick up its dollies and go home if the North did not alter the rules of the game. General Beauregard remarked before Fort Sumter that unless the Confederacy were baptized in blood it could not last six months.

Even after Sumter they did not believe the North would fight. The South was a unit; the North split between the Republicans and the Democrats who were counted on to remain the allies of the slave-holders, as they had always been. The retiring Buchanan administration did little to change this opinion and it was a terrible shock to the Confederates when such Northern Democrats as Stephen A. Douglas and John A. Logan went Unionist. The contemporary Richmond and New Orleans papers are full of denunciations of their "treachery."

Nor must the influence of Jefferson Davis and Judah P.

Benjamin be overlooked. They were genuine leaders, forming one of the perfectly matched historical teams of character and intellect—Rockingham and Pitt, Washington and Hamilton, Hindenburg and Ludendorff—and between them had worked out a case that presented the act of secession as right from every moral and legal standpoint. The moral right was based on the individual's privilege of doing what he wishes with his own—the Jeffersonian theory that a man is ultimately a self-sustaining tiller of the soil, with no obligations but those he assumes voluntarily, capable at all times of withdrawing into his own little cosmos and pulling the ladder in after him. The legal right was grounded in the Constitution's purposeful vagueness and the fact that in accepting the Constitution both Virginia and Rhode Island had categorically stated the right of secession without cavil from the other members of the compact.

From a juridical point of view the Southern position was difficult to assail. Lincoln attempted it in his inaugural— "It is safe to assert that no government ever had in its organic law a provision for its termination," but this was an experimental government, and the argument from precedent was without value. The legal right of secession was recognized among the intellectual classes of the East, the strongest supporters of the Union—"let the erring sisters go."

The real weakness of the Southern argument lay elsewhere—namely in the doctrine that every man is king of his castle. It is true that good government should abridge the liberty of the individual to the least possible extent; the nub of the question is what is possible. The concentration of society makes all the difference. If a farmer living five miles from the nearest neighbor wishes to beat a war-drum all night and fire cannon at half-hour intervals, there is no earthly reason why he should be estopped, but the case becomes different when the inhabitant of a city apartment wishes to do the same thing.

While Jefferson Davis was living on a remote farm, Abraham Lincoln dwelt in a city apartment. They were both right in this sense—that they were citizens of different worlds. The South retained the pastoral manor-house existence of the forefathers, at least among those classes which controlled the machinery of mass opinion. In the Northeast a more urban type of polity had been achieved—with the concomitant of stricter regulation of the individual—and the Northwest, though a farming community, was a farming country that lived in symbiosis with industrialization.

The unfortunate feature, the thing that prevented peaceful separation, was the fact that both worlds had existed for some generations under the same tent. If the North once admitted the right of secession, the process could never be halted; it must adopt the theory that any unit had a right to withdraw from an association it finds inconvenient. Pennsylvania could step out of the Union and set up the dynasty of King Simon I, and Allegheny County could secede from Pennsylvania and pass a law forbidding railroads to cross it. Outwardly an effort to safeguard the right of the individual, the Southern argument inwardly denied the individual everything but the right to be a hermit. It did not permit him to associate with his fellows or to achieve any of those forms of progress which are the result of contact with other individuals at the price of sacrificing one's own prejudices.

Indeed, the South admitted as much by a capital political mistake at the beginning of the contest—West Virginia. When the mountain counties tried to withdraw from the Old Dominion an army was hurried through the passes to recall them to their allegiance. Now if the right of secession exists at all, there is no reason why the state is the only unit that should possess it; if the Alabaman individual is to choose whether he will be ruled from Washington or Montgomery, the West Virginian individual certainly should have the same choice. The invasion of West Virginia vitiated Jefferson Davis' whole case. Of course Lincoln to a degree reversed his legal position when he accepted the new state into the Union, and this must have been obvious to Davis, who doubtless felt that since both parties were at fault, the one which could master the greatest forensic resources would be the victor. He entered the contest with complete confidence in his own intelligence, which was considerable; so far beyond that of Lincoln (as pure intellect), indeed, that he could have crushed him in a debate on any intellectual issue.

Davis, like Douglas, failed to appreciate that pure intellect is not the alkahest or that principles of political economy are often rationalizations of acts undertaken for nonpolitical reasons. Lincoln was making his case on the basis of a sympathy with humanity so broad and universal that the intellection of the Southerners became contemptible in comparison. He stood on the desirability of saving a Union which could offer its citizens something more than the maintenance of the *status quo*. He defied law and logic in the West Virginia case, but only when logic was viewed from Davis' narrow standpoint, and only when law was regarded as an end in itself, not as an instrument for improving human relations.

Finally, the South did not believe the North would fight because Davis and Benjamin fully expected to draw all the slave states into their Confederacy. If they had succeeded war would have been impossible for the North on strategic grounds alone—mark how narrow is the link, and how easily severed, between Northeast and Northwest. As matters stood, it was a task which every informed observer regarded as hopeless for the least military of republics to attempt the conquest of a united nation only twenty-five per cent less numerous than itself and covering a territory half as large as Europe. With Maryland, Kentucky, Missouri and Delaware added, the Confederacy would have had the majority in both population and territory, besides holding the national capital.

While the Union had to officer its raw armies with captains of fifty dragoons the Confederacy was at no such disadvantage. It was a simpler form of society, still no great distance from feudalism. In the North a man might become a world-wide figure in some field—say mousetrap construction or astronomy—and remain unknown to the large majority of his fellow citizens. In the South leadership in one field was still leadership in all. The Confederate leaders in peace stepped naturally into place as its generals in war. It was no mere freak that the President of the Confederacy should be a graduate of West Point or that one of its generals should be a bishop and most of them magnates. Military science was still the avocation of every gentleman.

Similarly, when the Southern armies took the field, they were already equipped with nearly every military quality. The excellence of Lee's cavalry service, an arm impossible to improvise, is significant. A Southern gentleman, even a Southern poor white, was brought up, like a Persian nobleman, to "ride, shoot and speak the truth." Their Northern opponents stepped from counting-house and factory with everything to learn—which means more than mere trigger-squeezing, when you remember that the Union armies lost heavily by illness through sheer ignorance of how to live in the open. The Northern soldier enjoyed but one advantage, the one thing the Southerner lacked—the capacity for discipline.

For if the Southern individualist knew how to handle arms without instruction, the Northern collectivist was equally familiar with the process of unquestioning reliance on his fellows, seeking development and self-expression in most fully executing the will of the general mentality—whether represented by the body politic in government or the high command in war. The Southerner, claiming the right to make all decisions for himself, often made them on insufficient data. Joe Johnston later told how his soldiers wanted to go home after Bull Run, under the impression the war had been decided. In a military sense it would have been quite possible for him to march into Washington on the heels of McDowell's fugitives; in a psychological sense, it was altogether impossible; his army was more disorganized by victory than McDowell's by defeat. Southern individualism dared not admit that one man has more ability to form judgments, even in a specialized field, than another man. It must deny the value of specialization.

In the West, of course, the Confederacy met armies made up of farmers who, if they were already on the one-way street toward specialization, had certainly not advanced far down that path. The Minnesotans and Iowans of the Army of the Tennessee were nearly as good with weapons as the Southerners themselves, and infinitely better at obeying their officers. Westerly, the new republic had no advantage but the ability of the high command, and the Union was rescued from the full effects of this by the geographical accident that made the opening campaign largely a naval one in which the North could exploit its mechanical genius to the fullest extent.

. . . On the whole, neither side had yet shown the ability to sustain a first-class war. The West Virginia campaign was insignificant; Bull Run a beautifully planned contest between armed mobs; McClellan's Peninsula campaign the burrowing of a military porcupine who could sting only when attacked; Lee's Peninsula campaign wrecked on Southern lack of cooperative ability; the Federal advance in the West was mainly the work of the navy.

In fact, the only battle both well planned and well fought in the whole first year was the minor combat at Mill Spring, where Union General George H. Thomas caught a heavy column of attack coming in on him, smashed the column into a line with a stroke like a hammer-blow, then delivered an oblique attack that rolled up the line into a mass of fugitives in a manner to warm the cockles of Frederick the Great, his heart. Thomas was only a division commander in the Army of the Cumberland, whose Virginian birth made his loyalty dubitable.

BOOK II. GENIUS IN THE ASCENDANT

14

THE DOLOR OF THE CRESCENT

IN THE early days New Orleans was much as before; "Dixie" and "The Bonnie Blue Flag" replaced "The Star-Spangled Banner"; Colonel Sherman and the other damyankees resigned from the Louisiana Military Institute to go north, that was all. The change came gradually; it was not till the fourth repetition that a boy noticed the clerks in his father's store had one by one been laid off. The cotton-mills slid down a gradient of shortened hours into immobility, and a febrile paralysis drifted slowly back through the city's veins, symptomatic being the shortened Mardi Gras and the groups of ladies who called at certain homes to sit circular in the parlor, one after another asking the same monotonous question—"Why doesn't your brother go to war?" "Why doesn't your brother go to war?" The Prussian consul forswore his allegiance and went to serve with Lee's army at the ramparts of Richmond; the Creole Legion was called out and sent ninety miles down the river to man Fort Jackson against the black fleet from the North.

The squadron hung about the mouth of the passes, crouching for the spring, while Admiral Farragut teetered his heavy frigates back and forth at the ends of tow-lines, trying to cross the bar. He was a character; a rock-faced old man whose hair turned up at the back of his neck because he forgot to visit the barber. A Southerner himself and married to a Virginian; they had sent round a delegation at the secession to ask him to lead the rebel navy. Farragut told them he would see them roast in hell-fire first; a little taken aback by such vehemence, one of the delegation murmured something about a man with such sentiments being hardly able to live in Norfolk. Farragut started, snorted and left the room; two hours later he had left the state as well, abandoning everything it had given him but the clothes he stood in. Since then, living in poverty and seclusion in New York.

He was still there when Gustavus Vasa Fox, the assistant naval secretary, called in Commodore Porter to discuss an attempt on New Orleans. Forts Jackson and St. Phillip were the obstacles, with sixty-seven and forty-nine heavy guns, at Plaquemine Bend, where the current ran deep and swift to detain advancing steamers. Beat the forts down with high-angle fire from a fleet of distant mortars, said Porter, and the town is ours; any ships we send will take it, once the forts are smothered. Porter was very junior; there had to be an admiral in at least nominal command, so all the old sea-dogs were summoned from retirement for examination. This one would not do for such a reason, that one for another. Fox and Montgomery Blair, who were examining the candidates, finally worked down the list to Farragut. When they broached the project he smiled all over and his face suffused with red:

"Why, gentlemen, I will undertake to take New Orleans and the whole Confederate navy as well with two-thirds of the force you have outlined."

He leaped up and began prowling the room like a tiger in a cage, talking all the while. When he had left, Fox made a pinwheel motion at the side of his head and remarked that general naval opinion of this Farragut was correct; a dashing fellow, but too mercurial. Blair had known the man for some time; he replied that this was just his manner, he was solid enough under the show, and Commodore Porter (whom both men greatly trusted) being in favor of the appointment, the commission was made out.

The rebels expected a New Orleans expedition some day; they had organized a strong river fleet, headed by two rams, *Louisiana* and *Manassas*, and were building a third, *Mississippi*, the most powerful warship in the world. But Farragut moved on ball-bearings, secret and swift, and in April, three months before they were ready for him, burst across the bars into the river with five big frigates, three sloops, nine gunboats and Porter's mortars.

April 18: at midnight the mortars began to rumble and thence for a dozen hours their dull inharmonious beat continued without cease, pounding Fort Jackson with a shell a minute. Yet the damage was not so terrible; men lived under the storm of fire and only nine guns were dismounted; a cautious vedette that crept up the river found them ware and wakeful and was turned back by shots. Porter wanted to land troops and make a siege in form; Farragut to go storming through with the frigates, cost what it may—his spies had brought word that the rebels were working day and night on *Mississippi*, she might come down and sweep them all into the gulf. They clashed; old Rock-face reminded his junior as to who was in command, and at three in the morning the fleet steamed upstream to make the desperate trial, ninety-day gunboat *Cayuga* in the lead, Farragut following in *Hartford*.

As the Union ships came round the bend bonfires sprang into being along the banks, and the stream was all adrift with huge fire-rafts, fifty feet across. Fort Jackson began to tune up; then Fort St. Phillip. The ships replied; Porter's mortars arched long trails of fire across the heavens. *Cayuga*, with shattered sides, lunged past the forts; out of the shadows three rebel vessels rushed to ram her. One she crippled with a heavy shell; it burst out all over with bright red flames and reeled into the bank. The second she avoided, the sloop *Varuna* came up astern to drive the third into flight. The Confederate ships were all around now; one rammed *Varuna*, another rammed her again, and down she went in the shallows, sinking her slayer with her last gun. The sloop *Oneida*, gunboat *Katahdin* got through; into them drifted Confederate vessels loaded with cheering troops to board and fight it out hand to hand. But the Union guns were too heavy; one after another the light rebel craft blew up or sank beneath their fire.

Down opposite the forts Farragut and his frigates had

slowed to engage the defenses. *Brooklyn* was badly hit, her wheel went, she began to drift; through the smoke came a cry, "The ram! The ram!" and *Manassas* charged, tearing a great hole in her side. The gunners gave never a whit; *Manassas* got a broadside that punctured her armor and sent her spinning helpless under the bows of another frigate. A big tug pushed a fire-raft against *Hartford*'s side while the forts thundered; the rigging caught, the admiral in it "seemed to be breathing nothing but flames" and lost his eyebrows; the gunners began to run. Over the uproar rose the old man's voice, thin and piercing. "Don't flinch, boys, or there's a hotter hell than this waiting! Give that rascally tug a shot!" They gave the rascally tug a shot, a broadside; her boilers burst, the fire-raft drifted clear. The big guns of the frigates swept the parapets of Jackson and St. Phillip with grape and the whole Union fleet was through into the upper river.

Up at the Crescent City the levee was black with crowds listening for the mutter of the distant guns. They fell silent and there was a long pause of anxiety. What ships would come? Then they saw them—tall masts, crossed yards, not our river-steamers, but sea-going frigates. The mob went wild; the quays were fired and the riff-raff of a Latin town cursed in futile rage or ran drunkenly through the streets, while downstream the oncoming warships floated through a tide starred with half-burned bales of cotton, streaked with long runnels of molasses. "I see the ships now as they come slowly round Slaughterhouse Point into full view, silent, grim and terrible; black with men, heavy with deadly portent, the long-vanished stars and stripes flying against the frowning sky. Oh, for the *Mississippi*! Oh, for the *Mississippi*! Just then, down she came. But how? Drifting helplessly, a mass of flames. The crowds on the levee howled and screamed with rage. The swarming decks answered never a word, but one old tar on the *Hartford* silently patted the black breech of a pivot-gun and blandly grinned. And now the rain came down in torrents."

So they took New Orleans, the great seaport, the largest, the wealthiest, the strongest city of the Southland. In Europe they understood what great seaports meant; the *Times* printed the news in mourning borders and Ambassador Mason wrote to Jefferson Davis—"The occupation of New Orleans by the enemy gives little hope now of any interference with regard to the blockade. It has struck our cause a fatal blow."

There was a second act. Ben Butler went out as commander of the army of occupation. No general, but this was not war, it was civil administration, where he knew his business. He suppressed banditry, choked off a yellow-fever epidemic, built drains, started commerce, made New Orleans cleaner and more habitable than it had ever been. But the Creoles were irreconcilable. They cooked up a tale (which may have been true) that he stole the silver spoons when invited out to dine, a tale (which was pure invention) that he had offered his troops the "beauty and booty" of the city. The "Why doesn't your brother go to war?" ladies crossed the street to spit in the faces of Union officers or turned their backs on Butler when they met him. ("These ladies evidently know which end of them looks best," he remarked acidly on one occasion.) A heaving, uneasy movement ran through the town, finding expression in minor vandalisms, the whole thing so amorphous as to be impossible to deal with, obliquely moving toward armed insurrection. Finally a woman emptied a pail of dirty water over Admiral Farragut's head and a man named Mumford pulled down the Union flag on the customs house and tore it to pieces.

That was enough. Butler hanged Mumford to the roll of drums and issued the famous "Woman order":

"Hereafter when any female shall by word, posture or movement, insult or show contempt for any officer or soldier of the United States she shall be regarded and held liable to be treated as a woman of the town plying her avocation."

Southern chivalry shuddered to the marrow of its bones. A reward of $10,000 was placed on Butler's head, and when the news got to Europe a shout of horror went up. The French ambassador protested at Washington. A question was asked in the Commons and Lord Palmerston replied that the order was unfit to be written in the English language. Butler retorted crushingly that it was taken almost word for word from the ordinances of the City of London, but it did very little good. The pressure on Lincoln became too strong, and he had to remove the "American Cyclops" from the one job he could do well and send him back to the field operations which he did so very badly.

15

SOMEBODY'S HAND SHOOK

U. S. GRANT, left in temporary charge of the Army of
the Mississippi when Halleck was translated to apoth-
eosis in Washington, found himself deep in enemy country,
but all spraddled out. Buell with the Army of the Cumberland, in indepedent command, was pounding slowly toward
Chattanooga and the gate of the hills. Halleck's bright idea
of building railroad as he went slowed him up, and guerrillas
popped from behind every bush to tear up the tracks as fast
as he laid them; Grant was drained bloodless to supply guards
for the line, and Bragg got to Chattanooga first after all, driving the Union outposts through the passes.

That meant trouble. Bragg, a long-headed, dry, punc-
tilious man, who walled himself in ice from the world, the
better to think, saw deep into questions of high strategy. West
of the Appalachian chain the natural movement of the North
in war as in peace was vertical (by his computation), from
the grainlands to the seaports of the Gulf. The movement of
the South was lateral, from the beeflands to the cities of the
Atlantic. The lines crossed; while the peoples were enemies
one must die if the other were to survive.

Jefferson Davis' policy had been war for self-defense
only, with cordons of protection for the lateral lines. That
method had failed; the cordons were pierced till only one
was left, through Vicksburg. Bragg's new scheme was to
reverse the Northern movement; go slashing along the
parallels of the Kentucky hills for Louisville and Cincinnati
in frank invasion, forcing the Union armies into unnatural

lateral movement and extended cordons that could be ruptured as Albert Sidney Johnston's had been.

He threw out a stream of cavalry to hide the move. Buell thought the Confederates meant to swing a great circle for a drive up the corridor between the Cumberland and Tennessee Rivers on Nashville, and remained well west, concentrating for battle at Murfreesboro in central Tennessee. It was not till the 30th August that he understood Bragg's purpose, and then in the light of the appalling news that 40,000 rebels had crossed the Cumberland and were rushing on Louisville. He set off after them, dropping detachments all the way to guard the precious railroads in case Bragg should feint north and cut in behind him.

What happened there is another story; the important thing at the moment is that Grant had sent to Buell two divisions. It paralyzed the Army of the Tennessee; he had three hundred miles of rail across an active front from Memphis eastward to cover, beside the vertical lines down from Columbus, whence he now drew supplies, as the rivers were too low for heavy traffic. Grant made the best of a bad business by planting forces at Memphis, Bolivar and Corinth, with his headquarters and a general reserve at Jackson, but there was no concealing the fact that Bragg's strategy had succeeded and the Northern armies had been forced into a bad defensive along lateral cordons.

South of the Memphis-Corinth panel were two Confederate forces; Earl Van Dorn, a tall, stately man, noted as a lady-killer, with 16,000 protecting Vicksburg, and Sterling Price, "Old Pop Price," with the same number at Tupelo on the vertical railroad. The latter gave Grant headaches by shifting about rapidly; Washburne of the staff woke at three one morning to find the general chewing the butt of a pencil and muttering over what Price would be up to next. On the 15th September he found out; a cavalry scout from Corinth discovered Price's whole army in Iuka and at the same time came word that Van Dorn was moving toward Holly Springs. One of two things—either the rebel commanders were pre-

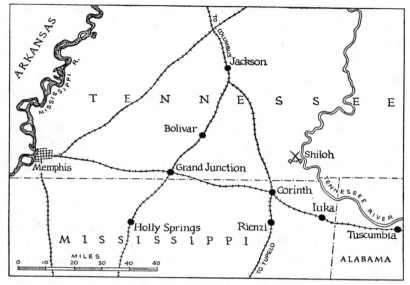

Iuka and Corinth

paring a concentric move on Corinth, or they were assembling to cross the Tennessee and go north to wipe out Buell from the rear while Bragg pinned him with a front attack.

Whichever way it was, Grant saw that the Confederates should have joined before moving. He could assassinate Price solus; Van Dorn was long distant on bad roads. Rosecrans' Corps, 9,000 strong, was ordered south and east from Corinth in a circuit to cut off Price's retreat. Ord's division from Bolivar, 8,000 more, came down from north and west to strike Price in rear when he faced Rosecrans; the reserve was hurried forward to hold Rienzi and keep Van Dorn from sticking his nose into the operation.

Ord arrived first, on the night of the 18th, and the trap was set. He was to fall on when he heard the sound of Rosecrans' cannon. Rosecrans, a majestic-looking man with the face and mind of an old Greek orator, pushed in lustily at dawn, striking the Confederate outposts across a bare knoll just south of the town. Price, dumbfounded and frightened at finding a Union army south of him, put in three-quarters of

his force in a smashing counterstroke that brought Rosecrans to a standstill, and the battle stabilized into a parallel-
order rifle fight with little advantage on either side. There
was a strong north wind; Ord never heard the guns and did
not move till he became impatient along toward evening. By
that time it was too late; Price had found a road leading
southeast that Rosecrans, in his excitement, had forgotten
to close, and pulled out. There was still a chance to cut up his
retreat but Rosecrans went to bed without giving the necessary orders, so that was lost, too. Price lost his trains and some
prisoners and it began to dawn on him, as it had on Johnston
before, that U. S. Grant was a poor man to take chances
with.

Also like Johnston before him, he retreated into Mississippi, where he joined Van Dorn; the two cooked up a plan
to stun Grant with a blow. They felt cautiously forward to
Grand Junction, at the center of the big triangle of roads,
with their united armies, but found Grant had abandoned
the effort to keep the Memphis-Corinth railroad operating,
so that blow landed in air. However, the point was propitious;
they could turn on Memphis, Bolivar or Corinth and whichever one they hit, it would hurt. Memphis was hopeless; the
river was full of Union warships with large, ugly cannon;
a move on Bolivar would bring both the Memphis and
Corinth forces onto their rear. Therefore it had to be Corinth.
Fortunately Van Dorn had a map of the forts there, sent
through by the star of the rebel spy service, Aurelia Burton.
Rosecrans' dispositions were faulty (he was in charge of the
place); he had his troops strung out around the weak line
of outer redoubts, and Battery Robinett, the keystone of the
inner defenses, was as yet without guns. The outer works
could easily be rolled up by a flank attack, and while the
Union forces were in disorder, a heavy column could be
driven through the soft spot at Robinett, splitting their army
in two. Van Dorn's superior numbers made the task easy;
he circled to the north to gain the added advantage of a
surprise attack.

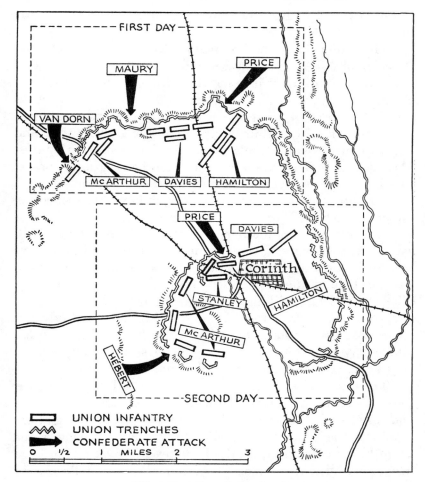

The Battle of Corinth

There was nobody to tell him that Aurelia Burton had been in a Federal prison for the last three weeks, or that Rosecrans knew all about her map and his plan. Battery Robinett bristled with masked artillery; Grant had anticipated Van Dorn's deduction. General McPherson, a new man, was coming down with 5,000 to take the Confederates in the rear as soon as they were committed to the attack on

Rosecrans, Ord with 7,000 more was moving to cut their line of retreat at Holly Springs.

The Union line was just behind the outer redoubts, the division of McArthur, Davies and Hamilton from west to east, Stanley's division in reserve, south of the town. At dawn the drums beat; the rebels came swarming through the woods on McArthur's left in an attack that, for all preparation, was half a surprise. McArthur held around a hill where forts and railroad meet; Van Dorn's other divisions came on against Davies. His defense was too good; a rebel regiment broke, and Davies' men went shouting forward in pursuit. It drew them in an eccentric from McArthur, and a split opened between. Maury of Van Dorn perceived the gap and threw a brigade into it, then another; McArthur's right, Davies' left, were taken in rear and went to pieces. Hamilton tried to save things by turning from his side, but Price struck him so hard he was held pinned. The Union front began to break up; McArthur lost his hill and the whole line reeled back.

The country was wooded and difficult, the rebel advance slow. Rosecrans brought Stanley up and halted things with a fierce bayonet charge beneath the westering sun, and as night came down drew within his inner lines.

The cannon hammered all night long; all night long the generals rode through their lines, shifting regiments. When morning came, Stanley's fresh division was in Battery Robinett, the Union center; McArthur to his left, Davies and Hamilton on his right, north of the town. Van Dorn ordered Hébert's division to attack McArthur and attract Rosecrans' reserves thither; with the action on that side well begun, Price's whole army was to slam straight through Battery Robinett. Everything went wrong with the Confederate arrangements; Hébert had a stomach-ache and, instead of beginning the attack at daybreak, sent his surgeon at nine o'clock to report illness. Van Dorn galloped off in a rage to lead the movement in person and, being in a rage, flung his men on in reckless, heavy masses that were riddled by McArthur's cool fire.

Price heard the crash of guns to the south and, deeming it meant Hébert's success, headed his columns for Battery Robinett. They ran into the masked artillery and such a storm of shot as no man in that army had seen; two regiments were practically wiped out in less than twenty minutes. The supports broke; Price rallied them and came on again, at the same time swinging his left against Davies. Battery Robinett was too strong; again there was a repulse with ghastly losses, but Davies' outnumbered wing gave way and Price's column got into town. For half an hour there was a savage street-fight, while the wild black eagle of the Eighth Wisconsin screamed from his perch on their standard. The rebels penetrated to the very yard of Rosecrans' headquarters and the general snapped pistols at them from the upper window, but Hamilton threw a brigade in from his wing, Stanley brought some artillery from the other, and the Confederate advance was driven out with gun and bayonet, utterly broken and disorganized. Van Dorn's last reserve was gone. Just then McPherson's skirmishers showed up in Price's rear and terrified what was left of his men. Van Dorn's army shambled hastily off into the forests south, with only one sound brigade to cover its retreat.

Rosecrans had his victorious soldiers paraded and rode through the lines congratulating them to the sweet music of their cheers; then treated them to a good meal and twenty-four hours' rest before taking up the pursuit. By that time it was too late; Ord, who had reached position with his 7,000, held up the rebels for six hours at the passage of a stream near Holly Springs, but Van Dorn, with no pursuit on his rear, easily flowed round the obstacle and back to safety in the jungles of central Mississippi. The defeat finished him as an army commander; when he arrived at Vicksburg he found an order to turn the command over to General J. C. Pemberton, an odd fish of a Pennsylvanian with a devotion to intellectual principle as pedantic as Jefferson Davis' own, who had married a Virginia wife and "went south" on the outbreak of war because he believed in states' rights. The Confederate President found him extremely *simpático*; he talked so profoundly about military matters in the Richmond drawing-rooms that he was believed to have considerable talent.

History repeats itself. Twice now the Confederates had surprised one of Grant's armies, twice it had meant the end of a commander and the ruin of his campaign—and twice the army had escaped because there was no pursuit.

16

WATER IS MORE DESIRABLE THAN BLOOD

ON AUGUST 27, General Braxton Bragg watered his horses in Cumberland River. All the bugles clamored for joy as the men in gray swung their muskets on their shoulders and took the northward-running roads. His army was high in mind and heart, more than 40,000 strong, with weapons for the 20,000 recruits who would join when Kentucky had been redeemed. Kirby Smith, with the flank-guard of 10,000 more, and Wheeler's horse to help him, had stormed the mountain issues and was marching on Cincinnati; Buell lay far behind at Nashville.

From the north those marching columns loomed gigantic through a haze of fear. Indiana put the last man under arms, the Kentucky legislature burned its records and fled. Buell was out of it, he could not get there in time; jails and hospitals were being scraped for defenders. "Bull" Nelson, who had led a division at Shiloh, went to Lexington to rally an army of home guards and raw recruits against Kirby Smith's advance. He had but 7,000, yet feeling cautiously toward the rebels, made contact near Richmond. Smith knew what kind of force faced him and went straight in. Nelson's outnumbered raw levies broke on the right flank, broke on the left; Wheeler's cavalry got across the retreat and slew or captured all but a bodyguard of heroic souls who cut their way through by the side of their twice-wounded general.

No more defense; the road to Cincinnati was clear, and on September 6 the rebel horsemen came trotting into the outskirts of Covington. The towns went under martial law;

Bragg's Invasion

banks and grog-shops closed, and 40,000 citizens, business-men, mechanics, wharf-rats turned out to dig trenches on the Kentucky shore while women carried their dishes down cellar or dispatched gold trinkets to friends in the East. Tissue-paper and 12,000 soldiers; what price the safety of the cities? Yet Smith only threw some shells into Covington and turned away. Cincinnati sent up a hosanna of relief, unaware that Bragg had called in his lieutenant for a trial of arms, with the West for his prize if he won.

At the passage of the Cumberland, Buell still had insisted Nashville was the object of the campaign and pursued languidly, around a circle through Bowling Green, leaving three divisions to hold the Nashville base under Thomas, his most trusted subordinate. Bragg outpaced the Nationals to Munfordville, captured the guard there and turned to bay across Buell's lifeline of supplies. He could have taken Louisville with ease, but preferred to wait for the Union army, which came tramping up dead weary, without reserves of bread or bullets, and faced with the necessity of attacking superior numbers in strong positions to obtain either.

Back at Nashville, Thomas, "Slow-trot" Thomas, the portly, dignified Virginian, who all along had declared Bragg meant invasion, scouted the trail of the Confederates for himself and found they had gone north. Grant sent in a new division from Corinth; he left it to cover Nashville, and gathering up the rest went to Munfordville in one titanic, seven-leagued stride. Buell's tired troops cheered themselves hoarse as the regiments came thundering in. It was late at night; over in the other camp Bragg, surprised at this manifestation from an army that was due to fight a certainly disastrous battle on the morrow, rushed to his picket-line, where he learned that Thomas and 20,000 fresh men would lead the attack next morning. Unfortunately for Braxton Bragg he knew what that meant; he had seen the mad rout pour through Mill Spring the first time Thomas delivered his stroke, a year before. Kirby Smith had not yet joined; the Kentuckians, instead of enlisting under his banners, were blowing up bridges and sniping his campfires in the dark o' the moon; he was outnumbered. It made him hesitate, and hesitating, doubt, and doubting, he retreated—through the Knobs, a little range of hills, to Frankfort, the capital of the state, while Buell marched on to make Louisville safe.

A hitch here. Oliver P. Morton, the perfervid Indiana governor, had come down to Louisville to ginger things up and quarreled with Buell, who said he was disrupting discipline. The general sent the worst possible emissary to discuss—"Bull" Nelson, the tall, fat, violent man, his temper unsweetened by adversity and wounds. He and Morton flashed angrily at each other over a bottle of Old Overholt; at the height of the wrangle, in came one of Morton's pets,

General J. C. Davis, with some question in which Nelson saw a masked sneer.

"So you both came up here to insult me, did you?" he bellowed, beside himself with rage, then "Get out of my sight, you contemptible puppy!" and struck Davis across the face. The chairs crashed to the floor as all three reached back; Davis was quickest on the draw and shot Nelson dead. That night Nelson's troops rioted through Louisville, crying for vengeance, and Morton wired Lincoln that Buell must go. Lincoln was willing; Thomas was the brains of the army in any case, and he was wired to take over. Thomas refused; the enemy was too near to hunt for another, so Buell was reinstated. Drawing in new levies that raised his force to 58,000, he began to push toward Bragg's position.

The Confederate leader felt secure along the line of the Kentucky River; he could make Buell fight a disadvantageous battle for the crossings. Meanwhile, he amused himself by installing his general, Hawes, as "Governor of Kentucky." As Hawes was reading his inaugural—"Kentuckians! The Confederate Army of the West has entered your state to help you free yourselves from a tyranny of a despotic ruler—" as he was reading this tripe, a cannon boomed from the west and Sill's division of Union troops appeared at the bridge-head. Governor Hawes left his manuscript on the lectern and ran for his life.

Sill at Frankfort was making a mere demonstration. Simultaneously Buell's whole army was pushing toward Richmond to get across Bragg's rear. The movement was well and secretly made, but there was a drought and the troops thirsty. The night camp was to be just short of Perryville. McCook's and Gilbert's corps pushed on a little farther and encamped near some pools that marked the line of a dying creek. Bragg's scouts, also hunting water, found them there. As the Confederate cavalry had also discovered Union elements between Frankfort and Perryville, he made the reasonable but erroneous deduction that Buell was advancing on a wide cordon of front stretched clear from one town to the other. His men needed water, too; leaving stout guards at the north bridges of the Kentucky, he rapidly switched four divisions—Cheatham, Hardee, Buckner, Anderson—southward, to win the water supply and at the same time to chip off the single corps he imagined as holding the right end of Buell's too-long, too-thin line.

It was two o'clock on the 8th October. McCook was on a sausage-shaped hill on the Union left, with a corps of recruits, among trees. South of him lay Sheridan's division of Gilbert on another eminence, with the rest of the corps some distance behind, across a deep valley. Southward and rearward was another Union corps; Thomas was in movement with a fourth, swinging round the other three to become the vanguard of the advance on Richmond. North and behind, Buell was coming up with two more. Bragg's four divisions, 20,000, were pointed straight into the center of the Union army.

It was two o'clock; the men were at ease, the officers smoking and talking, when Cheatham came unheralded through the trees onto McCook's flank, followed in twenty minutes by Hardee and Buckner. They were three to one of McCook; at the first volley three of the latter's brigadiers fell. Veterans might have stood the pressure, but his raw men, no. The officers lost control, the hill was carried with a whoop and McCook could rally only a few regiments around the brigade Gilbert sent to his help.

Cheatham, Hardee and Buckner flowed across the valley and flooded round Sheridan's hill, now joined by Anderson as well. But this was different; Sheridan's men were tried soldiers, their leader a very paladin. The infantry stood like a rock amid sheets of rifle fire that scorched the bushes bare; the Federal artillery achieved prodigies. Five times Hardee and Buckner rallied and came up that crest; five times they were hurled back down it, leaving long windrows of dead, and as the last tide ebbed, some cavalry crossed the valley from Gilbert to Sheridan's aid. The young general placed himself at their head for a flashing countercharge that went through Anderson's line, tearing it to pieces. Hardee and

Buckner were milked dry, Cheatham dispersed, and the Confederates went tumbling back in a confusion that a single fresh corps would have converted into rout.

Buell had hurried toward the shooting. He arrived when things were at their hottest but only ordered Crittenden's Corps up to support Sheridan while he sent an aide for his brain, Thomas. The messenger lost his way; it was two hours later, Sheridan had charged, the rebels were withdrawing unmolested when he found the Virginian. Thomas nearly had apoplexy; he saw in a twinkling that the attack on McCook must be an accident and Buell was missing a chance to bag the whole rebel army.

Too late now; Bragg had awakened, his divisions were streaming southward and away, the pursuit was hobbled by the same old lack of water. The armies sparked apart like particles of magnetism, Bragg toward his stronghold among the hills of Tennessee, Buell to Nashville and the congenial business of drilling green troops.

The Union commander was finished, a sound general, but he could not handle large masses. The Cabinet had time now to thresh out the question of a successor. Stanton demanded Thomas, in whose forthright drive he recognized a kindred spirit. Lincoln said no, Thomas had refused the place once, now he would have to wait his turn, opportunity should knock only once at any man's gate. Besides, Governor Morton was asking for Rosecrans and it was politically important to keep Morton happy. Rosecrans got the commission; Stanton signed it with a vicious dig of the pen and stood up:

"Well, you have made your choice of idiots!" he cried. "Now you can expect the news of a terrible disaster."

17

SECOND INTERLUDE

Dinner for Six

Mr. Motley alighted from the trap and looked around. The park through which he had been driven was cleared back before the house, a building of noble proportions but obviously dating from the Tudor, which Mr. Motley considered lacking in taste. Fortunately there were recent restorations in the sound Gothic manner that was to distinguish the Albert Memorial; Mr. Motley ascended the steps with a sensation of comfort filling his bosom as his eye caressed a minaret the architect had unexpectedly introduced into the ensemble.

His lordship met him in the hall, a hearty and straight-backed octogenarian with a tuft of whisker before each ear. Lady Palmerston was charming, and after the preliminaries, dismissed the two men for a walk in the grounds. Mr. Motley, who believed in candor, went to the point at once with a reference to the article in the week's *Spectator* in which it said that England would recognize the Confederacy in November. His lordship permitted himself a smile, and remarked that it was pure fiction; the Cabinet had no such intention—"Why, sir, do you suppose I would willingly deprive myself of the pleasure of hearing Mr. Bright defend Her Majesty's Ministry in the Commons?"

Then, seeing that Mr. Motley was taking himself seriously, he went on to discuss the matter in more detail, reiterating his assurance with a vigorous tossing of the head that made him look like an aged but still respectably potent stallion.

There were six at dinner, mostly of the political set, and when the cloth had been taken away the talk gravitated inevitably to American affairs. One of the guests, a horse-faced man whose name Mr. Motley had missed, remarked that Lord Malmesbury was hot as be damned for recognition, but that it was hardly surprising as he was up to his neck in Lancashire actions.

Mr. Motley observed that the whole insurrection was founded on the theory that Great Britain could not exist without American cotton, and felt that he had scored a point. His lordship stirred:

"We are up to that cotton dodge, but aside from our unwillingness to assist in the dismemberment of a friendly nation, there is rather stronger reason why our true policy is to keep quite clear of the conflict. The Ministry, sir, has no particular disposition to play cat-and-chestnuts for our neighbor across the Channel."

"Oho!" said Sir Charles, "*La Méxique*, eh?" and hummed a bar of the "*Chant du Depart.*"

"Still," put in someone else, "one must recognize that America would have little reason to complain of any want of sympathy on our part were this a conflict for the manumission of the slaves instead of some splitting of political hairs that no one but an American can understand. I speak freely."

"The advantage of a gathering like this is that everyone may speak freely," said Palmerston. "Mr. Motley has no official mission but to provide us with pleasant company, which he has fulfilled very agreeably. I think he knows that the practice of nations is to recognize *de facto* governments even less strong than the one in question and that we are under considerable pressure in that direction."

"For that matter, it is a war against slavery," replied Mr. Motley. "The election was on no other point, and the uprising is an outgrowth of the election."

"Aye, but not officially avowed as such," answered Sir

Charles, "and there's the rub! If Pam could say as much from official sources he could count on a round dozen votes from the psalm-singers to help put the Opposition dogs to rout. Yet your President specifically avoids the slavery question."

The horse-faced man laughed. "The lion and the lamb shall lie down together and a little black boy shall lead them—forgive me if the picture of the psalm-singers and our host acting together moves me to mirth. When you write to your President, Mr. Motley, don't fail to remind him that England always sympathizes with everybody's rebels but her own. Just now your Southern friends are the oppressed minority, but if Mr. Lincoln makes a crusade of it, why the slaves become a minority of the second degree, and hence have all our hearts."

18

THE IDIOT'S TALE

JOE JOHNSTON, recovered from his Seven Pines wound, was named leader of the West for the Confederacy and President Davis came out with him to survey the situation. The new coordinator regarded Bragg's delicate maneuverings with a jaundiced eye; the fellow was a mere ballet-dancer, a war against the Ironside Presbyterians of the Northwest could be won only by smashing them. Rosecrans had snuggled down into winter quarters at Nashville; he, Johnston, would take over Bragg's army and, with Pemberton from Vicksburg, close in on Grant from opposite directions by rapid marching and crack him like a nut. Bragg explained how illogical this would be. They had a long three-cornered jibber-jabber, and Jefferson Davis stuck by the general whose ratiocinative processes so reminded him of himself. After Johnston had stamped angrily from the room Davis remarked that there appeared to be some dissatisfaction with the—ah—want of military activity in the late campaign; perhaps a good blood-and-thunder battle would—ah—reduce criticism.

Bragg understood. His army lay at Murfreesboro, covering middle Tennessee. From this point he placed Rosecrans at Nashville under a kind of distant siege by pestering him with raiding parties. When the Union general came out to brush away the flies there would be a fight. Rosecrans, also harried by a government desirous of action, was nothing loath. The day after Christmas he broke up his winter quarters and moved slowly down toward Murfreesboro through an atmosphere of cavalry bickerings. On the 27th

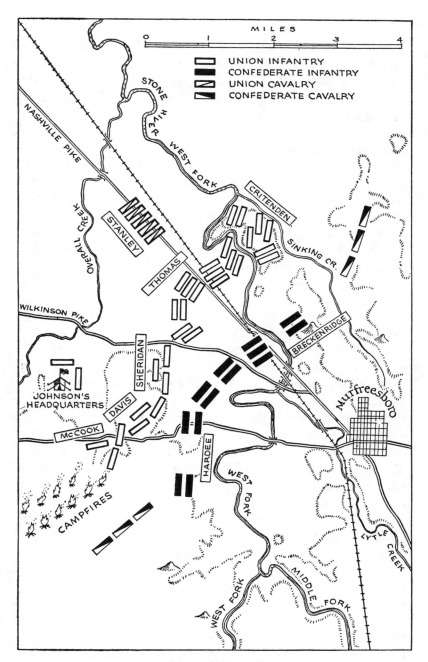

MILES

UNION INFANTRY
CONFEDERATE INFANTRY
UNION CAVALRY
CONFEDERATE CAVALRY

NASHVILLE PIKE

STONE RIVER

WEST FORK

OVERALL CREEK

STANLEY

CRITENDEN

SINKING CR.

THOMAS

WILKINSON PIKE

BRECKENRIDGE

SHERIDAN

DAVIS

JOHNSON'S
HEADQUARTERS

McCOOK

HARDEE

WEST FORK

Murfreesboro

CAMPFIRES

WEST FORK

MIDDLE FORK

LYTLE CREEK

Stone River, I

the resistance stiffened, with masses of Confederate infantry appearing. The next two or three days were spent in scouting and taking position, and on the 30th it became apparent that Bragg would accept battle with his army astride Stone River and Murfreesboro at his back.

Rosecrans was organized in three unequal corps. McCook, three divisions on the right; Crittenden, three on the left; Thomas, five divisions in the center—slightly less strong than the rebel army but not impossibly so. Rosecrans planned to use the river for a simple flank attack; Crittenden to cross with his own and two of Thomas' divisions, well north, eat up the Confederate right, swing down into their rear at Murfreesboro before Bragg could return his main body, which lay on the other side of the stream. McCook to keep safe the Union right—could he do it? "I can hold against anything for three hours," growled General Arthur McDowell McCook, and left the conference to order a line of fake campfires out beyond his flank, giving a mendacious appearance of length and strength to observers in the enemy's lines. The attack was to start right after breakfast.

Curiously, Braxton Bragg had conceived the same simple plan. Three days' wait had convinced him that Rosecrans was not coming forward; therefore he put an overpowering force on his left wing to break the Union right and lasso their whole army in the crook of the river—the old Shiloh plan reversed. The attack was for dawn; Hardee, his strongest hitter, to lead it; a big man with a bulging forehead and plenty behind it, author, linguist, philosopher.

R. W. Johnson, commanding the division on the extreme Union right, went to bed chuckling over the ruse of the campfires and rose late for an *al fresco* breakfast on griddle-cakes and brandy at headquarters two miles behind the line. His men were scattered, his artillery not even unlimbered, and neither McCook nor Rosecrans had thought it worth while to inspect. As he was tossing off a jorum there came a roar, then the shock of cannon, then a staff officer with the news that the rebels were upon him. He got to the saddle; before he reached the front one of his three brigade commanders was killed, another a prisoner, the whole division was utterly routed and Hardee coming along like a train of cars with 20,000 men behind him.

Davis—anti-Nelson Davis—was next in line. He drew back to the Wilkinson Pike to make front to the rebels, but they had swung so wide against the line they imagined behind the false campfires that they were already far in his rear. The sound of his cannon brought them on him from all directions, a typical Southern attack, dense crowds of men in butternut brown, bounding and yelling. His division broke, half of it was captured, his artillery went lost and the Confederates were sweeping around the last of McCook's three divisions half an hour from the start.

But this division was commanded by Phil Sheridan, the paladin of Perryville. As the rebels came through a cedar brake, shouting in full-throated triumph, he met them with a rousing bayonet charge along the whole front. The lines locked in one of the few hand-to-hand struggles of the war. Sheridan was ten times outnumbered, his flank was in air, his division simply melting before his eyes, but he would not give up. He pushed his artillery right up to the infantry line, where it dueled with the rebel guns at two hundred yards' distance and mastered them. Hardee's leading division was pounded to pieces against the defense; he had to bring up his reserves and even then it was only with his ammunition exhausted and rebel cavalry edging down to stab him in the back that Sheridan withdrew his battered and exhausted command.

Battered and exhausted, but he had gained time, of all things most precious. Rosecrans snatched Crittenden from his left and made a rallying point along the Nashville road. Stanley covered the operation with the cavalry of the army. Thomas drew back the right of his center, cool and precise, a parade-ground maneuver, though one of his divisions, that of Negley, had to face front and beat off an attack, then face rear and cut its way through a rebel advance, before the movement was complete.

A lull; Bragg and Hardee looked over the field. The

Union army had been driven from woods onto open ground. McCook was knocked out, Crittenden, far back, involved in the confusion of a too-rapid movement through a snowstorm of routed troops. Only Thomas remained, his position between the river and the Nashville Pike making a strained, unnatural angle. That angle was the weak point; if it could be cracked, the Army of the Cumberland would be thrown in the river. The success of the morning's attack had relieved Bragg of the necessity of keeping out a general reserve; he placed every man at Hardee's disposal to shatter the angle and, at two o'clock, on they came with a hurrah.

At the first gun of the morning Thomas had climbed into his full-dress uniform. Now he rode along the line, blazing with stars and gold braid, everywhere at once in spite of his stateliness of movement, steadying the troops with precept and example. He personally placed the batteries, personally directed where each company was to form, personally stood with the firing line while the red-hot assault came on, the most conspicuous man on the field—"Fighting under Thomas was like having a stone wall in front of you or a battery to cover you." The rebel attack was beaten back. It formed and came on again; again Thomas broke it up. The third charge found the whole Confederate army concentrated on the bloody angle; 1,000 men lost their lives in less than an hour, the fighting was fierce to desperation, even Sheridan's battle of the morning cambric tea by comparison, but Thomas would not yield an inch nor any soldier under him. Half past three; the rebels' columns halted.

Off behind Thomas the Union army was beginning to revive; Crittenden sent him a division, Sheridan surprisingly fell in on his flank with a couple of brigades raked up from nowhere. Half past four and dark shutting down under a cloud-draped sky; the rebel cannon fired a salvo and on they came in one last surge with bands playing them in and a swarm of cavalry on their left. Sea-wave and granite wall— for an hour more they raged against it but could not find the hole; then Thomas lifted his arm, the Union bugles blew rally, and the defenders, the weary defenders, rose for a counterstroke that ended Bragg's last chance. He would not win the West this day.

. . . At night there was a council of war in Rosecrans' headquarters. The division commanders made lugubrious reports of loss and disorganization; the Army of the Cumberland was beat, the only question how to save what they had left. Rosecrans was not so sure, there might be some tricks in the old dog yet, but they pressed despair onto him from all sides. At last the general sighed and turned to Stanley of the cavalry—"Is your command in shape to cover a retreat?"

Thomas had been drowsing with his hands crossed on his sword-hilt; the impact of the last word touched him to wakefulness. He looked round, then drew himself to his full height, with the lamplight throwing weird shadows on his leonine face:

"Retreat?" he boomed. "This army doesn't retreat. There is no better place to die than right here."

"By God, no!" cried young Sheridan, leaping to his feet.

Rosecrans smiled. "You see, gentlemen? Sterling, will you be good enough to telegraph Mitchell at Nashville for a trainload of small-arms ammunition? We will advance against the Confederate positions as soon as it arrives."

The new year came in cold and melancholy on two armies that had fought themselves to paralysis. Bragg felt cautiously here and there to ascertain the line of the Union retreat and, discovering there had been none, went back to his headquarters to think over such astounding conduct on the part of a defeated army. Rosecrans was waiting for bullets.

There is a high hill on the right bank of Stone River; conning his map, Bragg perceived that if artillery were posted there it would enfilade Thomas' line and blow him out of position. On the morning of January 2 he sent his cavalry to cross downstream and gather up the fragments of the Union army as they fled under his new attack, then ordered Breckinridge's division to take the hill at daybreak.

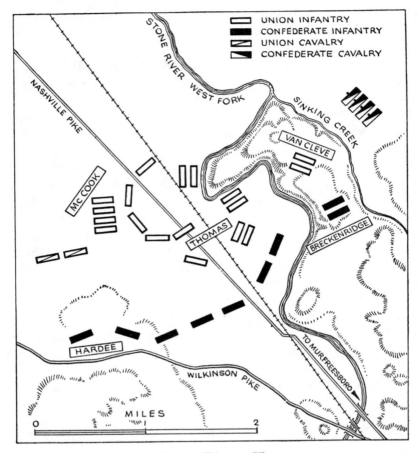

Stone River, II

To Breckinridge's astonishment he found Van Cleve of Crittenden in possession; as the first gray light filtered through the clouds a huge Union battery of fifty-eight guns opened up.

The hill was so far forward that the battery enfiladed the Confederate line from across the river; it began to shake, and Thomas showed unmistakable signs of massing for an advance. This could not be borne; Breckinridge went forward with orders to take that hill at any cost. He gained a foothold, but the Union artillery was too good; Negley and Palmer of Thomas crossed the river to aid Van Cleve; and Breckinridge was torn to tatters. The Union troops pressed on; some of Stanley's horsemen began to appear among their formations, they were headed for Murfreesboro and if they got it Bragg's whole army was gone. He hastily withdrew one, two, three divisions from the other bank to stop this menacing advance, and then abandoning all pretense of victory, formed a rearguard and led his shattered regiments out of the fight back along the road toward Chattanooga. Rosecrans had been too hammered to follow up, but he could telegraph Lincoln with no less than honesty—"We have fought the greatest battle of the war and are victorious."

So the hard combat of Stone River, the high point of the western Confederacy, came to an end, with more than a quarter of either army casualties. The margin between victory and defeat was narrow and consisted in this—that Bragg did not have a Thomas at his headquarters.

19

SEVEN TIMES AGAINST THE CITY

HERE is General William Tecumseh Sherman, a tall, untidy Westerner with a hard jaw, aggressively intelligent, anathema on all compromise. When he finished deflating Frémont, back in the confusion days, he had been offered command of the Army of the Cumberland—"And how many men will it take you to subdue the rebellion in the west?" "Two hundred thousand," quoth Sherman, and was held seriously suspect of treason (wasn't he the Sherman with connections in Louisiana?) or insanity. Buell got the post, with a fifth of Sherman's number; Sherman drifted into minor employments, bitter with the consciousness of great powers fallow. Then came Shiloh and the connection with Grant, who made him his right arm and man-of-advice, an arrangement in which Sherman found an interior justice. "I am a better soldier than he, but I lack his iron nerve. I would have retreated on the first day at Shiloh."

Van Dorn's claws were clipped at Corinth, Buell and Thomas handling Bragg; Grant felt strong enough for advance, and conferred with Sherman on the direction. Should it be east to catch Bragg between two armies or south against Vicksburg? Oh, Vicksburg by all means, said Sherman at once, "the possession of Vicksburg is the possession of America," without it the eastern Confederacy is a tree deprived of its taproot and must eventually wither.

The navy clutched for the prize while Van Dorn was beating at Battery Robinett. Farragut brought the frigates up from New Orleans; the gunboats, now under David Porter, steamed down from Memphis, and there was a spectacular double attack. Stone forts and wooden ships; part of Farragut's fleet was beaten back, the rest barely ran the batteries with heavy loss to themselves and none at all to the men on shore. The gunboats had no better luck; one blew up, another sank, and the attack was given over. The united fleet spent a week licking its wounds at the mouth of the Yazoo, then Farragut went back to New Orleans through a night of flame and thunder, Porter back to Memphis through days of cross-currents and miasma. Failure No. 1.

The losses of Corinth had hurt the rebels; they could not hold Grant longer, who drew in his Memphis wing and came swinging down to the line of the Tallahatchie behind a swarm of cavalry. It is a military stream, with high cut banks; he found it fortified at all points where foot or artillery might pass, but shook his cavalry through on a raid and found where the weak spots were. With enough men to make a feint that would keep the defenders from concentrating opposite him, he could storm the river line out of hand and go on to take Vicksburg in rear. He knew how to get the men; the single-track down from Columbus by which he was drawing supplies ate up a quarter of his force in guards; he would abandon it, basing on Memphis, so much nearer, and put the men thus gained into the battle-line. Halleck, of course, forbade the step from Washington—it was against military principles to base on an enemy town. Wait, said he; you will be heavily reinforced with new troops down the Columbus line.

Grant growled and marked time. While he waited the Confederate irregulars broke loose in his rear. A word about them; John Morgan, the Kentuckian "with a beautiful suit of hair," had organized the first band early in the war. They all went on horseback, they had no uniforms, no certain organization and no more discipline than a cageful of monkeys. They picked up men en route and discarded them the same way; the force might be 500 men today, 5,000 tomorrow, with those left behind becoming peaceful farmers.

They tore up railroads, burned depots of supplies, tapped telegraph wires and sent Union regiments chasing hither and yon under fake orders. To Union General Boyle, across the wires—"Good morning, Jerry! This telegraph is a great institution. My friend Ellsworth has in his portfolio all your dispatches for the last month. Signed, John Morgan." Bedford Forrest, with another band of the irregulars, captured a whole brigade and burned out the tunnels on Buell's vital railroads in the Kentucky campaign. Some leaders' methods were less military; more often they were not nice at all; Quantrill's gang assassinated a wounded officer in his bed and massacred the prisoners at Lawrence, Kansas. War on the lowest common denominator—plunder, glory and go as you please.

Morgan was out of it now; had found him a beautiful wife after Perryville, "was enervated by matrimony and would never be the same man again." Forrest remained; Bragg sent him across the Tennessee for a slash at Grant's alimentary canal between Columbus and Jackson. Van Dorn remained; Pemberton gave him all the cavalry of the western army, he picked up some night-riders and swung a great circle against Grant's advanced base at Holly Springs.

Bedford Forrest, a bearded giant of piratical aspect, who knew nothing of English grammar ("I git there fustest with the mostest," he answered on being asked his principles of making war) but everything about partizan cavalry, conducted his raid on the dispersion principle. He crossed the Tennessee in an old flatboat on the 15th December; on the 18th he wiped out 700 Union cavalry between Jackson and Columbus. On the 19th he started along the railroad, eating up the line and the small posts that protected it as a robin eats a worm. His flank-guards roamed fearlessly through the countryside, the telegraph wires went down everywhere and Union regiments wandered helplessly in a land of no information, searching for him while he made his way back to the Tennessee, the flatboat and eventually to the flanks of Bragg's command. Grant's supply line was ruined, it would

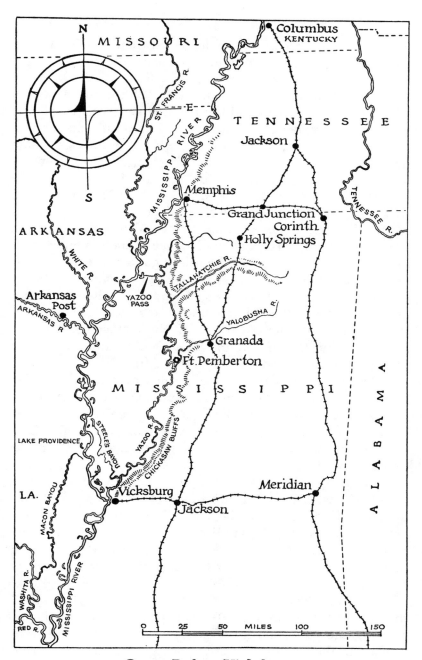

Grant Before Vicksburg

take months to rebuild it and for more than a week he had not even telegraphic communication with the North.

Van Dorn, burning to revenge the loss of Corinth, made his raid a hammer-blow. Grant heard of the move on the 19th, read its purpose aright and wired Colonel Murphy at Holly Springs to·double the guards and keep his guns shotted. It was a raw and rainy midnight when the message came through; Murphy sighed that morning would be time enough and pulled the covers round his ears. He had a nightmare of earthquake and woke to find one of Van Dorn's troopers shaking him. The Holly Springs depots, with $4,000,000 worth of stores, went up in one beautiful pillar of fire, and to make matters worse, Colonel Mizner of the Union cavalry so bungled the pursuit that the rebels got off scot-free. Grant bit a cigar in two when he got the news; he dismissed Mizner and ordered a court-martial on Murphy, but this would not provide food for 30,000 hungry men or restore the vanished rails down which he could get it. No assuagement; Grant must abandon the line of the Tallahatchie and go back to Memphis for food and a fresh start. Failure No. 2.

The lament of Van Dorn. He celebrated his victory by a midnight gambol with the light and lovely wife of one Dr. Peters. The doctor came home inopportunely at two A.M. and blew his brains out, which was too bad for the Confederacy as the brains had been better than most in the Confederate west.

For the present few brains were needed on that side; Grant had walked into a hurrah's nest of intrigue and misdirected effort at Memphis. He had a general of division named John A. McClernand, a boom-boom politician from Illinois, who had been at Shiloh. On his record as a mover of mass enthusiasms Grant sent him north to hurry the enlistment of the new levies Halleck promised. McClernand, like all his class, oblivious to every ideal but personal advancement, seized the forelock of opportunity and made the recruiting campaign a whirlwind speaking tour of the state, pitched in the key of "The only good general in the army is

ME. Grant is a shambling dipsomaniac, and I am tired of having him pick my brains." Politically it was a great success; 30,000 men trooped to the colors, and McClernand went to Washington for authority to use them in independent command. He was a Democrat of almost presidential caliber, and the mid-term elections looked doubtful. Lincoln, carried away by the dazzling prospect of such a capture for the Republicans, gave the plan his benison, and wrote out a secret order making McClernand Grant's equal in command and in the same district.

Meanwhile the new levies had begun to come into Memphis, where Sherman commanded in Grant's name. At this stage the main army was still on the Tallahatchie; Sherman perceived that if they held the rebels pinned along the stream, he could go far down river with the new regiments, cut in between Pemberton and Vicksburg, and either capture that general or his fortress. "Make it so," said Grant to the suggestion, "but, above all things, haste." Sherman hurried off in transports with 16,000 men, leaving word for the rest to follow as ready, and at December 26 was at the point where the Yazoo joins the Mississippi. Over his head towered the two-hundred-foot bluff which defends the inland from the valley all the way between Memphis and the Gulf—here named Chickasaw Bluffs. The wires were dead; he had no knowledge of Van Dorn's raid or Grant's retreat. When rebel gunshots sounded from the crest, he took them for mere pickets and ordered an assault. The men went at it with a will, but ran straight into the fire of Pemberton's whole army. The loss was terrific; Sherman sat down in the soggy bottom-lands where no man could sleep dry to wait for reinforcements.

But there were no reinforcements. McClernand had turned up at Memphis with his secret order, wired a five-thousand-word complaint to Washington about Sherman stealing his army, and went off with the men he found there to justify existence by doing something splendid. "Vicksburg is too big a boo for us," he remarked to Mr. Dana, the War

Department inspector, but there was a Confederate fort at Arkansas Post up country on the west side of the river which he considered a boo of the right size. He commandeered Porter's flotilla and went off to gobble it up. On arrival Arkansas Post also turned out too big a boo, so he went on downstream to the mouth of the Yazoo, stunned Sherman with his secret and carried off his force also for the private side-show in Arkansas. At the Post he had a fleet and four men to one; the victory was gained in half an hour and McClernand, basking in the irradiation of his own genius, sent telegrams north, asking prominent Illinoisans to write and tell Lincoln what a wonderful general he was. Failure No. 3.

Give the devil his due. Henry Wager Halleck, no general but at least a soldier, was the man who got McClernand's complaint. It was his first news of the secret order; he sought immediate audience with the President, damning the whole McClernand business as cheap politics and its author as a scoundrel in sesquipedalian but unexpectedly vigorous terms. Lincoln had the grace to be ashamed and, as McClernand was doing as badly as might be expected, wired Grant that he had "full and absolute authority" over the Army of the Tennessee, including John A. McClernand.

That settled the issue of command; remained the main problem—how to take Vicksburg? Useless to worry down from Memphis along the railroads; Van Dorn and Forrest had wrought too wildly well, the country was a desolation where supply lines were not. Grant would have to come up out of the quagmires somewhere against the foot of the bluffs. But Vicksburg, like Island No. 10, lies at the bight of a great bend of the Mississippi. He thought to take a leaf from Pope's book, canaling through the peninsula and taking the fortress from below. It was January now; the army went down river and camped in the slope opposite Vicksburg, while two corps went to work with shovels. All through February they toiled amid incredible difficulties; on March 7 came the wave of the spring freshets and Porter's gunboats raised steam to go through the channel. The obstinate river only flooded, without scouring, the new canal; the gunboats could not pass, and when one unarmed transport, with yo-heave-ho and snubbing, was dragged through the ooze, she ran into a brand-new rebel battery erected opposite the lower end of the ditch. Failure No. 4.

Lake Providence is a crescent-shaped frog pond on the west side, where the river once swung a loop. Six miles from it are the sources of the Washita, which leads into the Red River, which leads into the Mississippi again. The mouth was a hundred leagues below the city, but the highlands there were undefended far along. Cut through the six miles, you have a channel which transports and gunboats can follow for a long campaign up from the south against Vicksburg, but at least on dry ground. The cut was made; the river poured in, the first boat followed, riding on the crest—to tear her bottom out against underwater stumps. It was a check, but not a fatal check; an ingenious engineer remembered a St. Louis inventor who had built a machine for cutting off underwater stumps. Grant sent for it; it came, it worked, the stumps began to go; then a rebel sniper put a bullet through the boiler of the device and the sawing machine dissolved in a burst of steam and a fine rain of cog-wheels. Failure No. 5.

December to January, January to February, February to March, turning the corner into April. Five failures; Lincoln, Stanton and the country growing impatient, and the bluffs towering impassably over the Union army. There was a council of war on a gunboat, with Sherman arguing hotly for a return to Memphis and a proper campaign down a new-built railroad, McClernand sneering, and the other generals glum. Admiral Porter cut the knot; if the army would give him a canal to bring his gunboats into the Yazoo, he would go from that river to the Tallahatchie, shoot out the Confederate batteries along the banks and land Grant's army on the high ground. Grant gave him not one canal but two— through Yazoo Pass where the bayous link up with the northern end of the Yazoo and through Steele's Bayou where they tie in with the southern.

Yazoo Pass came first. Porter went in with six gunboats

and a brigade of infantry in transports. The height of water was all right but the rest of the conditions not. The way lay through dense jungle, the rebels had half-cut trees trailing in the water all along, and sharpshooters on the banks. The flotilla moved a mile a day, with the infantry pausing at every step to clear the woods while the sailors hacked at the obstructions. The Tallahatchie was too blocked to make the turn; Porter pressed on to the next side-river, the Yallabusha, on which Granada stands. At the mouth he found a big fort, Fort Pemberton, with a cherry-faced old man in white whiskers sitting on the parapet, yelling "Give them blizzards, boys! Give them blizzards!" The stream was too narrow for the gunboats to maneuver; the fort gave them such blizzards they had to go back and that was Failure No. 6.

At Steele's Bayou Porter had Sherman's support. The passage was excessively strait; the rebels blocked the way before and behind with hewn trees, and ambushed the iron-clads with masked batteries. For a week a lugubrious struggle, more assassination than war, raged through the tangle of growths, crocodiles and deadly snakes; at one time Porter even considered blowing up his ships and trying to escape with the crews, but Sherman pushed a half-brigade through to save the ships from overwhelming snipers by the narrowest of margins. Failure No. 7 and failure complete.

A hundred thousand miles away in Washington they heard nothing from the Mississippi but murmurs of soldiers dying like flies from river fever and snipers' bullets. Grant was seven times a failure, another Buell. The Illinois Congressional delegation came to Lincoln to demand his removal, declaring flatly that, unless the command were given to McClernand, the Republican party could never carry their state again. That touched the President narrowly; a new wrinkle leaped among the many on his forehead. He got to his feet and began pacing the room, to and fro, to and fro. Then he turned on the tormentors:

"I can't spare that man," he said. "He fights."

20

THE SUMMER OF DISCONTENT

LIFE went on. Parson Brownlow's book fell flat, in spite of careful puffing. There was no small change—pay your street-car fare in postage-stamps. The newspapers filled up with ads for artificial legs and the magazines with short stories in what was believed to be the Continental manner, with French catch-words for titles—*"Toujours Fidele," "Sans Coeur," "La Coquette."* Mr. Emerson was shocked to discover that an unknown scribbler named Whitman had blazoned an encouraging phrase from one of his letters across the cover of a volume of Caliban-like verse; and R. G. Graham's unguent would force luxuriant WHISKERS to grow on the smoothest skin. There was newspaper bitterness over the lack of patriotism among the immigrants; "No Irish Need Apply" was becoming a pendant to "Help Wanted." The general tone of society was restrained gloom; we stand on the lip of a volcano with the ground trembling beneath our feet and no man can see the end. Yet the North was not quitting; in Chicago 50,000 stood to shout the refrains of "We are coming, Father Abraham, three hundred thousand more" when the President called for enlistments:

> "To Canaan, to Canaan
> The Lord hath led us forth
> To plant upon the rebel towers
> The banners of the North."

was read with approval from New England pulpits, and

Halleck and Pope came out of the West on a wave of victory to set everything right.

What to do with General Pope? Removing McClellan was not to be thought of; he was a Democrat, intensely popular in the country, with elections coming on; the architect of the Potomac Army and its darling. Lounging in Camp Misery at Harrison's Landing the soldiers sang "McClellan is our man, man, man," and sulked orders from a capital that seethed with intrigue and bad temper. Congress chipped restively at the slavery question; an officer met you on the street to whisper that Stanton was conspiring for a *coup d'état*, Lincoln was sold out to the slave-holders and only Little Mac could save the country. The First Estate, feeling vaguely toward caste entity, would have McClellan for its leader or it would not play; yet McClellan was a punctured Napoleon, the hope of victory lay with the new man from the West.

Clever Lincoln, caught in the cleft, sought solution in intrigue beneath intrigue. He named Pope commander of an "Army of Virginia" for a strike southward overland. It was made up of the fragments round the Shenandoah; as it advanced, reinforcements would be needed, and they would be drawn from the Army of the Potomac till Little Mac was left general of a headquarters guard and a band of music.

Pope established his headquarters at Sperryville in northern Virginia and spent a month drawing in the divisions of his ghost-army from the Valley. They made two corps, Banks' and Sigel's, the worst troops in the East, downhearted and poorly trained. To buck them up the new general opened with a proclamation—"I have come from the West where we have always seen the backs of our enemies. I hear constantly of lines of retreat. Let us discard such ideas. Let us study the lines of retreat of our opponents and leave our own to take care of themselves. Disaster and shame are in the rear." The army was much insulted; Pope heard catcalls round his tent at night and the marching columns turned southward on the wrong foot under a cloudy pillar of growl.

They were headed for Gordonsville, a railroad junction

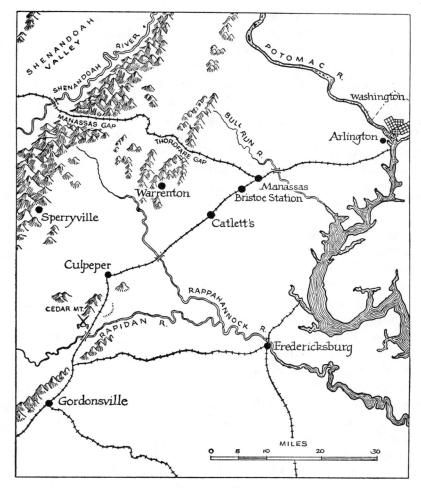

Pope's Campaign

vital to the Confederacy, controlling the route from Richmond to the Shenandoah; McDowell's Corps was coming
down the rails from Washington to meet them there. Pope
believed in cavalry; he appointed a man named Buford to
reorganize his, a lithe, strong captain, big and active. The
general tapped at Gordonsville while the army was organizing and found the place lightly held. But the tap warned

Lee; he sent Stonewall Jackson with 25,000 men up from Richmond to spoil the movement, while he watched Harrison's Landing in case Pope were making a diversion to uncover Richmond. Jackson, pushing straight ahead, got across the Rapidan while McDowell was still at Culpeper, Banks and Sigel west of Cedar Mountain. Pope, well served by Buford's horse, knew of the advance at once; drew Sigel in on McDowell at Culpeper and prepared a red-hot reception for Jackson. Banks, with two divisions, was to detain the Confederates at Cedar Mountain while the main force cut in behind them.

The orders were verbal; Colonel Roberts, a pot-valiant staff officer, rode into Banks' camp with them just as Jackson's head of column appeared around the turn of the hill. Seeing an opportunity for a surprise victory he changed the orders from "Hold" to "Attack" on his own recognizance, and Banks swung out into line, Williams' division on the right, Augur's on the left, 7,500 men. Jackson's lead division, Winder, had just time to fall into line before the blow came. Williams overlapped Winder's left, the line was flanked and crumbled after a short, sharp tussle. But Williams swung inward, exposing his own right; while Jackson's other two divisions, 20,000 strong, flowed around the Federal force, striking it front, flank and rear all at once, and sent it hurtling from the field in collapse. The Union artillery was wonderful, as usual; it made the last stand and smothered pursuit.

Change the pieces. There was a leak in Washington. Rebel spies got wind of Lincoln's plan; Lee dropped McClellan like a hot potato and came up country fast to throw his whole strength onto Pope before the reinforcements could reach him. Buford alertly spotted the onrushing avalanche, and Pope backed to the line of the Rappahannock. On the 21st August, Lee was there also, with better than two to one of men, and there were brisk passages of arms where he tried to break through the fords, with the Confederates having the worst of it. That night the first of the new troops joined

Pope, Reno's Corps and Reynolds' independent division. The Union defense line, however, was excessively long and tenuous; Lee sent Jackson upstream to try for a crossing among the mountains and at the same time sifted Stuart's cavalry across in the night, far down, for a raid round the Union left flank.

The weather was execrable, with thunder and a cloud-burst of rain; Stuart only touched the Union communications, burning a train at Catlett's, but Pope immediately pictured the main rebel concentration in that direction, shifted his weight thither and asked that Franklin's Corps from the Army of the Potomac be brought to him via Fredericksburg. Jackson got his crossing unopposed near Warrenton, and Lee had the measure of his opponent—a stout fellow in a combat but subject to muddle and overhaste. Very well; if he were that kind he should be given every opportunity to blunder. Jackson was sent with his whole wing, 25,000 men, on a tremendous, an incredible circuit up behind the Manassas Mountains, through Thorofare Gap, and thence down to Manassas and across Pope's windpipe.

Stuart was to hide the march, but Buford penetrated his screen, and try as he would, Jackson could not shake the inquisitive Union horsemen from his skirts. Pope got full information as to the movement and its direction, but it did him not the slightest good. The corps of Porter and Heintzelman had just come in from the Potomac, he knew his forte was battle and was determined to believe nothing that would prevent him from having one. A telegram was dispatched to Washington that Jackson was going to the Shenandoah and the pontoons were prepared for a river-crossing and a thrust southward against Lee. Five minutes later the Washington wires went dead; Jackson had just taken Bristoe Station and was astride the Union communications.

That night the Army of Virginia ate its last rations while Heintzelman put a regiment on a train to run down to Manassas and find out what was wrong with the telegraph. At four in the morning they came back without their train and with the appalling news that the northern sky was black with the smoke of the Manassas storehouses and thousands of rebels in possession of the place. Pope clapped his hand to his forehead and beagled like a maniac; he had clean forgotten Thorofare Gap. But he calmed down in an hour or two; after all, there was no shortage of food at headquarters, and he was a sanguine and pugnacious man—as might be expected of one who had proposed to make the Arizona desert a "blooming paradise" by the insertion of artesian wells. A message went off to Washington by runner that he was about to capture Jackson and his army; Buford was dropped behind to hoodwink Lee and the Army of the Potomac started a forced march to round up the invaders.

John Pope was never very articulate; under pressure of the effort to trap Jackson he became positively incoherent. His orders might as well have been written in Chinese; nobody knew what he had in mind, not even the general himself. Porter's Corps was marched at top speed for ten miles under a broiling sun; then turned square around and rushed back whence it had come at the same furious pace; Heintzelman's tramped eighteen weary miles, round and round a spiral to reach a town they had in plain view, three miles away when they started. Regiments crossed each other, got tangled in their own trains and stumbled hither and yon in an insane cat's cradle of movement, while the gagged soldiers subsisted for three days on unripe greencorn and two hours' sleep a night. Through it all one *idée fixe* dominated the general's mind, to wit, that Jackson would try to get across Bull Run and escape northward.

On the 27th Reno and Heintzelman reached Centerville and found the rebels had not crossed for the run north. "Then he must still be at Manassas!" opined Pope gleefully, and began spreading his corps in a wide net to catch them there. That night, Porter, all in order of battle, went into the ruins of Manassas in an "attack"—and found it tenantless. Two days before, Jackson's men had moved a little way

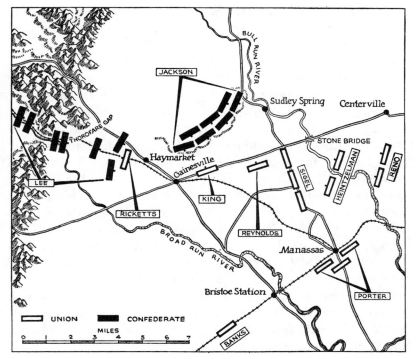

Gainesville

upstream to the old Bull Run battlefield and were now quietly seated there, resting their feet and consuming Union bacon while awaiting the arrival of Lee, who was rushing on through Thorofare Gap like an express train.

Yet the situation was not without peril for the Confederates. Fortune arranged it that Jackson's scouts, feeling toward Gainesville, at peep of dawn on the 28th, should sight a column of men in blue moving eastward and away. It was King, the center division of McDowell's Corps, pushed out to Haymarket in one of the antic convolutions of Pope's strategy, now being recalled for the grand assault on desolate Manassas. It never entered Jackson's head that the Federals were searching for his army, an object difficult to lose; he drew the conclusion any sane man would, that they were in retreat toward Alexandria and the full dinner-pail, and ordered an attack to spread confusion through discouraged ranks.

King's men, however, were not discouraged, only wild angry with hunger and futile marching; they turned in their tracks and counterattacked like a swarm of hornets. The first brigade Jackson put in was blown to bits; a savage battle raged for two hours over the possession of the end of a disused railroad embankment and Jackson had to swing a good half his force to that side before the sullen Union waves were silent. The sound of the guns attracted Reynolds' division and Sigel's whole corps; Heintzelman, turning back from Centerville, fell in next to Sigel and, on his own responsibility, ordered up Reno, who was behind him. Meanwhile, far out on Jackson's right, Ricketts' division of McDowell, isolated by accident, was corking the bottleneck of Thorofare Gap against Lee's advance. As the slow night of the 28th closed in, more than half the Union army was in position before Jackson, with his own help still distant. Another division to fend off Lee, and a quick blow would give the Stonewall as much as it could stand.

There was no one to deliver the blow. Pope had McDowell with him back at Manassas, deep in the fog of war, feverishly composing orders for another strategic monstrosity. Out on the important Union left, whence Lee was coming, the marplot Colonel Roberts had turned up at Ricketts' headquarters. Ricketts had stood a heavy pounding from Lee, and the rebels were all round him—what should he do? "I believe you had better retire to Bristoe Station," said Roberts. Ricketts obeyed with military promptitude; the cork slipped from Lee's bottle and before day he had joined hands with Jackson. That was not all—King, overworked and overworried, had a nervous breakdown, told his division to fly for their lives to Washington and then went into an epileptic fit. Hatch, who took over for him, gathered up the command, but not till they had fled to Porter's camp at Manassas.

First light on the 30th found the position of the armies reversed, with most of Lee's force prolonging Jackson's right and facing the left wing of the Union army under Reynolds, which hung in air. Buford's cavalry was worn out; neither man nor horse could move to scout or make a screen. Lee, with the advantage of Stuart's keen work, saw the opposition clear as crystal and decided merely to let Pope alone and see what further follies he would commit.

The appearance of King's division at Manassas made Pope's eyes stick out like the eyes of a lobster; he galloped off to the front, interviewed Sigel and Reynolds and pictured the situation as it had been on the previous afternoon, before Lee's arrival, of which he was unaware. If it were still so, a sweeping attack through Gainesville by McDowell and Porter would crush Jackson's right wing, and he ordered one in this pearl of ambiguity:

"Generals McDowell and Porter:
You will please move forward with your joint commands toward Gainesville. I desire that when communication is established with the rest of the army the whole command shall halt."

What he meant, he explained afterward, was that communication should be established by breaking through Jackson's line from the rear. Porter, already annoyed with Pope, failed to see it that way. The order did not make sense. In the morning, he advanced tentatively, like a small boy sticking one toe in a bathtub. Longstreet on Lee's right wing was not yet in position, but marked the advance and let brush be tied to the tails of some twenty horses which were ridden up and down in the dust to give the impression of a big column marching. Porter fell for it and came to a halt, blocking McDowell's path. The latter rode up, shouting angrily, "Porter, this is no place to fight a battle!" and the two fell into an argument, while Sigel and Heintzelman were attacking and being shot to pieces by the Confederates,

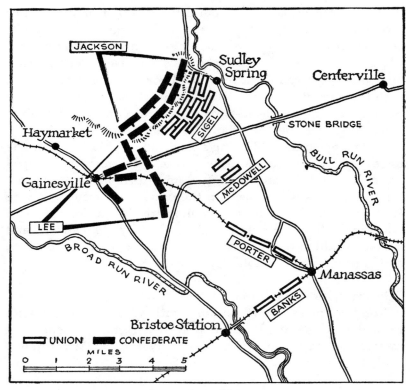

Second Bull Run

comfortably ensconced behind their embankment. Pope lost 8,000 men; telegraphed to Washington that he had won a great victory and ordered Porter wrathily up for another try on the morrow. Lee sat still, merely concentrating his artillery to sweep Jackson's embankment from the side.

Pope, still clutching the delusion that he had only Jackson in front of him, shuffled his corps during the night so that his men would be sufficiently tired before having to fight on the morrow. Porter had the end of the line, opposite the embankment. At five in the morning, he went in. The assault was gallant, but his men were under rifle fire from shelter in front and, as they got fully engaged, the pitiless enfilade of Lee's massed batteries burst upon their flank.

Porter's loss was terrific; whole regiments went down, he was hopelessly broken and Pope had to order Reynolds in to keep him from rout.

Just at this moment, Lee, who had been reaching his right around the Union rear, released Longstreet in a counterattack with Hood, the hardest hitter in the Confederacy, at its head. It fell on the part of the Federal line that had been most badly used—Porter and Reynolds—and rolled them away before it. The confusion spread; Jackson's men leaped up and advanced with a cheer, the Union army was pinched from front and flank. Reno tried in vain to stem the tide; Heintzelman broke, McDowell went rattled as in the first Bull Run and spent his force in vain piecemeal effort. There was no panic—McClellan had drilled them beyond that—just a Union army hammered out of sense by superior numbers at every contact, hopelessly outgeneraled. Only a heroic defense by one of Sigel's brigades at the bridge over Bull Run kept Lee from capturing them by corps; as it was, he took 7,000 prisoners and thirty guns and the Army of Virginia went flying back to Washington, confused and routed.

So the Second Bull Run ended like the first in defeat and bitterness. Pope was right—disaster and shame in the rear. Heintzelman and McDowell lost their posts; Porter was court-martialed and cashiered, and "as big a liar as John Pope" became a temporary adjunct of the American language.

2 1

FOREVER FREE

THEY were all there but Blair when the President came
in—grim Stanton, muscular features for once composed,
Welles whispering behind his forest of beard to Bates and
Smith; tall Seward, burly Chase. They had been talking
about him and the debate of yesterday on the proposal to
arm the blacks; Lincoln saw it in the hush and half-spent
words, but he was used to that by now. He ambled clumsily
to his place at the head of the table, a slight uplift at the
corners of his mouth as though in anticipation of some pleasant emotion, and when all had taken their places, produced
a book.

"This is the funniest thing I ever read," he remarked,
looking round, and opening at a marker, began to read in a
high-pitched voice—"High-handed outrage at Utiky, by
Artemas Ward." They heard him out, only Smith and Bates
frankly amused; Chase was unhappy, Stanton sternly dumb;
Seward smiled a fatherly and patronizing smile. The President wiped the tears of laughter from his eyes and his face
took on a graver accent.

"However, the reason I have called the present meeting
is to lay a proclamation before you—" and once more he
began to read, while they sat dumbfounded as the words
rolled on to their climax:

"Be it ordered that, on the first day of January in the
year of Our Lord, 1863, all persons held as slaves within any

state or designated part of a state, the people whereof shall be in rebellion against the United States shall be then, thenceforward and forever free.

"Done in the city of Washington, this twenty-second of July in the year of Our Lord, One thousand eight hundred and sixty-two, and of the Independence of the republic, the eighty-seventh."

As he ceased there was a moment's silence; then the whole pack burst into unanimous excited babble that fell quiet again as Lincoln raised his hand.

"My mind is made up, my resolution taken. This step is a necessity; in delaying it so long we have given dissatisfaction if not offense to many whose support we cannot afford to lose; and we have been condoning a moral wrong. I have called you together to ask your opinions on the date of issue and the form the proclamation shall take."

Moral wrong? A new Lincoln, different from the one who hoped for God's aid but must have Kentucky's. Only Welles understood; he had ridden in the carriage with Lincoln when the President came back from the cemetery on that dark day two months before when Stanton's son was buried, so soon after Lincoln had lain his own child there, had seen the momentary lifting of the mask, the doubt, the humility, the fear that he might be insufficient to the task, the need for spiritual sustention. "I have made a vow, a covenant with God—"

Stanton's prehensile mouth sprang open—Mr. President, if that is the case, I am in favor of issuing the proclamation at once.

Chase: It is a measure fraught with great danger, and would undoubtedly lead to universal emancipation. It goes beyond anything I would have recommended, yet I cannot but approve.

Seward: Will not the foreigners prevent abolition for the sake of cotton? That species of agriculture cannot be supported by free labor, and the deficiency of the staple will produce the ruin of industries by which they exist. If the present conflict becomes a war for the abolition of slavery England and France will recognize the Confederacy and make war upon us to maintain their supply of cotton.

"I had anticipated that objection, and surely it rests upon a misapprehension. England cannot well afford to enter a war to maintain the slave power, and it is also an adequate reply that the Confederate agents in Europe insist that the war has nothing to do with slavery."

—But, Mr. President, we ought not to put in jeopardy the patriotic element in the border states. The results of this proclamation would be to carry over those states en masse to the secessionists.

Lincoln looked up; it was Blair, just entered. "I have considered the danger, which is certainly serious, but the objection is certainly as great not to act. Slavery is the lever by which the secessionists maintain a hold on the border states. That lever I shall break before their faces."

All of them were intellectuals; none was fearless. They sat silent, bemused to an unreasoning dread by the emotional impact of a view wider than their compass, probing to find some reasonable basis for the tightening at their throats.

Seward spoke.—I am inclined to the measure as justifiable. On the point of expediency, however, the depression of the public mind consequent upon our recent reverses in the field is so great that I fear the effect of so important a step. It will be viewed as the last measure of an exhausted Government, a cry for help. Instead of Ethiopia stretching out her hands to us, we are extending ours to her. It will be considered as our last *shriek* on the retreat, a malicious effort to foment a servile rebellion.

Lincoln started; the point was new. "I shall do nothing in malice," he said slowly. "What I deal with is too vast for malicious dealing. . . . "

Blair leaped in eagerly—the border states, the political situation, the fall elections—

"No, no." The President moved impatiently, brushing aside the cloud of midges. "I will wait only on the military situation. If God gives us a victory in the next battle, I will consider it an indication of the Divine will that it is my duty to move forward in the cause of emancipation."

He stood up.

22

MARYLAND, MY MARYLAND

Y ou shall not imagine, either, that all is abounding grace and united effort within the Confederacy. Where are our little luxuries, our silks, our wheaten bread, our breakfast coffee? The sun wheels from east to west, the seasons pass, the long tide of victory flows in and the Yankees can never conquer us; yet still the northern sky is red with war and our husbands and our sons march away to return no more.

No more. Our own sweet land must bear the weight of many tramping feet because an old man in Richmond declares that we must prove before the world that we fight in self-defense. "The efforts and victories of the Southern Confederacy up to this time have been only the blundering blows of a blind giant. When the enemy rubs up against the military power, the army hits, sometimes with striking effect. But the success is all barren, isolated, and without ulterior consequences." Go to! Let us "transfer the war from the interior to the frontier, give the enemy some other realization of war than an immense money job by which they profit, aid the kindred folk of Maryland to recover their liberties." For south of the Potomac we are undeceived by Lincoln's mildness; we know him for an avaricious and bloody tyrant. who has authored frightful atrocities and holds his foot on prostrate Maryland's throat. Not even Robert Lee is immune from this, proving, if you will, how war acts on the intelligence like the curved mirrors of a hall of grotesques.

So the Army of Northern Virginia, an instrument perfectly attuned, which could march like fire, strike like a trip-hammer, swung pack on back and musket on shoulder and turned northward in hope and glory. The Northern army was leaderless and racked by defeat; it was not unlikely that pusillanimous Lincoln would hold it within the Washington redans while they conquered a peace on the Susquehanna. There is a ford of the Potomac near Leesburg, east of the mountains; on the 4th September the rebels made the passage, lifted the new flag in the breeze and called on the state to rise around them.

That same day Gideon Welles, Secretary of the Navy, was entering in his diary:

"Blair, who has known Pope intimately, says he is a braggart and a liar. He is certainly a failure here. Chase called on me with an address to the President stating that the signers did not deem it safe that McClellan should be entrusted with the army. The paper was signed by Stanton, Chase, Smith and Bates and a space was left between the two last for Blair and myself; Seward is not in town, purposely absent. I declined to sign. As we talked, Stanton entered, terribly agitated. He said in a suppressed voice and trembling with excitement that he was informed McClellan had been ordered to take command of the forces. He is mad at McClellan and determined to destroy him. God help us."

It was true. Halleck could do nothing but twirl dividers over a map and mutter about ration returns; Pope was hissed in the streets, the army in a state of utter misery and distrust, desertions piling up. Little Mac was a punctured Napoleon and Stanton hated him with a virulent hatred, but Lee was sweeping into Maryland, and if the demoralized army could not respond to this dose of its favorite drug, then God help us indeed.

It did respond, waking slowly as from a bad dream. Broken organizations took on cohesion again under the touch of the master organizer. Ladies driving through the shimmering haze of autumn around the capital heard the sunburned regiments singing while they cooked their lob-scouse beside the road:

> "I'll eat when I'm hungry and drink when I'm dry,
> And if the Johnnies don't kill me, I'll live till I die."

There was even a little cheering when Our Mac rode through the lines; General Stuart noted with surprise how much bite the Union cavalry had where it clashed with his along the fringes of the advance.

Lee had swung west and north from the crossing, through Crampton's Gap with 40,000 men. There were no good roads east of the mountains by which he could connect with Richmond; once he got through, however, the Union garrison at Harpers Ferry would be forced to pull out and his supply line could run down the Shenandoah. Maryland was a disappointment; the people only turned out to gaze stupidly at Stonewall Jackson "in his seedy homespun and a hat that any Northern beggar would consider an insult," and at the mongrel, half-barefooted crew that followed him. Were "Maryland, My Maryland" a thousand times inspiring it could not make them join their fortunes with such a troop of raggedocios.

On the 9th the rebels were pouring through the South Mountain passes, pointing west on Hagerstown; Stuart brought in word that McClellan had moved out of Washington, reorganizing as he came, with six army corps, 87,000 men, according to his own muster-rolls, as filched from the files by the espionage service. That noon there was a slight check; Stuart's lieutenant, Fitz Lee, feeling south with the left wing cavalry, reported that the Union garrison at Harpers Ferry was sticking it out. Lee was short of supplies and, with the country round him turned sour, must open communications through the Valley soon; the Harpers Ferry garrison was 11,000 men, enough to make trouble for anything smaller than a corps. He sent Jackson and his 20,000 back to smoke out the rats of that granary, dropped D. H.

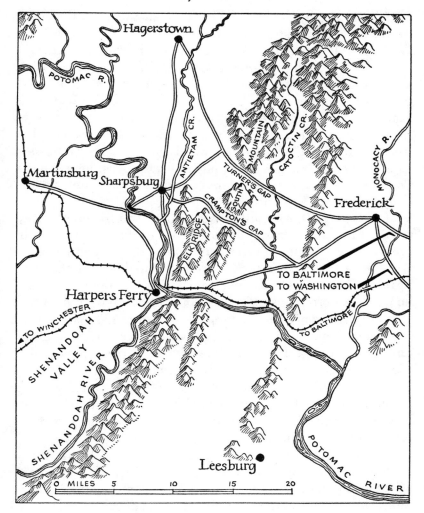

The Antietam Campaign

Hill's divisions as a rearguard at the South Mountain passes and pushed on northwest with the rest. It was dividing his army, but not dangerous; supine McClellan moved so cautiously that a concentration could be worked up before any attack from him became a menace, and long before the ponderous Federal columns could make the passes Jackson would have rejoined at Hagerstown.

The orders went in duplicate. That evening some of Averell's Union light horse clashed with a rebel formation south of Crampton's. A few shots streaked the dark; one of the gray riders toppled from his saddle and, when the body was examined for badges, Averell found a copy of Lee's order to Jackson. McClellan had it by 6:30 in the afternoon and it worked on him like the elixir of his lost youth, for he saw looming before his eyes the opportunity to thrust between the Confederate wings at Sharpsburg, hold off Jackson and destroy the rest of Lee's army.

But George B. McClellan would not spoil his men's sleep to win a battle. His night orders bade Franklin's Corps begin the thrust at Crampton's in the morning, Reno's and Hooker's with the cavalry to attack Turner's Gap later in the day. Franklin was a feel-your-way general, a cautious old man; he pressed on so painstakingly that a single division detained him at Crampton's all day long. The assault at Turner's Gap was hotter; Reno led it, swinging his hat as the men scrambled among the rocky screes. But the way was narrow, the cavalry useless; Reno was killed in the first advance and the fire went out of the attack till Hooker came up and went surging through the rebel line. By that time it was mid-afternoon; McClellan, riding to the front, decided it was glory enough for one day and ordered a halt.

Meanwhile panting messengers had carried the alarming news to Lee. He spun on a dime, marched back southward all day and half the night, taking up a strong position at Sharpsburg, behind the precipitous banks of Antietam Creek. Harpers Ferry and its 11,000 had surrendered that morning; the prisoners were sent south and Jackson was hurrying to join Lee by forced marches.

He might have spared the trouble. McClellan spent the whole day riding through his lines, drinking in the cheers with which he was everywhere greeted and forming a plan of battle. Toward evening he had achieved one, uninspired but perfectly sound—hold hard in the center, throw two or three army corps on Lee's floating left flank and, when that cracked, send Burnside, with what had been Reno's Corps, straight across the stream to break through the rebel right.

Hooker's Corps, supported by Mansfield's, was started to move at once; they crossed high up, came down the Hagerstown road and ran into the rebel flank-guard while taking position. There was a sharp little contest in the gathering gloom; Lee had to put in Stuart's cavalry to make good his line, but viewed the incident with profound gratitude. It told him where the attack would come in the morning; he shifted Jackson and Ewell with most of his artillery to cover that flank and pushed a heavy cloud of skirmishers into the woods and fields in front of the main line.

At birdsong Hooker was afoot, a brave, vain, insubordinate man who could lead a charge supremely well. His corps went in with all the drive he could give it, square on Jackson's front, whose men were not all come as yet. They ran into concentrated artillery fire and Lee's thick-sown skirmishers smothered the Union guns, but Hooker drove in so hard that Jackson had to call on Ewell. Still Hooker came on; the angle of the rebel line was pierced, the Federals cleared the East Wood and came storming up around the Dunker Church. Old Stonewall had for once his belly full; he rode to the front, shouting alternate prayers and objurations, but even he could not stop the onslaught. He had to send for more help; Stuart fell on Hooker's right with artillery and cavalry, slowed the advance, and rebels and Federals faced each other across the Hagerstown road firing murderous volleys. The losses they stood were almost incredible; Union Ricketts lost a third of his division, Confederate Lawton more than half his, and every regimental officer. By 7:30 the flame died down for sheer lack of fuel, both Hooker and Jackson wrecked and no longer war-worthy.

In fifteen minutes it blazed up again as Mansfield's Corps came hurrying down the Hagerstown road against the West Wood and Lee pulled Hood from his center to stay the shaking line. Mansfield fell at the first fire, but his troops rushed on. Hood met them with a counterattack; the lines clashed in a desperate, frightfully sanguinary musketry fight. Hood was outnumbered; he could not stand the pressure, his command was almost annihilated. The West Wood went lost, Mansfield's men carried the Dunker Church, and then were stopped dead as Stuart struck in once more on their one flank, D. H. Hill on the other. By nine o'clock they were fought past effort, a countercharge would have sent them and what was left of Hooker whirling from the field.

It never came; Lee had his hands full. Sumner, with another Union corps, had crossed the Antietam and headed a third attack, at the base of the West Wood, trying to break through behind Sharpsburg. He was an old cavalry officer who had never led foot before; he advanced in long lines without flankers, which will do for horsemen but not for infantry. The proof is that as his regiments approached the Confederate line they were taken flank by a surprise attack from McLaws' and Anderson's divisions of Longstreet, rushing to the rescue from below Sharpsburg. Sumner's lines were enfiladed, his men fell by hundreds and in half an hour his corps was routed and driven off.

Ten o'clock. McClellan, sitting back on the porch of his headquarters, imbibing cool drinks, had thoroughly bungled his battle and spoiled three army corps in piecemeal assaults. But there was fight in the Army of the Potomac yet, and Lee's position was become dubious. Jackson's, Hood's and Ewell's commands were no longer fully able to fight, the rebel line was bent double north of the town, Stuart was worn to tatters, and the Confederate right wing was weakened by successive withdrawals to stand off Hooker and Mansfield. McClellan ordered up a division of Franklin's Corps to rally Sumner and sent Burnside's in against the stone bridge at the far southern end of the position. Sumner's Corps were iron-souled New Englanders; they did rally, they came back north of Sharpsburg, they fought a titanic battle with McLaws and Early and every reserve Lee could gather for the possession of

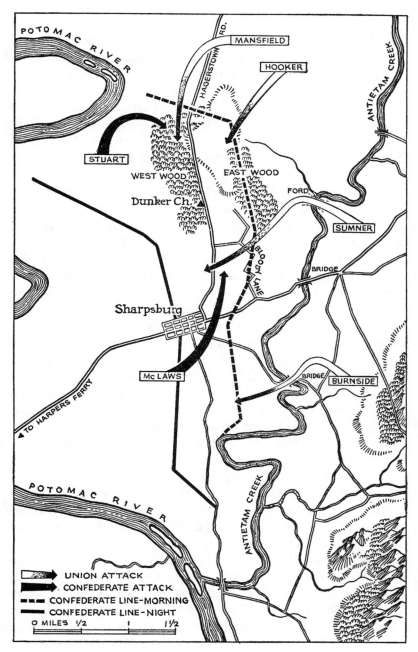

POTOMAC RIVER

HAGERSTOWN RD.

MANSFIELD

HOOKER

ANTIETAM CREEK

STUART

WEST WOOD

EAST WOOD

Dunker Ch.

FORD

SUMNER

BLOODY LANE

BRIDGE

Sharpsburg

McLAWS

BRIDGE

BURNSIDE

TO HARPERS FERRY

POTOMAC RIVER

ANTIETAM CREEK

UNION ATTACK
CONFEDERATE ATTACK
CONFEDERATE LINE-MORNING
CONFEDERATE LINE-NIGHT

0 MILES ½   1   1½

Antietam

a sunken road that acquired the deadly name of Bloody Lane. They carried it, they swept on into the outskirts of the blazing town and held one side of it while the rebels clung to the other, firing rifles and cannon muzzle to muzzle across the streets while burning roof-tops crashed about them. But they could get no further; McClellan remained on his porch, failing to send reinforcements or do anything else and at three or four o'clock this battle also died down to skirmisher fire.

Burnside on the Federal left belonged to the anti-McClellan union; he was pouting because he had not been given two corps instead of one and, when he got his orders, moved with the unhurrying pace of a glacier. It was full three o'clock when he got his column ready; then his artillery let go with a clap of thunder and he flung a column of General Crook's command at the bridge. A concentrated rebel fire blew the head of column into the air. Crook deployed skirmishers along the bank, seized a flag and led the next storm himself with a bugle sounding; one of the bravest efforts of the war. Five hundred men went down in a minute; Crook, marvelously untouched, led the rest right on and split the rebel line. Other regiments followed; they turned right and left to exploit the gain, but it was too late now, the fighting elsewhere had died down, and Lee could bring his last reserves from all over the field to form round the audacious attackers in a semicircle and bring them to a stop.

That was the last flicker; the battle of Antietam was over, the bitterest, the costliest yet fought in the war, with 12,000 of McClellan's, 11,000 of Lee's men lying on the field. By good tactics and a stout-hearted defense Lee had saved his army, but he had saved it crippled; the invasion of the North was over. That night the Union soldiers heard the rumble of wagons from the enemy lines and slept under the rain of occasional shells with which the Confederate artillery was covering their retreat. On their side, a botched, a bungled, a badly fought battle, the climax of a bungled campaign. It looked even worse from the distance of Washington when

McClellan's report arrived; he was sending up his usual howl for more troops, accompanied by one of his usual Oriental estimates of the enemy's force—they had 100,000, said he. Lincoln retorted by sending an inspector, who discovered that, though Little Mac was drawing pay for 87,000 on his muster-rolls, he had less than 60,000 in camp, all the rest away on leave to keep them sweet-tempered.

"Sending that man reinforcements is like shoveling flies across a room," said the President grimly, and forthwith removed McClellan as commander of the army, let the consequences be what they might.

Yet a victory for all that; for the first time the Army of the Potomac had seen butternut backs, and Lincoln had his indication of the Divine will. Five days later the Emancipation Proclamation flared like a comet across the world. Comet? No, a sun—"This is the dawning of a new day," said Chase as the President signed the paper. "The effect on our fortunes will be magical."

The effect was magical. The Lincoln men lost the fall elections, and the President had a hostile Congress to face.

23

THE DARK HEIGHT

AMBROSE BURNSIDE, who sulked at Antietam, received the baton. He was a pioneer in the art of personal salesmanship, simply oozing elusive charm and sterling worth from every pore; the only general in history to have a barber's specialty named after him. No one who talked with him for five minutes ever doubted that Burnside was a very fine man, although people who talked with him for ten were known to express skepticism as to his intellect. There was a blinding snowstorm the day Colonel Buckingham brought the good news down from Washington; Burnside met the messenger outdoors with a cordial handclasp while the flakes outlined in white the bridge of whisker across his face as he protested: "I do not want the command. I am not competent to command such a large army." It took an hour or two to beat down this maidenly modesty; then the new generalissimo went over to Sumner's headquarters and had a bottle of champagne opened while they sat down to work out a plan of action.

The army lay at Warrenton, in the shadow of the Blue Ridge, with a strong wing out in the Valley. The new enlistments were coming in strong; Burnside counted 113,000 men, in six army corps. Lee, keeping to a wary defensive in rock-bound positions among the hills, had been reinforced up to 80,000 by the Confederacy's new conscription law, but was still organized in the old way—no corps, two grand wings under Jackson and Longstreet, with D. H. Hill's independent division and Stuart's cavalry at the general's personal disposition.

Burnside inherited a plan for fighting straight ahead toward Gordonsville along Pope's old line, but that looked obvious and the idea of a winter campaign among the mountain spurs failed to appeal; better to deceive Lee with a covering attack on the Warrenton front, meanwhile shifting the gross of the army down the Rappahannock for a fast drive along the direct line from Fredericksburg on Richmond. Halleck disapproved the scheme, pointing out that Robert Lee was not an easy man to bamboozle, but disapproval from Halleck had become so chronic that it now stood at fifty per cent discount, and when Burnside went up to Washington and pulled out the Vox Humana stop full length at a Cabinet conference he came away with the official benison on his design.

On the morning of November 15 Sumner started the leftward glide with two corps; on the 19th they were opposite Fredericksburg. The Rappahannock is bad here, wide and deep, with commanding heights a little back from the edge on both sides; there was no bridge, and somebody—Halleck said Burnside, Burnside said Halleck—had forgotten to provide pontoons. Sumner's two corps amused themselves by building snow castles till the pontoons arrived on the 25th. Meanwhile Stuart had punctured the half-hearted cavalry screen behind which Burnside sought to hide his maneuver and Lee knew all about it. As the pontoon train plodded into the Union camp north of the river, Longstreet's wing of the rebel army came marching into the Confederate camp south of it. A few days later Burnside arrived with the Army of the Potomac; so did Lee with the Army of Northern Virginia, and went to work actively fortifying Marye's Hill, the high ridge behind the town.

Burnside was paralyzed with astonishment at finding the rebels there. He spent three weeks accumulating a stock of supplies and ideas. His imagination gave way under the strain; on the 12th December, after "a night of sleepless anxiety" spent in wandering vaguely through the camp, he dredged up from some well of wits' end the notion that he could force his way straight through the rebel position. Toward morning he prepared orders for the maddest enterprise of the war—bridging a wide stream, crossing it with 100,000 men and assailing nearly vertical hills crowned with fortifications, occupied by an army of 80,000 under the ablest tacticians of the age and well supplied with artillery. He himself did not seem to know quite what was to be done—"Seize some strong point on the other side and keep your whole force in position for a move toward Richmond," said his orders, nothing more precise.

The whole thing was hopeless; everyone but Burnside knew it. The soldiers stacked their knapsacks and wrote affecting letters home, including little trinkets—"Dear Mother: Tomorrow, if our present plans are carried out, we are to fight the great battle of the war. I have little hope of the plan succeeding; there will be great loss of life and I—"

The day dawned dark and late, with swirling fog, through which the artillery sent a dull vibration. Sumner, with the II and IX Corps (they had numbers now), bridged the stream on the Union right with heavy losses; Franklin, with the I and VI Corps, bridged the left. They ranked on the opposite shore amid the fields and houses, and the mist sprang back to show them to the Confederates, bayonets glimmering in the frosty winter light. The Union men were in the hollow of a cup; along Marye's rim, from side to side, a tornado of artillery fire burst upon them, mingled with the high crack of musketry. The supporting cannon from the northern side opened out, peal on peal, but the distance was too long; the shot popped harmless in the river or dropped among the Union troops, and they soon gave over.

Franklin on the left was first to strike, with Meade's Pennsylvania division in the van, straight up the hills with bayonets fixed and grim faces. Meade was resolute as you please, the Pennsylvanians very valiant; in spite of the hurricane of bullets that beat on them, they went right on, up and up, broke through the rebel line, captured a color and gained the crest. But Lee, surveying the movement calmly, saw their supports had been cut to pieces by the artillery; a reserve division was ordered up, new batteries planted. Meade's salient was encircled from every side, and he was slowly driven back from the hill into the town, leaving behind two-thirds of his strength.

Sumner on the other wing led the charge in person, his white hair flaring to the breeze. The hills were steeper here, the artillery fire worse; the II Corps stood it in the hopeless advance for two hours, till 5,000 men had fallen. Burnside, watching through his glasses, ordered Hooker with two more corps to drive the attack home. Hooker was the best assault-commander in the army but "the fire of the enemy now became still hotter. The stone wall was a sheet of flame that enveloped the head and flanks of the column. Officers and men fell so rapidly that orders could not be passed. . . . " Why plunge further into this sea of blood, this effort to batter down stone walls with living men? At four o'clock it was all over; the Army of the Potomac was a clove-shaped mass of dregs at the bottom of the cup, the hills around them littered with the bodies of 15,000 good men and true and Ambrose Everett Burnside, the personality expert, raging alternately at the "thieving poltroons" who composed his army and the "cowardly scalawags" who led it, was proposing to ride up Marye's Heights alone with his staff. They should have let him. It was not till night that he began to weep.

On the other side, Lee simply would not believe in the execution his guns had wrought. "They are demoralized!" cried Stonewall Jackson. "A night attack on them and we have them all. Let us all strip ourselves perfectly naked for identification and then charge them." Nudity in December had few charms for Lee, he said no, the great moment passed, and the Army of the Potomac slowly withdrew behind the ice-strewn Rappahannock, while the long-range guns in the Union batteries tolled a requiem for the fresh dead.

The beaten troops paused for a month, keeping a wretched Christmas amid rain and heartless despair; then Burnside had a new inspiration and dragged them up the river to force a passage at one of the fords. A storm of rain came on; the men waded ankle-deep, the pack trains foundered in bottomless mire, but Burnside dismounted the cavalry, used their horses to carry supplies, and pressed on. The march went a mile a day; Lee had every ford fortified and the Confederate outposts called through the driving sleet—"Hey, Yankees, shall we come over and help you build a bridge?" Burnside kept on. On the 21st January he reached United States Ford, and distributed orders for another frontal assault.

There was almost a mutiny. Franklin protested, Burnside overrode his objections; Franklin said the New Jersey regiments in his command would not fight as their state had just elected a Democratic Senator and might withdraw from the war. Burnside told him the excuse was frivolous (which was true) and drove him out of headquarters. Sumner protested; "Silence!" said Burnside. "The attack will be made in the morning." Hooker protested; he could not guarantee the conduct of his troops; the words ran hot and high. Hooker sent one of his brigadiers to Washington to beg Lincoln to prevent another Fredericksburg horror. Burnside went to Washington, too, with an order dismissing Hooker from the army as incompetent and cowardly, and opened the spigot of his personality again. This time it failed to draw; Lincoln told Burnside he need not bother about going back to the army and that was the end of the experiment in business methods as a means of conquering the Confederacy.

24

THE DITHYRAMB OF SHIVA

WHEN Lincoln removed Burnside from command, he passed Sumner and Franklin, who were next of seniority, to appoint Hooker. They went into miffed retirement, and with them went an era; the era of forcing-house generals. For Sumner and Franklin, like the other early Northern leaders, were men of great private rectitude and inconsiderable experience, in whose selection to command armies character and political expediency played almost equal parts. These were admittedly unreliable guides, but Lincoln had no others at the beginning of the war, and the experiment of rapid promotion for fortunate minor commanders had failed disastrously with McClellan and Pope.

Hooker and the new corps commanders who came up with him (Meade, Reynolds, Hancock, Sedgwick and Howard) were dogs from a different kennel; they had advanced quickly, it is true, but none of them was a half-pay captain one day and generalissimo of the United States armies three months later, like McClellan. They had time to observe and form some concept of the inner workings of the vast and complicated machine of which they were cogs, something McClellan never achieved.

Indeed, it was this very fact that made McClellan a good strategist and earned for him Lee's subsequent encomium as the best of the Union generals. For military strategy is an art of immense and infantile simplicity, demanding that the practitioner overlook the trees and contemplate the forest only. McClellan's trouble was that he overlooked too many trees, he concentrated his intelligence on the effort to place his opponent in a position where a lost battle must be disastrous, forgetting that before he could bag the prisoners the battle must be fought—this and the Cæsarian delusion that caused him to make such statements as "I am willing to become dictator, save the country and then perish by suicide to preserve her liberties."

He was the nearest thing to a Cæsar and his army the nearest to a Prætorian Guard the war produced; one recognizes in the attention he gave to his soldiers' creature-comforts, the freely granted leaves, the same tricks by which some emperor of the Roman decadence, says Maximin, raised himself to the throne. It is perhaps fortunate that McClellan had to do with Robert E. Lee instead of the Marcomanni and thus became a conquered and not a conquering hero, though it is unlikely that the nation would have stood for a McClellan dictatorship under any circumstances. The country already had a Cæsar who, whatever the state of the Dacian frontier, was giving increasing satisfaction in Latium, and McClellan's suicidal ardors, though appreciated, had an air at once baroque and ridiculous to a generation which read Petroleum V. Nasby. Lincoln was too much the epitome of the average American to be unseated by any such Alice's White Knight; he could have laughed a *coup d'état* out of existence with an off-color joke.

Pope was the exact antithesis of McClellan; he saw nothing but trees. It was his passion for detail that had brought him success among the Missouri guerrillas and at Island No. 10. The same characteristic lay behind his able handling of cavalry; it was two years before the Union horse was used with such dash again.

At the same time it was one of the highest tributes to Lee's ability that, though he had never met the man, he penetrated these manifestations and saw what lay behind them; then smothered Pope's intelligence by keeping in constant movement—giving him so many details to look at that he could not form them into a connected whole before the kaleidoscope had changed.

Yet Lee's own intellect was curiously opaque in certain directions. Nowhere do we find the slightest indication that he (or any man under him, for that matter) understood the portentous meaning of Antietam. With that knightly and gracious courtesy to the individual, to the commanding individual, that was characteristic of the Southern aristocracy, he assumed that it was McClellan who beat him there. He failed to realize that the battle was won before a single rifle cracked and that McClellan had done his best to lose it. He failed, just as the average Sothoron failed, to realize that the war was not a "money job" on the part of the North; he continued to believe in the indiscipline and poor fighting quality of Northern troops just as the average Southerner continued to believe he was the superior of any three Northerners in something he vaguely denominated "prowess." The only lesson Lee drew from Antietam was that he ought not to fight battles against such numerical odds, and he made the appeal that resulted in the Confederate conscription law and filled up his cadres to the strength they had at Fredericksburg.

Fredericksburg furnished an apparent justification of this view. It was a tremendous victory, in which the South apparently demonstrated that if its full strength were put forth, invasion could not succeed against it. Lee carried the analysis no further. If he had carried it further, indeed if he had correctly analyzed the conditions on the field at the time, he would have perceived that there was something wrong with his tremendous victory. He won the battle and severely damaged the Union army, but he had destroyed neither its will to come back for another battle nor its physical capacity for doing so, and he had really demonstrated nothing but the inability of the Northerners to win the Battle of Fredericksburg.

If he really wished to complete the proposition he should have taken Jackson's advice—not, indeed, about stripping naked for identification, but certainly about charging the enemy while they were in the reflux of defeat, with the organization half destroyed, their soldiers discouraged and in a position against a river where their own artillery could not support them. Most of the Confederates were relatively fresh and Lee had a large force of cavalry, which had not fought at all, opposite the Federal left wing. In precisely similar circumstances at Friedland, in 1807, Napoleon mercilessly destroyed a Russian army and ended a war.

Why did Lee not apply the crushing blow? Humanity, perhaps; the humanity which made him so admirable a character, and which men are required to set aside if they are to succeed in the bloody business of war. Yet this is only half the story. There was also a lack of depth to his analysis, as at Antietam. Indeed, had he grasped the full significance of that deadly clash, it is possible that he would have been fighting for the other side. For Antietam was the first note of the death-knell, the warning that the Southern system was mistaken. It is the first duty of every system to protect its existence against the violent contact of every other system.

The Confederacy had conspicuously failed to maintain its right to existence by peaceful means. The fact that there was a Confederacy was a demonstration that the rebel leaders considered peaceful means useless, and at the same time the demonstration of their limitations, their lack of constructive ability. They had abandoned all effort at compromise, had plunged headlong into secession and violence, not because they were deprived of property without due process of law, like the revolutionists of '76, but the mere threat that such aggression might one day become possible—at the collapse of only one of the safeguards against such aggression, the convenient arrangement by which the pro-slavery party should choose the President of the United States. There was plenty of executive ability in the South, but so little talent for organization, so scanty a diplomatic sense, that even with war and death staring them in the face Davis and his merry men had not intelligence enough to conceive any device that would protect them but the possession of this one office.

In a way, this is not surprising. Individualism, the 1863-Dixie species of individualism, is a destructive and not an organizing force. The moment your individualist begins to cohere with others, his individualism ceases to be; the majority must make decisions for the mass, which is just what the Southerners were kicking about. "Despotic majority," said Davis of the anti-slavery people. By the very theory on which the new republic was founded, the whole thing was a dithyramb of Shiva, and Jefferson Davis and his entourage so many Thuggars. Revolutions, of course, are always made by destroyers, but they usually consider themselves reformers who have some better cosmos of their own to substitute for the existing order. The Confederate rebellion was remarkable in this—that it was both more conservative and more radical than the type—more conservative in that it aimed at the maintenance of the economic *status quo*, more radical in that its guiding principle was the destruction of all restrainders, with no substitution of anything new.

Yet this system, fundamentally anarchic, was failing to provide means for its own preservation. It was not merely that the North could give the hollow and insincere McClellan more men than the South gave such a story-book hero as Lee; in war, numbers count for nothing—at Plassey, Robert Clive demolished odds of one hundred to one. It was not that the Army of Northern Virginia fought barefoot and in rags, for the management of supplies was the great defect of Lee's generalship. It was rather that the North had developed a fighting machine, an aggregation of military specialists, who in spite of all McClellan could do to lose Antietam, yet won it. The superiority of the Southern soldier in the first stages of the war had been moral; a lonely individual in a universe of his own, he had learned to care for himself in the most desperate circumstances. When outflanked or outnumbered he considered himself equal to the occasion and stood his ground. The hard discipline of two years of war had at last impressed upon the Northern private the fact that war was an activity more dangerous but not more recondite than his ordinary life; he already knew he was not an ordinary individual but a cooperating unit in a machine composed of some millions of his fellows. He had now discovered that if he were outflanked or outnumbered he need not despair; some cooperating unit of infantry would rise from the ground to outflank the outflankers; some cooperating levin-bolt of artillery from the blue would strike down the superior numbers. The rally of Sumner's Corps at Antietam is profoundly instructive; no beaten troops in the Union army, hardly any troops in any army, had ever come back after defeat for such an onslaught as they made there.

This new cohesion, this new fighting machine, received its supreme test at Fredericksburg, where, with everything obviously hopeless, the men in blue marched unflinchingly into certain death, pitifully confident in that cooperation of leaders and fellows they had been taught to expect. It was the failure of such cooperation that brought them to the edge of mutiny after the battle; they had trusted their discipline and they had been betrayed. Yet they would trust it again under another leader; their whole lives had been a training for that trust, they had learned now to apply it in war as in peace. The discipline, the one-for-all, had reached the mass intelligence and turned the mob into a fighting machine; when the young leaders who had been through the founder's fire of that hard school came to the top, it would become a thinking machine as well.

If the machine ever attained that goal it would go hard with the Confederacy, for the Confederacy was predicated on the belief that the trick cannot be accomplished; that once the individual abnegates freedom of will he abnegates freedom of intelligence as well. Lee could not apprehend the growth of a Northern military machine because such a thing was outside his mental horizon; like the countryman before the giraffe, he thought "there ain't no such animal." His life was dedicated to proving the theory that a man is born to the purple of ability, that it cannot be educed by specialization or culture, that the bankrupt tanner U. S. Grant will be a bankrupt tanner forever. If this be untrue a Negro is as good as a white man and slavery is wrong.

The Confederacy tripped over a slight mixture of theories here. Your sincere individualism demands *la carrière ouverte aux talents*, but the necessities of the African problem forced upon it an aristocracy of birth, ultimately pointing toward such a social absurdity as the Victorian England in which a man could be a bounder because he was in trade, no matter what his parts and attractiveness. It was really a kind of sham individualism, which requested that the divine afflatus hover only round well-born hands. Once the prerequisite was met, however, the South was singularly free from narrowness with regard to its heroes, any degree of eccentricity was permitted. Æsop was impossible, but Socrates a boon companion. Nobody thought any the worse of Earl Van Dorn for his lecheries or Stonewall Jackson for his prayers; General Ewell was considered very good company in spite of the fact that he had fits of imagining he was a bird, during which he placed his head on one side, emitting a speculative chirp from time to time as he pecked lightly at a few grains of wheat while others were enjoying their beefsteaks.

This made for a society gay and polished, even brilliant, quite unlike anything on the other side. It would have been impossible for a troop of Northern soldiers to find their general, as some of Stuart's men found him, surrounded by pretty girls in a Richmond street, his horse garlanded with roses and his arms full of them. The surprising thing is that this society was so sterile intellectually. By their amusements ye shall know them, and the general level of Southern amusement was about that of Huck Finn's Royal Nonesuch. Nor can this be attributed to the fact that the Southerners were not yet emerged from their colonial swaddling-clothes; the Porteños of Argentine, the Creoles of Santo Domingo, produced a respectable amount of culture under similar circumstances.

Perhaps it was because the South had an aristocracy without commercial backgrounds; the arts wither in open air, they demand the rubbing of intellect against intellect, the constant stimulus only the marketplace gives. Plantations produce nothing but Mæcenases; it is too easy a life; there is no *weltschmerz* and very little adultery, the primary constituents of two-thirds of literature. The commercial cities that served the South were all in the North; alone among the great historical aristocracies it was without a capital of its own. By seceding, it had deliberately thrown out of gear the intellectual motor which drove it, a fact which may in part explain the frenzied effort of the Confederate plantation aristocracy to establish a rapport with the English commercial aristocracy—although the Confederacy was outwardly concerned with the more material deprivations it suffered as the result of being cut off from the Northern intellectual centers.

These deprivations were serious enough to cause any man concern. The substitution of rye and corn for wheat was a commonplace and to be borne; it was the accumulation of small needs that threatened to mosquito-bite the Confederacy to death. Already in the summer of 1862 a man could not build a house because nails were unprocurable; a woman had difficulty sewing into garments the homespun cloth she made (with much difficulty) because needles were beyond price—literally; salt was as rare as silver, and Heros von Borcke saw Jackson's men gorging themselves with it by the handful at a captured Union magazine.

It was not that the South lacked the materials or the latent ability to produce these things, but there was no social pressure on anybody to get them produced. In fact, the social pressure was in the other direction. A man who started a salina or a nail-factory became, *ipso facto*, an "engrosser," a profiteer, and socially impossible. It was the same with supplying the fighting forces. Nobody wanted to play quartermaster, so the business usually fell into the hands of some Memphis Jew who conducted it for the benefit of his private profit. Corruption in the bookkeeping department touched a new all-time high in Jefferson Davis' republic.

Similarly, few of the Southern individualists cared much

about camp duty. The squalor and disorder of a Confederate camp, the informality with which the men treated their commanders, would have given a Union officer the dark blue horrors and did when they saw it. Robert E. Lee never inspected his camps; he shrank from what he would find. And after every battle a few thousand individualists straggled away to amuse themselves elsewhere till the next fight.

It is this that makes it so difficult to state the number of Confederates present at any given battle; compiling reports at the best of times smacked of that strait-jacketing of the mentality they loathed above all things under the canopy, and when the reports were compiled, they were usually inaccurate. General Hood's army returns almost invariably contain mistakes in simple addition. Mostly the mistake was in the direction of not counting all the men present, just as Union reports were apt to be inaccurate through a too-meticulous accuracy, by listing everybody who belonged to an organization, present, absent or prospective. Thus, although there were numerical advantages for the Northern armies in most battles, they are far less than generally stated, and certainly a long way from the mystic three-to-one figure every Southerner then and later has regarded with the same devotions as the Holy Trinity.

But the very fact that they believed in these odds, and believed themselves a match for them, adds to rather than detracts from the splendid valor with which they fought; and Lord Russell might well declare such a people unconquerable.

BOOK III. MAN AND MACHINE

25

THE ABSOLUTE MASTERPIECE

Spring came early that year; the ice slid down the Rappahannock under a veil of mist and a bright yellow sun
swept the heavens clear as a burnished shield the day the
President rode down from Washington to see whether the
army had recovered its tone.

"The Union boys are moving—" he heard them singing
from afar, O sound of happy augury,

"—on the left and on the right,
The bugle-call is sounding, the shelters we must strike;
Joe Hooker is our leader, he takes his whisky strong,
So our knapsacks we will sling and go marching along."

At the review the swaying lines cheered uproariously as
Hooker sat his horse beside Lincoln, his red moonface dis-
tending with pleasure over the compliments pumped into the
ears that flanked it. The bright guidons of the Pennsylvania
lancers finally fluttered past and everybody went into the
headquarters tent for a luncheon, at which the Princess Salm-
Salm kissed the President three times amid considerable
gaiety. Mrs. Lincoln was not present. . . .

Now, said the major-general commanding, let us make
a plan, a plan which shall take into account the fact that
we have seven full army corps, artillery abounding, and
11,000 horsemen, say 113,000 for duty, while Lee has only
65,000 and a conviction we never mean to do business, since
he has sent Longstreet down to the tip of Virginia to ex-

purgate the annoying little force the navy landed there a month ago. Let it be a plan like this; Stoneman, with the cavalry, shall go far above the point where Rappahannock joins Rapidan, cross one river, then the other, swing a great circle far in Lee's rear, cutting off his supplies and his retreat on Richmond as Stuart did to our army in the Seven Days. While the enemy are at sixes and sevens, Sedgwick, the strong, abrupt son of the Mayflower Compact, shall take his own corps and Reynolds' across the river at Fredericksburg, where Franklin tried in December, with red fire and parade, fixing the rebels' attention thither. Couch, with his corps and Sickles', shall march upstream to Banks' Ford with loutish secrecy, easy to penetrate. Lee will oblige by reading one of these as the true attack; while he faces one or the other, Meade, Howard and Slocum, three corps, 48,000 men, will cross the two rivers on Stoneman's track, come fast through the woods to strike the Confederate left flank— "and the rebel army will be the legitimate property of the Army of the Potomac." Wonderful; an absolute masterpiece! said the staff officers, and the general beamed.

Stoneman had two weeks' start with the Union horse; Averell's brigade of his command forded the Rappahannock on April 14 and had a brush with Fitz Lee's Confederate cavalry among the hills, very heartening, for the men in blue were best against some of Stuart's sabers for the first time in this war. That night it came on to rain bucketsful; the freshets rose to spate, the fords were drowned before morning and stayed that way for a fortnight more, locking Stoneman on the north bank, where Hooker cursed him by correspondence. "Who ever saw a dead cavalryman?" On the 27th the commanding general's patience went out the window; never mind these rascal manure-spreaders, let the movement begin;—and the three infantry corps rumbled upstream for the turning maneuver. On the 28th they crossed, with Stoneman behind, in so bad a temper that he drove his horses to death, moved himself right off the board and took no further part in the campaign. Stuart readily scouted the turning infantry, since there was no horse to cover their movements, but thought them headed for Gordonsville, on the slopes of the Blue Ridge, and flew off in that direction, on an eccentric. That same night Sedgwick's guns boomed through a heavy fog at Fredericksburg, and Jackson, holding Lee's right behind the town, reported the Federals crossing, while Couch's Corps was seen in movement near Banks' Ford.

Lee rose like a trout to Hooker's bait. He had six heavy divisions, each not quite as big as a Federal corps (proportion, $11 = 17$). Only the divisions of Anderson and McLaws were left to face Couch at Banks' Ford; the rest gathered opposite Sedgwick, who succeeded in conveying an impression of prodigious numbers by marching a couple of regiments round and round a block of houses. Hooker's striking force, quite unopposed, made its long circuit onto the Confederate left and rear. On the afternoon of the 30th, he had the road-junction of Chancellorsville controlling United States Ford, by which Couch joined him that day and most of Sickles' before dusk. Out in front, Meade and Slocum felt Anderson's pickets, and wanted to drive him to destruction then and there, which they could easily have done, but Hooker said no, the pear will fall into our laps now, bivouac for the night, and read this order to your troops:

"It is with heartfelt satisfaction that the commanding general announces to the army that the operations of the last three days have determined that our enemy must either ingloriously fly or give us battle on our own ground, where certain destruction awaits him."

By this time Lee had discovered the trick; leaving Early with one division on Marye's Heights to hold Sedgwick, he rushed back toward Chancellorsville and battle with the rest. The country between that town and Fredericksburg is open; between Chancellorsville and the Rapidan it is one huge mat of second-growth and chaparral, called the Wilderness. The Confederate leader was anxious to catch the Federals in

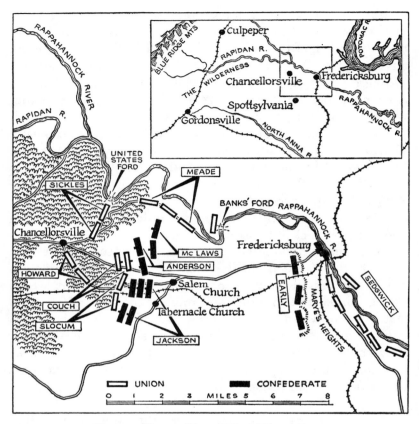

Chancellorsville—The First Day

this mess, when their numbers would count for little and rebel élan for much.

Hooker moved like a mastodon, ponderous and irresolute. It was noon before his troops got started, Meade on the north road out of Chancellorsville, Couch by the center, Slocum leading Howard out the south road. They were to form along the ridge from Banks' Ford to Tabernacle Church, dig in, and let the rebels beat themselves sore. Meade met no obstacle, but before Couch got clear of the forest he was set upon by Anderson. There was a hot fight; Couch ployed into column and thrust through the rebel center, but McLaws came up and got round both his flanks while he was doing it, driving in the advance. At the south end of the line Jackson hit Slocum hard with his three oversize divisions, broke down the Union general's floating right wing and threw him back. That was the end of the Confederate push; Slocum got his back against a high hill, where falling light and Union artillery stopped Jackson with losses heavier than he gave.

Lee's headquarters—conference by night. Hooker had shown himself faltering in maneuver, but things looked bad enough; Slocum and Couch were solidly intrenched on lofty crests, and scouts brought word that Meade had been recalled to Couch's left, where he was throwing up works. Sickles had been discovered on Slocum's right, between him and Howard; a reliable spy said Reynolds was on the march to United States Ford, and the ground trembled with the far-away beat of Sedgwick's guns, cannonading Marye's Heights for an obvious blow at the new Confederate rear. Retreat? Not through open country with Hooker's 100,000 on the trail. Stand? Not against Fighting Joe Hooker with such odds on his side. He would attack in the morning and nothing could stop him.

As Lee and Jackson talked in low tones, the door suddenly opened and in clanked—Stuart! humming "Jine the Cavalry." He had ridden hard all day, back from Gordonsville; the country was full of his horsemen, they had come on Howard's right flank on the road west of Chancellorsville, and found it all unprotected. Lee's eye lighted; he saw his way clear in a flash of inspiration. Jackson was to take his whole wing, three divisions, 35,000 men, in a wide-swinging circuit like that against Pope, fall on Howard's weak flank, break him and drive the Federal army into a pocket, away from United States Ford. Only Anderson and McLaws should stay; they to deploy and open a rafale of skirmisher fire against Couch and Slocum as though covering a powerful attack. Hooker's stomach for battle was sure to betray him, he would wait for the big fight where he was. But is there any road by which I can make the circuit through that brush in less than a month? inquired Jackson. Stuart had thought of that. He stuck his head out the door, "Ho, there!" and in walked a man in rusty black with a Bible in one hand, a backwoods preacher, wise to secret ways through the jungle.

The march began at midnight, Jackson, fidgeting with excitement, riding in the van. "His face was pale, his eyes flashed, he leaned far over his horse's neck, as though in that way to hurry the march. Out from his compressed lips burst the words again and again, 'Press forward! Press forward!' " Dawn found them still amid the chaparral. The rising column of dust roused Sickles and he carried the news to Hooker, who spread a map on a bed and leaned over it, muttering, "It can't be retreat without a fight. That's not Lee. Why, he's trying to flank me!"—and sent word to Howard to watch well his flank while, for his own part, he rushed Sickles' Corps forward in one heavy column to break connection between the flankers and Lee. Slocum, Couch and Meade he held inactive; Lee's skirmishers were deploying in clouds along their front, indicating a heavy attack coming there, which could best be resisted from the positions now held.

Howard's was the German corps, lately Sigel's; he was a sniffling godly Presbyterian, shocked at their rude ways, who did not like them or they him. Von Gilsa's brigade, out on the menaced flank, detected Jackson's coming before dinnertime and its general rode to Howard with an appeal— "The enemy are massing on my front. For God's sake, make disposition to receive them." Howard dropped a sneer about Dutch courage; Von Gilsa flung back to his command in a towering passion and the next moment Jackson was upon them. The road runs a narrow tunnel through the impenetrable bulwark of wilderness; Howard's men were strong out along it, facing south, whence Hooker had given them to think the attack would come. The rebels came hurrahing around the turn in column and fell on the outermost single man of Von Gilsa's flank, a hundred and fifty to one; when

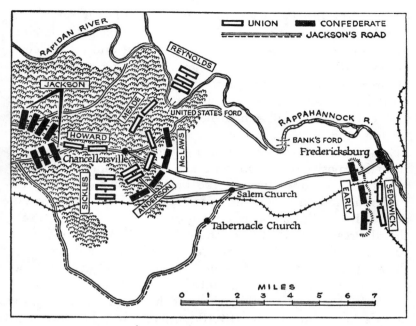

UNION   CONFEDERATE
JACKSON'S ROAD

Chancellorsville—Jackson's Attack

he dropped, they fell upon his neighbor, and his and his, right down the line. Courage, Dutch or other, was no good against the constant 150:1; tactics were no good, there lacked room to form a line perpendicular to the road, lacked time to meet column with column. As Jackson penetrated deeper, the fugitives piled up before his hurrying advance like driftwood on the crest of a flood, and the whole corps, what was left of the whole corps, went wailing through Chancellorsville in utter rout.

Hooker spied the tumult from a headquarters window where he sat puzzling why Sickles' lunge had found no opposition south. Illumination came sudden and dreadful; he leaped for the stairs and made ground just as the rebels topped the rise into the open space around the town. Warren, the staff engineer, swung the reserve artillery round to meet them, but Jackson came on so fast the gunners had no time to load. The only troops at hand were the headquarters cavalry, the 8th Pennsylvania, 400 men. Pleasanton of the staff hurled them at the rebel column; they met a withering fire, every man of the gallant band was hit and 80 per cent of them killed, but the rebel charge was checked for a precious ten minutes. The guns got unlimbered, they roared a furious salute, and Jackson stopped as though poleaxed. His men took cover, threw out skirmishers and began to work round the devoted battery, but Berry's division of Sickles came up on the run to save it, Slocum got a brigade turned round from his position, Couch sent another division. The fight raged like a flame through the bright spring evening, fed by fresh men on both sides; the musketry shot long streaks across the twilight, the red-hot guns dripped sparks. "Press them! Press them, Hill!" cried Jackson. "Cut them off from the ford!" But his men were weary with day-long struggle, they could not strike home against those fatal cannon, and the hysterical night of toil and shouting closed in.

The blow that would drive the last nail in the Union army's coffin must wait till daybreak—and Jackson rode forward to locate the weak spot. There was firing all round; the men of the 33d North Carolina were being hit by cannon balls out of the dark. When they saw shadowy forms moving on their front, they assumed an attack was toward, rose for a volley—and they slew Stonewall Jackson, the great general.

That saved the Union army. Jackson's whole staff went with him; A. P. Hill, next in line, was laid out by a Federal cannon ball; Lee had to call Stuart from the cavalry to take over, but, instead of giving him detailed orders, left him to make a tactical plan of his own, and Stuart made one without knowledge of Jackson's scheme for seizing the ford in the Union rear. He stretched his right to touch Anderson's left, carried a high knob of hill called Hazel Grove with a rousing charge from three sides at first daylight, and planted a thirty-gun battery on it, proposing to cave in the salient of Sickles' line. Lee approved; the Hazel Grove battery was admirably placed to enfilade Slocum as well as Sickles, and to take Couch in the rear; he would split the Union army in two at the center. The battery opened a slaughtering fire; Stuart, Anderson and McLaws all hurled their regiments against the lines the Federals held, and Hooker's salient began to shake round Chancellorsville.

Jackson's idea had been better; Stuart's move gave Hooker time to swing Reynolds and his fresh I Corps into position at right angles to Sickles' line for a smash at Stuart's flank that would sweep the field. Reynolds was ready to go; his men fretted feverishly as they saw the red flashes rim the horizon, he sent three times to Hooker for the order, the order that never came. What happened was this—a plunging shot from the thirty-gun battery hit the porch-pillar against which Hooker was leaning. It felled him to the ground, stunned; when he rose it was to pass through racking convulsions of pain and turn on his subordinates a face from which intelligence had fled. Yet he was the Commander-in-Chief, he remained conscious, he continued to give orders, his the responsibility, the power and the glory.

Sickles and Slocum held their ground under terrible losses; "They fought like devils," said rebel Mahone, but not all the sons Apollyon ever sired could stand the double fire, they were driven back and back from the red line. Chancellorsville went lost and the hill-tops and the road-line; Geary's division was almost wiped out in a counter-charge Hooker ordered but forgot to support, a battery was sacrificed to cover the retreat, and as the third evening of war round Chancellorsville shut down the Army of the Potomac stood on the last possible line of defense. But it was only pushed back, not broken; Meade held the all-important ford like iron, Couch was still full of fight, Reynolds closed ranks of granite behind the beaten corps to stay Lee's drive.

Off at Fredericksburg, Sedgwick had waited for two days for the order to attack, hearing the high roar of battle from the west. He could get no news; at last he grew impatient, put his divisions into column and, under an intense covering cannonade, punched right through Early's center. One of the rebel brigades flew off like a chip, away toward

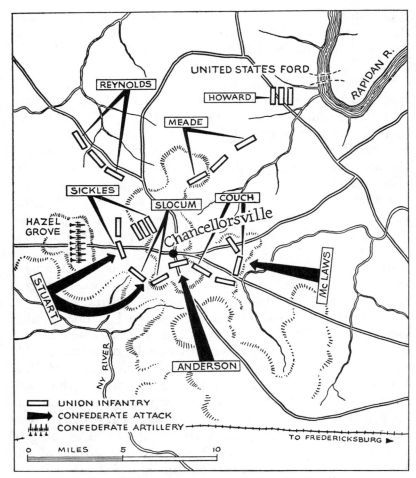

Chancellorsville—The Third Day

Richmond; the rest flowed back through the roads to Lee. Hooker was beat; the Confederate commander was sure of that. Leaving Stuart to harry the big Union army across the river, he right-about-faced with the divisions of Anderson and McLaws to ambush Sedgwick and annihilate him.

Too late to do more that night, the Union corps had camped near Banks' Ford. They marched with the day, but the rebel resistance stiffened and a skirmisher brought in a 14th Alabama badge from a Johnny Reb he had shot. The 14th Alabama was in Anderson's division; Sedgwick realized instantly that he was running into the jaws of Lee's whole army. He halted, retreated to a horseshoe of ragged ravines and set his men digging in for dear life. Before they had scooped out more than belly-pits, the onslaught came, and it was both fierce and long-sustained, but Sedgwick rode calmly through the storm and the line held fast. Toward evening Early put a brigade into column for one last effort, with the war-cry "Remember Jackson!" but a Vermont regiment as hard as the hills that gave them birth stood up to receive it hand to hand and the retreat of the Union army was secure.

Retreat? Aye, retreat, for Chancellorsville was the truest, the most splendid victory Robert Lee ever won, against all odds and a commander who had half shut a trap round his army—an absolute masterpiece, beyond which no further art is possible. It discouraged Lincoln deeply and, to make matters worse, his wife found out about the Princess Salm-Salm's kisses that same night and he had to sleep on the "mad couch" out in the hall.

26

FEVERED INTERLUDE

1. The Black Joke

New York.

The room was full of men, over whose heads floated a thin haze of tobacco-smoke. The wheel stood on a table, with two soldiers beside it, leaning on their bayoneted muskets. They were old soldiers, invalided out, tall men with beards and long, mournful faces. One of them had the clover of the II Corps in his cap. The man with the blindfold groped for the hole and pulled out another slip of paper, which Captain Ehrhardt accepted from his hand. "Joseph F. O'Neill," he read in a clear voice.

"And I'll not go!" cried a man in shabby clothes whose face looked as though it had been chewed. "You can tell Old Abe to put that in his pipe and smoke it!"

There was a chorus of groans and whistles. "And him with a wife, too!" "That's the stuff, Joey!" "Draft some of the rich bastards!" "Hurrah for the Golden Circle!" Outside, the faces against the dirty window vanished suddenly, then returned as a louder roar from the street drowned that within. From the platform by the wheel a sea of moving heads could be seen, brimming Third Avenue from side to side and reaching back into Forty-sixth Street. A compact group of men in black shirts and firemen's hats pushed their way to the entrance. One of them shook a bottle at the flag over the door. "Here's the Black Joke!" "Hurrah for the Twenty-third Volunteer Firemen!"

The man with the blindfold hesitated uncertainly, cocking his ear toward the uproar. "Let the draft proceed," said Captain Ehrhardt loudly. He was handed another slip. "Thomas P. Cassidy!"

"Wheeeew!" "Captain Tom, hey Tom, you're drafted." "They're drafting the Black Joke." "To hell with the government!" Outside a black arm was raised and a pistol shot cracked sharply; with a bellow the men of the Black Joke charged the front of the store, which shattered in a shower of glass. "Holy Mother of God," cried a woman with a baby and the whole street seemed to surge toward the platform. The wheel went down with a smash, the man with the blindfold snatched it off, gave one agonized glance, then followed the captain and the veterans through the back door.

"Break it up." "Burn it." "Larry, get some coal-oil." A giant with a hatchet was chopping madly at the furniture, the walls; another beat the edge of the platform with a crowbar. Someone produced a lucifer match, and the bright little flame danced up amid the splintered wood and the fragments of the draft slips. "Everybody out, let 'er burn!" In the street the whole mob was yelling at once, the upper windows had already been smashed and stones were banging against the adjoining buildings. As the fire took hold on the coal-oil a puff of dark smoke came rolling out to be greeted with cheers. In front they began to sing "We'll hang Abe Lincoln on a sour-apple tree," and the crowd pulled back a little to let the corner buildings burn. Suddenly a new tide swept through them, they headed westward through the rolling smoke along Forty-sixth Street. "They've got Kennedy!" "Kill him!" "To hell with the Metropolitans!" "Hurrah for the Pope!"

They had caught Kennedy, the police superintendent. He was down, on his face against a building, the center of a semicircle, with a couple of rat-like children kicking at his head. "Father, I've bruk his back." "Ha, ha, that's the boy, give it to him." Across the street there was a shattering of glass as the window of Grosset's Liquor Store yielded. The man with the crowbar forced his way through, trailing a long strip of cloth. "We'll show them a flag," he shouted, and, bending over the prostrate man, dipped a finger in the clotting blood and dabbled NO DRAFT across the banner in staring letters.

There was a roar of approval as he displayed this piece of craftsmanship. "Come on," he cried, "let's go burn the *Tribune*. We'll hang Horace Greeley on a so-o-o-o-u-u-u-r apple tree. . . . " The mob bellowed the chorus as it fell in, joined by affluents from every side street. A man with a bandage and a bloody head marked time with a policeman's club; at Forty-second Street they were pushing down the telegraph poles with a yo-heave-ho. From Lexington came the sound of yelling and an illuminating sentence ran through the mass—"They burned out the nigger orphan asylum."

"Hang all the niggers!" "No draft!" "Down with the rich!" At Thirty-eighth the Bull's Head was a mass of flames with a couple of wrecked fire-carts in front of it. The street was filled with broken liquor kegs and cases, one of them cradling a dead policeman, but the bottles were empty, the first comers had all the luck. Brooks' Clothing Store had been gutted, some of the mob were still at work in the upper floors, throwing out fashionable bonnets, with which the crowd below crowned themselves, the ribbons fluttering around grimy faces.

There was another heave. "Here comes the coppers!" "No, it's the military!" Ahead, across the avenue, a ragged blue line of militia was formed, their muskets at queer angles. There was a young officer in front of the line; you could see his sword-hand shaking. The mob swayed to a halt, shouting imprecations. "How are you, Abe's monkeys." "Kill the niggerlovers!" Stones began to fly, both from the back ranks of the crowd and from the roof-tops. Somewhere a pistol went off; a soldier who had been struck by a stone raised his musket and fired; before the officer could stop them there was a ragged volley. Somebody screamed; the man with the banner coughed and stumbled, and the mob, with a shriek of rage, plunged forward again as the line of militia took to their heels.

At the Red Bird Livery Stable most of those who were pulling the horses out, loudly avowing their intention of forming a troop of cavalry, were drunk, and cheering for the Archbishop, who, they said, had refused to intervene. The most fun was farther downtown. A bunch of niggers had been caught; they were dragging them by the heels across the cobbles. When the crowd went on to raid the armory just after dark, they left five of them hanging to lamp-posts, with fires burning under them. They were dead by that time, of course. The middle one was named Big Sue the Turtle, and she was a procuress.

Then it began to rain.

2. RAGAMUFFIN MARCH

Richmond.

When the President came out on the steps of the Capitol the street was already filled with women. Nobody could ever explain how they got there or what caused them to gather. "If you do not disperse—" he began angrily, but they all screamed at him together, and seeing he could not make himself heard, he turned back toward the door.

"Shall I have the Provost-Marshal's guard called, Mr. Davis?" asked one of the secretaries anxiously.

"Yes, yes, by all means," said the President, "such an affair is more disgraceful than a Union victory. It is an outrage on the fair name of the Confederacy!"

He went back to the window to look down into the street, but they recognized him and began to shriek again— "Bread!" "Union!" Mr. Davis had a sudden inspiration. He opened the window and, throwing up his hand, obtained a temporary silence.

"If any of you are in distress," he said, "I will be glad to have you call on me, and furnish you with a sum of money—"

That set them off again. "It's worthless!" screamed a harridan right below him. "No more starvation! We want bread and the Union!"

The President closed the window and began to pace the floor angrily, while the mob of women, after a time, trailed off to break into the commissary stores and help themselves to bacon.

The *Enquirer* referred to them next day (on an inside page) as "a handful of prostitutes, professional thieves, Irish and Yankee hags, gallows-birds from all lands but our own," but as the adjoining column held a long and very interesting article on the question of whether German prisoners should be hung, nobody gave the women much attention.

27

WHEN THE WAVE BROKE

RISE up! men of Virginia, for the hour of good luck has
come. "Jackson was taken from us to the shades of
Paradise," but victory rises behind victory, each greater
than the last, till the South is all one peal of exultation. "If
General Lee wishes rations," the high commissary wrote
across his requisition, "if General Lee be in need of rations,
let him seek them in Pennsylvania." In England Lord Russell wrote to Lord Palmerston—whether the moment had
not come to offer the Queen's justice in this quarrel? In
Mexico an Austrian prince bound a new diadem around
his brows while the ministers shouted *"Vive l'Empereur!"*
and went in to write an offer of alliance from the federated
empires to the republic of the South. Along the Rappahannock the army of that young republic turned north with
80,000 muskets to conquer a peace; and in Washington the
Cabinet of the old bellowed across the table, while the soldiers made plaint of the "drunk-murdering-arson dynasty
of Hooker."

Yet the drunk-murdering-arson dynasty had a friend;
Chase of the Treasury, the tall, imposing, portly man with
ambition enough to strike for the rule of a world and enough
ability to support any ambition. A man of order and method,
who found the President irresolute, without unity or system,
though of honest intention. By order and careful method he
had builded him a party, a congress within the Congress,
"The Radicals," or fire-and-sword men, so strong that when
Lincoln and Stanton wanted Reynolds to lead the army they

must needs keep the Radical, Hooker, instead. Stanton raved and swore, would resign rather than have Hooker leader; Chase only smiled, elaborately distant as Buddha, and Lincoln had to calm the tempestuous little Secretary in an anteroom.

Hooker had an excuse; he was not defeated at Chancellorsville, had retired only because he lacked elbow-room to fight south of the river—a pure question of strategy. Lincoln, Stanton and Halleck held a conference; Old Brains went down to headquarters and, making ambidextrous use of his training in war and law, wrung the truth from Hooker after a stiff cross-questioning. The man had lost his nerve; mentally, he shook like an aspen; was wanting in the simple resolution to carry through any plan, found lions in every path. That settled it; "It's a bad time to swap horses when you're crossing a stream," but Hooker must not be allowed to command the army in another great battle. Yet what to do? Chase and his Congressional camorra stood immovable against any change. Let Hooker lose a thousand battles, let General Couch resign the service rather than serve under such a leader; he should not, he could not be removed.

Up from the south, huge and menacing, rolled Lee and his 80,000. He slid west along the rivers; on June 12 rebel cavalry was reported in the Shenandoah Valley. Milroy, whom Jackson beat among the hills the year before, had 11,000 men at Winchester. Pugnacious Milroy; when scouts brought the news of Lee's advance, he thought it a raid and stayed to fight. But it was Ewell's Corps, the vanguard of an army; Milroy's outposts were driven in, the supplies stopped coming and unseen cannon fired into him from the night. He threw his guns down a well and tried to escape by rapid marching, but the roads were beset, half his command lost their way across fields in the dark and made Harpers Ferry with only 2,000 left. Rebel cavalry rode through the passes of the Blue Ridge; a reconnaissance showed there were still Confederates at Fredericksburg. "If the head of

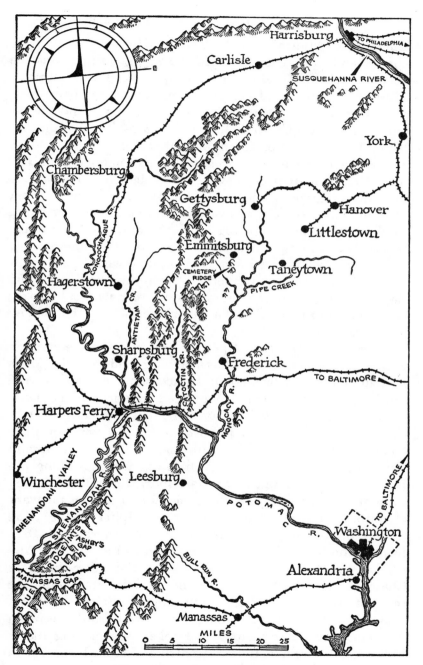

The Gettysburg Campaign

Lee's army," Lincoln wrote down to Hooker, "is at Winchester and the tail at Fredericksburg, the animal must be very slim somewhere. Could you not break him?" "Impossible," said Hooker. "I cannot divine his intentions as long as he fills the country with a cloud of cavalry," and then—ominous postscript, McClellan *redivivus!*—"I am outnumbered, I need a reinforcement of 25,000 men."

Yet Hooker was not ill-served by his mounted arm. Buford, Gregg, Kilpatrick, new leaders, they had new riders in their ranks, plainsmen from the West, who gave Stuart blow for blow all along the valleys, and had the upper hand, so that the rebels were driven back into the Blue Ridge passes and Lee was held wide west on the line toward Sharpsburg and Hagerstown. Nor could he win any information as to Hooker's movements—"They are still along the Rappahannock," the general told Longstreet, whereas Hooker had a corps at Frederick and another marching in the shadow of Washington.

The capital was full of prickly-heat and strange rumors; a spy in the streets of Chambersburg had counted Lee's marching host up to 90,000; Halleck was sold out to the rebel cause. Out on the fringe of Lee's advance, the Pennsylvania roads were choked; farmers, driving cattle before them, Negroes flying to the woods for the peril of their bodies. The state was wild with alarm; fourteen thousand citizens turned out at Pittsburgh to dig trenches along the line of Braddock's defeat; in Harrisburg the militia drilled through the streets with fowling pieces and scythes for want of muskets. Business stopped on Philadelphia 'change; the pastors offered to form a regiment, the veterans of 1812 formed another and the governor wired to Lincoln that McClellan should be reappointed. In the Cabinet Salmon P. Chase smiled, Buddhistic and bland, he was introducing the reign of law and order among our tangled affairs.

Or was he? That man did not live who could overreach Abraham Lincoln by intrigue. Hooker was moving like a pachyderm around a circle concentric to Lee's advance, with

Washington as its pivot, gnashing his teeth at the corps commanders and wailing that if he had not reinforcements he couldn't be responsible for the issue. Stanton showed the appeal to Lincoln; they answered no, General Hooker, you shall have no more men—what of it? On the 27th June rebel Early, "Old Jubilee" Early, a sarcastic, hard-bitten man, ransomed the city of York for $100,000 and a thousand pairs of shoes and Hooker wrote a bad-tempered note to Washington: "I must have more men. This is my resignation else."

That night Colonel Hardie, aide to the President, rode out toward Frederick—in civilian clothes, since raiders from Stuart's command were all about. The streets of the towns were full of drunken men, the roads foul with vehicles and stragglers camping in the ditch. He found a countryman who, for fifty dollars, agreed to take him through in an ancient wagon; at three in the morning they heard the sentry's challenge in front of V Corps headquarters, and Hardie went up to rout General Meade out of bed. The general started up in his nightshirt, his eyes fuzzy with sleep. He had quarreled with Hooker that very day—"Am I under arrest?" when he saw Hardie and the crowding uniforms behind him. "No. Hooker has resigned. You are appointed Commander-in-Chief of the Army of the Potomac."

Chase never heard of it till Hooker arrived in Washington a day later. He began an angry protest; Lincoln's eyes opened in innocent astonishment. "The acceptance of an army resignation is not a matter for your department." And the great Poo-Bah could only bite his nails.

Poo-Bah put to silence; but Early's advance-guard was planting batteries against Harrisburg and Lee's army spread in a wide circle, from Chambersburg through Carlisle and York, hesitating—Baltimore or Philadelphia? That night Ewell's scouts brought in a German farmer; he had a Washington paper with definite intelligence that the Union army was north of the Potomac and feeling westward toward the rebel communications. Unpleasant shock—the rich countryside provided food without stint, but powder must come up the long road from Richmond. Quick as thought, Lee shifted plans; there was a road center at Gettysburg, east and south of the Cumberland chain; he could concentrate there, turn south along the Monocacy in mass, drive through the scattered Federal corps and conquer his peace by laying siege to Washington. The army was in three corps since Jackson's death—Longstreet, Ewell and A. P. Hill; Longstreet was ordered in on Gettysburg by way of Carlisle and the north, Hill from Chambersburg and west, Ewell from York and east. The threads drew in.

Meade, haggard with sleeplessness as he strove to master the detail of his huge machine on the eve of decisive conflict, was hurrying on, himself drawing in threads. Only one change he made—three young captains of cavalry, just out of West Point, to be generals—Farnsworth, Merritt, Custer. The threat to Lee's communications would draw the rebels down the Monocacy, he was sure; let the engineers fortify a strong position along Pipe Creek, we will retire there and await attack. Reynolds' I Corps and Buford's horse were to hold an outpost at Gettysburg with Howard's XI Corps in support. General Sykes and the V Corps out to Hanover, Slocum and the XII Corps to Emmitsburg, the rest to press on with all speed for Taneytown and headquarters— these were the orders for the first of July.

Heth's division of Hill's advance struck a Union cavalry picket west of Gettysburg before nine. They drove them in slowly; as the horsemen retreated the zing of bullets came out of a wood on the slope of a low hill behind. "That's all right," called Heth, "only some of that Pennsylvania militia," and sent two brigades to clear the way for his column. They swung forward carelessly; as they reached the edge of the wood, the fire rose to surprising crescendo, and out of the underbrush onto their flank burst a storm of men with bayonets low and all in line—the Iron Brigade. A yell of surprise went up, "T'aint no milishy! Lookit them black hats! That's the Army of the Potomac!" and then Heth's

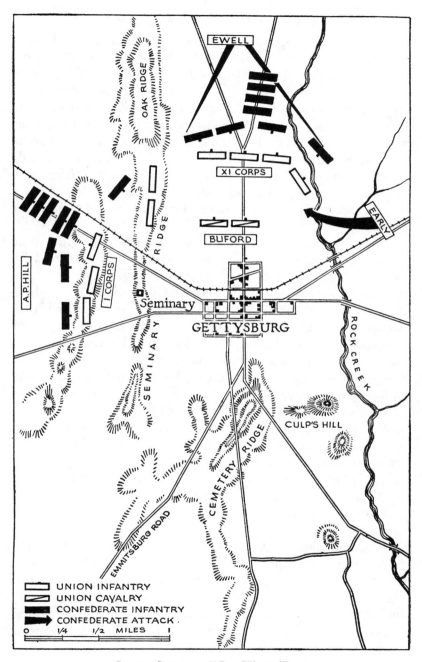

Gettysburg—The First Day

two brigades were swept into rout, smashed, one brigadier killed, the other captured. The battle for the world was on.

Heth, surprised, but still confident that it could only be an outpost, spread his skirmishers, ordered up some artillery and began to attack in force. The pulsing musketry rose to a roar as more of Hill's men came up and joined in. They worked round both ends of the hill, the firing became a regular rafale, but the Federals held hard, with spirited little countercharges at every opportunity. A tall officer rode among them, the soul of their stand; some rebel sharpshooter drew a bead on him, and down he went, shot through the head.

It was Reynolds; "None died there with more glory than he, though many died and there was much glory," said his foe. From the belfry of the Lutheran Seminary on the ridge behind he had looked afar, looked with seeing eye, and beheld every road from north and west tide-brimmed with the oncoming river in gray. If the streams met at Gettysburg unopposed, they would push between the Union corps; the Army of the Potomac was lost, and Washington and the war. Reynolds looked once more; behind him and the town upthrust a long, high crest, Cemetery Ridge, admirable for a place of arms. He dashed off notes to Meade, to Howard, to Slocum, to Sykes, to the III Corps at Littlestown—hurry on, in God's name, we must fight here. Himself he rode forward to hold back an army with his single corps and to keep his rendezvous with the sharpshooter's bullet.

Doubleday, Abner Doubleday, brave, stolid and steady, took over when Reynolds fell; by eleven in the morning he had most of the corps in line and the artillery blazing. Heth was beaten back, but Hill's whole corps was on the field, three to one of Doubleday. The rebels' corps artillery came up to batter a hole in the Union position and a column of assault formed to exploit it. Northward Ewell was beginning to arrive, with nothing to hold him but Buford's horse, which spent itself in frantic skirmish fighting to gain time. At noon, with the whole position alive with bursting shells and men dying a score a minute, Howard and his Germans arrived.

The new leader climbed the belfry, judged Ewell's advance the more dangerous, and attacked him at the double-quick. The Germans went in raging like wild Teutonic boars to avenge Chancellorsville; Ewell was stopped, but Hill's assault came on against Doubleday, wave after wave. The I Corps held on, repulsing them all, though it lost two-thirds of its numbers; in one regiment the blows of death struck down the hierarchy of command through colonel, lieutenant-colonel, two majors and five captains to leave a lieutenant senior officer. Two o'clock, three o'clock, no intermission in the ceaseless attacks with fresh troops; at half past the hour division Early came on the scene from the east against Howard's right flank. He caught the Germans at the crest of a countercharge against Ewell and broke their flank; Ewell came on in front, the rout spread from right to left along the Union line and the tattered remnants of the two corps flowed back through the town to Cemetery Ridge, with Hill and Ewell hotfoot on their heels.

Reynolds' morning chit had found Meade at breakfast. He left the coffee on the table and ran out to order the army forward on Gettysburg without halt for food or rest. A little after noon came word that Reynolds was down and the I Corps hard hit; Howard doubted whether the position could be held. "Damn it, it must be held!" said Meade and sent on Winfield Hancock to take command. Winfield Hancock, his most trusted leader, the Beau Brummell of the army, another McClellan for popularity, another Hooker in his stomach for conflict. He gathered the reserve artillery and some of Kilpatrick's horse that had just come from a scout, and they went on at the trot, claiming priority over infantry on the roads, since they could move faster. Hancock got to Cemetery Ridge at four, the crucial moment, with the cavalry and guns pounding along behind.

When the beaten troops saw the dandy general ride along their line their hearts lifted; they gave a yell and tightened belts. Hancock's guns opened up against the rebels; young Kilpatrick rode toward Hill's flank as though at the head of fifty squadrons. Hill and Ewell had already taken some nasty knocks; dismayed by this bold front, they recoiled to wait for orders from Longstreet and Lee. Half an hour later Sickles and the III Corps came up on the Union side, tramp, tramp, tramp, with the XII Corps right behind, and the position was saved.

Meade arrived at one in the morning, hollow-eyed and bad-tempered. Lee was already on hand, conferring with Longstreet as he rode through the lines in flickering torchlight. The latter was against fighting on the ground, an offensive battle with their 75,000 against the Federals' 80,000. Maneuver round their left flank, was his sage advice, we are the more rapid marchers. But no, we cannot do that, said Lee, Stuart is away on a raid, we lack cavalry to cover such a movement, the Union horse is both numerous and good, with Buford and Kilpatrick; they would slice our wings to pieces as we turned. Depend upon it, general (he went on) this new leader of theirs is like the rest—play on his mind with quick blows, he will lose his power of coordination. Longstreet wanted to argue the matter as not proven; the man Meade had certainly concentrated with surprising speed, this might be a new brand of Union general. Lee silenced him for a hair-splitter and gave orders for this plan —Ewell to throw a heavy column on the extreme Union right, where another hill, Culp's, flanked Cemetery, Longstreet himself to lead a simultaneous attack against the Union left, break it down, and, meeting Ewell's column behind the Union lines, basket their army. The details are yours to work out, General; now get some sleep.

In the morning Longstreet felt forward slowly, hoping the Federals would attack first. He found them quiescent, their line in front of Cemetery, running out to a sharp salient on the rise crowned by a peach orchard. It was Sickles' Corps, the III, which had been ordered to fight to the last along a line that would protect the arrival of Sykes' V and Sedgwick's

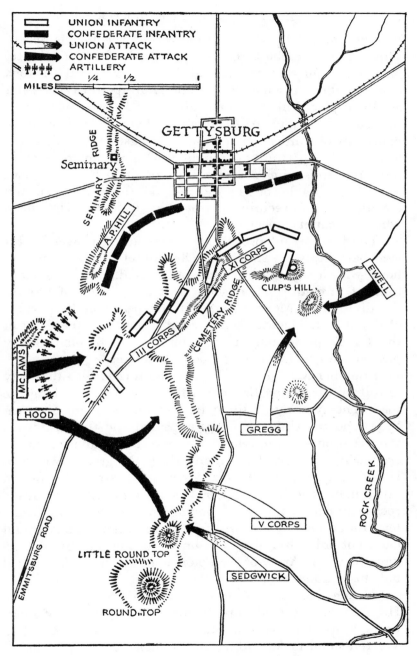

Legend:
- UNION INFANTRY
- CONFEDERATE INFANTRY
- UNION ATTACK
- CONFEDERATE ATTACK
- ARTILLERY

MILES 0   1/4   1/2   1

GETTYSBURG

Seminary

SEMINARY RIDGE

A.P. HILL

XI CORPS

CULP'S HILL

EWELL

III CORPS

CEMETERY RIDGE

McLAWS

HOOD

GREGG

ROCK CREEK

V CORPS

LITTLE ROUND TOP

SEDGWICK

ROUND TOP

EMMITSBURG ROAD

Gettysburg—The Second Day

VI corps on a field where Meade was as yet much inferior. This was Dan Sickles, the politician, who had shot Philip Barton Key for an intrigue with his wife which never took place; he thought some glory would do his political prospects good and placed his men in a salient far forward of the correct position to gain it. A salient is always bad; it gives so many opportunities for enfilade. Longstreet, seizing the forelock of opportunity, brought up his whole corps artillery, 160 guns, ringed around this point to blow out both lines of the angle, but he did not like the battle-plan and dawdled about executing his part in it. It was high noon when his battery opened.

The fire was intense; Sickles' men suffered severely, his own batteries were smothered, he himself hurled from his horse with a leg smashed by a cannonball. Birney replaced him; at three-thirty Longstreet sent his column of assault, the division of McLaws, against the peach orchard ridge of the salient. The attackers carried it, broke in the point of the III Corps formation in a bitter struggle and slowly pushed the Federal flanks in both directions.

Brigadier Kershaw of McLaws had turned the other way to roll up the Union line north toward Cemetery along the road. The tyranny of time; he had almost made it when Sykes and the Union V Corps appeared and the battle was stabilized once more. Longstreet sent Hood's division to get around Humphreys' flank then, where the ground was low. Hood was a tall, thin Texan, tawny, awkward and strong, a "wild man" and fierce fighter. His quick eye caught a steep, rocky eminence, the Little Round Top, higher than Cemetery Ridge and just south of it, from whence guns would flank not only Humphreys in one direction, but Sykes, Birney, the whole Army of the Potomac in the other. He turned half his command toward it.

Meade, busy at the north end of his long line, where Hill's activity seemed to portend attack, sent Chief of Engineers Warren to see how matters were going on the left. Warren could make nothing of the melee he saw; for better vision rode onto where Little Round Top thrust its pillar above the battle. He saw the III Corps retiring slowly under slanting lines of fire, saw Sykes' fresh men muster for the charge, and then caught the sheen of Hood's bayonets as his men began to climb Round Top.

In a flash Warren recognized the crisis; if the rebels got that hill, the Union flank was crushed and the army gone. He leaped his horse down the slope, on his own authority snatched two of Sykes' brigades out of formation and took them to Little Round Top. The 20th Maine reached the summit, breathless, just before the first of Hood's brigades, which had stopped for a rest on the way up, and plunged into a terrific nightmare of a battle. A New York regiment joined them, then the rest of Warren's chance-met men, and a battery, pulled up the precipices by hand. The defenders lost brigadiers Vincent and Weed, Hood put in three times their force, the ammunition all went, and they struggled hand to hand, stabbing, throwing stones and growling like wolves. Warren was the soul of the defense, an enchanted figure, his clothes tattered by bullets, his ceremonial sword dripping blood.

McLaws had now finished with the III Corps and was hammering at the cut between Round Top and Cemetery. Sykes' V Corps met him in front; the battle swayed and hung with charge and countercharge to and fro across the bloody ground. Hancock came onto the field, steadying the swaying line with fragments of regiments gathered from everywhere. A cannon ball carried away Hood's arm; Longstreet rode forward in person to lead the Confederate advance, but as the event hung doubtful, Sedgwick and steady VI Corps came down the road in a swirl of dust and the rebels rocked back into the sunset, somber and gray.

What had happened to Ewell and the simultaneous column? He swung wide round Cemetery Ridge and made ready for his blow at Culp's Hill. "There is always a reason why converging columns do not converge"; this time, the vagueness of orders on a plan that needed stop-watch timing. Ewell waited for Longstreet. It was five miles by road from flank around to Confederate flank, the messenger was late. By time the order to go in reached Ewell, Sedgwick was on the field and Hood off it, the effort was forlorn.

Culp's Hill is double; Geary's division of Slocum's XII Corps held the northern peak, with trenches, but Meade had ordered most of the men out to go to Sickles' help. Nevertheless, Ewell's first division was shattered by artillery fire as it scaled the steep sides of Rock Creek; he resolutely put in another division and came on with a hurrah through the gathering dark to carry the southern peak, but that was the end. Gregg had been posted farther south with a Union cavalry division in reserve; he turned his artillery in the direction of the uproar, then sent in his men, dismounted. Ewell detached men to stave them off, but dared not advance farther with the northern peak of Culp's untaken, and Gregg's ghostly riders, like the vampires of some military Walpurgis night, rearing at him out of the dark, and the second day of Gettysburg was over.

That night Stuart's horse rode into the rebel camp, eager but so fagged after their longest raid that men fell asleep while their horses were crossing a fence, and the command would be of no use for another twenty-four hours; behind them the *corps d'élite*, Pickett's Virginia division. Lee's voice rang; in calm exaltation he explained his plan for the morrow. The Federals' best troops were fought out, their right had been effectively turned by Ewell, their left smashed by Hood. Meade must have reinforced both wings from his center; there could be but few troops left there, and those inferior, probably militia. Bury them under a cascade of fire from the guns which had so well prepared McLaws' advance, then drive 15,000 men with Pickett leading like a thunderbolt straight through the weak spot, on and on to victory, to conquest and to peace.

Longstreet doubted; the Federals had too much artillery at the center. He did not think any 15,000 men God ever made could drive across that valley into it; wished to outflank the Federals by a long move to the right, where a night scout had reported (inaccurately, as it happened) they had nothing beyond the Round Top. Lee only repeated the attack order, in a tone that was as near an approach to temper as he ever came. The artillery? A staff officer said it could be beaten down by our guns, and once more Lee said, "Attack"; and Longstreet, feeling such a depression as he had never known, went forth to translate the order into details.

In the morning, in the still and peaceful morning, the long valley lay dreaming in the summer haze, faintly dotted with dead men. Here and there a skirmisher's musket cracked; the sun rose to zenith and past. The Confederate horses toiled, pulling guns into position, tube by tube down Seminary Ridge. At one o'clock, they stood fast in a quiet so deep a whisper would have broken it. Lee nodded; Alexander of the artillery threw up his arm and with a roar that made the world tremble, 160 cannon let go together.

One-thirty; two o'clock; Cemetery Ridge was white with shellbursts; the reply of the Union artillery had weakened and died. Out around Culp's Hill there had been a fight that morning, where Meade put in the XII Corps against Ewell, and in a wild combat succeeded in flanking him and driving him back across Rock Creek. It was all over now. Beyond the flank eastward cavalry slashed and hammered, where Stuart sent Wade Hampton charging home. The new commander, Custer, rode against him with long blond ringlets streaming behind him like a crest, crying "Come on, you Wolverines!" to the 7th Michigan. Stuart was matched and overmatched; the rebel horsemen borne before the hurricane for the first time in their lives.

On the other wing Longstreet drove in a partial attack against the Round Tops. Kilpatrick was there; he hurled young Farnsworth and his horsemen into the flank of the attackers. Farnsworth fell, his brigade was riddled by the fire they bore, but the rebel advance was stopped, no help for Pickett from that quarter.

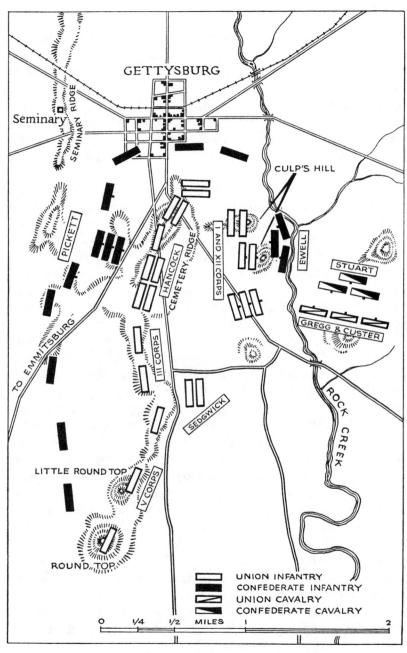

GETTYSBURG

Seminary

SEMINARY RIDGE

CULP'S HILL

PICKETT

HANCOCK

CEMETERY RIDGE

I AND XII CORPS

EWELL

STUART

GREGG & CUSTER

ROCK CREEK

TO EMMITSBURG

III CORPS

SEDGWICK

LITTLE ROUND TOP

V CORPS

ROUND TOP

UNION INFANTRY
CONFEDERATE INFANTRY
UNION CAVALRY
CONFEDERATE CAVALRY

0   1/4   1/2   MILES   1   2

Gettysburg—The Third Day

Two o'clock; the Virginians and Carolinians ranked in a little wood and swept out into the open, shoulder to shoulder, in long gray lines, with shining bayonets. General Garnett rode by, just out of hospital, buttoned to the neck in his old blue coat; Armistead and his iron beard went by, Kemper of the proud face. "Good-by boys, see you in Washington!" "One—two—three—four, right dress, there," called the sergeants. Fifteen thousand fighting men—Colonel Freemantle of the British army surveyed them with pleasure and turned to Longstreet, by his side. "I wouldn't have missed this for anything in the world," he said warmly. Longstreet laughed harshly. "The devil you wouldn't! I would like to have missed it very much," he said.

Pickett rode up, his auburn hair escaping from his jaunty cap. "General, shall I advance?"—jubilantly. Longstreet bowed, turning away his head; he could bear to speak no word. Pickett stood in his stirrups and raised his sword. "Forward!"

Longstreet was right, and Lee had miscalculated; it was not militia, it was Hancock and the II Corps, the best in the Union service, that they were going against, with Hunt and the reserve artillery behind, silent only to let the guns cool. As Pickett stormed out into the open, one—two—three—four, right dress and take your time, the whole diapason blazed out. Gaps showed in the gray lines, long lanes down which you could drive a carriage. "Close up! Right dress!" and they came on, down the slope. Hancock's guns changed to shells, then to canister. The gray lines came on magnificently, heads held high, leaving a long red trail behind them. They guided left, the supports split rightward, the Union musketry spoke up. Pettigrew's brigade began to shake in the advancing column; their commander rallied them. All along the Union line from Round Top north the artillery was firing now, a tornado of fire. Right on they went through it all. Pettigrew gave a great shout, Armistead and Kemper and Garnett took it up, and with the rebel yell on their lips, the 15,000 swung forward at the run, like a tidal wave, amid a tumult that seemed to split the skies.

Kemper fell as they reached the crest; Garnett was down as they got in among the first line of guns. A young officer's voice rose to a scream, "I'll give them one more shot, Webb!" and as Armistead collapsed the Virginians stormed through the Union batteries and broke the Union line. But Hancock, sitting on an eminence with blood pouring from a wounded artery, was yelling triumph as Webb's Pennsylvanians, Hall's New Englanders wheeled and went past him, blades and heads low, to meet charge with countercharge. The Virginians were torn from front and flank; the artillery never stopped shooting them down, they had no strength left to meet Webb and Hall—and the high tide of the Confederacy broke in tears and blood and despair, ebbing back to the sound of "It's all my fault" from the anguished lips of Robert Lee.

. . . The next day the papers had it all; Lee in full retreat toward Virginia. Baltimore and Philadelphia and New York woke from a dream of terror to toll bells for an Independence Day that held more of relief than joy. At the height of the celebration the wires flashed an incredible piece of news. An aide had ridden into Holly Springs, plastered with mud, incoherent with excitement; he said Grant was in Vicksburg, the Confederate army of the west cut off and our general and troops safe.

28

THE REVOLT OF THE TURTLE

W HAT to make of Ulysses Grant, behind the black cigar, his clothes looking as though thrown to fall where they might on his stocky frame, his pockets blistered with the letters he never answered? By the newspaper correspondents, whom he kicked out of camp, nothing. "Our noble army is being wasted by the foolish, drunken, stupid Grant. I have no personal feeling about it; but I know he is an ass." By the commercial Jews, drummed out of camp for cotton speculation-peculation, even less—"There never was a more thoroughly disgusted, demoralized, disheartened army than this." By Henry Adams of the naked sensibilities, more, but that unfavorable—"His officers could never follow a mental process in his thought. They were not sure he did think. A type pre-intellectual, archaic; he had been extinct for ages."

Wrong! This was 1863; they also thought Krakatao extinct in those days, it had snow on top. There was nothing amiss with the quality of Grant's brain; only his veins ran glaciers, his mental thermostat habitually stood at −273° Centigrade. Drink? He suckled like a carp before the war, but found a higher stimulant in the crash of battle and boozed no more. The heat of emergency, which made others boil over, rave, sing and swear, call on their Gods for what they had not themselves, only brought this tortoise to the comfortable temperature of activity. The evidence—his dispatches, usually so stodgy—those written in the midst of battle ring clear and sharp as a chime of bells. Under such pressures his mind absorbed details as easily and unconsciously as a sponge takes up drops of water; he saw whole entities as readily as McClellan, but saw them as compositions of detail, and when he found a detail that did not relate to the rest, simply dropped it out of the completed picture. Also write down this about him; he was never jealous or envious of any man.

This was emergency; seven failures before Vicksburg, with the army marooned among bayous and sharpshooters, and Washington sending out an inspector with the possibility of removal behind. The soldiers amused themselves with a religious revival: "Here, you have let that Illinois regiment get ahead of us," rapped out the colonel of the 78th Ohio to his adjutant. "Detail thirty men for baptism immediately." The waters dried; it became possible to move by foot across the soggy bottom-lands, and Grant marched McClernand's Corps down the west bank of the Mississippi to Hard Times, below Vicksburg. Hard Times faces Grand Gulf; Porter ran the gunboats through and scored Failure No. 8 against the batteries along the cliffside there. An ox-bow stood in Grant's way; he had it bridged and sat on a log with General Sherman by night, the whole scene lit by bonfires of pitch-pine, the bridges swaying beneath the military tramp of marching men, with their accouterments gleaming redly.

Sherman: What are you going to do?

Grant: Cross here and reach the high ground.

Sherman: That would be putting yourself voluntarily in a position which the enemy would be glad to maneuver a year to get you in. Go back till high ground can be reached on the east side; build a road, fortify, establish a depot of supplies.

Grant: That will take us back to Memphis.

Sherman: Exactly. The very place I would go.

Grant: The country is tired of retreats. I shall cross here.

Sherman: But your communications? You cannot get supplies down the west bank.

Grant: No communications. We will live off the country.

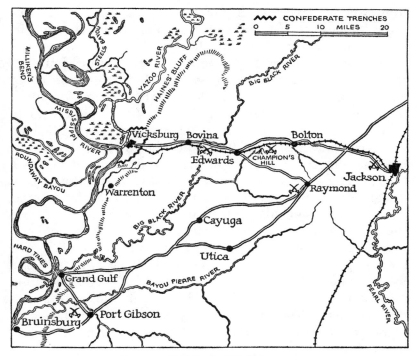

Grant Behind Vicksburg

Sherman's jaw dropped and his eyes sprang open in wild amaze; he knew as well as any man that failure meant a starved army and a cashiered general, but for once he found no word, only sat staring as the regiments rocked past through the firelight.

On the last day of April a gunboat stood in and fired some shells at Bruinsburg; before morning, McClernand's Corps was across, 16,000 strong, and marching for high ground. The rebels had a division, Bowen's, at Grand Gulf; it came down to meet McClernand and the advance-guards clashed at Port Gibson, in a country of buttes and narrow ravines, stifled with cane and underbrush. McClernand fell on heartily; the rebels held him back for a time on their difficult ground, but Logan with a division of McPherson's Corps came up, burst through Bowen's right flank and sent him whirling away with 1,000 men lost. . . . That same night Stonewall Jackson was tramping through the Virginia scrub to reach Howard's flank at Chancellorsville.

Pemberton had 50,000 men, more than Grant, but scattered, some at Haines' Bluff, where Sherman was making a feint, some flying from the field of Port Gibson with Bowen, some back at Jackson, the main force at Vicksburg. He called in all but the Jackson wing by telegraph and sat still for a week, convinced that Grant would not live away from the river and must come straight along the highland to break his knuckles against the fortified bluffs of Warrenton. Grant disagreed; on the 5th he had heard of the Jackson force, knew it had risen to 12,000 men with Joe Johnston to lead them, and determined to knock it out, then turn on Pemberton. He appeared at all sorts of odd places along the marching column, impassive as a hitching post but possessed by a demon of hurry—"with all dispatch," "overwhelming importance of celerity," "no delay" beat like metronomes through his orders. He was everywhere at once; he never passed a marching regiment but to urge them to march faster, faster.

On the morning of the 12th McPherson's advance struck a line of vedettes outside Raymond, pushed through them and found the rebels drawn up on a hill behind a stream. It was Gregg's brigade, coming out of Jackson to fall on the Union rear when Grant turned toward Warrenton. McPherson had a corps, 15,000 men; he swung round both Gregg's flanks, carried the height in a fast charge, captured the rebel guns and sent what was left of them into Jackson as a mass of fugitives.

Two days later Grant's army was around the town. Johnston had begun to fortify, but he was caught half-prepared. He posted his men in the trenches, wiring frantically for reinforcements. Too late; before the key stopped clicking Sherman had stormed his lines at one spot, McPherson had cut through another. Grant came into town so fast that when he stepped into the mill, he found the looms still spinning

army cloth with "C. S. A." woven in each bolt. Lesson—
never kick a man when he's down—the year before some
of these same Union soldiers had been led through Jackson,
footsore, hungry prisoners from Shiloh; when they asked
for food the generous Mississippians threw clods at them
for damyankees. Now they burned the place out, enjoying
themselves very much.

The country was bad for scouting and Pemberton had
few horse; it was the 11th May before he learned that Grant
was pointed on Jackson. By this time he was 42,000 strong,
enough to fight; he had a touch of inspiration—strike south,
sever the umbilical cord of communications that must bind
Grant to the river at Grand Gulf, then round up the starving Union army. On the morning of the 14th his advance
elements crossed the Big Black toward Cayuga and Pemberton learned to his horror that Grant's movement was already
full born, with no communications at all. That same night
came a despairing telegram from Johnston—"Turn at once
. . . too late—" and then the wire went dead as Sherman's
bluecoats dashed into the Jackson streets.

Pemberton turned round and hurried back toward Jackson as fast as his bandy legs would carry him, but that last
broken message had the right of it—too late. Just outside
Edwards' Station, his cavalry points were taken and he
realized that the Army of the Tennessee was upon him. He
tried to retreat and slip away around a Union flank. Too
late; the roads were full of Federal troops, they would eat
up a retreat. There is a high hill just south of the main road,
Champion's Hill. Pemberton ordered up his artillery here
and formed for a stand, with Stevenson's division holding
the hill, those of Bowen and Loring across the southward
roads.

The Union army was coming west on parallel routes.
McClernand had the advance out of Richmond with four
divisions, Grant himself found Hovey with a division on the
north road and rode with it toward Champion's Hill, speed,
speed. The rebels' guns there opened just as a messenger ar-

rived from McClernand to say he had found more Confederates in line across the fields on his front. Grant made a plan out of hand, the old plan of Iuka and Corinth, sound, simple and brilliant—send Hovey against Champion's Hill with drive enough to attract Pemberton's reserves thither; then let McClernand with his big four divisions break through the weak Confederate line before him, fall on their rear as they faced Hovey and bag them all. The time for delivery of the message would be just enough to let Hovey's attack draw Pemberton's eye. He wrote the order, then rode in with Hovey's van.

They rushed the hill through a hot fire and, carried along by Grant's energy, gained the southern peak, piercing the Confederate center. Pemberton, alarmed at the prospect this opened, drew reinforcements from Loring and Bowen. Laggard McClernand ruined the plan by failing to press home; Pemberton's reserves collected round Hovey and drove him out. But Grant was not done yet; Logan and Crocker of McPherson had come up while the fight was going on. In a moment Grant changed plans from breaking one rebel flank to breaking the other, and sent the two new divisions round the head of the hill to attack it from the north.

The eminence was slotted with ravines and swept by artillery fire, but Logan and Crocker lapped clear round the Confederate left, went up the crest with irresistible dash and hurled the defenders down the other side into rout, their organization completely broken. The pursuit was so hot that Grant's men got the only crossings of Baker's Creek before the division of Loring, retiring under McClernand's languid pressure. Loring found the passes held and wandered south along the stream, leaving wagons, cannon, finally muskets and cooking utensils, and weeks later filtered through to Mobile with a few worn-out men.

That night a spy reached Grant's camp; he had been long among the rebels, they had made him official courier and he bore a dispatch from Johnston to Pemberton—Come north with all haste, leave Vicksburg to its fate, but save your army. Too late. Grant sent Sherman and McPherson to drive the flying enemy with speed behind the Big Black to spoil any such movement. The next morning they were before the bridge there; the rebels had a *tête-de-pont*, with trenches and artillery, to hold the crossing. As Grant rode along, surveying it, a colonel he did not know accosted him with a message. When Halleck in Washington had heard of the campaign, the mere thought of such audacity nearly drove him out of his mind; the rash leader was unreachable by telegraph (no communications!) but this officer had ridden day and night with peremptory orders that the army should be returned to the west bank of the Mississippi. "That will be difficult under the present circumstances," remarked Grant.

"Shall I report, sir, that you refuse to obey?" demanded the colonel, angrily. At that moment there was an outburst of cheering; both men turned round to see General Lawler go past in his shirt-sleeves, leading a charge for the *tête-de-pont*. The Confederate line burst like a rotten melon; Grant filed the peremptory order among the other forgotten correspondence in his pocket and a day and a half later the Army of the Tennessee laid Vicksburg under siege.

As Sherman stood looking down from the Chickasaw Bluffs he had striven in vain to win the year before, he said to Grant: "Until this moment I never believed in your success. But this *is* a campaign; this is a success, if we never take the town." It was—one of the most tremendous on record; in seventeen days Grant had marched 130 miles, split the Confederate forces in two, won five battles and besieged their greatest stronghold. Pemberton had lost 14,000 men, Grant barely 2,000—Julius Cæsar could have done no more.

Now the siege. The works were very strong; on the first day Grant tried an assault. It broke down with loss, like Lee's at Malvern Hill; just as the general ordered withdrawal there came a note from McClernand that he had partial possession of two forts and wanted pressure elsewhere to help him win them. Sherman was sent in again;

there was another repulse with more loss, and then Grant discovered that McClernand had been drawing the long bow; he had gained nothing but the ditches before his two forts. To round the matter out the politician-general issued a vainglorious order of the day saying that if Sherman and McPherson had done their parts as bravely as he, the place would have been taken. Grant learned of the order first through the newspapers; within the hour McClernand's explanation was demanded; within twenty-four he had been sent home to do his growling in Illinois and Ord had been appointed to his corps.

The siege. Heavy guns came down the river; day and night they threw shells into the place, while the parallels crept close. Every house was shot through, the inhabitants lived in holes in the clay. "Mother didn't want to have a cave. She was afraid the roof would come down and said she would rather be killed outright than buried alive. A shell passed through the room just as we left the breakfast table, and one side of the house looked like a peppershaker, it was so full of Minié balls. Mrs. Lovatt and her baby were killed by a cannon ball that day." Provisions ran desperately short, flour cost $1,000 a barrel, meat $250 a pound.

Bill of Fare, Vicksburg Hotel

SOUP
Mule Tail

BOILED
Mule bacon and poke greens. Mule ham, canvassed.

ROAST
Mule sirloin

DESSERT
White oak acorns
Beech-nuts
Blackberry-leaf tea

All through May and June this went on, while Johnston

strove to gather an army of relief in the background. He got it up to 30,000, but Stanton was rushing more men to Grant on every boat down river. On the 28th June Sherman turned to face Johnston with 40,000 men and blood in his eye; the army of relief retreated hurriedly. Curious symbolical note —as Sherman rode through a plantation yard he saw a book lying in the mud and dismounted to rescue it. It was a copy of "The Constitution of the United States" and on the fly-leaf was written—"My property—Jefferson Davis."

All through May and June. On the first day of July there was only one moldy biscuit apiece for the garrison and somebody left a note on General Pemberton's doorstep—"I tell you plainly men are not going to lie here and perish. Hunger will compel a man to do almost anything.—One of your soldiers." He called a council of war; the generals agreed that further resistance was futile and too late; and on the fourth of July, the glorious fourth, the greatest fourth since '76, the flag came down, the Confederate army stacked arms, and Grant's men marched into "the Gibraltar of the West" singing "The Battle-Cry of Freedom." Six days later the steamer *Imperial* ran through unarmed from St. Louis to New Orleans and Lincoln proclaimed exultantly, "The Father of Waters once more flows unvexed to the sea."

29

TORQUEMADA?

THERE was a man named Bickley. He was a surgeon of high degree, rich beyond the necessity of labor, wedded to a lady from New Orleans, and dwelling on an estate where he stewed in the romantic juices of Cagliostro and Walter Scott. This was in '54; William Walker, the comet of the Isthmus, was trailing his momentary glory through the southern skies and Dr. B. was thrilled to the inner recesses of his being by the thought—"There, with the grace of God, go I." Literary romantics seldom leave wife and three meals a day for filibustering expeditions in Nicaragua. Bickley took his adventure internally by drawing up plans for an Invisible Empire, the Knights of the Golden Circle, with passwords, temples, tylers, grand, lesser and supreme councils and a terrifying ritual which included a live snake suspended over the head of the neophyte and an oath to curdle his blood:

> "Whoever dares our cause reveal,
> Shall test the strength of knightly steel;
> And when the torture proves too dull,
> We'll scrape the brains from out his skull
> And place a lamp within the shell
> To light his soul from here to hell."

Object of the Empire—to rescue Mexico from barbarism. On a trip to Louisiana, Bickley initiated some of his wife's relatives as a parlor game. To his astonishment they took it seriously and brought so many friends to share the delicious horrors that he began to believe in it himself. Die-hard slavery men took it up, who could see no safety for their institution but in conquering territory southward to balance the great northwest, forever free by geodesy. The thing snowballed through the uncertain years of Buchanan's administration; at the election, there were 50,000 members, largely in Texas, where the conquest of Mexico seemed a not-unrealizable project.

Then the guns began to shoot, and "We will have to stop off at the Capitol in Washington on our way to Mexico" wrote Supreme Grand Imperial Potentate Bickley. During '61 the Golden Circle spread beyond the line of fire into the Northern states, drawing in any number of incognito copperheads under the leadership of another romantic proslavery medico, one Bowles. A year later, when Governor Morton began to tap their Indiana lines through a counterespionage service, there was an Empire in his state with 15,000 subjects. They formed a prodigious (or absurd—one never knows) plot to seize Indianapolis arsenal under cover of a picnic. Morton called out a brigade of militia which anticipated about 1,000 revolver-bearing knights at the gates in the "Battle of Pogue's Run," an engagement in which several persons received bloody noses.

In Illinois the organization got control of the Democratic key-men and went political; they carried an election and jammed a resolution to recognize the Confederacy through the lower house. There is evidence that this was only the first stage of another grandiose and Bickley-esque plot— formation of a Northwest Confederacy, including Wisconsin, Minnesota and Michigan. In Ohio and Kentucky the chevaliers took direct action; Edmund Wright's wife was poisoned and his home burned when he campaigned against them; old Mr. Bobe, who told General Buell which direction the rebel column had taken, was called out and shot on his doorstep. The thing flowered all through the West in secret meetings and queer emblems—a peeled hickory pole upright in the yard, a butternut, the head from a copper cent, a star. Its operations slid down toward mere organized vandalism as the inevitable attraction of the mask drew in social misfits to drown out the few romantic Bickleys.

What to do with these bugs and he-witches? What to do with the Black Joke, the Baltimore blood-tubs, the thousand and one petty commerciants who shouted "Haro for individual liberty!" when the society that gave and guarded their homes asked them to leave profit-taking for its protection? With the silk gloves who cried Peace, peace, and wrote letters to individual soldiers telling them they could stop the war by deserting and coming home? With Frank Howard, who summoned his audience to rise against the vulgar and brutal despotism that ground them down? . . . Abraham Lincoln, examining sentence of court-martial—"Must I shoot a simple-minded soldier-boy who deserts while I must not touch a hair of the wily agitator who induced him to desert?"

No: Pardon the soldier-boy and throw Frank Howard into Fort Lafayette. There let him complain to the turnkey that the bed is hard—"My son sleeps harder tonight on a stone ledge at Malvern Hill, and a hundred libertarians like you cry against his blood." Whereupon your wily agitator's wily lawyer procures a legal document, and *exeunt omnes* to the air of "Sweet Land of Liberty." There are no laws against wrong thinking and the Constitution protects every man in the expression of whatever thoughts he has in mind.

Difficulty the second—the Golden Circle guarded its own with threat and midnight knife. No evidence; juries would not convict—"There are always some of them," said Lincoln, a trifle bitterly, "more anxious to hang the panel than to hang the traitor." Or evidence that came too late, when the Golden Circle was in control, as when the Illinois legislature suddenly passes its sympathy-with-the-enemy resolution before any can hinder. A government that cannot punish or prevent is no government; one day it will move too late and utterly dissolve in some black joke.

Mr. Secretary Stanton, a man without inhibitions, took the short and rough way with intolerables. When Frank Howard got his writ of Habeas corpus; when wily agitators exercised the indubitable right of free speech, he sent them to places where they would never hear the dogs bark. How many of them? Nobody knows, for he kept no records. Some thousands in all, justly and unjustly lumped together—the editor of the disloyal *New York News* and the crippled hawker who sold it in Naugatuck railroad station. All illegally arrested, condemned without court or cause, since there was no other way. The population of Canada increased by evaporation and freedom shrieked louder than when Kosciusko fell.

For there were honest men, old constitutionalists and Silver Grays, melancholy over the paradox of a nation founded in liberty fouling its origins to preserve—existence? or the Republican Party? How to mark these sincere friends of liberty from sincere friends of the Confederacy? The difference is indistinguishable, said grim Stanton, it is the paradox of being Silver Gray when black and white are at war— all opposition is aid to the enemy—off with their heads! and Wendell Phillips, taking the man for the master, shouted that Lincoln was a more unlimited despot than any this side of China.

Was he miscast? Count Gurowski, that disinterested observer, thought so, confiding to his diary that the President was "pure, but surrounded by atomistic Torquemadas." Let us see—

General Ambrose Everett Burnside had retired from active service to command of the Department of the Ohio, which included three states. In one of them flourished the prince of dissidents, Clement L. Vallandigham, his mouth wreathed with a perpetual sneer; shallow, flippant, reckless, full of strange doctrine that had a meretricious shimmer of easy solution, very appealing to the war-weary mind—"The war for the Union is in your hands, a most bloody and costly failure. There is mourning in every home. Make an armistice.

Call a constitutional convention. The Union will re-establish itself."

In '63 he ran for governor in Ohio, harping his song of a single note—"The dead, the dead, the numerous dead; think of Fredericksburg. Let us make peace." Lincoln was disturbed; the elections were going badly; Burnside, with whom any mention of Fredericksburg was a sore point, more so. He issued an order, General Order No. 38—"The habit of declaring sympathies for the enemy will not be allowed." Vallandigham retorted by a monster mass-meeting against the war. There was a float with young women in cheese-cloth representing the thirty-four states, a parade of men wearing butternuts and penny-heads, followed by refreshments and inflammatory speeches, which reached their apogee in an oration from the tribune of the people himself. "I have the most supreme contempt for General Order No. 38. I have the most supreme contempt for King Lincoln. Come up, united, and hurl the tyrant from his throne. The men in power in this country are attempting to establish a despotism more cruel and oppressive than any that ever existed. Do you know that a proposition has been made for the re-establishment of the Union and the refusal, in Lincoln's handwriting, is still in existence? He does not wish to end the war. He will continue it as long as there are any contractors or officers to enrich."

Under the rostrum, disguised by butternut badges, were two staff captains in plain clothes making shorthand notes. When Vallandigham got this far they nodded to each other and snapped shut their books. The next morning a file of soldiers called on Mr. Vallandigham for breakfast; he lunched on beans and bully-beef in a prison cell and faced a court-martial before sunset.

Speech was in fact and intent seditious, decided the court. Accused is guilty as charged; sentenced to perpetual imprisonment. Approved—Ambrose E. Burnside, Major-General.

It was a *cause célèbre*, the greatest of the war. The papers leaped into headlines, North and South. Vallandigham was a scoundrel, a hero, a martyr, a traitor, the subject of millions of words, from which the passion has so little died that even today it is impossible to find any estimate of the man or his works that can be called altogether without bias. The center of everything, he sat in his jail cell, happy as a grig, drinking in publicity beyond his wildest dreams, while Lincoln paced the floor at midnight, wondering what to do.

What to do? It is a sorry task making war on martyrs. But Vallandigham released would be a blanket permit to black jokes, blood-tubs and Golden Circle chevaliers to go as far as they liked without fear of punishment. But Vallandigham silent in jail spoke a thousand times more eloquently than Vallandigham at liberty, where his silly lies recoiled on themselves. The Ohio election was doubtful— what if he won it, a governor in jail?

Then came inspiration. Lincoln sat down and wrote an order, grinning as he wrote. Sentence of prison commuted to banishment to the Confederacy, where the tribune of the people could enjoy the liberty he praised so highly. Under presidential order a file of soldiers gathered up the prisoner's belongings with minute care, packed them in a black trunk and then sent trunk and politician to General Bragg with a trumpet and a flag of truce.

As Lincoln had foreseen he would, Vallandigham raged; he wanted to go home. He wrote to Congressmen, businessmen, newspapers. Even copperheads found irresistible the spectacle of an uninjured martyr begging to return to the tyranny of King Lincoln and resume his chains. To complete the picture, Vallandigham began to howl about how little liberty there was in the Confederacy, so Jefferson Davis had him ejected from that too; he went to Nassau on a blockade-runner and the only publicity he got after that was his appearance as the leading figure in Edward Everett Hale's "Man Without a Country" which was not at all the kind he wanted.

All's well that ends well if you can make a definite end;

there remained, however, General Burnside and Doctors Bickley and Bowles. The personality general had been enchanted with the result of his Vallandigham case; it put him back on the front page, where he felt he belonged. Anxious for more glory as a censor of thoughts, he made a sudden raid on the *Chicago Times*, filled the office with soldiers and the street with patrols, and announced that the paper, being disloyal, would appear no more. This time Lincoln could not turn it off with a laugh. Twenty thousand people attended the indignation meeting in Chicago Court House Square; the mayor, the governor and generals all down the line telegraphed to Lincoln that this sort of thing must stop. He agreed; the suppression was canceled by executive order and Burnside got a rap over the knuckles. To make the point perfectly clear, the President ordered a general jail delivery of wily agitators.

No consequences; fortune willed it that on that very day two men in gray uniforms appeared before the Nashville lines, asking for passes north. They were, they said, surgeons from Ohio, held against their will in the service of the Confederacy since the fighting began. The story sounded fishy to General Rosecrans, who was deep enough to give them the papers without batting an eyelash but also to detail a couple of men to follow them. One of the medical men got off the train at New Albany, Indiana, whereas his pass said Ohio. The detectives followed, arrested him on the station platform and searched his baggage. They found the great seal of the Knights of the Golden Circle, an assortment of keys, stars, passwords and ciphers and, finally, documents that proved their prisoner was none other than the Supreme Grand Imperial Potentate himself, Dr. George Bickley.

The other traveler, who was Bowles, had seen the arrest. He slipped into the train's washroom and then out the window. One of the trackers jumped after him, missed his quarry in the night, ran to the nearest telegraph station and got in touch with Governor Morton's counter-espionage headquarters. Posses scoured the countryside; they caught Bowles in a "castle" of the order, brandishing a pistol and making arrangements for an uprising to coincide with a rebel cavalry raid. There was a fine crop of courts-martial, with real evidence this time; Bowles was hanged out of hand, Bickley went behind the bars, whither a good many of the Illinois chevaliers presently followed him and the Golden Circle was effectively eliminated from the combination.

30

FOURTH INTERLUDE

DEDICATION

IT WAS eleven o'clock on a November morning.

Mr. Everett had spoken for two hours, faultless in intonation and gesture. He stepped back, his figure beautifully erect in spite of the years, his white hair shining like the snow on a mountain peak, proud and dignified, while the audience pattered applause, and turned to look at the headstones in the Gettysburg National Cemetery he had so nobly dedicated as the President shambled awkwardly forward, in one hand holding the old yellow envelope on which he had scribbled a few notes while on the train. People whispered and stirred, there was even a slight titter as he began to speak in the thin, high-pitched voice, so much at contrast with Everett's orotund periods:

"Four score and seven years ago our fathers brought forth on this continent, a new nation, conceived in Liberty, and dedicated to the proposition that all men are created equal.

"Now we are engaged in a great civil war, testing whether that nation, or any nation so conceived and so dedicated, can long endure. We are met on a great battlefield of that war. We have come to dedicate a portion of that field, as a final resting place for those who here gave their lives that that nation might live. It is altogether fitting and proper that we should do this.

"But, in a larger sense, we cannot dedicate—we cannot

consecrate—we cannot hallow—this ground. The brave men, living and dead, who struggled here, have consecrated it, far above our poor power to add or detract. The world will little note, nor long remember what we say here, but it can never forget what they did here. It is for us the living, rather, to be dedicated here to the unfinished work which they who fought here have thus far so nobly advanced. It is rather for us to be here dedicated to the great task remaining before us —that from these honored dead we take increased devotion to that cause for which they gave the last full measure of devotion—that we here highly resolve that these dead shall not have died in vain—that this nation, under God, shall have a new birth of freedom—and that government of the people, by the people, for the people, shall not perish from the earth."

He turned away. In the audience there was not a hand-clap, not a murmur. They stood as though struck dumb.

Mr. Everett turned to Mr. Seward on the platform, shaking his head:—"It is not what I expected from him. I am disappointed."

"No," agreed Mr. Seward. "He has made a failure, and I am sorry for it. His speech is not equal to him."

3 I

BRAGG IS A GOOD DOG . . .

THE town was by the ears over the concluding installments of "The Moonstone"; would it turn out after all that Franklyn Blake was the murderer? Bernard Koch got 411 Negroes aboard ship for the Ile à Vache colonization project and the financiers who backed the scheme held a gratulatory meeting, at which champagne was opened—three crops of cotton a year and the labor cost nil! Imagine! The Unsleeping Eye discussed the punishment of Judge Waite for enforcing the polygamy laws, but three regiments of Californa volunteers arrived to protect Deseret from the Indians and Brigham Young decided to bear his cross in patience. Over the mountains the National Charity Flour Sack reached Virginia City, where it fetched $3,000 at auction, after which the editor of the *Territorial Enterprise* used it for a pillow when he made up his bed on the imposing-stone. Toward both Deseret and Virginia City slowly crept the railroad, chivvied along by the Congressional grant of $32,000 a mile, which had been opposed by Elihu Washburne on the ground that there would never be any passengers for the Pacific Coast. His speech strongly affected the members of the Biological Society, which met the next afternoon under the presidency of Count Pourtalis, and the discussion turned to California matters, particularly to the giant squids which lurk in the caves along tide-level and strangle Chinamen when they come down to the beach to wash clothes. Mr. Emerson called—

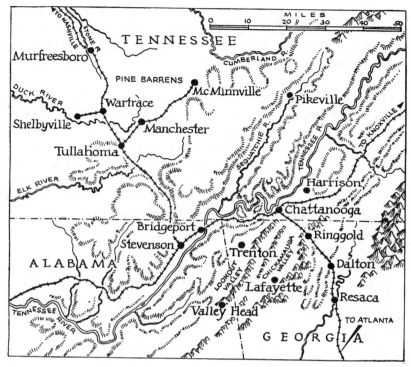

The Tennessee Mountain Campaign

Futile—"Beat you louder, heavier drums; you bugles wilder blow."

In central Tennessee Bragg and Rosecrans faced each other. They were men much alike; if war were a chess-game played with animate but somehow indestructible pieces, both of them would have been great soldiers, but battles took all the fun out of it. While Lee marched on to his high tide and Grant slugged at Pemberton among the marshes they sat still, inventing reasons why they could not fight.

In both camps the technique was similar. General Bragg rose for morning prayers and, being of a morose temperament, spent an hour or two brooding on his wrongs before calling in one of his generals for a quarrel—"Be pleased to inform me to what extent you have encouraged General

Polk in his acknowledged disobedience"—then dispatched a wire to President Davis, setting forth his inability to accomplish anything while surrounded by such scandal-mongering villains. General Rosecrans did his squabbling by telegraph, a less wearing method. He was out for early mass and, being of a poetic temperament, rode around for an hour or two with Father Tracey, discussing the influence of God and the beauties of nature, then returned to headquarters and dashed off a bad-tempered telegram to Halleck, demanding more cavalry; he could accomplish nothing without it. Halleck, a good nagger, retorted in kind—"Your actions with regard to Governor Johnson are disapproved"; "I must protest against the expense to which you put the government for telegrams"; "You have already more cavalry than any other general in the field." Being legally minded, the Chief of Staff had the general always in the wrong. But, right or wrong, nothing could make Rosecrans move from Murfreesboro till he had the horsemen he wanted, and six months drifted by from the day when Bragg withdrew from the banks of Stone River.

Really, the problem before both armies was considerable. Bragg was inferior in force, his best regiments constantly drafted off for the relief of Vicksburg, but lay strongly intrenched along the Duck River Valley, with the high pine barrens of Tennessee rising, terrace after terrace on his right, mountains left and rear. The country is savage and desolate, strewn with the wreckage of an Archean mountain-chain, with no vegetation but a poverty-grass which horses will not eat. Below the porous top-soil lies a pan of bitter clay that holds every drop of rain to make the surface an impossible quagmire after a storm, then sheds water so rapidly as to make the country a howling Sahara twelve hours later. Bragg felt nervous about his left wing, where the hills were passable if difficult; he concentrated his gross around Shelbyville to protect it, with only a corps at Wartrace on the main railroad line, center, and some cavalry heads in the barrens, right, to cut up Federal raiding parties among the narrow, winding defiles.

He was sure an army could not pass the barrens; therefore Rosecrans determined to march by that route. On the 23d June, Mitchell, the astronomer-general, who left his circles to ride on a horse to his grave, led his cavalry in a heavy feint direct against the front of the Shelbyville intrenchments. Behind him came Granger's small corps, behind Granger, McCook's full-size one, obliquing off toward Wartrace; behind both, Crittenden's. They were to press Bragg hard, but not too hard, so he would stay in position. Wheelhorse Thomas had the heavy task with his oversize corps of five divisions; he was to make the great swing through the barrens, come down into the Duck River Valley and cut the rebels from behind. The army had twelve days' provision of bread and bacon; as it set out the rain came down in sheets.

The first clash was on the 24th June, Midsummer Day, when Willich of McCook's Union corps seized a high gully north of Wartrace. Hardee, a stout fighter, whose incredible modesty alone kept him from command of an army, held the rebel flank here. He was surprised to find Federal troops rising out of the barrens, but threw in a division against Willich with hearty good will. There was a hot, swaying battle, decided by the arrival of the Union division of Davis on Hardee's flank; the flank broke down and McCook got through the pass.

Eastward, Thomas was out of soundings in mud, but plowed right along to win the critical point, Hoover's Gap, from a Confederate cavalry post. It was a narrow defile, the only outlet from the barrens. Hardee heard of Union troops at Hoover's Gap the night of his fight with Willich and Davis; more and more astonished at this irruption of bluecoats through impassable obstacles, he faced round his whole command to the northeast. McCook pressed him close; it simplified Hardee's problem for him to imagine Thomas' advance was only a flying wing of cavalry. Accepting this comforting supposition, he sent a couple of brigades to drive Thomas back into the defile; they came on the scene to find the hills black with artillery and 20,000 Yankees swarming all over the mountainside. The two brigades ran away with great speed, Hardee's command dissolved, the Confederate army was flanked and driven west of the railroad.

Thomas dropped a division to keep liaison with McCook and went on to Manchester with his main body to cut the rebel retreat. Rosecrans joined him there on the 26th. While astronomer Mitchell amused Bragg with his cavalry parade before Shelbyville, the whole Union army was slid leftward, then pushed ahead down to the mountain spurs overlooking Tullahoma. It was a hard march; the wagons cut hub-deep in roads like soggy sponge, the artillery had to be dragged by hand, but on the 30th everyone was in position and Braxton Bragg in a peck of trouble. He had to quit Tennessee in a hurry or fight his way up out of the railroad valley against superior numbers on commanding hills. After a day spent in abusing Hardee for not beating Thomas in a battle he could not have fought, and Forrest of the cavalry for not being in the barrens and in Shelbyville both at once, he chose retreat, a very good idea. Sheridan drove in hard behind him with a division but the Confederates set up a rearguard at the Elk River, dropped their sick, their stores and some of their guns and, thus lightened, escaped through the mountains and away to Chattanooga.

The country from Tullahoma to the Tennessee River is poor as Job's turkey; it supplied nothing. The railroad life-line had been cut up during the retreat. Rosecrans went into camp for a month to rebuild and double-track it, establishing an advanced base at Stevenson, while war-worn men and horses recruited their strength, for the campaigning had been exhausting. His men were confident; the movements had been well performed; the only thing he had not accomplished was the destruction of the rebel army. But the next problem was twice as hard; Rosecrans must assail an enemy of known strategic ability across a deep, swift river, and the Cumberland Mountains, tall pillars of granite, shot with narrow gorges running perpendicular to his line of advance. The easiest route was north along the river, then down through the parallels of the valleys; it had the disadvantage of being also the only possible way for an army, with Bragg watching all the river-crossings north of Chattanooga.

Rosecrans, as before, chose an impossible way, straight up and across the precipices. If the rebels spied him, it was sure ruin among those rocky funnels, but he did not mean they should. Dust for Bragg's eyes—on the 16th August, Crittenden swung his corps north up the river, with some light horse clear up at Pikeville, to hint a far northern crossing. On the 21st Crittenden's artillery threw shells into Chattanooga from across the river and his infantry appeared as though to force a passage. As a final touch of illusion Rosecrans had Burnside bring 10,000 recruits and militia down the east Tennessee valleys to Knoxville as though to cut in behind Chattanooga along the railroad.

Bragg was gulled to the queen's taste. He drew his masses northward and never even thought of Bridgeport, where Brannan and Reynolds of Thomas crossed on the 29th in rowboats, threw up a quick trestle-bridge and led the army over. On September 5 Thomas had clambered toilsomely over the first mountain range and was concentrated at Trenton with advance elements forward to seize the passes through Lookout Mountain. On the 9th he had Negley's division through into Chickamauga Valley. It had been difficult to find the enemy among the hills; nobody knew just what Bragg was doing, but now information came in a flood. Thomas' scouts located some rebels at Lafayette, a dozen deserters came in to say Bragg's army had abandoned Chattanooga to fly toward Atlanta in misery and disarray. Rosecrans had succeeded once more; he exultantly hurried McCook's Corps south across the mountains through Valley Head to cut off Bragg's retreat; Crittenden was to come through Chattanooga onto the Confederate rear by the way of Ringgold, Thomas, to push straight ahead.

Mistake: Bragg was fresh, strong and full of fight; he had met craft with craft. The deserters were fakes, sent in to tempt Rosecrans into careless dispersion of his force. The rebels had 15,000 new men from Mississippi, Longstreet and

12,000 more were racing from Virginia over the thundering rails at forty miles an hour. Bragg outnumbered Rosecrans' whole army now; he had Thomas' Corps almost under his guns, with the two Union wings far away from their center. Bragg's hour, and the Confederacy's—break Thomas, spread the Federal wings; march quick-step down the valleys to crush lone Crittenden in Chattanooga with a bridgeless river at his back; bottle Thomas in the valleys and throw the weight of his whole army on McCook—no plan was wrong.

But Bragg's deception deceived too well, beguiling even its maker; he fumbled. On the 12th his cavalry clashed with Crittenden's south of Ringgold; scouts said McCook was far south of him, there were Union men (of Thomas' Corps) in all the passes. D. H. Hill from Virginia arrived to find Bragg looking worn and prematurely old. "It is living in a house whose wall is honeycombed with rat-holes," he said, despairingly; "too many rats pop from too many holes. Who knows what lies behind those peaks," and he made an oratorical gesture toward the mountain crests. Instead of dealing his blow with hot speed like Jackson at Chancellorsville, he dawdled ten miles in the rear, watching rat-holes through other men's eyes. On the night of the 12th he made up his mind for the crush-Crittenden plan. Polk, of all his generals the least amical, was given the advance, and foot-slogged slowly toward Ringgold where he should have moved like a thunderbolt. At eleven the next night he reported that he had taken a strong defensive position and wanted reinforcements to hold it. He had been supposed to attack; Bragg rode to the front, his rage mounting at every step, found Polk quietly reading a newspaper and cursed him out in language that would have made a mule-driver jealous. Polk had been a bishop before the war; he was shocked into entering a long slanging-match which the troops heard with amusement and disgust. Then the whole army turned west into Chickamauga Valley to split Thomas and Crittenden and fall on the former.

Too late; Rosecrans, well served by the cavalry on which he had spent so much effort, had taken warning. Thomas blocked the rebel advance with felled trees and prepared for battle. Crittenden was ordered in on him; McCook, who would never invent gunpowder, could smell it miles and weeks away; at the prospect of battle he quickened his steps and went driving north along the valley in one tremendous burst, fifty-seven miles in a day and a half. His weary troops tramped into position on the night of the 17th, just as fierce cavalry bickerings, sure omen of battle, began along Chickamauga Creek. That night Rosecrans had his staff wire to a selected mailing list of preachers throughout the North for their prayers; he was about to fight the great battle of the west with 56,000 men against the Confederate 67,000.

Bragg's battle-plan was to outflank the Union left and roll right down the line, cutting the link with Chattanooga and hurling Rosecrans back to destruction among the cliffs. The divisions of Walker and Bushrod Johnson forded the creek at daybreak on the 19th for the flanking blow, but the Union cavalry had kept too good a screen and Bragg had guessed wrong on position; Walker, instead of flanking the Union left, plunged headlong into the front of Brannan's division of Thomas. Walker charged home; a roaring conflict blazed up, swift as a forest-fire. Brannan lost ground; Thomas sent Baird and R. W. Johnson with two fresh divisions to his aid and he won it back. Walker called up Bushrod Johnson and burst through Baird's line; Thomas threw in the divisions of Reynolds and Palmer (borrowed from Crittenden) on Walker's flanks and carried him back to the stream.

"You're not fighting conscripts now!" shouted Walker's men, Virginians, as they charged. "And you're not fighting the New York store clerks!" retorted the westerners under Thomas.

Bragg rode up on the rebel side; he had concentrated heavily behind Walker to make sure of breaking that Union left flank; now he threw in two more divisions, Cheatham and Stewart, and sent his whole line forward in a swinging charge. The rebel divisions were bigger than similar Union formations and every man in them felt the battle was make or break for the Confederacy, since Lee had risked existence to send Longstreet's men west for one masterful stroke. Under Bragg's urging they came on like a cloudburst, brushed division Palmer away, broke through what was left of Brannan, drove Reynolds and R. W. Johnson in. Crittenden sent Van Cleve's division; Van Cleve could not hold the Confederates, they came right on, they were a quarter of a mile from the vital road that would cut the Union retreat, old Thomas was riding down his line, bellowing like a bull for a stand when McCook came through the trees on the run with Davis and Sheridan, and Rosecrans got the reserve artillery up.

The line re-formed on Davis, the guns slowed the rebel charge and Sheridan went storming into the flank of the assaulting column just as Thomas ordered a counterstroke against the rebel front. For a time there was a hard struggle, both sides using thick columns that multiplied striking power, but also losses, in geometrical ratio; then the rebels gave.

It was only noon; the battle had barely begun. Bragg saw he could not force Thomas' position and withdrew Bushrod Johnson for a thrust at the Union center. Hood led it, the hardest hitter in the Confederate army, with the divisions of Law and Hindman in addition to Johnson. At two o'clock they struck Reynolds and Van Cleve. Van Cleve reeled back, the rebels got into the gap and the Union center was broken right through to Rosecrans' headquarters, but Thomas sent two divisions from the left, McCook another from the right, and as dark shut down the rebel salient was pinched out under their combined efforts and a cross-fire from the artillery. Battle drawn; many killed.

The troops of both sides slept on their arms in pools of blood; for the generals there was no sleep at all. Thomas re-formed his wing on a long ridge of ground, with divisions Negley, Baird, Johnson (this was the same Johnson who built the misfortunate watch-fires of Stone River), Palmer and Reynolds down from the left; then Wood and Van Cleve, and

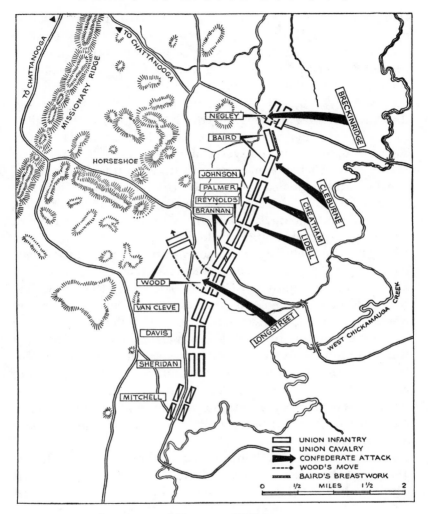

The Second Day at Chickamauga

on the right McCook's Corps, the divisions of Davis and Sheridan, with Granger's three brigades, not enough for a corps, in reserve.

Bragg had no more mental flexibility than a Scottish divine; his plan was ever the same, turn and crush the Union left, but he rearranged his high commands to get more power.

Polk, for all his crankiness a good battle-captain, had the right with five divisions, Longstreet the left and center with six. Polk was to stretch his wing to get round Thomas' left, then attack, each division down the line falling on as it heard the crash of musketry from its right.

The day broke dark and windless, with clinging fog. Breckinridge of Polk's right groped to contact with Negley, found him farther north than expected, but formed behind a screen of mist and delivered a massed assault from close range. Negley's front shattered, his division threaded out and Breckinridge wheeled to take Baird in flank as Cleburne struck his front. Baird had been flank-guard the night before; his men spent the dark hours throwing up a log breastwork *en potence*. Breckinridge could not dent it; the sun burst through and Cleburne went to smash against Baird's batteries now they had light to shoot by. At ten he gave over and dropped back, fought out. By this time Cheatham, Walker and Liddell had been put in against Johnson, Palmer and Reynolds. They assaulted with force and determination, one regiment coming forward as fast as another fell back, a third stepping into the tracks of the second and the rallied first relieving the third. Thomas had no reliefs, every man was in, with Breckinridge still hammering the north end of his line. He had to appeal for reinforcements, and finally reached such an extremity that he asked for Sheridan and his division.

Rosecrans ordered them up and, as the flame of battle ran along the line, rode down behind his center, making all tight. As he passed Brannan's position he noticed a regiment out of line. "Tell General Wood to close that gap," he flung over his shoulder to Major Bond of the staff and Bond hastily wrote the order, the famous muddled order of Chickamauga:

"To General Wood—

The general commanding direct that you close up on Reynolds as fast as possible, and support him.

Bond"

Wood was dumbfounded; Brannan's division lay between him and Reynolds, a quarter of a mile long. But he was a soldier and in battle; he had lately had a wigging for questioning orders, he saluted and obeyed. The troops were pulled out of line, started on the march round Brannan to Reynolds. Just at that moment Longstreet's skirmishers began to close. An intelligent major, noticing the skirmisher-fire was not returned, sent for the general. Longstreet investigated in person, confirmed the astounding fact that a gate had opened in the center of the Union line, hurled Stewart's division at the gap, and then poured the whole of his gigantic wing, six divisions, 30,000 fighting men, in behind Stewart. They spread in both directions, shouting victory, victory, onto flank and rear of the surprised Federals. In ten minutes the divisions of Van Cleve and Brannan had all been captured except the men who threw down their arms and ran. Davis' division broke up; Sheridan and Wood, each caught in movement by rebels from every side, could make no head against the torrent. Their officers lost control, the best and bravest fell, the rest fled. Mitchell's cavalry tried to cover and was dashed to pieces. The artillery was captured and the ammunition train; Rosecrans' headquarters went, the general was borne from the field in the mob of fugitives, down roads blocked with abandoned wagons and splintered gun carriages. Panic.

It was after dark when he reached Chattanooga in the midst of the flying men. The first person he spoke to was Garfield of the staff. "Do you think there is any chance?" asked Garfield, and the two dismounted and placed their ears to the ground to catch the rumble of cannon which might indicate some vestige of defense. No sound. Rosecrans got to his feet and turned toward Garfield:

"Ride to the front," he said, speaking like a man in a dream. "Ride to the front. Find General Thomas, if he is still alive. Tell him to cover the retreat with Granger's men. I will wire to have Cincinnati and Louisville put in order for a siege."

Thomas was still alive. Riding anxiously down his line

that noon he had seen a dark mass of troops come over the rise on his right, thought them Sheridan and the promised aids, and saw to his horror that their uniforms were gray. His line was already hard beset; of the rest of the army he could know only that it had met with some disaster. Behind him lay a convex of hill, Horseshoe Ridge. The first wave of the new rebel assault he halted with a patchwork of troops flung in in reckless countercharge, the rest of the corps he drew back to the ridge.

Just in time—the rebels were all around him. Cleburne came back to join Breckinridge on the north of the horseshoe; Bushrod Johnson, Preston, Stewart, Law of Virginia and finally hard-driving Hood fell on the southern side, sweeping up the slopes, mass after mass, shouting in the fearless passion of sure triumph. The moment was too desperate for enthusiasms; Thomas rode soberly along the line, "Steady, there, steady. Shoot low and pick your man." Mass after mass the waves of assault rolled back, then up again, through the long afternoon. Thomas' regiments had frayed to a single thin line; officers were handling muskets like privates, Granger's reserve had come and been used up too, but whenever any of them looked up, there he was, strong and impassive against the red twilight over the mountains, looking ten feet tall to their superheated imaginations, literally carrying the whole army on his shoulders. At dark the ammunition ran out; the dead were robbed of their bullet-pouches, and that ammunition was gone too, with a circle of red flashes picking out the crest of one more charge from Longstreet. (It was at that moment Garfield listened in vain for distant guns.) "Fix bayonets!" ordered Thomas quietly, and cocked his pistol. The last charge struck, there was a boiling melee of clubbed muskets and silver-flashing bayonets under a solemn harvest moon, and then that charge, too, rolled back down the hill and the Union army was saved. Longstreet rode to Bragg—"I need reinforcements to finish them." "I have none to give you; all our divisions are so beaten as to be worthless."

Be content, General Bragg, it was a Confederate victory;

Thomas will be drawing back to Chattanooga in the morning and you may besiege the Army of the Cumberland there. A victory—that cost the victors 23,000 in killed and wounded, the heaviest butcher's bill of the war—"One more like this and I am ruined"—but a victory.

Rosecrans lived for thirty years after and was counted a useful citizen, but the shadow of that awful moment of defeat never left his face and he was a broken man forever. As for Thomas, he got the command of the army and the name without which he is never mentioned—the Rock of Chickamauga. The day news of the appointment reached the army in its lines at Chattanooga the soldiers broke ranks at morning parade and cheered like crazy men—and the new general of the Army of Cumberland pulled his hat down on his nose to hide his school-girl blushes.

3 2

. . . BUT HOLDFAST IS BETTER

GRANT's army had been split; a third of it to Missouri, a third to Arkansas, himself to chase guerrillas in Mississippi, scoundrel fly-by-nights who shook your hand one day and shot you in the back the next. The system was rough but efficacious, leaving no room for questions later— "The general regrets to report that on the march back to camp eight guerrilla prisoners fell off a log and broke their necks."

Grant was doing little or nothing; his horse threw him and he could hardly move for pain when the message came— "Report to Indianapolis at once." At Cairo an officer handed him a secret dispatch—go on to Louisville. In Louisville he hobbled aboard a train on crutches, and found a little man in a fudge of chin-whisker and an appalling waistcoat pacing rapidly, his mouth clapping open and shut like a steel trap as he disgorged puffs of words. It was Stanton; the Army of the Cumberland was besieged in Chattanooga, it must be relieved at once. Grant pulled at his cigar. "Hooker has been sent from the East with the XI and XII Corps. He is at Nashville now. You are in command of all armies west of the Alleghanies. Here is your commission. Good-by. Good luck."

The bankrupt tanner left the room military dictator of a territory larger than Europe, and wired to Thomas that Chattanooga must be held at all costs. "Till we starve," replied stout Thomas. He was near it; Bragg had guns and inexpugnable trenches on Lookout Mountain, cutting the only ingress south of the river. North of it was one poor mountain track; it foundered under the weight of trucking food for 40,000 men. To complete the debacle, Confederate Wheeler had led out a dashing cavalry raid, captured all Thomas' disponible wagons near Bridgeport and made a bonfire of them. Even the mountain track could not be used after that. Eleven thousand horses and mules died in the besieged city; the brigade headquarters existed on parched corn, the regiments on thin gruel. Retreat was no longer possible, the artillery and ammunition could not be moved without animals, the army would be defenseless. Mr. Dana had never seen anything so lamentable and hopeless; he believed the army would have to surrender.

So did Jefferson Davis, who came west to look down on 'the prisoned Federals from the head of Pulpit Rock, the eyrie of Mount Lookout. "Before another week that army is my own!" he cried, unconsciously or consciously quoting Napoleon. ("Fine view," observed one of his staff, looking down about the same moment; "But a poor prospect," retorted General Longstreet, gazing with distaste at the presidential stern.)

Napoleon, the darling dream of the rebel President's heart. Had not he, too, spent his early years at West Point-Brienne? Had not he, too, commanded a Battery of the Fearless at Chapultepec-Toulon, risen to lead armies in an hour of revolt and invasion? Was not he, too, a philosopher, orator and strategist? Alas that his figure was long and lank, ladies did not swoon over his classic profile nor armed men shout when he thrust a hand inside a uniform to clutch his left mammary! He held a conference with General Bragg; they could count on the delay-psychology of that old Aulic Council of Lincoln, Halleck and Stanton. Grant would undoubtedly be kept in the West, building railroad till Chattanooga fell; let Longstreet take his corps on a flying march to Knoxville and capture the force Burnside had there as well, how Napoleonic!

Psychology is a wonderful thing, but the two Napoleons erred by the calendar; they did not know the half-gods had bowed themselves from the stage in a Louisville trainshed two days before, and they were dealing with Ulysses Grant, a man who vitiated psychologic rules by sheer spirit. "In him, the energy alone counted; such men were forces of nature, they made short work of scholars. The fact was certain; it crushed argument and intellect at once." Before he even reached Chattanooga, Grant had sent the damaging fact of Hooker's Corps to Bridgeport; two days later the damning fact of Sherman's Corps was hurrying on by forced marches, and he had approved Engineer "Baldy" Smith's plan for revictualing the town.

Where the Tennessee swings its loop round the buttress of Raccoon Mountain there are some low hills behind which the walls cease, leaving a practicable ferry, Brown's Ferry. To reach it a road crosses from the right bank at Kelly's Ferry, cuts between Raccoon and the foothills through a high-walled gorge, crosses the ferry and dives into Chattanooga behind the abutments of Moccasin Point by means of a third ferry, the whole making a line roughly straight across two of the Tennessee's loops. The gorge was deep enough to be safe from Lookout Mountain's plunging fire, but the rebels had an outpost in it and another at Kelly's. If warned, they could easily throw a corps into the place; silent surprise alone stood a chance.

On the night of October 27 Hooker marched his two corps (Howard and Slocum) to Kelly's Ferry and hid them in the woods on the right bank, no lights, no sound. Thomas loaded 1,300 picked men under General Hazen into pontoon boats; with fog on the water, drifted gently down the stream, not a man speaking, not an oar dipping for fear of noise. At 3:30 the current wafted them round the base of Raccoon; they slid in toward the post at Kelly's Ferry, where a dying fire and a sleepy sentinel kept ward. The man had just time to give a shout as the boats bumped and Hazen's 1,300 swarmed ashore to smother the outpost. Some of them rushed on into the gorge; the rest signaled Hooker by shout and torch, who hurried men across in other boats. As they plied ax and hammer on a pontoon-bridge under guttering lights the Confederate guns on Lookout woke up, but firing down into mist

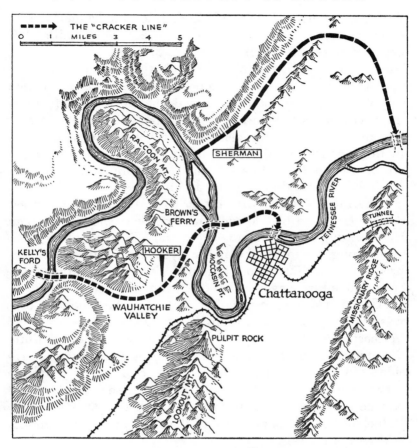

The Fighting Around Chattanooga

and dark, they hit nobody. In an hour the bridge was finished;
Hooker's corps artillery came rumbling over to take position
in the foothills and blast the head off the brigade Bragg sent
to see what was going on. After them came column on column
of foot, and then the slow wagons with their blessed cargoes
of food. "Full rations, boys! The cracker line's open!" and the
siege of Chattanooga was raised at a cost of six men by
chance balls.

Bragg was discontent to leave it that way. The next night
he massed Kershaw's and Law's divisions in Wauhatchie

Valley and hurled them at Hooker's line in a dramatic night attack, with the cannon reverberating among the hills. The brunt of the combat fell on Geary's division. He held hard; Howard and his Dutchmen came charging up to help, and just at the crisis the noise stampeded the mules in the Union camp. They put up their tails and dashed for the Confederate lines with squeals of terror; in the dark, made more intense by cannon-flashes, the rebels took it for a cavalry charge, an ill thing to face at any time, doubly so at night where eye and foot cannot coordinate to save one from milling hooves. The rebels broke, they fled, the position was safe.

Sherman reported with his corps on the 15th November, raising Grant to 60,000 men, and he began to think about battle. Bragg's position on Lookout and Missionary Ridge was very strong and fortified elaborately; it would have to be surprise again, a difficult matter, since the Confederates on the crests had a bird's-eye view of every move below.

Grant had an answer for that, too; Sherman's Corps was marched into town, then out again downstream around Moccasin Point, with parade and music, while *soi-disant* deserters carried Bragg the news the corps was going to Burnside's aid. Out of sight behind the Moccasin Hills, Sherman turned sharp east into a hidden valley. At daybreak on the 23d he surprised a crossing at the north foot of Missionary Ridge, pushed in fast and carried the outer peak of that mountain with a hurrah.

Simultaneously Hooker had been ordered to demonstrate at the foot of Lookout. That was too passive a rôle for fighting Joe, the vain man; "May I take the height?" he asked. "If you can," said Grant, eyeing him narrowly. He put the whole two corps (now made one and called the XX Corps) in the line of battle with an exhortation to remember that the men they were facing had declared they were "Eastern counter-jumpers" whom they could always beat. They stormed that huge mountain in snarling fury, while the army in the valley looked on with bated breath, catching fitful glimpses of struggling men through rifts in the clouds that swept low

around the peaks. Suddenly a long shaft of sun picked out
Pulpit Rock like a celestial searchlight; at that very moment
a man mounted the crag and a whiff of breeze blew out the
flag he carried. It was the stars and stripes; the valley rang
with cheers as the Confederate line, all broken and in rout,
tumbled down the reverse slope into Chattanooga Valley. The
triumph bettered rather than worsened Bragg's position; he
suffered for lack of Longstreet, but was now concentrated
along Missionary Ridge. Grant thought he had the key. He
had swung his left, then his right, pivoting on Thomas; now
the left again—let Sherman drive right ahead and roll up
their line while Hooker locked it in position with the threat of
another move around the flank he had already struck.

The plan went agley. Hooker had too far to go, and across
an unbridged stream; his threat drew only a few regiments,
an outpost of observation, then Bragg simply ignored him.
At the railway tunnel through Missionary Ridge Sherman
ran into a vertical-sided ravine, not marked on the maps. It
took the swing out of his attack. The rebels had time to assemble; Hardee, opposite Sherman, was heavily reinforced,
and Sherman had to fight his best merely to hold on. By
afternoon he was sending to Grant for help. The general
looked round; the only troops at hand were Thomas'. He sent
them to attack the Confederate rifle-pits at the foot of Missionary, a feint to relieve the pressure on Sherman, of whom
the general still conceived as charged with the main business
of the day.

The men moved out of town in parade formation, deployed into line, went forward with a rush and carried the
lightly held rifle-pits. From above a stinging, unanswerable,
intolerable rain of bullets beat down onto them. There was
no cover. They hesitated; then Sheridan stood up, shouted
"Here's how!" drained his half-pint of whisky, slung the
flask up the slope and began to climb after it. The whole line
suddenly went insane; from one end to the other they leaped
out of the trenches as one man and fled—but forward.

That mountain is still there; with foothold and handhold

you can climb it in half a day. The Army of the Cumberland went up it, musket in hand, with sixty cannon thundering in their faces, against two lines of trenches filled with soldiers who had rifles and every intent of killing the climbers. They went up singing discordant songs, yelling like savages, taking no account of their losses. In one regiment a bugler with his leg shot off sat on an outcrop of rock blowing Charge! till he fainted. Like flies they went straight over vertical pinnacles; like snakes through narrow chimneys a goat could not have negotiated. It was incredible, it was magnificent, it was not war, it was not anything, it was monstrous paradox. Grant in the valley stood transfixed with astonishment for once in his life. "By whose orders are those men going up there?" he demanded.

"By their own, I fancy," remarked Thomas calmly, and turned his glasses to catch a better view of the Confederates fleeing from their trenches half way up as the horde of maniacs burst in upon them. Sheridan, Baird, Whitaker, Hazen reached the crest all at once at different points, went right over the trenches at the top, bayonetted the gunners at their cannon and, without a pause to form, flung themselves into the midst of the Confederate army. There was no time to organize a stand, no time to set up a rearguard. Whole regiments were cut off, Bragg's headquarters went, the yard was filled with shouting madmen before his staff could get out of the building, he himself missed capture by an eyelash. "Here's your commander!" he cried, riding among the fugitives. "Here's your jackass," they answered, threw down their muskets and ran twice as fast. The center and left of the Confederate army went whirling away into the hills in utter wreck, leaving their artillery, their wagons and everything else they possessed. Hardee pulled out from the right barely in time and, by sacrificing a battery at the next pass, managed to hold up the pursuit long enough for the rout to get away into the heart of Georgia.

After that, what happened at Knoxville was no longer important; as a matter of fact, Longstreet beat a retreat.

"God bless you all," telegraphed Lincoln fervently when the news came through, and Congress passed a law reviving the grade of Lieutenant-General, vacant since George Washington. Grant got the appointment, of course, with the command of all the armies of the United States. That involved the demotion of Henry W. Halleck, but nobody complained about that, not even Halleck, for he was appeased by an appointment as Chief of Staff, a post in which he could gratify his avuncular soul by fiddling with reports and ration returns all day long.

33

THE ANACONDA AGAIN

THE South limped toward independence on one leg. How to convince the world of national greatness, when it can only see the new flag tossing above the fog of war, only hear the new voice grotesquely muffled behind the iron wall of the Federal navy? Iron wall; day and night the rollers trundled across the ribbons of burning steel, the heavy hammers drove their rivets home and flat, snub-nosed monitors floated down the tide to make the lack of all things within the lines ever more beyond assoil. The Confederacy wanted bacon, butter, coffee, tea, soap, starch and glue; the earth beneath old smoke-houses was tried out for its salt content; there was an absurd resort to flint and steel (no matches), a ridiculously hampering shortage of postage-stamps. Counterfeiting flourished amain on a currency so wretchedly printed that the imitation was better than the original.

Beyond assoil: blockade runners picked their way down inlets, then flashed through the night for Nassau with trails of sparks behind their gasping funnels. The captain made a fortune and all the sailors had new clothes—but on the next trip, U.S.S. *Canandaigua*, just out of the Atlantic Yards, with a sixteen-knot turn of speed and 9 IX-inch Parrotts, was off the port. The blockade runner could not outfoot her; the Parrotts began to speak, the blockade runner hove to at dawn with a shot in her gizzards and the sailors could wear their new clothes in billy-o.

Break the blockade, then, by main force. In Savannah, the women gave their jewels to build a new ironclad, a super-

Merrimac, hight *Atlanta*. She went down Wasaw Sound with a new flag and a parade of excursion boats to see the ruin of the blockading fleet. At four-thirteen in the morning, the monitor *Weehawken* slipped her cable and headed toward the new colossus; at five-two, *Atlanta* fired and missed with a broadside. *Weehawken* closed in silently to five hundred yards. At five-fifteen her turret spun, her big gun boomed and a hundred-pound shot slammed the *Atlanta's* flank. It burst the plates, slaying eight men and stretching forty-seven more on the deck, some wounded, some merely stunned. The second shot cracked her pilot house, wounded the two pilots and laid out the helmsman; the third, fourth and fifth penetrated the casemate on the track of the first. *Atlanta* filled with steam, confusion and death; the captain was down, the ship could not shoot or steer, she was a wreck and down came her flag.

Break the blockade by stealth and craft. A clever engineer named Hundley concocted a machine for underwater transportation—the *David*, "mechanical whale" or "peripatetic coffin." "A most brave device to murder their flat bottoms," the cultured Mr. Hundley described it, in a quotation from rare Ben Jonson. Nine men sat in a row to work velocipede-like paddles which propelled the thing; it carried its sting in its tail, a keg of powder with a detonator. On her trial trip the mechanical whale stuck its nose in the mud and stifled the contents; on the next trip they left the hatch-combings open for air, the water dashed in and drowned another crew. Yet there were found other nine to drive the peripatetic coffin down Charleston harbor by night to murder the flat bottom of U. S. frigate *Housatanic*. It worked; the powder exploded, *Housatanic's* ribs caved in, she sank in a whirlpool of steam and shouting, but the mechanical whale was sucked down into the boiling eddy and that was the end of Mr. Hundley's idea for fifty years.

The blockade would not be broken; the iron wall crept in as upon the prisoner of Salamanca. Hatteras and the North Carolina sounds had been taken in the summer of

'61; in November of the same year big warships came up out of the blue to batter into surrender the forts on Hilton Head; in March, Fernandina in Florida, Fort Pulaski soon after. April saw the fall of St. Mary's and St. Augustine in Florida, and Brunswick on the Georgia coast; in August Corpus Christi and Galveston in Texas were taken; in October of that year Sabine Pass and the Confederacy's link with the world through Mexico. That summer Connecticut Yankees raised and harvested the sea-island cotton. With every one of these forts the Confederacy lost a seaport, over every seaport floated the old flag, against them raged impotent exasperation. "Tell your master," said the rebel doctors to the wounded prisoners from Fredericksburg,—"tell your master, Lincoln, to raise the blockade and we will tend to you. We have not enough medicaments for our own wounds."

How useless!—to deal with an iron wall by railing at its component atoms. Yet the man in Salamanca pit would not drink the poison because he had the hope that an army of relief would break the gears of the devilish mechanism that drove him inward, and so it proved. So too did the Confederacy hope and labor, with Mr. Slidell in Paris, Mr. Mason in London, striving to raise an army to break the gears. The appointments should have been reversed. Slidell had almost Franklin's skill, but Napoleon III was Sudophile already, only he would take no action without England's connivance, which Mr. Mason was the wrong man to win. He was weighty and sincere, with a mouthful of statistics and a sense of humor bounded by flannel underwear, whereas the society into which he had been thrust revolved upon an axis of intelligent eccentricity, lubricated with witticisms. Mr. Swinburne was startling drawing-rooms with his macaw-like screeches and his incredible memory; Mr. William Morris found the half-dozen eggs the cook prepared for breakfast palatable if somewhat high; Mr. Landor threw his cook out the window and the Prince put ice in his soup while Mr. Mason stared in bewilderment and got himself disliked. Even Thackeray, who was convinced that Lincoln was a brute and Seward a cad, was obliged to confess that the Confederate emissary was a nincompoop.

Mr. Charles Francis Adams, on the other hand, though representing the brute and the cad, possessed just the right degree of charming eccentricity. He disapproved of knee-breeches, he smoked in the house (instead of the stables, as good manners demanded) and he paid a debt of organized society by calling Lord Palmerston a liar in the most graceful and unexceptionable manner. By the middle of the second year he had received the accolade; they said he was "quite mad" and flocked to his dinners, afterward repeating his remarks as they might those of an educated Tumbo from Dahomey. Though American, and hence not quite human, he was interesting, while Mr. Mason was just a man like the rest of us, rather on the City side.

For the gentlemen of percentages and stocks, however, the Masonic solidity possessed a certain fascination. Though he came not a hairsbreadth nearer his objectives of recognition and armed mediation, Mr. Mason had no difficulty in floating loans, or even in finding backers for a flyer in piracy. The Lairds of Birkenhead were behind it; they built a ship, *Oreto*, to specifications for a British navy cruiser, but gunless. She cleared from Liverpool for South America with a cargo marked "Machinery." Off Madeira she met another ship which, oddly enough, had sailed the same day as she, with a large passenger list of Southern gentlemen. There was a mysterious interchange; the "machinery" came up out of the hold to be mounted on the gun-deck, the British flag came down, the rebel flag went up and the Confederate States cruiser *Alabama* stood out to sweep the sea.

It was the golden age of those wonderful tall vessels, the clipper ships. They were fast, but *Alabama*, with her steam power, faster; she harried them terribly all up and down the Atlantic from Norway to the Cape of Storms. A dozen, a hundred, were taken and burned; her decks were packed with prisoners, her lazaret held five hundred pounds of gold. She even dared a rush through the blockade to Galveston.

The admiral off the port took her for a blockade runner and sent the light cruiser *Hatteras* in chase. *Hatteras* gained; toward twilight the ships were close, when *Alabama* swung sharp round and opened fire with all her heavy guns. Captain Blake of *Hatteras* was overmatched; he tried to close and board, but the raider had the speed of him as well as the guns, and kept her distance to make it an artillery duel. In ten minutes *Hatteras* lost her walking-beam; the pivot-gun was hit, a big shell tore a hole in her side, and down she went, waving surrender across the hurrying dark water.

Alabama went on to another cruise; the damage was terrific, the clippers began to transfer to British registry, at least a dozen warships sought her in vain. It lasted till '64, that chase, when the raider visited Cherbourg for coal. Captain Winslow of the U.S.S. *Kearsarge* heard of the visit and brought his cruiser down to block the port. Semmes of *Alabama* sent him a challenge; the press got the news and excitement went up to fever heat. A French battleship escorted *Alabama* to the three-mile limit; 15,000 spectators lined the cliffs and the railroads ran special trains from Paris.

In full view of the gallery the cruisers began to swing long circles around each other, *Alabama* firing rapidly in crashing broadsides, *Kearsarge* slowly, gun by gun, every shot timed. The spectators could see the splinters flying and the big ships wince like living things as the shot went home but they were too far away to make out who was getting the best of it. At the end of an hour the Confederate ship suddenly threw up her sails and turned shoreward. She never made it; *Kearsarge* closed in, *Alabama*'s stern gave a flick like the tail of a duck and she dived for the bottom of the sea, half a mile down.

She left behind a bad precedent and a fine crop of protests. The Lairds, encouraged by dividends, floated out more raiders—*Shenandoah, Rappahannock, Sumter, Nashville*—which ruined the clipper trade and captured the whalers in the Bering Sea. Mr. Adams consumed reams of paper telling

Lord Russell that England would have to pay through the nose for this some day, which was true although his lordship would never live to see it. His lordship did nothing; the protests coincided with the Fredericksburg blood-bath and one angry American the more did not seem to matter. The Lairds, encouraged to boldness, laid down two huge ironclad rams, informing his lordship that they were for the Turkish government.

Mr. Adams, who had tapped all the sources of information society so bountifully provides, was not taken in. He assembled his proofs and demanded that Lord Russell do something about those rams before they started fighting American warships. His lordship addressed a discreet inquiry to the Lairds; the Lairds replied that the rams had been sold by Turkey to Denmark, and got the Crown Law Officer to say that in any case there was no legal basis for interference. Lord Russell informed Mr. Adams that he did not quite see what he could do . . . and at this precise moment came the momentous news of Gettysburg and Vicksburg. The town, all pro-South in spite of a personal feeling for the eccentric Adams, was struck dumb. Nobody spoke of the American war any more, that is, nobody that mattered, for it was the starving weavers of the Midlands, unimportant masses, who held a meeting that ended in a vote of shouting enthusiasm for a message to Mr. Adams—"We are pinched a bit for lack of cotton here, but for God's sake don't give up. We are with you; good luck to every stroke."

Mr. Adams, buoyed up by victory, took a high tone— "I am ignorant of the precise legal aspects of the question, but if these vessels escape, it is superfluous to point out to your lordship that this is war." His lordship was flabbergasted; the eccentric American talked like an Englishman! But he did not want war, oh dear no, especially since the experiments in constructing Ericsson turrets in Her Majesty's dockyard had not been successful, and the grapevine telegraph said the seven new American cruisers would travel at the vertiginous speed of sixteen knots. Besides

Argyll was pounding the government in the Lords and Mr.
John Bright making a tremendous fuss in the lower house;
it would never do to risk an overturn on such a point. He
stopped the sailing of the rams by executive order, and that
was the end of the Confederacy's hope of finding a lion to
pull its chestnuts from the fire.

The iron wall moved in.

34

AUTUMN MANEUVERS

Along, the Rapidan, the old Rapidan, river of war, the armies faced each other drearily. October, and dejection beneath the falling rain; the cavalry rode picket and hoped for fresh milk, the infantry played dominoes with a set from which the double four was missing. Engineer officers must consider the safety factor first; it makes them occupational pessimists, and George Gordon Meade, ex- of the U. S. Engineers, did not feel strong enough to attack. Mathematical reason lay with him; Halleck had taken a division from his army to hold down riotous New York, more than a corps for side-shows along the South Carolina coast, and now two corps more to relieve Thomas in Chattanooga. The council of generals agreed on defense without rapture, spirits and flags hung limp and General Meade hoped that the order relieving him of command would not be too rudely phrased.

Beyond the river the young Turks gathered round General Lee—Ewell with his piping krawk, jovial Early booming like a cannon behind a fog of beard, gay Stuart, the heart-breaker, all stars and grace, a song on his lips and in his heart. No doubts harassed them; Gettysburg had been an accident, a *je ne sais quoi*, fought on foreign soil and under an evil star. The men were poor in accouterments, but sound in body and of great heart; *Les Misérables*, Lee's Miserables, they never could be beaten. Let us deal with this Federal army as we have with the others, drive them, drive them.

Lee faced the young men with that calm, benignant air which he alone shared with General Washington; if he exulted in his heart at being the leader of such a band of brothers, or despaired amid lost battles and abandoned hopes, he gave no sign. His face remained serene with inner peace. What does the result matter, sobeit the duty be well performed? He, too, had learned, in the dark hour when Pickett's men came flooding back from Cemetery height, this lesson—despise no man.

"General Meade," he said slowly, "is an exceedingly able officer, and if I make any mistake before him he will be prompt to take advantage of it." Still Meade was an engineer, an occupational skeptic and slow to move, as he had shown on the retreat from Pennsylvania. Let the thrust be lightning fast and he might lose his mental balance as Pope had lost his on this same ground—ages ago.

They planned it together, a wide sweep left around the flank of the depleted Union army where it lay along the river east of the railroad. A low range of hills, Clarke's Mountain, would hide the move from prying Federals. Stuart led; on the 9th October his riders clashed with Kilpatrick's Union horsemen along the Robertson River, with the Confederate army rolling up behind to Madison Court House. Kilpatrick, an original, was also a good soldier. He saw the danger, stayed to fight and, though beaten, gained a precious dozen hours by resolute resistance. On the night of the tenth, Stuart got round his wings and drove him through Culpeper in rout; the next morning Lee's main guard came swinging into that town.

The thrust was too fast; Lee had outmarched his supply trains and had to wait for them to come up. It was not fast enough; on the 10th Meade had got behind the Rappahannock, with French's III Corps at Sulphur Springs as his flank-guard. Nothing developed the next day, which was the one Lee spent at Culpeper; Meade hurried the V and VI Corps back across the stream for a riposte at Lee's rear, imagining that the Confederates were taking a long circle among the spurs of the Blue Ridge. French was to follow them in.

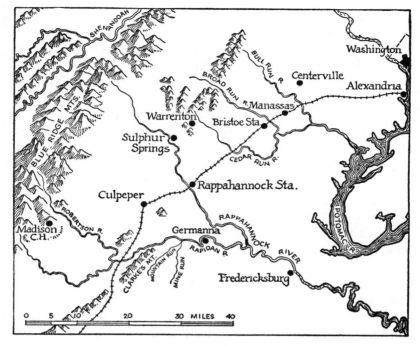

Lee's Blow

Meade was right, of course, but had counted without Lee's speed or French's hesitancy. Once they had supplies the Confederates were off on the wings of the wind for Warrenton. French delayed; twilight found him still at Sulphur Springs, isolated, with outpost guns cracking all around him as rebel divisions came up to hem him in. Disaster? Not quite—Gregg was with him, Gregg and Custer, and the cavalry put up so active a front, with partial charges and little ambushes among the groves, that Lee never suspected French's presence. He took it for a cavalry rearguard, not worth driving hard, and bade his tired men rest. During the night French got away to join the other Union corps behind Cedar Run, whither Meade had withdrawn them at the news from Sulphur Springs.

Score one for the Confederate side as well; that night

Stuart pushed ahead with his vanguard of cavalry, found himself between two Union corps. His men slept in the woods without fires; at daybreak they appeared with a shout on the flank of the II Corps. The II Corps retreated in haste, believing everything but the truth—namely, that they outnumbered these bold intruders three to one.

Meade would not stand at Broad Run either; it left his right flank open to those attacks through the mountain gaps that had ruined Pope, but A. P. Hill, who led Lee's vanguard, drove in so fast that he forced the V Corps to a stand at Bristoe Station. The corps was badly overmatched, but had Warren, the hero of Round Top, for a commander, a man with an uncanny eye for a position. He anchored his left wing on a railroad embankment with the corps artillery to sweep the approaches, and maneuvered his right to tempt an attack. Hill made it with energy, ran into a fire that blew his column head to hell and turned the promising advance into a bloody repulse. Lee came up with Ewell's wing to find everything disorganized at the front, Meade inexpugnably intrenched at Centerville, and the campaign a washout. Hill tried to excuse himself—"Well, general," said Lee, "bury those poor men and let us say no more about it."

Nothing more was said, but the railroad had been torn up during the push, the army had no supplies and must retreat to get them. Meade followed up slowly, rebuilding railroad as he came, with Kilpatrick handling the cavalry on pursuit. "Kill-cavalry" they called him in the service; he drove his mounts hard, arriving at Warrenton on horses whose tongues were hanging out to find Stuart for a battle. Kilpatrick detached Custer with a reserve for emergencies and steered into the fight. It hung equal; Custer could not resist the temptation to make a thrilling charge and went in with a cheer, confound the orders. Just at that moment Fitz Lee and the rebel horsemen Stuart had hidden for such a case came galloping onto Kilpatrick's flank, the Union formations broke up and were driven back on the main army.

It did not matter; both forces were along the Rappahannock again in early November. Lee meant to dispute the passage; he had a bridgehead at Rappahannock Station, with artillery supports and Hay's brigade of Early. Meade sent Warren against the bridgehead, whose keen engineering eye caught a defect in the layout of the position. He secretly massed his artillery, opened a surprise fire that knocked out Hay's supports, rushed the bridgehead and snared the whole brigade—"the saddest chapter in the history of this army," thought Lee, withdrawing to the Rapidan and his old position.

His right, under Early, lay from Clarke's Mountain to an affluent of the Rapidan, Mine Run, with Stuart watching the lower fords; the left was beyond the railroad, under Hill, with a gap between, where the mountain prevented crossing. Meade scouted the position and believed it could be broken. Not by a thrust into the gap from across the river, but crash through Stuart's cavalry screen at the lower fords and a lightning-fast march around Early's flank and rear to cut in between the widespread rebel wings from behind.

It was all worked out on a minute schedule based on timed marching speed over measured roads. The trains and heavy artillery stayed behind; iron rations and fast marching, boys, and start at dawn on the 26th November. Warren and the V Corps were to make the long swing south, through Culpeper Mine Ford, with the I Corps behind; the II Corps to cross at Germanna Ford; French, with the III and VI corps, to cross at Jacob's Mill Ford and pin Early in the corner of Mine Run and the Rapidan with an abrupt attack.

First fault—the river rose, the pontoon bridges were too short, the engineers had to piece out with trestling and hours went by. Second fault—Kilpatrick failed to smother Stuart, he scouted Warren's movement and carried the news to Lee. By nightfall Hill was rushing from the western end of the line to a concentration for battle. Third and fatal fault— French of the III Corps, "a gay companion, full of wit and sparkling humor," gave a merry party at headquarters and left details to his subordinates. They got mixed on roads and never crossed till morning of the 27th. The movement had no pivot, Early was not pinned; he strung his men out along Mine Run and spent all day and night throwing up fortifications behind the stream.

In the morning, when French did get across, Lee was on the ground with Hill's wing. He attacked French so furiously that the general had to call on the VI Corps for help, and when Warren got up to the other end of the Mine Run line in the afternoon it was fortified beyond any possibility of attack. Even the soldiers knew it; Meade saw them pinning scraps of paper to their blouses with names written thereupon so the bodies could be identified after the repulse.

Lee had the bind on the situation now. The Federals were all strung out, with no trenches and little food; by fast work, he could punish them severely. He left Early to hold the Mine Run lines, swung Hill south in a wide curve to roll up Meade's line from the flank, and at daybreak next morning sent the regiments forward in a regular Stonewall Jackson attack amid a chorus of hurrahs.

Surprise—the hurrahs roused nothing but a few startled rabbits. Hill's men charged on for half a mile through empty forest, then halted and threw out scouts, to discover that Meade had adroitly decamped during the night. Tweedledum and Tweedledee were back where they had started along the Rapidan, that old river of war, and the game had been declared a draw after exchanging pawns. The war went on.

35

THE INDECISIVENESS OF DECISIONS

SIR EDWARD CREASY considered Gettysburg one of the fifteen decisive battles of the world, and with Gettysburg, Stephen V. Benét sweep the pieces from the board, holding the result no longer in doubt; the mate will follow in a given number of moves. It is probable that a Jung word-association test on most people, with "Civil War" as the impulse-phrase, would produce either "Gettysburg" or "Gettysburg Address" as a response.

This is reasonable with regard to the address, which contains all of American aspiration and consecration, of reverence for the past and hope for the future, from the Declaration of Independence to the release of the slaves. But it is profoundly untrue with regard to the battle, which decided nothing except that the South could not conquer the North. The South had never supposed that it could; more, it had never wanted to. The whole Southern scheme of life was based on the idea that only beings on a lower plane of existence should be conquered, and the Yankee, though an inferior and rather obnoxious organism, was tacitly accorded the status of a reasonable being.

The invasion of the Southern states by the armies of the Union was immediately political in its object—to secure possession of the fountainheads of authority and return those states to their allegiance, a kind of exalted police duty. When Grant took Vicksburg a large part of his army ceased field operations to enter directly upon such political duties. The National army in Missouri did hardly anything else. Lee's invasion of Pennsylvania, on the other hand, was political only at the second remove; it did not aim at destroying the established governments in the Northern states, but only at subjecting them to a certain amount of pressure. It was undertaken for purely military reasons, and although most of the failures of the Confederacy were political (failure to win the border states, to persuade England to intervene) the Gettysburg offensive failed on military and not on political grounds.

In view of the fact that the event of the battle was so shocking to contemporaries who had come to regard the words "Lee" and "victory" as synonymous, it is worth while discovering what those grounds were. Pickett's magnificent charge has an inevitable attraction for the eye; one tends to be satisfied with the explanation that it was made and repulsed and that Lee admitted it was an error of judgment to order it. But this does not carry us far in the direction of discovering why the error in judgment occurred or why the charge was repulsed. It was not merely that the movement was too bold, or wrong in a technical, chess-game sense; the maneuver round Pope's flank at Second Manassas was just as bold, the encircling columns at Savage Station were just as bad tactically, Jackson's sweep at Chancellorsville was positively foolhardy—but all of them succeeded brilliantly.

Lee himself thought the explanation was the lack of Jackson; he was mistaken. The Army of Northern Virginia was all it had ever been in personnel and leadership, and Lee's own judgment was less bad than he and some of the recent critics who claim he underestimated Meade would like to have us think. He read Meade's mind as closely as he had Pope's or Hooker's—an unenterprising man with considerable ability at handling defensive positions. It was not Meade he underestimated but the Army of the Potomac, the Northern people, the thing he had failed to comprehend from the first. For if any one fact emerges from the tangled account of Gettysburg it is this—that the Union victory was achieved by no one man, but by the cooperation of a large number of men, each appearing, as though by a miracle, in exactly the right place.

When the II Corps is caught isolated on the first day, it is Reynolds, the most complete soldier in the army, who sees the importance of Gettysburg and places the corps in position to hold it; when he falls, it is Doubleday, a fourth-rate tactician simply too unskillful to retreat, who keeps the corps there; of all possible officers, it has to be Howard, burning to erase the stigma of Chancellorsville, who next comes on the field; and as the rebels are making their sunset attack, who should turn up but reckless Judson Kilpatrick to overawe them with an insane cavalry movement. It is the same on the second day; Warren, the engineer, appears at Little Round Top at the crucial moment; the perfectly drilled V Corps arrives to stop Hood. The stars in their courses fought against the Confederacy, right on through Pickett's charge that would have gone through any line not held by Hancock. Such a chapter of coincidence is impossible; when accident is repeated a dozen times the accidental explanation will no longer serve and we must look further.

The accidental explanation will not serve. Gettysburg is simply one step farther along the line than Chancellorsville. If Antietam should have been a portent to Lee, Chancellorsville should have sent cold shivers up his spine. He won a great victory there, but it was a strategic victory only, a triumph over the mind of Joseph Hooker, not over the Union army. In all the previous battles minor Union commanders had failed or regiments had broken. At Chancellorsville their conduct was as flawless as that of the Confederates, only the general did not know how to use his machine. "Be sure to put in *all* your men" was Lincoln's parting caution to Hooker before the battle, but the combination had been too big for him to grasp, and two of his corps only got in to cover the retreat.

Hooker had been trying to manage the complicated attacking maneuver; Meade was not only a better soldier, he also had a simpler problem; he simply could not help putting in all his men. Lee attacked him at every point in succession; all he had to do was keep a clear head and stand his ground. He had seen enough of war by this time—any of the Union generals had seen enough of war by this time—to do that; the rest followed as logically as conclusion succeeds premise. The appearances of Reynolds, Doubleday, Kilpatrick and the others at the right moments were not accidents but incidents; the Union infantry was full of generals who knew how to take advantage of the ground, the cavalry was loaded with valiant youths. What Lee attacked at Glendale was an armed mob; what he attacked at Second Bull Run was a group of quarrelsome old men; at Chancellorsville, he attacked a man; but at Gettysburg he came into collision with a system. The Army of the Potomac had developed to such an extent it no longer needed brains; it needed only someone to see that it did not fall over its own feet, which Meade was quite capable of doing.

He had not Lee's intellect, but he had an instrument infinitely more powerful than Lee's, and in the succeeding Mine Run campaign the combination worked out to a state of perfect equilibrium, which may be expressed mathematically:

$$\text{Army of Northern Virginia} + \text{Lee} = \text{Army of the Potomac} + \text{Meade}$$
$$2 + 4 = 4 + 2$$

The danger for the Confederacy obviously lay in the fact that its figures were constant; it could hardly improve upon the tactical genius of Lee, which was a maximum, nor could it increase the numbers of its soldiers, whereas the Army of the Potomac was guaranteed an unlimited supply of recruits and might some day produce a general who was a 3 or even a 4.

In other words, in the political factor, the thing that made the Army of the Potomac a 4 with an inexhaustible reservoir of other 4s behind it was the real danger; the spirit of voluntary combination. The South, a democracy of the classical type, believed combination on such a scale, such regulation, impossible without the sacrifice of individuality; they conceived of the Republic as the narrowly knitted federal league prescribed by the letter of the Constitution. They looked upon it much as Chios or Mitylene on the Athenian League of Pericles.

They did not realize that the North had developed a much stronger and more imperial structure, a type of polity new in the world. Combination is not new in the world; the Romans were a people of combination; the Germans are, so are the Japanese. But all the classical combinations had obtained their strength by making the individual one grain of sugar in the sack, with no thought or will or direction save those furnished by the mass. They ruthlessly harried the oddity, even the oddity of genius, such as Scipio or Schubert. The Northern type of combination—which became the American type, since it triumphed—was something much more complex and valuable, and constitutes this nation's one outstanding contribution to the science of human relations, a contribution not even yet thoroughly understood.

It lies not in that spirit of voluntary combination alone, but in the ability to form combinations for certain objectives, maintaining perfect freedom of action in all other respects; to divide the mind into water-tight compartments, as it were, to give complete obedience in one direction while maintaining complete independence in others. The ideal has not always been attained, it is true; it tends to shade into the more restrictive type of combination, as in the case of prohibition; but it has remained the ideal, and the ideal has been held in an amazing number of cases.

Americans are a race of "joiners"; they should exult over the fact, it is their greatest title to fame. It enables them to form an association for the improvement of musical taste without inquiring into the social status of the members, and one for sending a rocket to the moon without examining their private morals. In Europe such bodies would be impossible unless the members were *gemütlich, sympathique,* all around the compass; every association is necessarily a general association, throwing the members together at all points.

Americans are a race of joiners; it has enabled them to form those strange caravans that subdued a continent, and those research bodies which are the glory of science. The husking-bee, the house-building-bee, are the characteristic American institutions. Once their purpose is accomplished, they disband and no more is heard of them.

This implies an extraordinary flexibility of mind and a high degree of tolerance. The fault, the fatal fault of the Confederacy was that its system possessed neither. Tolerance was reserved for the small circle of the elect. It was intolerant of any but received opinion; it was inflexible, Chinese, dead, static. It was not without splendid virtues; ability (when found in the right places) made its way more swiftly to the top through the loose Southern organization than through the tighter organization of Northern society. But such ability, unless it were genius itself, arrived at the top not quite capable of performing its tasks. The Northern system furnished talent with such an elaborate apparatus of training and support that it became the equal of genius. It is not without significance that the Southern commanders at the beginning of the war—Lee, Longstreet, Johnston, Bragg, Forrest—were still the Southern commanders at the end of the war, mostly older men, while the Union, with an air of prestidigitation, was producing such young tigers as Sheridan, Custer, Wilson, Upton and Kilpatrick. The South, like most aristocracies, was deficient in education, both of the corporate body and of the individual member.

It also had the other common aristocratic defect, interior disunity. Your people of combination finds its problems simplified; it can continue to serve an idea, the purpose of the group, although the personal representative of that idea may be somewhat unlovely. Individualism can offer only personality as a focus for devotion, and the South was, unfortunately, not rich in attractive personalities. Jefferson Davis was a brilliant intellectual but the last man in the world to excite sentimental enthusiasms, as cold as an iceberg; and his most prominent and capable assistant, Judah P. Benjamin, was draped in the strangeness of the alien. The successive commanders in the West (after the fall of Albert Sidney Johnston)—Joe Johnston, Pemberton, Bragg —were all of the Davis type, forceful, intellectual, precise and chilling. Their very existence generated quarrel and complaint.

All the more, then, does the personality of Robert E. Lee stand out against this background. He had that rarest of qualities, character, the unmistakable willingness to follow his view of the right, be the consequences what they would; the unselfed ability to subordinate his own feelings to the general good. He had a strong sense of justice overlaid with so deep a sympathy for human shortcomings that he was never unable to forgive the wrong and parole the prisoner. And, as it happened, he was the intellectual as well as the moral superior of the other Confederate leaders. It was no wonder that he acquired a personal following not surpassed by that of Washington, perhaps not equaled by that of Washington. "Country be damned!" exclaimed Henry Wise in the hour when everything was crumbling, at Appomattox. "There is no country. There has been no country, general, for a year or more. You are the country for these men. They have fought for you. If you demand the sacrifice there are still thousands of us who will die for you."

As time went on, as defeat sharpened the tempers and dulled the minds of the other rebel leaders, Lee became the only cohesive force within the Confederacy; in the last days the government practically abdicated in favor of a kind of Lee dictatorship, which might have saved the day if it had come sooner. For it is the virtue of the aristocratic democracy that it can produce such characters, that it can find men to entrust with its liberties during an emergency when monarchy alone, the single control, will give it the strength to beat off the attacks to which it is subjected.

Lee's one defect as a leader was that he really was the kind of plaster saint Lincoln is in danger of being made by admiring schoolboys. There was something unearthly about the man's best moments. He was foreordained to failure by a devotion to duty so inhuman that it would not let him step a hair's breadth beyond the legal bounds of his office, even to save the Confederacy. He had no humor and none of that talent for intrigue without which real statesmanship is unattainable.

Lincoln, on the other hand, would have delighted Machiavelli. One can picture the astute Florentine in ecstasies over the maneuver for eliminating Hooker and the Chase-led "Radicals"—"A masterpiece of duplicity!" Yet Lincoln bore as good a moral character as Lee; better, for he took his morals into the tumults of the market-place while the Southerner was hiding his precious integrity behind the monastery wall of Duty. There is not a single step in the Hooker business where Lincoln can be shown to have acted with anything but the utmost sincerity and frankness; that is what makes it so interesting—it is intrigue on a new basis, strictly moral. Look at the record—Lincoln objected to retaining Hooker on grounds of his inefficiency; he was overruled by the pro-Hooker faction. He denied the general the reinforcements he had asked because Hooker had already shown himself incapable of bringing what troops he had into action and because he already had more troops than Lee; when the general protested by resigning he accepted the resignation.

The only point at which a weakness can be suspected is in permitting the radicals to foist Hooker upon him, and even here Lincoln was obedient to the spirit of the state over which he presided; a spirit of control by the general intelligence instead of individual intelligence.

The North obtained its monarchial singleness of control by combination; the South essayed to obtain it through personality, but it moved too slowly. By his personal prestige, Lee might cover the effects of the terrible defeat of Gettysburg, and he did so. Nobody in the South felt that Gettysburg was anything but a repairable error of judgment, like McClellan's during the Seven Days. But Lee commanded only the Army of Northern Virginia; his authority could do nothing to gloss over the fatal blows the Confederacy received in the West. In the last analysis, the rock on which the new republic split was the Rock of Chickamauga. Technically, the battle was a victory; actually it was a defeat, the most crushing, the most decisive any Southern army suffered.

At Gettysburg the rebels fought on "foreign" soil and against superior numbers; but there was no possible method of explaining or palliating Chickamauga, fought on ground of the Southerners' own choosing under D. H. Hill, Hood and Longstreet, against inferior numbers and with the additional advantage of Wood's terrible mistake. With the whole deck stacked in his favor the Southern soldier had failed to destroy or even seriously to cripple the Union army; at a terrible cost in lives, he had merely succeeded in confirming the Army of the Cumberland in possession of the prize of the campaign—Chattanooga.

Says D. H. Hill:—"After Chickamauga the élan of the Southern soldier was never seen again. He fought stoutly to the last, but after Chickamauga with the sullenness of despair and without enthusiasm or hope." He realized dimly, but with that marvelous clairvoyance the popular mind sometimes attains, something his commanders never realized at all—that he was not fighting human beings but elemental forces; not men, but a machine—a gigantic robot which had found its Napoleon in George H. Thomas. Nothing remained but to play out the string as best he might in that high spirit of duty of which Robert E. Lee was the standard-bearer.

And yet, such is the indecisiveness of all decisions arrived at merely by military force, Chickamauga really accomplished little more than a confirmation of Gettysburg.

Chickamauga-Chattanooga was the Eylau-Friedland of the Confederacy as Gettysburg had been its Austerlitz. Both sets of battles inflicted terrible wounds in a military sense; neither could guarantee that the patient would not survive; not even that he would fail to recover in time for a Leipsic triumph. Nationality is a precious metal that resists the most powerful reagents. Neither acid egalitarianism nor the crushing weight of Napoleonic power could keep down a Prussia much more thoroughly pulverized than the Confederacy. Poland persisted, an insoluble entity, in spite of being held in emulsion for a century and a half. An admission not merely of powerlessness but of changed standards must be secured, and the Confederacy had not even admitted military defeat, far less made the political *peccavi* that would re-create a Union not pinned together with bayonets. The existence and extent of the guerrilla warfare in the West, the number of men it took not to suppress it, but to keep it within bounds, is proof of that.

In fact, through this whole third period of the war there is evidence of a resurgent Southern political spirit, an awakened consciousness of the value of the prize the Confederacy had thus far allowed Lincoln to carry off by default. On the morning of July 4 a steamer bearing a white flag dropped down the James from Richmond. Among those aboard was Alexander Stephens, Vice-President of the Confederacy, the best negotiator in her territory and a man whose long resistance to secession would presumably make him *persona grata* in Washington. His commission bade him arrange at what point prisoners should be exchanged, an absurdity on the face of it, like making General Lee a deputy sheriff to keep soldiers from singing at night. The point was that the siege of Vicksburg was dragging interminably and the decisive battle being fought in Pennsylvania; the Richmond government wanted its best man in the capital either to negotiate a peace with Lincoln or to wring one from him by pressing the Congressional leaders in the event of Lee's victory. Unfortunately for Stephens' mission the news of

Gettysburg and Vicksburg reached Washington before he did; he was told (by note) that the method of exchanging prisoners at present was satisfactory and sent home with a flea in his ear.

On the whole, however, the Southern political offensive was less obvious and direct than this; it was more the movement of an idea expressing itself in different forms as it entered the individual brains of the actors in the drama; the Southern idea, the thesis of individualism for which the South stood, rising into active form. In all forms it was a protest against the regimentation which was all the Southerners could see in the Northern spirit of combination. It took a violent and brutal form in the draft riots because the rioters were brutal and violent men; Dr. Bickley was a phantaster, so the Golden Circle took a fantastic form; Vallandigham, the demagogue, and Horatio Seymour, the intelligent and far-seeing Governor of New York, gave it other forms still, but Stanton was right—the spirit behind all these manifestations was the same, and it was seditious in the sense that it was opposed to the war aims of the Union.

Lincoln dealt this spirit two terrific blows—the Emancipation Proclamation and the release of the political prisoners accompanied by the order to stop suppressing newspapers, no matter what their offenses. The first, so far from confusing the war for the Union with a war to end slavery, showed to the individualists and the world that the Union and human liberty were, as Daniel Webster had said, "one and inseparable." It showed the individualists that they were really fighting, not for the freer expression of their own individuality but for the suppression of the individualities of others; it appealed from the intellectual to the moral. The second of Lincoln's strokes, which has received insufficient prominence, demonstrated to the individuals that their worries were groundless; that they were losing no liberties, not even that of vilifying the President, if they joined their fortunes with those of the cooperative state. No political organization they could conceive could give them more freedom than this—

that they might hold public meetings during a great war and express opposition to that war and its purpose without cavil.

It cut the whole ground from under the feet of the Democratic party and transferred the debate to another sphere. When the political campaign of 1864 opened, the issue was no longer the expediency of the war or the re-establishment of the Union, but the method of carrying on the war and of rebinding the Union. It changed the incidence of the Democratic attack from President Lincoln to General Lincoln. By that token it made the attack stronger, for if the statesman had rendered his position inexpugnable, the ability of the captain was open to question.

Lincoln himself was perfectly conscious of this; one of his greatest moments was that in which he called the new Lieutenant-general, Ulysses S. Grant, to Washington, and placed him in control of the military affairs of the nation. He had done somewhat the same with McClellan and Halleck before, but always with reservations, always submitting suggestions for movements, making stipulations for the presence of McDowell's Corps before Washington or a column in East Tennessee. This time he removed his hands from the levers.

The step has been presented as one of supreme self-abnegation; actually, it was nothing of the sort, although it doubtless took something of the abnegatory spirit to carry it through. It was merely that Abraham Lincoln had at last realized that the full power of the prodigious machine of a modern nation at war can be developed only by the use of specialists in every department; "For the body is not one member, but many; for to one is given by spirit the word of wisdom; to another the working of miracles; to another prophecy." From the beginning he had permitted the specialist Chase to handle the department of finance as he pleased; there is traceable throughout the war a steady diminution, not of the Lincoln influence, but of Lincoln interference in the Navy and State Departments, and with the appointment of Grant the process reached the final stage and a specialist was given a free hand in the army.

Perhaps, after all, Lincoln had been willing to give a military specialist a free hand at any time, but had been unable to discern the requisite signs of ability in any of his generals. With very good reason he felt himself as able a military man as McClellan or Pope or Halleck or even Hooker. When Lincoln suggested advance along certain particular lines to any of these worthies, they put forward horse-fly objections about which there was a large amount of buzz, and no logically satisfying completeness. Half an hour's conference with Grant showed how differently his mind worked. Lincoln suggested a plan of campaign; Grant grunted and, without even commenting on it, offered an alternative scheme for war *à l'outrance* that went beyond Lincoln's imagination. The President relaxed with a sigh of gratitude and never interfered again.

So Grant went down into Virginia, prepared to treat time, ground and even men as expendable material, to try what the battle-ax could do against the rapier. And, behind him, William Tecumseh Sherman, the sword of the republic, the giant of the West, was set free at last with 100,000 men at his back and Atlanta for his goal.

BOOK IV. TO THE STARS

36

THE DEVIL IS LET LOOSE

WHAT followed was the greatest campaign in American history, one of the greatest in any history, possessing for the military student the same passionate thrill of inspired performance as a Beethoven symphony for the musician or a da Vinci portrait for the painter. During the five months since Chattanooga both armies had become perfectly attuned instruments; the high commands were accurately balanced for the rôles they assumed. Sherman's fire was mitigated by the solidity of his lieutenant, Thomas; Joseph Johnston had replaced Bragg for the Confederacy, a wary defensive man, enlivened by the boldness of his helper, Hood. The prize was worthy the contestants; Atlanta was the great city of the Confederacy, the plexus of the railroads connecting Richmond with the deep South, the indispensable center of all heavy industries, cannon and powder factories, rolling mills and depots of supply. The Union army had 98,000 men, the Confederate 71,000—exactly the odds which would permit the former to attack with even chances across the bastions of the Appalachian ridges.

Johnston thought they must attack with shouts and flashing cannon; "Cump" Sherman, he knew the man from old days at the Academy, a sanguine, liquid fellow with a bad nervous system, given to outbursts of temper, who would drive in like fury and tumble back as fast, leaving the way open for a powerful counterstroke. There was only one way he could come—straight down the railroad from Chattanooga. The Confederates spent the winter stretching breastworks thirteen feet thick across this line between the breakneck precipices around Dalton and gathering their forces for the blow. It was heavy work; Jefferson Davis, galled to the quick at being forced to dismiss his favorite, Bragg, haggled over every pound of beans, and Johnston had no art of conciliation to make things easier.

Sherman's trouble was transport; only one line down to base at Ringgold and a hundred thousand unproductive mouths to feed, with the country naked as a prima donna's bosom. They ground up corncobs to make their bread till he appointed an energetic Colonel Anderson director of rails, sent him to Nashville to steal locomotives from the northern lines and closed the supply road to civilian traffic. The population howled; the nabobs who were making a good thing out of contraband cotton turned the political thumbscrews on Lincoln, who begged Sherman to withdraw the order. "The railroad cannot supply the army and the people, too, one of them must quit," retorted the general. "I will not change the order and I beg of you to be satisfied that the clamor is humbug." Two years ago this would have been cause for dismissal, but now Lincoln merely used it to convince the politicians that he was unable to do anything with these rude warriors and they dried up, while Sherman stripped his army to the buff for work. One wagon to a regiment, no tents even for officers, no change of clothes, not even kitchen utensils. Three weeks out a Confederate exchange officer found the commanding general squatted by a roadside, coat unbuttoned, his face dark with a combined accumulation of red beard and black dirt, probing in a tomato can with a pocket knife for lumps of meat and carrot.

This program would not do for Thomas, however, who felt ill if there was a speck of dust on his boots and told an officer that the fate of an army might depend upon a buckle. He refused to eliminate his creature-comforts as flatly as Sherman to change the railroad order. The rest of them laughed at "Thomas' circus" or "Tom town," but the old man was the shield of the army, the boss round which Sherman could spin his arabesques of maneuver.

Example; on the first operation of the campaign. The army came down the roads to a stand before the buttress of Rocky Face Mountain with the Army of the Ohio (13,000) on the left under Schofield, a new man, a philosopher with a long wide beard, suspect as a dude and intellectual till one day the men saw him chewing tobacco—"He's all right, boys, look how he handles that cud." Thomas had three corps (Army of the Cumberland—61,000) in the center, McPherson two corps (Army of the Tennessee—24,000) on the right. Schofield tapped at the summits but between granite and gunnery made no headway; Thomas massed as though for assault and Johnston thought he had tempted his rash adversary. He was mistaken; the country was savage as Turkestan, without maps, but Thomas remembered having ridden through a narrow gorge, Snake Creek Gap, years before. It debouched on the banks of the Oostanaula near Resaca, behind the rebel flank and onto their railroad line. Sherman snapped at the plan his lieutenant drew; on the 9th May the Armies of the Cumberland and Ohio made a noisy pretense of attack that kept the Confederates within their lines at no sacrifice of life, while McPherson filed to the right through an awesome ravine where the sun never reached bottom, into the broken ground around Resaca.

The rebels had a cavalry division in the town. They came out and annoyed McPherson, who took them for the precursors of a bigger force and intrenched in the gut of the pass. Sherman's messenger galloped through mud and rain to urge him on, but the news rode faster to Johnston down the electric telegraph, and he had two army corps on hand by train before McPherson nerved himself to try assault. Next day the Union pressure on the Dalton lines relaxed; Johnston thought Sherman had followed the Army of the Tennessee down to Resaca, and made an attack with the design of breaking down the Federal rearguard and cutting Sherman's lifeline railroad. Mistake again; Sherman had sent only a corps to McPherson. The attack fell on Thomas and, like most attacks on the Rock of Chickamauga, broke down with loss. Johnston dared stay no longer in his fortress with McPherson hammering at his rear, and that night left for Resaca. Sherman wins this round, the Dalton lines are flanked—but he must tell McPherson, "Well, Mac, you have missed the greatest opportunity of your life."

A creek, Camp Creek, covered the west front of Resaca, with high hills behind it. Johnston had his three corps in a semicircle of fortifications from south to north, Polk, Hardee and Hood. Hood discovered that Thomas' left flank was bare and launched a stirring charge against Howard's Corps, which held it. He got not far; Sherman had discovered the weakness and threw Hooker against Hood's flank as the rebel went in. Hood was badly mauled before he could get out, but Johnston reinforced him from Hardee and ordered a stroke on Schofield for daybreak.

Before it took place there was trouble at the other end of the line, where Polk had intrenched a commanding height on the west side of Camp Creek mouth. Osterhaus, "Sow-belly Osterhaus" of Logan's Corps of McPherson, stormed a bridge and penetrated Polk's line; from the height he gained he smothered the west hill trenches under a cross-fire and won them, too. Logan got his artillery onto the eminence and, as twilight came down, shot out the railroad bridge, Johnston's only line of retreat, and began to rain shells into the streets of the town. Simultaneously, McPherson got a corps, Dodge's, across the Oostanaula lower down, and came swinging up river with a stormcloud of cavalry round him. Johnston canceled Hood's attack order and beat a hurried retreat on a pontoon bridge; next morning Sherman was in Resaca with the second round won.

Shift scenes for the next act; the mountain passes are passed, here we are in the rolling prairie between the Oostanaula and the Etowah, with Sherman getting his food down a long neck of railway line as sensitive as a giraffe's, and Johnston sitting right on his base, drawing in continual reinforcements. Rebel scouts said Sherman was moving in close column, concentrated for battle. Johnston laid a deadly ambush at Adairsville, with both flanks forward on

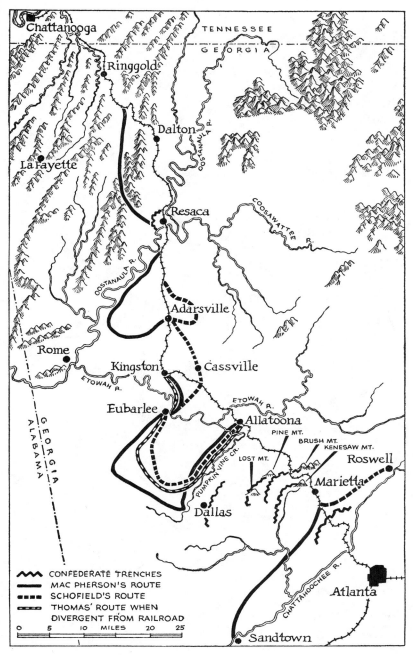

The Atlanta Campaign—Sherman and Johnston

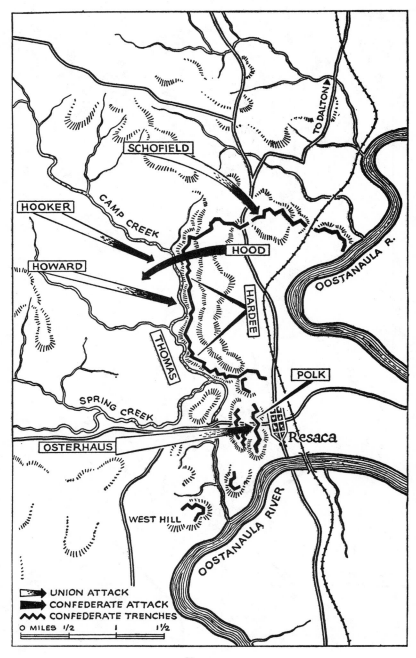

Resaca

hills, concealed, center intrenched across the intervening valley, to catch Sherman's column in a narrow funnel and crowd it to death. On the 16th, afternoon, Howard's Corps of Thomas came up out of a stream the men had crossed by wading naked with packs held overhead, to find the rear-guards stiffening; the air smelled of battle. Howard spread skirmishers and punched through the screen before him, then formed line with orders "attack at dawn."

Johnston's midnight orders were the same, but at two in the morning a wild-eyed aide roused him with the news that Garrard's Union light horse had ridden into Rome the previous noon, followed by a division of infantry, the van-guard of McPherson's whole army, which now lay outside and behind his left wing, ready to strike. Half an hour later came another Job's messenger with tidings that Schofield had worked round the Confederate right flank. Instead of trapper, Johnston was trapped; Sherman had capped his funnel with a bell of which Thomas was the clapper. He might hurt Thomas, but certain annihilation was coming from the flanks if he stopped to do it. The men were got out of their tents in the cold dawn hours for a comfortless rapid retreat past hummocks of burning stores.

The old horse could still prance, however; Johnston sent only Hardee down the normal road to Kingston, himself taking Polk and Hood cross-country to Cassville. Sherman, as he expected, followed Hardee with Thomas and McPher-son; only Schofield spread toward Cassville. The rebels tore up the railroad in retreat, twisted the rails, burned the ties and blew out the bridges; that would detain the gross of the Union army while Polk and Hood were to turn and demolish Schofield. Hardly had the rebels got into position, however, when their astonished ears caught the "fweet-weet" of a locomotive whistle and Hardee came tumbling in on the main body, with the horizon from west to east behind him a-shimmer with Union bayonets. Sherman's railroaders had actually rebuilt that line as fast as the troops marched, and Thomas had driven Hardee remorselessly before him, no chance for a stand. "That man Sherman," said a disgusted Georgian, "will never go to hell. He'll outflank the devil and get past Peter and all the heavenly hosts." Retreat again; this time across the Etowah, where it runs deep and swift through a rocky gorge north of Allatoona, and a passage may not be forced.

Sherman did not try to force a passage; the detachments he made for rail guards had brought down his numbers to nearly equal Johnston's and though General Blair was coming from the west with a new corps, 10,000 strong, he had to be careful. He gave Blair a rendezvous at Eubarbee, the engineers threw a bridge at that point, and the army, with twenty days' rations for a move away from its supports, crossed the Etowah into a new kind of country—a tangle of loblolly pine thicket so dense one cannot see twenty feet in any direction, interspersed with quicksand pools and high bosses of mountain which would be called mesas farther west. The direction was Dallas; from that point the army could cut in behind the Allatoona defile at Ackworth and get back to the railroad line.

Geary of Hooker's Corps struck rebel outposts near Dallas on the evening at May 25, and there was fighting. Hooker found the Confederates intrenched on hills behind Pumpkin Vine Creek, but kept feeding his divisions in on the left as fast as they came up, and near New Hope Church delivered an assault with all his old spirit. Howard heard the tumult and, gathering all Schofield's men (who were on the road with him), rushed through the dark of a gathering night to fall on at Hooker's left, near Pickett's Mill. A storm came up; thunder, lightning and artillery fire cracked across the night as the armies locked in fierce grapple, but at six in the morning, with Palmer's Corps of Thomas coming up behind Hooker and the Army of the Tennessee falling in on his right, the assault had to give over with nothing gained and many men lost.

The next day there was a continuous hot skirmisher fire along the line; officers dared not appear on horseback, the

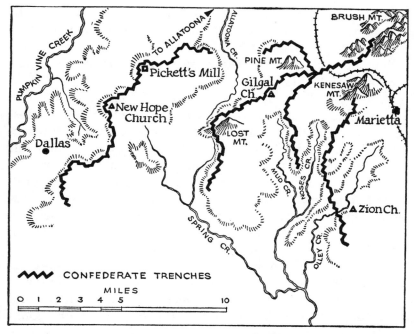

The Fighting Around Marietta

sharpshooters picked them off. Men called the place "the Hell Hole." On the third day Howard tried the Confederate right again, thought he had outflanked it and went in full steam, but only fell into a re-entrant angle of Hood's line and was severely punished. Sherman's line was a mess, with divisions, brigades and regiments everywhere as they had come in down the back roads, and army commanders did not know the location of half their men. The Union leader adroitly used the fact to build up a new movement, by picking the pieces of Schofield's Army of the Ohio out of line and filing them left, behind the rest, for a wide flanking sweep toward Allatoona. Johnston spotted signs of activity around his left; he thought the Federals would try to do the same thing again, and ploying Hardee's Corps into heavy columns, tried to hurl it through McPherson's center, the hinge of the movement as he imagined it. McPherson received them with a concave line and a centered artillery fire that brought men down by hundreds; meanwhile Schofield and the cavalry worked around behind Johnston's right flank, captured Allatoona and the river-crossings and compromised the whole Confederate line.

As usual the general advance found Johnston vanished into the pinelands southward. Sherman held Schofield fast in his new position while he slid Thomas and McPherson around behind him to base on the railroad line, then felt forward; General Hazen noted that the men in his brigade were letting their hair grow "till they looked like prophets." Down in Atlanta, Braxton Bragg had arrived as the personal representative of Jefferson Davis. He surveyed the operations of his successor (and enemy) Johnston with a jaundiced eye and reported to the President that the man was destroying the morale of the rebel army by constant retreat under heavy losses. Joseph E. Brown, the truculent and not too intelligent governor of Georgia, threatened General Johnston with civil arrest if he persisted in his obnoxious habit of interrupting commercial railroad traffic for his supply trains. And on the 5th June Sherman's vanguard made contact with the new Confederate position.

It was the usual thing; double revetted trenches with slashed timber and *chevaux-de-frise*—frizzy horses—out in front, stretching from the mesa of Lost Mountain to that of Brush Mountain with Pine Mountain making a salient in the center. The lines covered every point of attack; they were prodigious—too prodigious, declared Sherman, riding along to inspect them from afar, at least ten miles overlong for such numbers as Johnston had, there must be a weak spot somewhere. He was opposite Pine Mountain as he spoke; at that moment his horse shied to the kick of Minié ball and he looked up to see a party of rebel officers on an outcrop looking down. "Give them a shot," he called to a battery near by. The third shell fell on a group and slew the Confederate bishop-general, Polk. "Blizzards" Loring, who once held Grant off on the Yazoo, got his corps.

The steady snap of skirmisher fire rose crescendo as divisions all along the line pecked to find the soft spot; day and night they tapped away. The spring rains had come; the streams were up and the roads quagmires; out on the flanks life was frugal; the wagons with supplies could not get through. It prohibited the flanking move Sherman would have made, but on the 15th Thomas seeped men into the interstices of the Confederate line caused by the rough ground around the foot of Pine Mountain and pinched out that salient. Johnston drew men from his right to take up the shock and held the new line behind. On this McPherson tried the weakened lines at the foot of Brush Mountain and made a lodgement among its spurs; Johnston had to reinforce from his left, whereupon Schofield assailed the disgarnished wing and broke through near Gilgal Church.

Johnston had foreseen this would be the weak point; he merely withdrew to a new line of trenches behind Mud Creek. The maneuver left him, however, with a bad right-angled salient in his center. Thomas posted batteries at the angle and enfiladed the line in both directions. That was the 17th; in the morning the Nationals woke up to find Johnston gone again, back to another line of forts reaching from Kenesaw Mountain down Noses Creek. As they tramped across country to face it, General Hazen noted how the corpses of the last days' fighting seemed to have settled into the ground, the tall fresh grasses growing round them till they presented a weird appearance of flatness, of two-dimensionality.

Sherman was in a good deal of a pickle; he could not outflank to his left around Kenesaw, that would leave Johnston nearer the Allatoona base than he, and the wary Confederate would break up his supply-line. In the other direction the rebel trenches ran far down Noses Creek. The rain went on, the roads were drowned, it was impossible to truck supplies down to the right flank for a circling move at that end. Thomas suggested building regular siege approaches, but No, answered Sherman, Johnston will only construct one trench behind another as fast as we move forward. He ordered an intense artillery fire along the creek, then a formal assault around Kenesaw, where Johnston would think himself strongest and would therefore have fewest men.

It went surging in with desperate gallantry, but it failed, 2,500 men killed or hurt, among the latter a young topographical officer, Lieutenant Ambrose Bierce, who was invalided out to far-away California. But the effort was not altogether resultless, for during the battle Schofield had gained a foothold across Noses Creek. He developed it; the rains dried up as though Kenesaw Battle had been a signal, and, supplies coming through, he pushed on, with Stoneman's cavalry working through to raid deep behind Johnston's lines. The advance held so much of menace that Johnston drew Hood's Corps from his other wing to stop it. Brave Hood signalized his arrival by another attack, trying to break the link between Schofield and Hooker's Corps of Thomas, which stood next in line. Like every other the assault failed. Jacob Cox was at the point, a remarkable man of all the talents, world-famous as an authority on microscopy and cathedral architecture, literator, politician, artist, soldier—everything. He commanded a division of Schofield's; scouted the attack, massed reserves behind his line and delivered a crushing counter that caught Hood's men on the ebb, loose and disordered. They gave; Cox won through to Zion Church, Hooker joined in the advance and Johnston's flank was broken again.

That night, July 2, while Sherman's council of generals was laughing over the droll figure Howard made when Davis told one of his dirty stories (had the courage of his convictions, did Howard; he even dared lecture Sherman for curing a headache with whisky "when a Seidlitz powder would do you more good")—while they were laughing, Johnston's guns began to throb and they ran out to find him covering another retreat with cannon fire.

Sherman rode up with the advance; they had won Marietta, but all around and about the crossing of the next river, the Chattahoochee, there was another immense series of forts, redoubts and artillery. Thomas was locked in position around them; McPherson went downstream to Sandtown and began planting batteries as though to force a crossing, drawing the attention of Johnston's river-guards. Cox, with a single division, had gone the other way. Near Roswell, there is a fish-dam and a ford at a creek mouth. The intelligent Cox hid some men behind a hill. At a signal a swarm of pontoons pulled out the mouth of the creek while his infantry went stumbling and slipping across the stones of the fish-dam. The Confederate artillery picket opposite fired one shot and fled; a pontoon bridge was run over, and by night most of Schofield's Corps was on the south side.

The rest of the army followed; Johnston had to cross, too, and the last great barrier before Atlanta was passed. In the city there was panic; the Georgia delegation at the Richmond Congress snarled bitterly at Jefferson Davis as the author of their woes, who in turn snarled at Johnston, who told Bragg he saw no means of stopping Sherman short of Atlanta itself. "My opinion of his abilities is somewhat higher than that the newspaper editors entertain." The wires to Richmond crackled; on the night of the 11th July an order spun down them removing Johnston.

When the rebel soldiers heard the news they lifted their heads and turned toward the invader with new hope; anything was better than this slow decay with Sherman always on their flanks. Fabius Cunctator had failed them; but now they had been given a leader to lead them to battle—Hood, one-armed Hood, with the heart and face of a lion, renowned for his bravery in an army whose outstanding characteristic was courage. Look out, Sherman, here we come.

37

MORITURI TE SALUTENT

WILLARD's Hotel for Gentlemen and Ladies swarmed with officers in March, most of them in full dress and all of them in full importance. The ranking provost of the Army of Louisiana, who had experienced the rigors of a hard campaign at the bar of the Palmetto House in New Orleans, was expounding military strategy to an audience of newspaper men. Richard Dana, whose two years before the mast had given him a low opinion of bar-fly officers, looked up from the layout of two ink-bottles and a vinegar-cruet in time to see a short, round-shouldered, seedy-looking man come through the door, leading a boy by the hand. The eye was drawn by the fellow's peculiar gait, a lurching heave, as though the next step would bring him down on his nose—and then Mr. Dana gulped at the sight of three stars on his shoulder-straps. He jumped up, but others had made the discovery before him and the whole lobby hummed with "Grant—Grant." Mr. Dana experienced a vivid sense of disappointment; like most people in the East he had expected a kind of super-Burnside, a splendid, booming Lohengrin, armored in personality, and this dull stump—!

The squat man, as oblivious of the crowd's disapproval as he had been of its indifference, signed the register and, still towing his son, pitched along to his room. The next morning he was closeted with Lincoln. It must have been a curious interview. There were no witnesses, but one inevitably wonders what these two, so alike in their rugose exteriors, so alike in their possession of the inner light which enables its owner to disregard every exterior, had to say to each other. A curious interview, terminating in mutual approval and confidence.

Then came meeting with Meade and Halleck and plans for the campaign. The others gaped at the huge simplicity of Grant's concept; let the Army of the Potomac follow Lee wherever he went, clutching him in so fierce a grip that he could neither help the other Southern generals nor himself maneuver, while a minor force—the Army of the James—struck through from Fort Monroe up the Peninsula of Virginia close behind Lee and the great western army under Sherman stormed Atlanta and wheeled onto his rear from far behind him—the tactics of Iuka and Corinth repeated on the grandest scale with the whole nation for a field. There was a silence.

"I don't understand these military technicalities," said Lincoln, "but as near as I can make out, you propose to hold the leg while Sherman takes off the skin."

"That's about the size of it," replied Grant, and turned to Meade; he, Grant, would accompany the Army of the Potomac but Meade would remain its general—would General Meade suggest any changes? Yes, said Meade, there are too many corps and they are too small, let us combine them into four. It was done—the II Corps, with Hancock of Cemetery Ridge, now whole of his wound, for commander; V Corps, under Warren of Round Top; VI Corps under Sedgwick, "Good Uncle John" Sedgwick, big-boned man who carried a heart of gold behind a high, vigorous face that would have looked splendid under a helmet; and IX Corps under Burnside, too slow of wit to be the head of an army, yet stout enough to be the arm of one . . . but whom shall we have to command the cavalry? Buford had died in bed in December, Gregg was too mentally fluid, blazing enthusiasm one moment, utter despair the next; Custer a gallant idiot who could lead a charge but do little else; Kilpatrick a madman, Pleasanton an intriguer—they canvassed the list. Halleck cut the knot—"How would Sheridan do?"

"The very man!" cried Grant, clapping his knee and dispatched a telegram for him within the hour.

The new trooper, on arrival, proved doubtful of his own qualifications. He liked service with the infantry; had met Grant only once and Meade never, was not sure he could come up to their exacting standards—or, to put it plainly, preferred the freer rein of the armies of the west, where a whole division would turn out on parade to bleat at a commander whose behavior they considered sheep-like. Grant eyed him through a cloud of cigar-smoke, answering in monosyllables, then remarked that the Chief of Cavalry would have a free hand here on one condition—that he kept Jeb Stuart out of mischief. Sheridan emitted an explosive sigh of relief and accepted the charge, but his worst apprehensions were borne out when he reached the front and found all the horsemen strung out in long picket lines around the camp. There was a stormy interview with Meade before Grant would allow him to concentrate; then the army was ready.

The advance started on May 5th, synchronous with Sherman's. In the morning the slow wagons rumbled down to Germanna Ford, where the crossing had been made before Mine Run, with long snakes of infantry filling the roads around them. Lee did not rebut their passage; they filed over into the Wilderness, a deserted mining region with knolls and oakbound ridges peering above a tangle of undergrowth dense to suffocation on either side of the cow-paths they were pursuing. Around them "the little green leaves were just opening and purple violets in great quantities by the wayside."

Hancock's II Corps had the lead behind the screen of riders with Warren right behind, and Sedgwick in his rear, Burnside still distant. At 7:30 in the morning, Warren's flankers reported the enemy along Orange Turnpike. This would be Lee's vanguard. The news sped back to Meade's headquarters at the Wilderness Tavern, who ordered Warren to swing into line and attack with his whole force, while Sedgwick came in on his right. The opponent was Ewell, whom Lee had hurried forward with matchless audacity to surprise and crush the flank of the Army of the Potomac among the tangled trees where Grant's heavy surplus of numbers would do him no good.

Griffin of Warren's advance struck Ewell's center hard and, though every tree was a trench and every knob a fortress, burst through his first line, broke the second and threw both back onto the reserves. This was the Army of Northern Virginia, not used to giving way; the resistance was desperate, the losses heavy. Griffin was on a narrow front that became disordered as he advanced; on his right the VI Corps got tangled in roadless woodland and did not support him. Ewell worked round this wing, flanked Griffin's line with skirmishers and drove it in, then pushed back his center. Griffin, with his division all cut to pieces, came riding back to headquarters about noon, his face flushed and stern, to curse Meade because his men had been uselessly sacrificed. Out on the left of this first battle, Ewell had worked through the woods in open order to envelop the flank of another of Warren's divisions, Wadsworth. The attack came as a surprise, Wadsworth's flank gave way, he lost some guns and prisoners and was rushed back nearly to Wilderness Tavern, where artillery, a patch of open ground and heroic efforts by Warren himself brought matters to a stand. The struggle settled down to a murderous rifle-fight from cover, with a hundred men killed every minute and the soldiers on both sides burrowing into the ground like moles.

At three o'clock Sedgwick's VI Corps began to arrive on the right, just in time to halt a flanking movement Ewell had started from that direction. At four Ewell tried to drive in Warren's center, but failed, and the lines crystallized along emergency fortifications while the battle soared up south and east, where Hancock had struck Lee's second corps, A. P. Hill, along and about the Orange Plank Road. Hill put up a viciously effective defensive battle from ravines and copses; in that tangle they could not get round his flanks, simply straight push and never mind the losses, but Hancock was a good driver and kept putting fresh troops in. By sunset, Hill's lines were beginning to melt and his formations were badly shattered. Another hour's daylight would have done him in, but Grant was not Joshua to make the sun stand still, and it sank down on a shocking scene of blood among the spring violets just as Sedgwick delivered and failed in one more assault.

Both commanders were surprised; Grant by Lee's boldness and skill of tactic; Lee by Grant's resolution. Each was sure his own quality would win on the morrow. Lee reorganized Hill's men for a stand; they and Ewell were to hold fast, trenches and forest being their sure defense. His third corps, Longstreet's, came up during the night; he planned to swing it wide onto Hancock's flank, as he had swung Jackson on Howard at Chancellorsville, rolling up the Federal line. Stuart and the cavalry would work a wider circuit around Longstreet's circuit; as the attack succeeded, they would complete the rout of the huddled and helpless Union army. On the other side Grant now had Burnside's IX Corps in hand. Hancock was to press straight ahead through Hill's front, but guarding well his left flank where Grant suspected Lee of being about to attack him. Burnside would come in between Hancock and Warren, taking Hill's weakened formations between two fires. Each commander, in short, knew what the other intended to do, and thought his own plan better.

At five Hancock opened the ball. Hill, hard hit on the previous day, was rushed backward down Orange Plank Road. Hancock exultantly pulled in his left flank-guards to keep the attack swinging, and Lee ordered his trains prepared for instant retreat on Richmond. There was no need; ten minutes after the order Longstreet struck the weakened left wing of the II Corps and it collapsed. To Hancock an aide with deadly fear in his eyes dashed up—"General Mott's division has broken, sir, and is coming back." As he spoke a crowd of troops, all disorderly, some with guns and some without, came through the woods, followed by an outburst of yells and shouting. Hancock's flank was gone, the army was compromised.

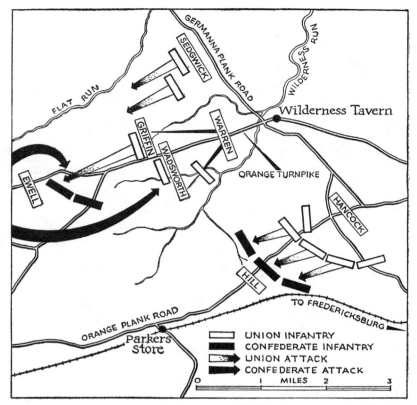

The Wilderness—The First Day

But Hancock himself was worth half an army. He rode among the fugitives, shouting—"Halt here! Halt here!" in a voice like a trumpet. The soldiers rallied around the beloved general; Grant sent him the army reserve. "It was a welcome sight to see them coming along that road, Hays riding at their head, a strong-built, rough sort of man, with a tawny beard, calm as the May morning. 'Left—prime—forward!' and they disappeared into the woods to waken the musketry with double violence. In a few moments Hays was carried past, covered with blood, shot through the head." With charge and countercharge the onslaught was stayed; Longstreet rode forward, trying to get it in motion again, took a bad wound, and the fire died out of the rebel attack.

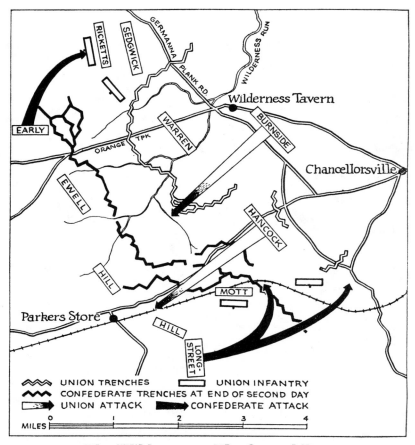

The Wilderness—The Second Day

Neither did anything come of Stuart's move; somewhere in the Wilderness south of Hancock's battle, he ran head-on into Sheridan, and locked in a motionless battle of dismounted horsemen among the thickets.

In the center Burnside was slow, did not get into position, and left Wadsworth's division of Warren to bear the brunt of the fight. Ewell attacked; Wadsworth was killed and his division riddled, but he had stopped them, and now all along the line of battle settled down to "a struggle blind as midnight, in a jungle where regiments stumbled on each other and on the enemy by turns, sometimes firing into their own ranks, guided only by the cheers and shooting that rose from the depths about them." The Union troops moved by compass. The dry leaves underfoot caught fire and the woods were full of drifting smoke that added to the grim haziness of the grapple; the wounded burned to death where they lay. Toward twilight Lee tried one more furious assault against the Union right. Ricketts' division of Sedgwick held the post—"Milroy's weary boys" they were called, garrison troops from the Shenandoah, not previously judged good enough for field work. They stampeded and the Union flank was almost turned. But Grant, stout-hearted as ever, was there, and so was Sedgwick; the gap was made good, the VI Corps counterattacked and the fight went on.

On into the dark when the armies halted to take count of their loss. The Army of the Potomac had suffered frightfully, 17,000 men down, more than twice as many as the rebels had lost. The new general from the West had fared no better than the others against Lee, the war would never end and the Union troops crawled out of their lines and began to head away eastward along the dark roads.

"Licked again, by crackey!"

At Chancellorsville House there is a three-corner. The road to the left led back across the Rappahannock, back to the Potomac, out of that grim wood to fortifications, comfort and safety; that on the right led past the rebel front, deeper than ever into the perilous and uncertain Wilderness. As the defeated troops came slogging down to the turn, the dispirited soldiers saw dimly a man in an old blue coat sitting horseback at the cross-roads with a cigar in his mouth. He silently motioned the guides of each regiment down the right-hand road. Grant.

They stared a moment—and then the slanting lines of steel took the road to terror and death, upborne on an uncontrollable wave of cheering. "That night the men were happy."

They could never be beaten now.

38

THE FEUD OF THE TITANS

THIS marks the difference between two men—when Grant and Lee drew breath after their first ringing passage at arms, the latter was surprised and troubled, the former merely surprised. "Lee will be retreating southward tonight," said the Union general and found it was not so. He wasted not a moment crying over spilt blood. Done!—and let General Warren lead his V Corps to Spottsylvania Court House, inside and behind the Confederate right flank.

Lee was equally sure he had won a victory. "Those people," (he never called them "enemy," more credit to him) "are in full retreat to Fredericksburg," he declared confidently, when the countryfolk brought him news that Grant's trains were in motion on the night after the battle— and sent Longstreet's Corps (commanded by Anderson instead of its wounded general) to take position on the flank of the retreating foe for a morning attack that should complete the rout.

The night was lurid with forest-fires; cinder-laden smoke drifted down all the ravines and Anderson's men could find no place to camp. They pressed on to the open ground around Spottsylvania Court House, and reached it before Warren, who had been delayed by a mixup in orders and roads jammed with cavalry. At peep of day men in dirty blue caps badged with the Maltese cross of the V Corps came crashing through the bushes against Anderson and the battle blazed up once more in full-mouthed fury.

Lee, a more complicated or less specialized mechanism

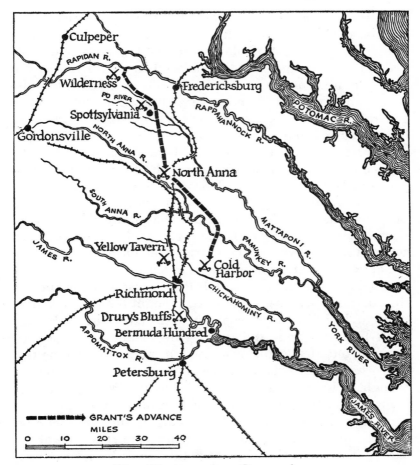

The Hammering Campaign

than his opponent, heard the news with incredulity and mis-
giving. Something incomprehensible had happened; he had
fought on ground of his choosing, his tactical touch had never
been more exquisite, Longstreet's assault had been delivered
with indomitable fervor, the Federals were beaten back at
every point under losses that should have shaken them to the
core, but the old sword, the invincible Durandal, had failed
to bite. Instead of taking refuge behind the Rappahannock,
the obstinate Nationals were circling his flank for an attack,

exactly as though they had won. The shock produced in Lee the first stages of a mental disintegration which it had hitherto been his privilege to inflict upon others. An imponderable had entered the equation; the victory had been Pyrrhic, if a victory at all. For the first time in his life he failed to write to his wife for a week, and never again did he undertake a general assault on Grant's army; his own losses had been so heavy that nothing but victory could justify them.

. . . Spottsylvania. The 9th May saw continuous skirmisher warfare as the armies felt each other along the new position. Lee, a master battlefield engineer, fortified along an acute angle with Spottsylvania in the center; Anderson's Corps on his left, Ewell's around the point, Hill's (under Early for the moment) on the right, while attackers must come in on an awkward eccentric. Warren had struck near the apex of the angle; Sedgwick circled the point and found it so heavily held that Grant felt there must be a weakness at the other end and, when Hancock brought his II Corps up at twilight, had him try the spot where the river Po ran through Lee's line, splitting Anderson's wing. Hancock almost got through, but Meade misunderstood the maneuver and neither supported the II Corps nor drove it home. In the morning Lee brought reinforcements across the angle from Early, and Hancock lost his gain in a day of determined fighting.

Sedgwick, meanwhile, had found a spot in the rebel trench line where the abatis was thin. He rode forward to survey it, the last thing he ever did, for as he stood among the trees a sharpshooter drew a bead on him and "Good Uncle John" pitched dead onto his face. Wright, a tall, powerful, impassive curly-headed man, slow at forming judgments, obstinate at holding to them, took over the VI Corps in his room. He planned an assault for the soft spot and asked Meade for supports. Meade sent him Mott's division of Hancock, a double mistake, for Hancock's offensive starved for lack of men, and the division was so racked by its experience in the Wilderness as to be no longer fit for heavy duty. Colonel Upton led the attack through the dawn; it went surging over the Confederate trench in a wave, captured 1,000

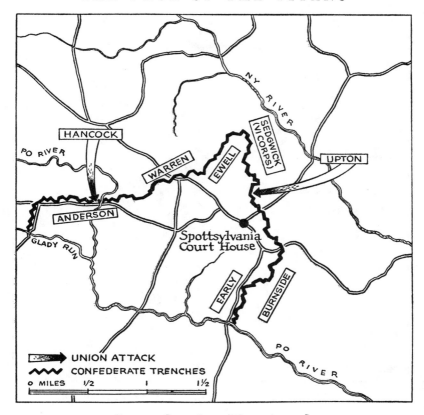

Spottsylvania—First Attack

men and some guns. But it was a rapier-thrust, not a hammer-stroke; Mott's supports broke under the fire they met, and a swinging countercharge led by Ewell himself killed nearly all Upton's valiant band and threw the rest out again.

No gain, and the casualty lists enormous, but next morning Grant reported to Lincoln—"We have now ended the sixth day of very heavy fighting. Our losses have been heavy, but so have those of the enemy. I propose to fight it out on this line if it takes all summer." Electric phrases; they went through the nation in a vitalizing current, as the sight of the unconquerable general at the cross-roads had given a new spirit to his army three nights before.

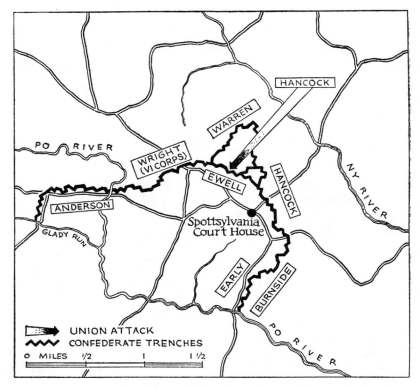

Spottsylvania—Second Attack

Moreover Grant was not yet done at Spottsylvania. The weak point of Lee's formation was the tip of that angle; he switched Hancock's Corps from his right to face it during the 11th and planned a surprise attack for the next morning early. The day broke in swirling mist; Hancock's men formed in silence and swept forward without a shot, without a cheer, through the dim light. "I remember the thin picket line of the enemy, with their bewildered look," said a man in that silent column. "There was a little pattering of bullets and I saw a few of our men on the ground. One discharge of the cannon I remember, and then we were up on the works with our hands full of guns, prisoners and colors." Aye, guns, prisoners, colors, for the charge had gone right over everything like an avalanche. A whole Confederate division was captured, with two generals—Johnson, "very dignified and downcast in defeat," and "a nasty little man named Steuart." "I shall not shake hands with you under the present circumstances," the latter told Hancock when he offered him breakfast; "And I should not offer to shake hands with you under any circumstances," retorted the Union general.

Lee's center was broken; the remnants of Ewell's Corps came flooding back through Spottsylvania, the Army of Northern Virginia was *in extremis*. His face set in hard lines, the general rode among them with uplifted sword, majestic on his huge white horse, to lead a countercharge in person, for if Grant held that angle all was lost. Anderson sent regiments to fall in, Early sent a division, Ewell's men rallied—"General Lee to the rear!" they cried. "We must take that angle," he replied and rode on, statuesque and terrible. "General Lee to the rear!" They held him back by main force—"We'll take it for you," and swarmed past him to the front, disorderly and fanatic, with tears in their eyes, prayers and curses on their lips. The artillery was pushed up by hand till it stood muzzle to muzzle with the Union guns; the Federals were hurled back to the trench line. But not out; neither would Hancock's men quit, they clung like bulldogs to the inner and then the outer face of the parapet:

"Nothing but piled-up logs separated the combatants. Our men would reach over the logs and fire into the faces of the enemy, would stab over with their bayonets; many were shot and stabbed through the crevices; men mounted the works, and with muskets handed them kept up a continual fire until they were shot down." Parties pulled piles of dead men out of the way to get into the trench and themselves die. It was the most ferocious fighting of the war, all day long, and when the Confederates staggered back through the evening to a new line of trench Lee had cut across the base of Bloody Angle, they had lost a fifth of their whole army and Grant more than a tenth of his.

No gain; or was it no gain?—never before had Robert

Lee found his army in so desperate case that he must himself ride among the bullets. That night there was a windy quarrel at Union headquarters, with Sheridan and Meade slanging each other like fishwives. "Why did your cavalry get to Spottsylvania before the rebels?" demanded Meade. "Because your orders crippled me," retorted Sheridan. "General Grant, where is my free hand?" "Go now," said Grant, "ride through to Richmond if you can."

Sheridan stamped out to lead his horsemen in a long swinging raid around the rebel right. That same night with the dead still uninterred, Grant began to move again, taking each rightmost corps in turn around behind the others to put it in on his left—first Wright, then Warren, then Hancock, extending his lines toward the North Anna River. Lee's alert scouts brought him news of the move, which he might have punished severely had it been made a year earlier with McClellan or Hooker facing him, but Grant's blows had left him too weak to hazard offensive battle. He could only shift corps parallel to the advance, and a continual hot dribble of firing went on among the thickets as the armies moved in daily contact. The spirits of the Union troops were up, the dogged old army found its head at last. When a wounded man was carried past Meade he twisted on his stretcher to shout— "Don't give up the ship! I am willing to lose my leg if necessary, but fight them! Fight them!" A cannon ball thudded into the ground three feet from where Grant was writing a letter, throwing muck all over him. He shook it off and went on writing imperturbably—"Ulysses don't scare worth a damn," said the passing soldiers as they tramped along— "There's the man who won't take his orders from Bobby Lee." He had changed his plan in mid-career for a bolder one; instead of following Lee, he was moving now to make Lee follow him.

Out behind the rebel lines toward Richmond Sheridan got through to cut Lee's supply lines briefly, and his men were hungry, but Stuart won a tumbling, fighting race to get first into the Richmond defenses and faced him from behind a line of redoubts. That was well, but Stuart came out to fight; there was a series of cavalry combats round Yellow Tavern and the end was not well. In one of them Stuart, the Bayard of the Confederacy, went down with a bullet through his lungs and never spoke again. He had been Lee's right eye as Jackson had been his right hand; from that day forth the Army of Northern Virginia stumbled half-blind into the daily battle.

Sheridan's outriders reached leftward till they touched the Army of the James, then in the midst of a burlesque and tragic maneuver from the head of navigation. Tragic, because all that blood was spent in the Wilderness to make this move easy; burlesque because Ben Butler commanded and every move that shambling Cocles made was accompanied by the sound of popping bladders. He had come up the James under a forest of masts on May 5, 35,000 strong, landed his armada at Bermuda Hundred and immediately began to quarrel with everybody—with the navy because it would not take monitors of fifteen-foot draft up a river ten feet deep; with his soldiers because they shouted "Who stole the silver spoons?" when he rode past; with his corps commanders because they insisted that the objective should be Petersburg, the cerebellum of Richmond. Five railroads entered the rebel capital, three of them through Petersburg, and the most vital. The corps commanders pointed out that Confederate Beauregard had a good-sized army within call of Petersburg; if the advance were direct north on Richmond, he would call in his troops and fall in on the Union rear. "I don't trust them West Point fellows," said General Butler, "they're trying to keep me from being successful," and ordered a march for the rebel capital.

It stalled before a line of forts at Drury's Bluffs. Butler sat down for a siege; Beauregard brought up his men from the Carolinas and, on the morning of the 15th, a day of rolling vapors close to the ground, came drumming out of Petersburg against the Federal rear. Butler's left wing dissolved, his right wing never had a chance to fight, and he beat a hasty and disastrous retreat to Bermuda Hundred, leaving behind many prisoners, dead men and guns.

No gain; but no matter, the real contest was north among the bushes, now along the line of the North Anna, a shallow stream confined between fifty-foot bluffs, with the rebels on the southern side. Warren had the Union right; he threw a pontoon bridge, got some artillery across and established a bridgehead, then began to pass over his foot. While he was at it, Hill's Confederate Corps came piling through the tangle in a sudden vehement attack that broke one of his divisions. They rallied round the guns and the effort cost Hill dear; Warren kept pouring men across the bridge, the rebels were driven backward in a bushwhacking struggle that lasted till the V Corps men were halted by a heavy line of forts late in the evening.

It was a day of hard fighting; on the other wing Hancock's men had rushed a bridge and worked forward through wood and dale under heavy fire till they, too, came up against a trench line, reaching southeast. Burnside in the center could not cross the ford on his front; the Confederates had intrenched the far back with artillery, and he lost 1,000 men trying to force their position. Wright's VI Corps followed Warren's and developed Lee's line on the Union right—trenched and redoubted everywhere. That made the position clear; Lee had fortified another acute angle, this time with the point resting on the North Anna, so it could not be caved in. The Union position was far from good, with the wings separated by a wide river that would have to be crossed twice. Lee might have thrown his full strength on either wing. Once more he dared not; Grant clutched him with arms of iron, the lightest movement would bring a rejoinder of such power that nothing less than crushing success could justify the losses it would entail—and Lee had already tried crushing Hancock with little luck.

The North Anna lines locked on the 24th May, the next two days were spent in tapping battles in a minor key. On the night of the 26th, dark as Egypt with pouring rain, Grant made a swift withdrawal and, veiled in cavalry as a comet in light, marched all night south and east. Near Hanover Court the Annas, North and South, unite to form the Pamunkey. He was forward enough to steal a crossing below that point, at the mouth of Totopotomoy Creek, then turned west along the Richmond roads. Lee was surprised by the movement (once more he had wired President Davis that Grant was retreating), but he had interior lines and, when mud held up the Union armies, got across the roads just in time. Hancock's and Warren's corps had a vicious artillery duel with Ewell's and Early's on the 27th and got the best of it when Early dared a local attack, but the rebels intrenched a line behind while the fighting was in progress and they could not be broken through for a real victory.

Grant began to work leftward once more; he had hurried Sheridan around that wing already to seize the road junction at Cold Harbor. Butler's army was hopelessly penned now; Grant cleverly drew from Bermuda Hundred one of his corps, the XVIII, commanded by the quaint but capable "Baldy" Smith who built the Chattanooga cracker-line ("I have more hair than the men who call me 'Baldy,' " he used to complain), and brought it up the Chickahominy by water. Smith disbarked and rushed forward, with one of Wright's divisions coming down from the north to lend a hand and Sheridan's cavalry on the wings. Right behind Cold Harbor he ran into a high ridge of ground, fortified to the hilt, and the forts filled with men in gray. Check again—Lee had drawn in most of Beauregard's army to fill up his weakened battalions and stood across the path once more.

Grant brought his whole army down to the position; so did Lee his. No gain. The ceaseless vigilance, the strain of daily battles, was beginning to tell at Union headquarters; everyone's nerves were frayed. Grant gruffed at the adjutants; Meade took a perverse pleasure in making his staff uncomfortable, colonels hardly dared speak to him, his voice "sounded like cutting an iron bar with a hacksaw," and he made the Judge-Advocate-General go without his supper like a naughty schoolboy. The atmosphere was as explosive as fire-damp. As the result of some snarling exchange Grant swore he would break through by main strength and ordered a general frontal assault for daybreak on June 3—the only thing he ever regretted in his military career. It lasted just ten minutes; in those six hundred seconds the Army of the Potomac lost 5,000 men and went reeling back to its lines, wounded and bleeding. "It is terrible," said Warren. "All day long a perpetual funeral procession goes by my headquarters."

Poor Warren, he was appalled, had come to doubt. Outside, the country and the world were doubting too, aghast as the tale of losses came out of Virginia; such sanguinary fighting had never been seen in history—over 50,000 men down on the Union side in a month's warfare, and still the Confederates stood unbroken before them. Only two men held on, undismayed; fortunately they were the only two who counted any longer—Ulysses Grant and Abraham Lincoln. They knew—and now Robert Lee knew, too. The iron arms held him close; he could not move, he could not breathe, all his delicate tactical skill was wasted in this dreadful, dumb slugging match, this duel between idiots in which the strongest man would stand on his feet at the end. He could see the end of Grant's movements, swinging ever round his left, till the Union army should reach the south side of Richmond—and then?

"We must destroy the Federal army before they get to the James River," he told Early. "If they get there it will become a siege and then merely a question of time." A shadow crossed his face;—"We must destroy them!" he cried, his voice going thin. The foundations of his world were slipping—he had lost the power to destroy; his men were beginning to desert.

39

SUSPENSE

A QUESTION of time; but only three men had that secret and the North was aghast. "Butcher Grant," the papers began to call him—"Grant's march is a funeral march; not a home but mourns its dead," they said. Self-sacrificing patriotism is a fever which must burn itself out or destroy the patient; the world was weary of blood and treasure spent and generals' pictures. "We are now receiving one-half as many men as we are discharging; volunteering has ceased," wrote Halleck to Grant. The new recruits who filled the gaps of his battle losses were drafted men, pressed soldiers, marching into the volcano with stony faces and hearts brimming with dread. "Tenting Tonight," saddest of melodies, was the song of the hour:

> "Many are the hearts that are weary tonight,
> Waiting for the war to cease;
> Many are the eyes that are looking for the light,
> To see the dawn of peace."

The journals had lost their spirit; instead of "Eye-Witness of the Latest Battle" they published ringing editorials about Le Bon Ton, thus:

"The caprices of Paris fashions are becoming more and more eccentric; these liberties place ladies in the dilemma of either following fashions not suited to their years or of subjecting themselves to ridicule by the opposite course." Or told melancholy anecdotes: "A citizen of Boston has made a wager of an apple to be doubled for every day beyond the opening of the campaign that Grant delays in taking Richmond. If his wager were settled to date it would cost him $82,632." Gold stood at 285, the war would never end and Horace Greeley, that great keeper of the public pulse, wrote to Lincoln to make an end—"I know that nine-tenths of the whole American people are anxious for peace on almost any terms, and utterly sick of human slaughter and devastation. I firmly believe that were the election to take place tomorrow, the Democratic majority in this state and Pennsylvania would be 100,000 and we should lose Connecticut also."

He was well advised to make his plea on such grounds; it was a presidential year and Lincoln wished to succeed himself, believing in full humility that he could solve the riddle by patience where others would bring only passion to the task. He knew those others; there were foes of that stamp in his own household. Since August of '63, and the ousting of Joe Hooker, Chase had been writing letters steeped in the humility, not of Lincoln, but of Uriah Heep. "If I were controlled by mere personal sentiments I should prefer the election of Lincoln. But I think a man of different qualities will be needed."

So thought a good many other people, Mr. Chase, particularly if the other qualities included a tight-lipped merciless determination to wipe the South from the face of the world. The furies were unleashed; you cannot have a war without them. Congress was in the hands of the Radicals, the vindictive, gloomy Puritan Eumenides, at their head Charles Sumner, beaten once with a stick by a South Carolina slaveholder, warped in mind and body by those blows, living on only to avenge them in fire and blood. Behind him stood Thaddeus Stevens, a Radical and rabid; charity was a word in the dictionary to him and mercy a bait to trap fools; the only emotion he understood was terror, but of that he was master. And able—both men had brilliant parts. They thought Lincoln a mealy-mouthed hypocrite, too soft for this stern war, and when he showed signs of gentleness toward the states already conquered—"If one-tenth of the voters take oath of fealty to the Constitution and establish a state government, it will be recognized," he had written—when he showed signs of mercy, they jammed a fierce fire-and-sword bill through at the end of the session; slave property to be forfeit, slave-holders to accept Negro citizenship before being allowed in the Union—to your knees and lick our boots!

Lincoln slew the bill with a pocket veto and explained the reasons in a public proclamation. That did not suit the vindictives' book; they launched a bitter manifesto against him—"studied outrage on the legislative authority," "Lincoln should suppress the rebellion and leave the political reorganization to Congress," "service of his personal ambition." A Chase-for-President Committee was formed, headed by five senators. The party at large favored giving Lincoln his second term, but he might be chicaned out of it by beating him in the nominating convention if an issue could be found that would make a sensible talking point. A tradition for one-term Presidents had grown up during eight administrations without a re-election; the vindictives adroitly used it to combine a bleat about "Lincoln's Cæsarism" with their own appeal for "more vigorous prosecution of the war," which meant more vigorous persecution of the South, and began a still-hunt for convention delegates.

Lincoln was forearmed; he sent the Blairs, his favorite political men-of-business, to Ohio, where they hastily assembled a caucus of the legislature and had him named as the state's favorite candidate. Ohio was Chase's own state; the move knocked the bottom out of his barrel, and he withdrew his name, with an apology to the President.

The matter was not allowed to rest. Francis P. Blair, the savior of Missouri, held the dual post of Congressman and Brigadier-General. The military campaign was about to open; he would be off with the army and immune to political attack, so he seized the opportunity of his last day in the House to get up and denounce Chase's underhand dealings. For good measure he added that the Secretary of the Treasury had found fat jobs for all his useless relatives, and was paying avaricious interest on government borrowings from the house of Jay Cooke, with which he had some vague connection, and then posted off to join Sherman before Atlanta, laughing out loud.

He might well laugh; Chase was mortally offended. He had been a persistent resigner since the beginning of the administration, withdrawing each demission only after being adequately buttered with phrases about his indispensability. Now he found a trumpery pretext to turn out a masterpiece among letters of resignation, full of sly sarcasm and mock abnegation, accusing Lincoln of having promoted Blair's attack and inferentially demanding public apology. To his mortification the President's only reply was the appointment of W. P. Fessenden as Secretary of the Treasury. Chase was already out of the fight for convention delegates; he could not get back into it before Lincoln was nominated by acclamation, and the Radicals were left on the outside of everything, biting their nails and planning revenges. A rump of them even went to the length of nominating the forgotten Frémont for the presidency on a new ticket of their own.

Those who remained in line were bitter. "I am introducing you to Mr. Arnold," Thaddeus Stevens told a visitor in Washington, "because he is an oddity, the only Lincoln man left in Congress." The House was a slough of despond; Congress sent up a resolution asking the President "to appoint a day of humiliation and prayer, asking the people to convene in their usual places of worship to confess and repent of their manifold sins, to implore the compassion of the Almighty, and if consistent with His will, implore Him not to destroy us as a nation."

Nor was occasion lacking; to run with Lincoln the convention had selected Andrew Johnson of Tennessee, equally distinguished for his addiction to strong waters and his lush oratory, a Southern Democrat who still believed in the Union, politically a kind of winged amphibian monster, unfitted for progress either in air or water. The nomination was itself a confession of weakness; on the heels of it came the news of the bootless assault at Kenesaw and the blood-bath of Cold Harbor, still further to depress hearts and spirits.

The Democrats were jubilant; they scented victory, and their convention in Chicago was one long pæan to harmony and the hope of unseating the "shambling ape" in the White House. It was a strange gathering, chiefly of men with many woes. Horatio Seymour, governor of New York, was there, lamenting the draft and the riots it had brought to his state. Frank Howard was there with a description of the horrors of life in a military prison; the jailers had not allowed him to publish a card in the Baltimore papers protesting that he had been unlawfully condemned. General McClellan was there; he told the tale of how Lincoln's jealousy had ruined his efforts in the Peninsula with a pathetic dignity of self-pity that left few dry eyes in the hall, and they nominated him for the presidency. Vallandigham was there, his face twisted in the everlasting sneer; he drew the keynote resolution of the platform:

"This convention does explicitly declare that after four years of failure to restore the Union by the experiment of war, justice, humanity, liberty and the public welfare demand that immediate efforts be made for the cessation of hostilities."

"The war is a failure!" the papers summed it up next day, and Horace Greeley begged Lincoln to resign in a long editorial that called for some other Republican candidate, one who would have the people's confidence—Ben Butler or Frémont for choice. "Mr. Lincoln is already beaten. He can never be elected."

Dark days. Thurlow Weed, the Republican leader for New York State, called on the President to tell him he could not be returned to office. It became dark as he talked; after the visitor left, Lincoln sat down and entered in his private journal—"This morning, as for many days past, it seems exceedingly probable that this administration will not be re-elected. Then it will be my duty to so cooperate with the President-elect to save the Union between the election and the inauguration, as he will have secured his election on the grounds that he cannot possibly save it afterwards."

The voting would start in another month; unless something supervened—

He got to his feet and stepped to the window; far down the avenue someone was whistling faintly . . . "to see the dawn of peace."

40

MORNING STAR

ATLANTA stands on a high plateau, girt round with smoking chimneys; to every side the streams flow down and away. From the northeast the main railroad from Richmond ascends the height, to the southwest other main lines slide down the long gradient to Macon and Mobile. Sherman was across the Chattahoochee north of the city, with his supplies coming by rail to Marietta, thence by wagon-circuit through Roswell. Across his front lay Peachtree Creek, a military stream, which means one that proper defense will hold against any but inspired attack. The weather was hot, the rations slow, but the men were in high spirits, for the slow days of bloody chess games were gone, and they were coming to hand-grips at last. Every man in both armies knew the appointment of Hood meant headlong battle—"Will the people at home keep up their pluck till we fight it out?" was all their letters asked, and those at home on both sides echoed back—"All now depends on that army before Atlanta; if it fails the game is up." Suspense and double suspense; here lay the crisis.

Sherman made the town of Buckhead, behind Peachtree Creek, the cornucopia of his advance. Thomas swung right and straight across the stream on Atlanta with his three big army corps; Schofield, with his one, went left to cross just where the stream forks; McPherson took his three corps (he had Blair's new one) on a wider swing, beyond Decatur, for Grant had written that Lee and Hood might exchange troops by the northeast railroad and it was important to block that line.

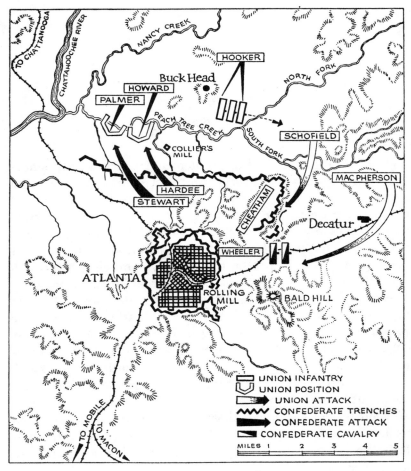

Peachtree Creek

The affluents of Peachtree course through deep gorges from the Atlanta plateau, splitting the country into finger-like peninsulas; along the metacarpal crest lay Hood intrenched, watchful as a lynx. The Georgia militia had been called out; with garrison troops from the Floridas and Alabama they would hold the fortified lines, leaving free a striking force of 65,000 men. By the 19th July, he knew how to use it; his scouts brought word that McPherson had cut the railroad east of Decatur, with Schofield close up on him, while Thomas' columns were crossing Peachtree to climb the backs of the finger-ridges. Through blunder or blindness the parts had been too far spread, a four-mile gap had opened between the halves of the Union army. Hood's chance—he would thrust between and hit Thomas with his whole strength. The weakest of the three Confederate corps, Cheatham's, was left with the militia to hold off Schofield; the other two (Hardee's and Stewart's) displayed their colors and poured out of the forts along the piny ridges to the attack, waving bayonets and bowie knives and shouting encouragement from band to band.

It had been blindness, not blunder, in the National army; the maps were bad, showing Peachtree Creek shorter than it was, and Thomas had edged persistently westward to make room for Schofield. On the morning of the 20th, with his three column heads across, he discovered that he had made too much room. It was impossible to connect up across the intervening ravines; Hooker's XX Corps was withdrawn behind the stream to go around and link hands with Schofield, and while he was in motion, just mid-afternoon, Hood's attack came piling into the head of the center column around Collier's Mill.

Howard and the Germans were on that front; never since the evil day of Chancellorsville had they failed to set up breastworks and post artillery at a halt; the attack found them with everything in position, just finishing dinner. Along the bare spurs of hill the rebels raged in vain against this line, and reeled back with gaping holes torn in their formations, but they worked strong parties through the tree-lined ravines and turned the flanks of each of Howard's divisions in succession. The stubborn Dutchmen would not break; they faced round to form hollow circles that stood like volcanic islands in the sea of gray, spouting flame. Thomas rode to the sound of the fighting from the other side of the creek; recalled one of Hooker's divisions and brought up the whole army reserve of artillery which fired right into the Confeder-

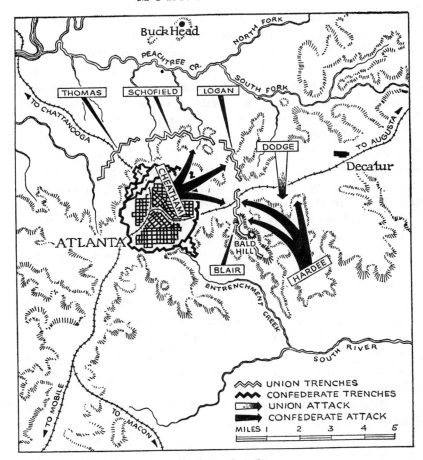

The Battle of Atlanta

ate line of advance. Hardee and Stewart suffered frightfully; they had to draw out for a rally, but formed for another attack with fresh troops in the van about five o'clock of a sweltering day.

It might have gone through, but never was delivered. Out on the other flank Schofield had swung in against Cheatham and was giving him all he could handle; the rebels could not spare a man to oppose McPherson, who had come through Decatur at noon, and was hurrying down the railroad line at a furious pace. Hood had only Wheeler's cavalry to check him; the horsemen dismounted and took advantage of every tree and accident of ground, but the Union leader drove so fast and hard that by four o'clock he had them backed into the main fortifications of Atlanta. A high bald hill was seized and fortified; from it one of McPherson's batteries began to plop shells into the big rolling mill that supplied half the Confederacy with steel; underneath the fire his infantry boiled up against the forts and it was only a question of time before they would break through. Cheatham had to send a division to hold them back; it left him short-handed against Schofield's onslaught and still McPherson pressed on. No help for it; Hood must recall Hardee from the attack on Thomas and make a hurried, scrambling defense at the inner lines. The battle had cost him 8,000 men and not hurt Sherman a whit; once more Thomas alone was equal to an army.

During the next day Sherman flung his coils close around the city. Hood watched a chance to strike and saw it in the position of McPherson's line, which ended in the air at the bald hill. On the night of the 21st, he sent Hardee's Corps by a circuit out of the intrenchments to attack the rear of McPherson's position between the bald hill and Decatur, break him and roll up the Union line. The rebels ranked in the dark; at daybreak they rushed hurrahing forward onto the rear of Blair's XVII Corps where it had intrenched facing the city.

By all the rules Blair was beat, but these were Grant's own veterans of the west and panic-proof. They jumped over the parapets of their trenches and fought from the other side with a constancy wonderful to behold. McPherson had Dodge's XVI Corps in reserve, where it had been pinched out of the contracting circle of Union armies; he hurried to the front with it and established a new line south of the railroad. Hardee's men flooded into the gap between Blair and Dodge; McPherson rode to stop them with a patchwork of regiments, and rode right into a rebel volley that killed him instantly, the knightliest figure in the Union army and one of the most brilliant men—his letters read like a philosopher's notebook.

No matter now; Hardee was surging in. Hood had brought Cheatham out of the fortifications and flung his corps straight against the hard-driven XVII Corps on its old front which had become its rear to face Hardee; against Schofield also and Logan's XV Corps on the other end. Blair's men had to leap back over their barricades to face Cheatham; they held like rocks, but it was touch and go when Cheatham got through the gap between them and Logan and almost linked hands with Hardee. Sherman in person saved the day, that fidgeting eccentric man who became cool as Kanchenjunga when the guns began to shoot; he raced up with Schofield's corps artillery as an escort at a slam-bang gallop over stones and tree. They turned on a dime, flung loose the limbers and opened from a hundred yards into Cheatham's massed columns. The butternuts could not bear it, they went back all raddled and teased out. Logan's men began to cheer; he mounted a parapet, shouted "Come on!" and led a wild, disorderly charge that spread all along the Union line, everybody taking it up. Cheatham broke, Hardee broke, and once more the Confederates went tumbling back into their defenses with 8,000 lost. It went into the books as the Battle of Atlanta.

The northeast railroad had been thoroughly cut; Hood was strengthening a line along Entrenchment Creek and Sherman saw he could not flank Atlanta from that side without exposing his communications. Meanwhile the supply rails from Chattanooga had been carried down and across the Chattahoochee; it was better to base on that line. He began to turn north around Atlanta to the other side, the old maneuver, taking the Army of the Tennessee, division by division, around behind the rest to prolong his right. The process was enlivened by a generals' squabble over who should have McPherson's place at the head of the Army of the Tennessee. Hooker wanted it; he was vain, pompous, flashy and wrongheaded, inveighing against his competitor,

Logan, as an amateur soldier of the McClernand stamp. Logan was subject to dazzling fits of inspiration, but needed them because he knew so little about the technical side of soldiering that he generally posted his men badly; he told Sherman that Hooker was an amateur politician of the Burnside type, and the general settled the quarrel by giving the post to neither. Howard got it—no driver, but sure and skillful. Hooker asked to be "relieved from command in an army where rank and merit are ignored." To his disgust Sherman obliged and sent for Slocum to take over the XX Corps, a handsome, blond young man, cultured within an inch of his life, who had done good work on the three red days of Gettysburg and been on garrison duty since. Stanley took over Howard's IV Corps.

Hood's losses had been terrific; Sherman thought he was done and would sit quiet, but Howard said—"No, I knew him at West Point, and he is indomitable." He was right; the wounded lion was a lion still. The Union lines round Atlanta were trenched and fortified to impregnability; no hope there, but he might catch Howard's Army of the Tennessee in movement at the tip of Sherman's right flank and crush it. There was a change in his commands also; since the battle of Atlanta S. D. Lee had taken over Cheatham's Corps. Hood sent the new commander out the Lickskillet Road on the 28th to form a concave basket in which to catch the head of Howard's advance at Ezra Church; while Lee held it, Stewart's Corps was to swing wider behind, take the Federal line in rear and break it up.

Lee's attack fell on Logan; he met the first rush like a tiger with a furious counterstroke in a tearing shock of battle. The Confederates rallied and came back on three sides around him. But the XV Corps, like all Sherman's men, had reached a counsel of perfection; neither numbers nor overwhelming fire nor unfavorable position could daunt them; they were invincible. Howard himself was with them; he brought more artillery to sweep the open spaces; with its aid, Logan's single corps stood off two-thirds of the Confed-

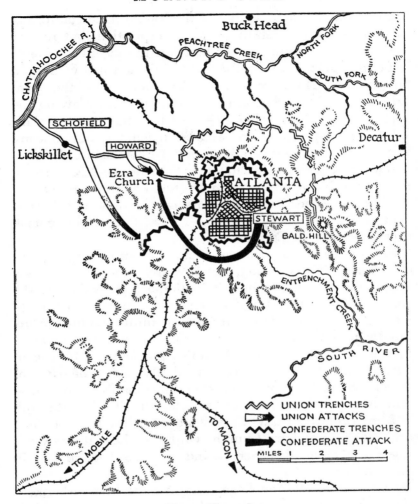

Ezra Church

erate army, though the rebel officers rushed in so recklessly that they lost four generals of division and Stewart fell wounded at the head of his corps. Toward evening Blair and Dodge came up at the double-quick on Logan's flanks and drove the attackers from the field with losses that reached seven to one of their own.

Sherman already had Schofield swinging around behind Thomas and Howard to prolong the line southward. He knew Hood was stretching his trenches out from Atlanta to protect the Macon railroad, now his only, and therefore vital, supply-line. A quick blow while the rebels were disordered by defeat might snatch the line from them and win Atlanta out of hand. Palmer's XIV Corps was detached from Thomas' army, added to Schofield's and an attack in force ordered. The stroke never came off; Palmer, a square-faced man with little bright eyes, full of intelligence and malice, insisted he was senior to Schofield and refused to act under his orders. Sherman summarily removed Palmer and gave his corps to Davis (who slew "Bull" Nelson in the Louisville hotel room), but there had been a day's delay and the opportunity was gone.

The lines locked; big siege guns came down from Chattanooga to send their projectiles screaming into Atlanta, chalked with "A Kiss for Jeff Davis." All day long it went on; at night cotton balls soaked with turpentine burned between the parallels and sharpshooters picked off everything living, but Sherman boiled with impatience. "They hold us with inferior forces," he cried. "Faster! Faster! Move up the guns." The weight of the war and the world rested on his shoulders; Grant was holding Lee, somehow he must break the deadlock that held him.

There was a chance that cavalry, useless in a siege, might do it. Stoneman and Kilpatrick went out in long swaying raids to break Hood's supply line. Stoneman fell into an ambush near Macon and got himself captured; Kilpatrick did indeed cut the line but only for a day. Sherman became irritable, did not sleep, could not sleep as the clock ticked on inexorably past August 5—10—15—20—25 with the elections rushing on like the clap of doom and nothing done.

August 25 and nothing done; on the morning of the 27th the siege guns began to go silent and that evening an old woman stumbled into Hood's headquarters. She had been within the Union lines the night before; they were striking

tents and loading wagons for a move; to her request for food
they said they had none to give. Hood knew Wheeler and
the rebel horse had been raiding toward Tennessee and
Sherman's communications; he saw it all now, they must
have touched a vital spot. He leaped to his feet, his face trans-
figured—"Sherman has been starved out," he shouted. "We
have won!" And within the hour his scouts located the Union
rearguard out toward Sandtown. The church-bells of Atlanta pealed forth joy, and a special train brought ladies and
musicians up from Macon for a victory ball, but in the midst
of the gay clamor there came a low, tremulous growl of artillery far away southward and the officers in their bright
uniforms one by one hurried from the room and to battle.

Hood's error; dupe of his illusions, he never dreamed
that Sherman was so bold, for the Union leader had cut
clear loose from railroad and supplies to describe an immense
arc south around Atlanta. The rebels would want ere he
wanted; it was harvest time with fresh roasting corn in the
cob, and Hood mured in a city where no crops were. On the
30th the Union army crossed and fatally hurt the Mobile
railroad; Hood heard of them that night. Like Pemberton
when Grant had made a similar stroke, his mind went numb;
all mazy, he somehow formed a dream picture of Sherman
making a grand general assault on his city and, holding
fast to his strong lines with Stewart's Corps and the militia,
he sent the corps of Hardee and S. D. Lee south to Jonesboro
on a train of cars to meet the single Union corps he expected
to find there.

At mid-afternoon on the 31st Hardee clashed with Howard's advance; the rebels attacked thinking Howard was
alone, and took a severe beating from the cross-fire of three
corps. "They no longer come on as fiercely as they did once,"
observed General Hazen. "They seem to know they are
beaten and nothing they do can alter the result." Beaten they
were; Schofield crowded up behind Howard, cut the line between Hardee and Atlanta, and chased the last train back
into the city. Thomas' three corps came pushing up behind;

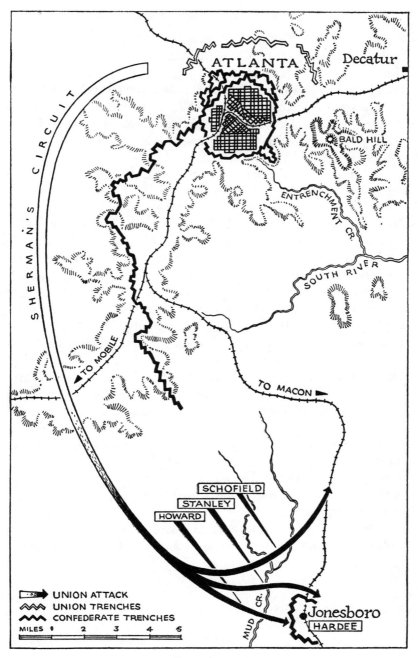

Jonesboro

Sherman rode with them; at four in the morning, groggy for lack of sleep, he trotted past flaring bonfires into Howard's lines to ask how the battle had gone. When Howard told him he realized instantly that Hardee was cut off and might be captured. Weariness dropped from him like a cloak; he spat out orders. Howard and his men were to attack forthwith, pinning Hardee to his lines; Davis' XIV Corps to strike the north end of the rebel line and bend it back to a fish-hook; Stanley's IV Corps to circle round and scoop up the rebel force from the inside of the fish-hook.

It all went well but Stanley's part, the important one. He dawdled, got mixed in difficult ground; Hardee was badly damaged, but not captured; he stood his ground all day, his lines only broke in the twilight and, though he suffered 5,000 loss, he got away into the dark with most of his little army.

That night Sherman sat on a stump, writing an angry dispatch to Stanley, when there came the sound of heavy explosions from the north, boom, boom, boom. The general started, a fold of worry leaped into his forehead—did it mean that Hood was throwing his strength on Schofield's lone corps? Then, long in the distance beyond the circling campfires, an elfin cheer sprang up and echoed nearer and nearer, swelling to a great roar of sound as the whole army took it up, yelling and cavorting oddly in the firelight. Atlanta had fallen, that great city; the explosions were Slocum's salutes as he led the Army of the West into the glum streets with torches and music, and the news was passed from mouth to mouth down twenty miles of picket line to reach the weary general's ears.

He tore up the dispatch to Stanley and, as the pieces fluttered to the ground, wrote one short line to Lincoln— "Atlanta is ours, and fairly won."

4 1

THE GHOST OF 1812

DAVID GLASGOW FARRAGUT, the oak-faced veteran of the curling locks, remained in command of the Gulf blockade after taking New Orleans. The port of Mobile irritated him like an old wound; three great rivers flowed into its bay from the coal and iron country, where fast gunboats and torpedo vessels were built that came down to pester the Union cruisers past endurance. Farragut loathed this type of warfare—"I have always deemed it unworthy of a chivalrous nation"—yet could find no means to abate the nuisance, his fleet being all wooden frigates, and Mobile Bay defended by two huge fortresses, Gaines and Morgan. The New Orleans trick would not work; suppose the forts were merely passed at whatever cost in ships, what then? They could not be cut off —and there was heavy doubt that he could pass them.

Farragut wrote querulous letters to Washington, telling his wish for ironclads to batter down those forts, but if wishes were navies the world would go to sea. No result; this one lacked boilers, that one's turret would not work, the hoisting gear of a third needed overhauling, more monitors were needed for the siege of Charleston, where the rebels had three ironclads in harbor. The battledore game lasted for a year; then the old man steamed away from his charge and turned up in Washington to present the demand in person. There was reason for impatience; the barrier forts grew daily more formidable, the rebels were planting torpedoes (which we should call mines—a beer-keg full of gunpowder) in the channel and, worst of all, they had the last and greatest of the Confederate rams, *Tennessee*, building up the bay. She was a monster, clad in mail of proof five inches thick; on the 18th May she drifted down the harbor and moored under Fort Morgan. The engines were not right; she could not go out and assassinate the blockading fleet as hoped. Mechanics came down from Selma and hammered away in her vitals for two months while the crew practiced gunnery overhead; on August 4, a day of breathless heat, they got her ready but that same morning the lookout on Fort Morgan's parapet saw low-slung hulls slide across the horizon, and four powerful monitors, *Winnebago*, *Manhattan*, *Tecumseh*, *Chickasaw*, steamed in among Farragut's wooden ships.

Understand the picture; it was in the darkest hour, with the Army of the Potomac bleeding to death in the Wilderness, Sherman held before Atlanta and the Democrats rampant for a new presidency. "I get right sick at such bad news from the North," the admiral had written only the day before. Time was; he bounded to the quarterdeck like a lad of sixteen when they told him the monitors had come, signaled all ships to clear for action. "I am going into Mobile Bay at dawn if God is my leader, as I hope He is."

The ships advanced in two columns, monitors on the right headed by *Tecumseh*, seven wooden frigates on the left, headed by *Brooklyn*. Farragut wished to lead the line in *Hartford*, but they talked him out of it, *Brooklyn* mounting heavy bow-guns that would be useful in the approach. To her side each frigate had a gunboat lashed; if she were disabled, the smaller vessel's engines would carry her out of danger. With battleflags at every mast the fleet headed for the neck of the passage after these simple arrangements.

The fast frigates gained on the monitors; from their decks one could see the triple tier of guns in Fort Morgan rising up the slope. There was a flash from the water-battery, a low booming report, and a geyser leaped up at *Brooklyn*'s side. Her bow-gun fired; the burst of the shell hung suspended high in the air above the fort. It was 7:10.

The range was found; all three tiers of Fort Morgan suddenly sheathed themselves in a garment of flame; out from behind the hill of fire steamed the *Tennessee* and three gunboats to post themselves across the head of the Union line and open a slow, raking fire. *Brooklyn* was hit and hit again; a huge shot plunged into *Hartford's* mainmast, throwing all over the ship a cloud of singing splinters that cut like knives. A shell from *Tennessee* struck the gunboat at *Hartford's* side and a burst of brilliant orange flame leaped out. The decks were shrouded in smoke; old Farragut climbed into the rigging to get a better view and, needing both hands for his glasses, tied himself there like a banner, his long white hair blowing back under the uniform cap, his face, pale with age and hard as a rock, giving him the aspect of a ghost from the great sea-fighting days of 1812. All down the line ships were hitting and being hit; the shot beat against the iron sides of the monitors with the uproar of a thousand forges. It was 7:17.

The fire of the water-battery died out as shrapnel from the monitors drove the gunners to the bomb-proofs, but the other guns of the fort hammered away. The frigate *Oneida's* boiler burst; *Brooklyn* was on fire; *Winnebago's* turret was jammed by a heavy shot. Captain Perkins of *Chickasaw*, wild with excitement, jumped out of his pilot house and did a *pas seul* on top of his turret, with missles whizzing all about him. "Engage more closely," signaled Farragut; Captain Craven of the monitor *Tecumseh* put on steam and headed straight for the rebel ram, across a line of half-submerged floating objects marked by a red buoy. There was a muffled, deadly shock, a huge fountain of water mounted to the skies at the monitor's side, her stern, with the propellers still revolving, lifted clear, and in thirty seconds she disappeared. One valiant deed—as the ship went down, Captain Craven stepped aside from the door of the pilot-house, saying, "You first, sir," to the pilot. There was no second; the man took one step, the vessel seemed to fall away from under him, and the next moment he was swimming. It was 7:20.

Brooklyn hesitated before the line of mines, stopped one

engine and swung around, bows to the fort, taking a raking fire that swept her decks from end to end. *Hartford* was right behind and *Richmond* right behind her; a moment's confusion, they would tangle and the whole fleet go to the bottom under the plunging fire that never ceased. "What's wrong there?" demanded Farragut from the rigging. "Torpedoes! Torpedoes!" "Damn the torpedoes! Full speed ahead!" he shouted. *Hartford* leaped forward to lead the battle-line; behind her it straightened out as though by magic, and the Union fleet swept on through the hurricane of fire into the bay. In the flagship's hull they could hear the snap of the torpedo-primers as she scraped across their line, but they did not go off. It was 7:22.

They paused above the forts, out of range, to take count. Not a ship undamaged, and some disabled, many men dead. But one of the Confederate gunboats was on a sandbank burning like a torch, another had sunk and a third was flying up the river. A wet fog began to blow in from the west. Farragut called his captains aboard for a conference—"This is all useless as long as the *Tennessee* remains afloat," said one of them. "The frigates' guns cannot hurt her." It was true; at that moment Confederate Admiral Buchanan was being gratified that the inspection of his ship revealed only some inconsiderable dents in her steely plates. In the Union fleet the men had finished breakfast, and the damage parties spread to their work. There was a shout—"Here comes the ram!" and *Tennessee* left the shelter of Fort Morgan and headed straight for *Hartford*, sure of her invulnerability, her big guns booming. It was 9:15.

The fast wooden ships outstripped the monitors, hurrying toward the monster. Their guns were useless; orders were to ram. *Monongahela* spun a circle and charged into *Tennessee*'s side under full head of steam; the shock almost brought down the tall ship's swaying masts, she reeled back from it with her bows torn away, her side shattered by the ram's gunfire, but the damage she inflicted was only a leak you could have plugged with a pocket-handkerchief. *Lacka-*

wanna charged, and pulled back from the charge with wrenched bows and a gaping hole where *Tennessee*'s shot went through; *Hartford* locked with the ram; her wardroom caught fire: but her shot rattled harmlessly off the titan's sides. It was 9:31.

Just then Lieutenant Wharton of *Tennessee* looked out a side embrasure and saw "a hideous-looking monster creeping up on our port side, whose slowly revolving turret revealed the cavernous depths of a mammoth gun. 'Stand clear!' I shouted; a moment later 450 pounds of iron admitted daylight into our sides." It was the monitor *Manhattan*; a man who stood against *Tennessee*'s casemate wall was reduced to jelly by the mere impact of her shot. *Tennessee* turned slowly to face the new antagonist; behind her Perkins, still bounding like a gazelle on his turret-top, brought *Chickasaw* up to physical contact, and hammered at the ram's stern plates, *Tennessee*'s smokestack went and the casemate filled with fumes; her steering gear was shot away, her plates began to crack, one port shutter was burst in, the rest jammed, she could no longer turn, her speed fell off, the admiral was wounded, and still the ding-dong of the monitors' double repeated blows went on. No help for it; the invulnerable was wounded, the invincible vanquished. A junior lieutenant waved a tablecloth from her hatch in token of surrender and the battle of Mobile Bay was over. It was just 9:42.

Two days later the monitors hammered Fort Gaines into scrap. Fort Morgan stood a siege by land and sea, but capitulated on August 22, and the Confederacy no longer had a seaport on the Gulf.

42

GLORY, HALLELUJAH!

COLD HARBOR was a defeat, a racking defeat. It left the Army of the Potomac shaken; the ominous little slips of paper that men pinned on their breasts before a battle to identify the body put in their appearance again. When soldiers think more of death than victory, defeat is likely to be their portion.

Cold Harbor was a defeat, not a disaster; Grant kept his power of movement and Lee had lost his, who never won a battle or a campaign but by swift maneuver. Within a week the long blue columns were flowing out of the lines away from the grumbling guns to the southward. A cavalry division under James H. Wilson, a slight brown man with pinched cheeks and a big brain-case, an engineer whom Grant had taken from his theodolites to sit on a stamping charger, covered their flank by a quick drive toward Richmond across the old battlefields of Glendale and Savage Station, between the Chickahominy and the James.

On the morning of the 13th they met the cavalry of the rebel flank-guard there, under W. H. F. Lee (still another Lee—there seemed to be a rule in the Confederacy that every other commander should be named Lee or Stuart, but the Stuarts were considerate enough to spell the last name different). Lee reported to Lee and the Confederate general sent out scouts who found Grant's Cold Harbor lines deserted; he began shifting Anderson's Corps south of the Chickahominy. Anderson drove in hard to develop the full strength of the Union movement. Wilson's men, fighting dismounted

among the trees, were armed with the new repeating carbines their general had introduced, which delivered such
a volume of fire that Anderson was convinced he was facing
at least two of the Union infantry corps and so reported. He
convinced Lee, who saw it all now—Grant was trying to
cut in behind his left flank north of Richmond—McClellan's
old plan. Hastily he withdrew the rest of his army from Cold
Harbor and intrenched a long staggering line from the
point of Riddell's Shop to the James, with Malvern Hill its
southern bastion.

The rebels spent the day digging in while a heavy
skirmisher fire rattled down the new front. At twilight
Beauregard telegraphed from Petersburg that he, too, was
hard pressed; next morning he sent a staff officer to tell Lee
that Union troops were crossing the James. "He must be in
error," answered Lee. "They are probably some of Butler's
men returning to his lines. The Army of the Potomac is
heavily engaged on my front." To make matters certain he
ordered local raiding attacks; everywhere they were turned
back to an echoing outburst of musket and artillery fire.

He expected attack; Hill reported heavy firing in the
center, and Lee rode there, taking the reserves and heavy
artillery for a brisk counterstroke when Grant's columns
should appear through the woods. Beauregard's second messenger found him late in the afternoon and repeated that
Petersburg horizon was blue with National uniforms. Lee
would not believe, he dared not believe—"If they get to
the James it will become merely a question of time"—with
the energy of despair he clung to his own picture of the situation. Grant was facing him, would attack, would be counterattacked and there destroyed on the ground of McClellan's
defeats.

But Grant did not attack; Beauregard was right, it was
true, all true, the thing Lee most feared had come upon
him, the Union thousands were closing in on the vital nexus
of Petersburg. While the Confederates toyed cautiously with
the cordon of repeating carbines that faced them, not daring

to venture full-bodied assault, "Baldy" Smith's XVIII Corps
was taking outer redoubts of Petersburg; behind him Hancock was forming the II Corps, Burnside was crossing the
IX Corps over that night and Wright and the VI were waiting for boats.

The situation was tense as a drumhead, with both commanders walking tightwires; if Lee attacked in force he
might catch the Army of the Potomac astride the James and
cut it to pieces. Beauregard nearly went frantic as his outer
redans fell, one after another; he had only 4,000 men in a
place built for 40,000, was arming the sutlers, clerks and
telegraphers, but the XVIII Corps, instead of driving boldly
in, made careful reconnaissance of each redoubt, bombarded,
flanked and encircled it, then moved in with agonizing deliberation to smother the corporal's guard inside. On the evening of the 15th, Grant, anxiously watching his rear north
of the river (where Wilson and his carbines held out like
heroes), sent Smith a message—he was to call on Hancock
for any reinforcements he needed and slam through. Smith
lumbered along in his own easy way; Hancock's men did
not get into action that night. Later in the evening, Captain
Chisolm, last and most trusted of Beauregard's aides, was
in Lee's tents, declaring vehemently, "Unless you come at
once, God Almighty alone can save Richmond."

A messenger interrupted; the telegraph connection with
Petersburg had gone dead midway through a message and
a train that started from Richmond a few hours before had
clattered back with news that the Federals had the connecting railroad under artillery fire. That made certainty; Lee
read the doom of his hopes and nation. He turned toward Captain Chisolm with a sad smile—"I hope God Almighty will
save it."

There remained duty; the Confederate general began
to issue crisp orders; outside, the bugles blew through the
thick dark of the summer evening. When Smith, aided by
Hancock's troops, urged on by Hancock's drive, dashed
against the inner lines of Petersburg the next morning, Hoke
and Johnson were in the trenches already and more divisions

of the Army of Northern Virginia coming up every hour.

The fighting continued all day, with fresh men on both sides; on the following morning Meade arrived in person with Warren and the V Corps, but the general attack he ordered only won some of the outer works of the fortress and it was the same old deadlock.

The east front of Petersburg is narrow; when fighting closed on the night of the 18th the Union position there was already well intrenched and two corps were enough to hold it. With the rest Grant began moving by the left to slice across Lee's three irreplaceable railroads below Petersburg. One, the Norfolk road, runs southeast from the city; Grant won that on the second day of battle, when Burnside got up. One, the South Side Railroad, goes south of west; it was beyond his reach. The center one, the Weldon road, runs straight south; the II Corps was headed for it, the corps flank fairly close to the Petersburg lines, with Wright's VI Corps moving parallel but farther south. Both corps were to make a great half-wheel with the right wing of the II Corps as the pivot.

The country was the usual forest and sand of the Virginia littoral, much ribboned with ravines. An accident of ground separated Wright's right and the II Corps' left as they turned north, and Birney, temporarily in command of the II Corps (Hancock out with a wound), neither connected up again nor sent out proper flank-guards. Every copse held a rebel picket; Lee knew of the gap within the hour and rammed Hill and his corps into it. The II Corps' flank was taken in reverse and began to break up; Birney hurried to the spot, but he was just a good division commander, with neither Hancock's high spirit to lead a rally nor Hancock's quick eye to choose a sound position. Brigade after brigade went to pieces under his eyes till the whole corps was streaming rearward. Hill tried to carry on and turn the break into a general rout, but Wright held like a rock on one wing, Warren received him with salvos of artillery from the other and he was glad to get away.

That ended the westward movement; both armies dug in,

the coehorns and sappers came down from Washington and the siege of Petersburg began, long echoing bombardments and men standing on trench-steps in rain and fair weather to shoot at any slightest sign of movement in the lines opposite.

Burnside's IX Corps held the portion of the siege-lines opposite a salient, called Elliott's, behind which lay a high hill, Cemetery Hill, dominating the whole Petersburg defensive system. There was in the corps a regiment of swart miners from the Schuylkill, the 48th Pennsylvania, who had enlisted under the master-miner, a Colonel Pleasants. Pleasants surveyed the salient from an observation post—"My men and I," he said, "can mine that salient, blow it into the air, and leave a gap through which an army may rush to storm Cemetery Hill." Approved, said Burnside, and passed the idea to Meade. Approved, said Meade, and the miners began to dig. It took them a month; the greatest problem was what to do with the dirt, but they put most of it in sandbags to use for parapeting and the rebels never suspected. When the tunnel was hollowed out, the 48th Pennsylvania carried powder in, the men racing perilously down the communication lines with tiny kegs of the explosive slung under their necks, like St. Bernard dogs in the Marjolaine. At daybreak on July 30 the mine was finished, the fuse was laid, the artillery reserve of the army concealed in the thickets behind the Union lines to bury Lee's trenches in shells as the storming column went forward.

Burnside's Corps was to make the assault, naturally; the division of Ledlie had the lead, closely supported by the black regiments commanded by General Ferrero—the first real test of how ex-slaves would fight against their masters. On either side the XVIII and the V Corps were to take up the attack as soon as Burnside started.

At half-past four the fuse was touched off; ten minutes later there was a shock that seemed to make the world tremble, and a tremendous geyser of earth rushed up toward the skies with men's bodies dancing on its summit. The Union artillery opened with a roar—and Ledlie's storming column stood in its trenches, staring curiously at the spectacle of shattered Confederate lines and graybacks running, waiting for orders. Finally the regimental commanders took the initiative; they moved, but not above ground in long, nimble waves as a storming column should; rather down the open cut left by the mine, in a tight-packed mass. They reached the crater the explosion had left and there they stayed, a few trying to climb the steep sides, which were all of twenty-five feet high. Behind them the black troops advanced down the same narrow cut to pile into the same crater till eight or nine thousand men were packed there in a breathless, tangled mass. There seemed to be no one to lead, no one to tell them what to do. The rebels began to recover; a gun opened from Cemetery Hill, a patter of skirmisher fire came from the flanks.

A colonel extricated himself from the mass and dashed back to seek orders. In the IX Corps intrenchments he found the advance regiments of the supporting XVIII Corps vainly trying to get through the abatis that Burnside had forgotten to clear, while Colonel de Chanal, the French observer, stood at one side wringing his hands and crying *"Cette perte de temps! Mais cette effroyable perte de temps!"* The colonel looked farther; safe in a bomb-proof behind the trenches he found three gentlemen seated—Ledlie, Ferrero and one he did not know, the commanders who were leading the assault. Ledlie, a tall, thin, neurotic-looking man, had just told a good story and the others were laughing. "For God's sake, give us some orders!" demanded the colonel, trying to keep the disgust out of his voice. "Oh—ah—have the men get out of the crater and go forward," said Ledlie, and helped himself from the bottle.

The colonel worked his way through a hail of bullets to find that the rebels had altogether recovered. Cemetery Hill was lined with batteries; shells were pouring into the crater, Confederates were perched at the edge of it, firing down into the mass. They got 4,000 of the stormers and the rest managed to return to the Union lines.

That finished Burnside; he went north on a "leave" that lasted the rest of his life and took Ledlie and his little jokes with him. "Baldy" Smith also disappeared; on top of his Petersburg failure he had had the bad judgment to become involved in a controversy with the politically potent Butler. Into their places stepped Parke and Ord, the former a spare, severe man who gave weak troops hard drill till they moved like machines; the latter a sturdy, rubicund Irishman, full of quaint conceits and atrocious puns, but a first-class fighting man.

The Army of the Potomac needed men like that; it had been losing tone, the rout of the II Corps and Burnside's failure proved it, there were too many recruits in the ranks. So now it settled down to a siege with the election coming on— never forget the election, it is an essential element in the combination, deeply affecting military strategy. For Lee it was the one element of hope—"I hope," he wrote to Davis, "that your excellency will put no reliance on what I can do individually, for I feel that will be very little. The enemy has a strong position and is able to deal us more injury than from any other point he has ever taken."

Very little; but there was left one more of those wonderful tricks of fence, the first and best of all the thrusts in tierce. The Petersburg lines were solid as skill could make them; Lee could hold there with reduced forces, sparing men for a campaign down the Shenandoah, the old threat against Washington that had upset Lincoln's equilibrium in the days of McClellan's black week. It might, it just might, shake the bulldog loose. The opportunity for such a campaign was ideal, the Union commanders themselves had made it, thus:

A brick in the structure of Grant's grand plan for the year had been a series of flashing raids up the Valley to Richmond's back door. Franz Sigel, the patriotic but uninspired dumpling from Missouri, made the first raid, coincident with the general advance in the early days of May. He flashed like a cart-horse; the rebels caught him up at New Market, wrecked his little army with one hurried charge and sent the tatters flying. Old General Hunter tried it next, with 16,000 men. He got through to Staunton and the railroads west from Richmond, but stayed too long. Lee sent a corps under Early, which cut across Hunter's communications, captured his breadline, and sent his starving men on a mad march through the West Virginia gorges without their artillery or wagons and with a hundred dropping from hunger every mile. The Valley lay open to the end; along its smooth roads went Jubal Early, the wide-bearded, profane man, with 30,000 men behind him and nothing at all in front.

On the 5th July he crossed the Potomac and a sudden thrill of fear shot through Washington; the next day a Confederate cavalry wing laid Hagerstown under $20,000 contribution on threat of burning the city and the Baltimore & Ohio Railroad was broken through. On the 8th Early's army passed South Mountain into Frederick; the papers leaped into screaming headlines, the roads ran caravans of fear, the militia was being called out and Lincoln telegraphed feverishly to Grant, for there was not a man to defend Washington. Lew Wallace, the author-general, in disgrace since he failed at Shiloh, was the only commander available; he gathered a motley force of 7,000 men, convalescents from the hospitals, armed police, bellicose clerks, and went out to dispute the passage of the Monocacy. Early laughingly cut the absurd army to pieces, sent the remnants whirling up the Baltimore road and marched on to take the capital. He arrived along Seventh Street just before noon on the 11th and heard the bells ringing to call the citizens to arms.

The day was breathless; Washington lay smoking with dust at the focus of its grid of roads as the rebels topped a rise that brought them into sight of Major L'Enfant's dome. Weary men, tramping since dawn, they fell out to rest while General Early rode forward to sweep the forts with his glass. They were formidable; as he watched, a gun boomed and a shell soared past to burst over the woods where his frontline lay—hundred-pounder by its explosion. He hesitated;

called a council on the question of attack, a fatal hesitation, for at that moment the forts held only a few militia, but as the council of war talked a line of ships turned in at the city piers and the VI Corps from the Army of the Potomac, strong, competent men, with General Wright at their head, marched through streets lined with flags and cheers to save the National capital.

They moved out at once in order of battle and Early turned away. That afternoon a division of the XIX Corps, just in from the war in the West, joined them; Wright took command and harried the Confederates back to their nest in the Valley. The agile rebels were not caught; the VI Corps countermarched and took ship for Petersburg. Early shuttled down the Valley right behind them, routed the local garrisons in a brief engagement at Kernstown, kept on across the Potomac for a second time, with a wing of cavalry flung clear north to Chambersburg in Pennsylvania. It is a town of size; Early demanded $500,000 from the mayor as the price of its safety. There was not that much money in Chambersburg; therefore the inhabitants were driven from their homes out into the hot July fields with such belongings as they could carry in their hands and every building in the city put to the torch.

Needless, for Chambersburg was of no slightest military importance, just a town without forts, factories, magazines, or soldiers; stupid, because it filled the storehouse of the grapes of wrath. The whole North was incensed, a nation of Charles Sumners; Grant left his siege-lines and came to Washington, where he found Lincoln simmering with the terrible rage of a patient man. These raids must end; let an army big enough to follow Early to the death be put into the Valley and never let him go, for the war is a failure and McClellan President if we cannot stop this.

I will send two corps, said Grant, and, since cavalry is good in that open land, a corps of cavalry as well, 50,000 men all told. It must be a pilgrimage of terror; the rebels escape us always by living off the farms of that rich valley while our columns go halt-footed, tied to their wagon-trains. We must ravage the Shenandoah from end to end, make it useless as a nursery and avenue of armies. Approved, said Lincoln. But who shall wield the lightning and the sword?

They discussed this general and that—Hunter, he was too much the Indian fighter, could handle fifty soldiers but not 50,000; Franklin, able but old and slow, Lincoln would not have him in spite of Grant's inexplicable fondness for the man; Meade, a great soldier on foot but not at the head of masses of cavalry—Sheridan!

Sheridan, doubtful ever of his capacity, would rather be a subordinate commander in the expedition, was not sure old senior officers like Averell and Hunter would work under a junior—"Remove them!" Grant ground out harshly. "You are in full command; act on your judgment and responsibility." Sheridan removed Hunter then and there; Grant approved the paper without word of comment. The new army commander stood up and saluted—"I will leave them nothing but their eyes to weep with," he said, and left the room to take command of the crucial campaign at the crux of the war.

At Halltown in the Shenandoah he gathered his new army—VI Corps, General Wright, three divisions; XIX Corps, General Emory, two divisions; VIII Corps, General Crook (Crook who led a charge along the bridge of death at Antietam), two divisions; cavalry, three divisions, young General Torbert to lead them, with the bright blades in the army to ride by his side—Custer, Merritt, Devin, Wilson.

The Army of the Shenandoah was no secret; Lee knew of it and its mission. Let it strike home, and his army would be left dependent for its rations on two slender lines of rail reaching down into the Carolinas with Grant's grim legions edging slowly in; he dared not lose the Shenandoah. The Petersburg lines were further strengthened, the conscription age extended—"He is robbing the cradle and the grave for men," said Grant—and somehow he spared Longstreet's Corps, the divisions of Kershaw and Field, to go to Early's aid.

The Valley campaign had suddenly become the vital campaign, with the elections hurrying on and every eye on Sheridan.

For a month the armies circled like fighting cats in the lower Valley, Sheridan testing his organization, Early trying to break and to keep broken the Baltimore & Ohio Railroad. Then Grant tapped at Petersburg again, Lee had to recall Longstreet's Corps. The night their badges appeared on the Petersburg lines Grant wired Sheridan, two words— *"Go in."* The day was marching on.

Sheridan lay at Berryville; Early at Winchester with a wing of horse out at Martinsburg on the railroad—he had taken his opponent's measure in the month of fencing, believed him a solid, unenterprising fellow, staggering under a task too big for his brain. A fortified defile, where the Berryville road crosses Opequon Creek, would hold him in play. The morning of the 10th September, a bright and brilliant day of harvest, saw Sheridan on the march by three o'clock; at five, Wilson, with the vanguard of cavalry, struck Early's fortified defile, submerged the rebel lines in a storm of troopers and forced the passage of the creek. The Union infantry pushed in behind to take up line, Sheridan's intention being to pin the rebels in front with the VI Corps, swing the XIX past it to his own left with Wilson's men out beyond, and while these men held, bring the VIII Corps down in an oblique attack on the left wing of the enemy where they stood at the edge of a low plateau. A hitch; precise, formal Wright marched to battle with all his ambulances and baggage wagons behind. They stuck in the ravine and the XIX could not get through; by nine o'clock Early had called in his outliers and was in full strength against Wright.

By time Sheridan had ridden to the ravine and shouted to "Get those damned wagons into the ditch!" a murderous combat had clenched down in front. There had been no time for field works, both lines were in the open, both full of the spirit of victory. Just as the XIX Corps began to reach the field and began to be fed in where the VIII should have

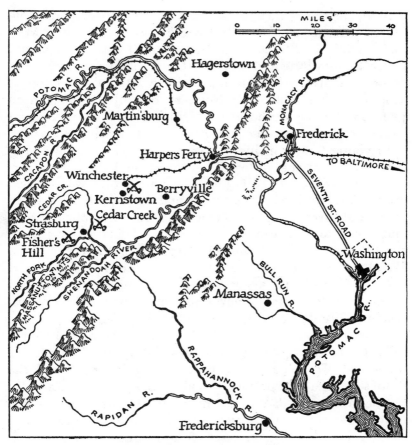

Sheridan in the Valley

been, Early found the weak spot where a road created a gap on its left flank; flung Rodes' division into it, and carried away one of Wright's brigades. But the gain could not be held; a battery of heroes from Maine stood their ground all alone, artillery against infantry, and shot the heart out of Rodes' charge.

Sheridan in person brought the VIII to the field, changed plans and thrust it leftward, where Emory and the XIX should have been. Crook gained a commanding eminence from which his guns began to enfilade the rebel line. They paused, began to turn back, formed a new line; and now fell into deeper trouble still. On the Confederate right Wilson's cavalry had fallen on; there seemed thousands of them, Early thought them the whole Union mounted force and turned all his own horse and artillery in that direction to keep from being flanked. Now, as his infantry began to yield in the center, he was horrified to see another great cloud of horsemen descending on his left wing—Torbert, with young Custer in his velvet coat and yellow curls leading them in at the gallop. They burst on Early like a tornado, the rebel left collapsed, the whole line was carried away. Early formed a rearguard and tried to make a stand in the outskirts of the town where he had some old trenches and a hill to help him. Custer and Torbert went right up the hill and over; Wilson got through on the other flank, Wright, Crook and Emory broke down the infantry center, and the Confederate army was driven through the twilight streets in utter rout. "I never saw our troops in such confusion before. It was sad, humiliating, disgusting."

The victory rang through the North like a shout on a hill; it was in the Valley, Jackson's Valley, the Confederate homeland. Congress voted Sheridan a gold sword and the thanks of a grateful nation—"God bless you," wired Lincoln, but before daybreak the next morning Sheridan had his victorious regiments pouring southward on every road, the cavalry on the van, no rest, "follow them to the death." Behind him, he left a trail of destruction, barns and ripe fields blazing in the September sunlight. Remember Chambersburg.

Early pulled up at Strasburg, where the Valley is narrowed to two defiles by the interjection of the Massanutton Mountains. A narrow stream, Tumbling Run, crosses the neck of the west Valley; behind it rises a buttress of mountain, Fisher's Hill. Here he fortified, one wing covered by the tall Massanuttons, the other by North Mountain; the deep ravine, all rocky ledges and shaggy with pine, protected his front. Cavalry was useless against the position, which was why he chose it. He felt and said that he could hold it against Napoleon, dismantled the caissons and stood the ammunition boxes around the guns for a siege because he would not be needing to move. Sheridan arrived the same night with the leaders of the VI Corps, closed his lines tight around and reconnoitered. There was no ingress, and from the summit of Fisher's Hill the rebels could look on every move his troops made. Still—

The VI and XIX Corps were brought up to face Early's trench lines next morning. There was a day-long skirmishing fight in which they took positions along Tumbling Run. Crook and the VIII Corps were not in it; they were hidden behind a fold of hill, far in the rear. As twilight came they moved forward, slowly, gently, far on the Union right, the Confederate left, in Indian file along the piny slopes of North Mountain, where a goat might cling, utterly silent, weapons wrapped to hide the clang. The sun dived down; Crook's men flung loose the wrappings on their guns and went charging forward onto the rebel flank and rear. The twilight was suddenly shot with flame; a startled shout of fear ran down Early's line—"We are flanked! Flanked!" They began to give, to run; Ricketts on the VI Corps right fell on in front, the XIX Corps cheered and began to scramble up the wild beasts' dens straight into the teeth of Early's forts, with Sheridan shouting "Forward, forward everything!" every time he was asked for orders. Everything went forward, the rebel formations lost cohesion, men fled away into the mountains, bolted up the Valley under the shadows of night, leaving flags, artillery and 1,000 prisoners behind.

The North went wild with joy; salutes of a hundred guns were fired from Grant's positions before Petersburg and by Sherman's soldiers in Atlanta; Mr. Ticknor noticed men stopped each other in the street to shake hands, but Sheridan marched on through storm and sunshine to lay waste the fertile Valley clear down to Staunton and the western railroads. His cavalry harried the rebel retreat; then he turned back past the ruined farms, which would never again in this war support an army.

On October 18th he camped on some hills behind a brooklet, Cedar Creek, near the battlefield of Fisher's Hill. Sheridan himself was at Winchester in the rear that night on his way back from a consultation with Stanton; there was the question of how many troops to hold the outlets of the Shenandoah against rebel guerrillas, now that his army's work was done. Neither he nor anyone else yet knew it, but Early was just behind him, outside his camplines. The Valley defeats were not to be borne; Lee had added Longstreet's whole corps to the army there again, and they had marched like wildfire, day and night, living on their iron ration, silent as stalking leopards, to deal the Union army a stunning blow at peep of day.

Sheridan's men were asleep in their tents, the VIII Corps farthest south. It was false dawn, with an icy autumn fog clinging to the ground; there came one single crash of musketry and the next moment the camp street was filled with Kershaw's Confederates, wild-looking men, yelling like maniacs. The VIII Corps never had a chance, those not captured floated away across the hills, a cloud of flying men with their own artillery, now in the rebels' hands, firing into them from behind. The XIX Corps, next in line, had time to wake and get out of their tents; then the rebels were all around one flank, rolled up their line before it could form properly, burst through their front and flank and hurled them down the road on the track of the flying VIII Corps. Crook and Emory were swept away in the flood; two division commanders yielded up their lives in a vain effort to make a rally. The XIX Corps guns went, too, the rebels had 1,500 prisoners, the rest of the two corps were dispersed, men had lost officers, officers had lost men, and it would take them a week to reorganize.

Now it was nine o'clock; the sun was up and hot. The starved Confederates, who had not eaten well for months, less on their mad march, were in the midst of a camp of plenty;

they fell out by scores to plunder and eat, in spite of the exertions of their officers. Early ventured one tentative movement on the VI Corps, but it faded in the Union rearguards' fire, and the splendid Federal cavalry, now in the saddle and moving, began to dog his flanks. It would take time to complete the rout; he paused to let his men eat while he arranged an attack in form to demolish the one corps they had remaining.

Sheridan, far back, woke to an ominous grumble of cannon. He leaped to the door, to the saddle, spurred his big black horse to speed and headed for the battle. Within half an hour he was riding past ambulances and provision wagons trotting north, sure presage of a defeat; then one, a dozen, a score, a whole cloud of leaderless, disorganized soldiers, their backs to the fighting. He stood in his stirrups—"Turn around, boys!" he shouted. "We're going back." The routed men looked, stopped, saw who it was, and then turned, as though just waking from a dream. A little cheer rose; they began to pass the word along—"Turn, boys, turn, we're going back. Here's Phil Sheridan!"

He rode on, surrounded by an escort that grew every moment in numbers and excitement, till it became a blue sea, crested with a shining foam of bayonets. It was noon as he reached the Union line; the sea had become an army— "Where's the Sixth Corps?" he demanded first. It was there, and sound; Wright had labored like Hercules, a last rebel charge had just been brought to a stand, his guns were all in position and shooting, Custer was champing at the bit at the head of 8,000 eager horsemen on one flank, Merritt and Torbert mustering on the other.

Sheridan rode down the battle-line, swinging his cap, where everyone could see him. Everything was in position, the lines straightened, straightened, composed of soldiers once more, who yelled as they saw him. He kept them in leash for an hour of mounting tension, then gave the word. The line swept forward, Crook's men, Emory's men, Wright's men, all mingled together behind any officers and standards they saw.

The tide was turned and the war was turned. The dismayed rebels, sure of their victory only half an hour before, had prolonged line left and right for fear of the cavalry; they had prolonged so far the line was thin; it broke in a dozen places when Sheridan led against it the charging infantry, crazy with enthusiasm, as he had led them up Missionary Ridge. Then the cavalry did charge; Custer from one flank like a whirlwind; Merritt down from the other. The rebels could not stop them; they could stop nothing, they were fought out, done. The triumphant soldiers of the Union went right back through their own camp, went on through the rebel camp and on and on. Early lost the twenty-two guns he had captured that morning; he lost all his own artillery; he lost his ambulances, his wagons; the magnificent Union cavalry was all over him in the pursuit, they gathered in hundreds of prisoners, the Confederate force was reduced to its component individual elements, flung back up the Valley, broken forever, and the Shenandoah campaigns were ended in a triumph doubly sweet because wrenched from the jaws of disaster.

43

CONFOUND THEIR POLITICS

SELF-PITY is useless as a cohesive force; you cannot build a wall with weak bricks, and the Democrat leaders were finding it out. "The war is a failure!" they wailed, amid tremendous enthusiasm at Chicago, and went forth singing their carol of peace, good will to all men but Abraham Lincoln. A thousand spellbinders took up the shout; "The war is a failure!" headlined the organization press dutifully, but the convention was only two days old when they had to print "Atlanta is ours and fairly won" in the next column, a juxtaposition ill-adapted to make the first statement sound convincing. "The war is a failure!" but Farragut had won Mobile; a failure, and Sheridan telegraphed yesterday from Fisher's Hill that "only darkness has saved the whole of Early's army from destruction."

What kind of failure do you mean, you queer men in Chicago? In a fortnight, a week, overnight, the situation had changed; the Democrats, with data and syllogism all complete, looked on a world inverted; Sherman and Sheridan had introduced a defect into the major premise, they had to explain and balance paradoxes, a great trick if you can work it, but not easy when the explanations must be given by many men of many minds, with nothing in common but a sense of frustration.

McClellan was first in the field; by time the formal notice of nomination reached him for a formal speech of acceptance it was as plain as the nose on his face that "justice, humanity, liberty and the public welfare" did not "demand an immediate cessation of hostilities." "No peace can be permanent without Union," he told the delegates. "I could not look in the face of the gallant comrades and tell them that their labors and the sacrifices of so many of our slain had been in vain; that we had abandoned the Union for which we so often periled our lives." It was a fighting speech, but the man was not there to make fighting speeches; it threw the Chicago platform out the window. The dazed delegates walked home, holding their heads. Here was strange doctrine for a Democrat; the most sword-swallowing Radical in Chase's drawing-room could not have proclaimed more resolution to fight to the end. If the election, then, is only a personal choice between Lincoln and McClellan, between master and lackey—

Seymour and Winthrop of New York came next, all about profiteers and personal liberty. The war is a failure because of the high cost of living. Sherman and Sheridan answered that argument, too; with every victory gold took another drop, the dollar another jump, and the Germans, a thrifty race, bought so many United States bonds they exhausted the supply. The hoarded dollars came out of their holes and a wave of prosperity made this argument sound silly.

Vallandigham and his crew struck up resounding airs on the personal liberty harp—think, he bade the electors, of all the innocent men rotting in dungeons because the tyrant in the White House willed it so. The war is a failure because Lincoln is a despot. Thoughts are things impossible to control; the electors thought, but they thought on the spectacle of Vallandigham himself standing there with a whole hide, uttering libels against the despot without let or hindrance.

Many men, many minds, and no explanation that satisfied. The Democrats, feeling the set of the tide, descended to personalities; McClellan referred to Lincoln's shady jokes; the *New York World* tagged him as a "filthy story teller," but unfortunately the *Richmond Examiner* had an editorial at the same time—"The obscene ape of Illinois is about to be deposed. He was, in the eyes of all mankind, an unanswerable argument for our secession." The Republican papers sent the two editorials around the country together, a deadly parallel.

Many men, many minds, and it was futile and petty and mean, small yellow dogs in a row barking at the moon in different keys, for no matter how they explained they could not explain away Atlanta and Mobile and Fisher's Hill. "The fact is certain." Such victories won even the Radicals back to the fold; they came out of their sulks to give Lincoln a boost. Governor Andrew of Massachusetts, "Our Merry-Andrew," the toughest radical of them all, wrote to his state's Congressmen that it was the plain duty of every practical man to support Lincoln. Senator Sumner and Thaddeus Stevens made bitter grimaces but also speeches for the President. Lincoln caught at the forelock of the occasion. There was a hush-hush conference; Montgomery Blair, the bugaboo of all Radicals, was swapped against Frémont; the first resigned from the Cabinet, the latter from candidacy, and the choice became a simple one—Lincoln or McClellan and no beclouding issues. Even Chase came out of his retirement and toured the West, orating from every point in his grandiloquent, energetic style, beating down Democratic debaters as though they had been struck with an iron club.

The result was hardly longer in doubt; when Pennsylvania, Ohio and Indiana voted in October, Lincoln had increased his 1860 pluralities to clean majorities in all three, and nearly all the Democratic Congressmen were turned out. Nicolay noticed the President's step was springier the day the news came through, and a day later it was springier yet, for that was the day of Sheridan's great victory at Cedar Creek, and with it the last chance of the rebellion to triumph over a divided North went glimmering. When the votes were all in McClellan had just three states. The war would be carried to whatever conclusion Lincoln could give it; this time the nation had given him a blank check.

44

BRING THE GOOD OLD BUGLE, BOYS

Hood turned west and north from his defeats at Atlanta. The marching columns moved as light as thistledown, for he had spent 35,000 men and the trains of an army beating his fists against Sherman; the splendid force that stood on Peachtree Creek was become the ghost of an army, a band of walking shadows, with regiments a hundred strong. He moved light and fast, dispensing with wagons to subsist by requisition on the country. In the green fields of Alabama, the weary and disheartened men recruited their strength and new soldiers filled out the skeleton brigades; Forrest, the incomparable partizan, was summoned from the Mississippi country with the 11,000 horsemen who had been roaming up and down the corridors of the West and the rebel leader, Briareus-like, drew strength from the earth for one more wrestle.

For the lion was a lion still; he had lost the game at Atlanta, a defensive game, for which he was not fitted; now it was over and he was free to begin a new one, on his own rules, in which the lion should be the hunter. Sherman dangled at Atlanta, a trapeze performer perilously suspended over nothing at the end of a single wire of railroad. Cut the line, he must perish.

Hood rested briefly, then swung wide west, light and fleet, for a slash at Allatoona, where lay Sherman's advanced base of supplies. He missed; the garrison held out against a day of assaults, with brave General Corse cheering them on in spite of a cheek-bone shot away, and "Hold the fort for I am coming," Sherman's signal across the hills, was written into the hymnals. But when Sherman clutched at Hood he missed also; the rebel got away quickly, turned farther north and had a go at Resaca. He promised the white soldiers of the garrison their lives if they surrendered without a fight; the Negro troops would have to take their chances. Vastly encouraged by this ferocious announcement, the garrison braced belts and repulsed him with loss. He disappeared into Alabama again under a mantle of fury, before Sherman's relieving force could strike him. The next thing Sherman heard, Hood had crossed the Tennessee at Muscle Shoals, and was pointing up into the old fighting ground around Nashville, evidently meaning to cut the Union supply line at the roots by capture of that city.

November had come and Lincoln was safely in for another term; it was the hour when daring could be dared. "A Union army in South Carolina will mean the end of the Confederacy," Sherman told Howard. "Without the aid of the Gulf states the Richmond government cannot get money for itself or supplies for Lee's army." He pulled a map across the table. "We will leave Hood behind and march clear across Georgia to Savannah or Charleston. Cut loose, break the roads, do irreparable damage. The move will ultimately place this army on Lee's rear."

The startled subordinate stared, trying to assimilate the idea—"And our communications?"

"Abandon them. Live off the country. Thomas shall be left to take care of Hood and destroy him. He is equal to any emergency."

Howard went out, shaking his head. He did not know that Sherman had foreseen Hood's steps like a crystal-gazer and, ever since the day Slocum marched into Atlanta, had been urging the project of a plunge into Georgia on the high command at Washington. Everybody there doubted—"I am anxious, even fearful," wrote Lincoln. How could one tell what the army would find in the heart of a hostile land, with no supplies but what it could pick up from the ground? The precedents were not good; Napoleon Bonaparte had made such a march; it gave Tschaikowsky a theme for an overture and Meissonier one for a painting, but it gave the poor devils who marched with him death under three feet of snow. Even Grant, the bold, worried; withheld his permission till Hood crossed the Tennessee, but then said Go.

The army was carefully examined and divided. The sick, the wounded, the unfit, went back to Nashville by railroad. With them went the IV Corps and the XXIII, 22,000 men, not enough to stop Hood, but Thomas should have the new recruits in the West and a couple of divisions from Missouri. There was an amiable discussion over cavalry commanders; young Wilson, who had just come out from the East—"He will add fifty per cent to the effectiveness of your cavalry," Grant had written—went back with Thomas while Sherman chose Kilpatrick—"I know he is a hell of a damned fool, but I want just that sort of man to command my cavalry on this expedition."

On November 12 the last train left, the two generals shook hands, and the long line of communications withered away behind like a tadpole's tail. The railroad was destroyed, the bridges burned. Sherman's engineers went through the machine-shops of Atlanta with hammers; afterward the population was expelled and the town laid in ashes; it would never again be of any use to the Confederacy. Then, with 60,000 men in two great wings under Slocum and Howard, the Army of the West set its back to the west and its face toward the sea and marched forth to "make Georgia howl." The men who had rushed so gaily into the streets to hail the outbreak of war were now to learn what war was like—at first hand.

The army moved in huge snakes along parallel roads, and Georgia howled. Fat senators made speeches, full of Southern bellicosity—"Georgians, be firm! Never before have you had so good a chance to destroy the enemy; remove all food from the invader's path; destroy the roads, rise in arms. Death is preferable to the loss of liberty." The governor decreed a levee-en-masse. But the men who had the spirit to rise were far away, with Hood on the banks of the Tennessee, or lying face down among the Wilderness thickets. Only

Wheeler's cavalry, a bare 6,000, hung round the skirts of the marching columns, trying to drive in skirmisher lines. The skirmisher lines took cover and shot the horsemen from their saddles. Wheeler could not save a house or stay the march a day.

The army marched. The enemy appeared seldom, then only little gusts of militia or cavalry, helpless before the veterans of the West. The weather was high and fine; by day they tramped and ate luxuriously. At night they gathered round the campfires to smoke and sing or tell stories of winters in Minnesota and buffalo-hunting on the plains. The general walked among the camps, unshaven, rough as any bummer of them all and they held torchlight parades for him through the pines—"Ho, Uncle Billy," they cried.

Milledgeville was the state capital; when they reached the place a battalion of Howard's wing played absurd comedy in the legislative chamber, with a mock session and speeches in the best Dixie manner about bleeding soil and invaders' rude hands. There were no bills to lay on the table; they laid a protesting sergeant there instead. In the midst of a fiery peroration someone stuck his head in a window to shout "Sherman is coming!" and the "legislators" stampeded for the door with falsetto screams of imitation terror.

The army marched. When it struck a railroad a brigade pried up the tracks along the whole length of its front with one-two-three; another brigade stacked the ties in cob-houses and set the piles alight. The rails were laid across the fires; when they became red-hot in the center a gang of men seized their ends and wound them around trees. These were "Sherman's hairpins." Foraging parties moved out from the wings like hordes of locusts. They blew out the bridges; they pounded the roads to mire; they cut down fruit-trees; the horses they took to pull the artillery; they left the inhabitants enough for bare subsistence. They moved in wasteful plenty, destroying what they could not use so that no other army should ever pass that way. These were "Sherman's bummers." When they met resistance, they burned the house till nothing was left but a pair of blackened chimneys—

"Sherman's monuments." Behind the line of march the
slaves left their plantations to follow the army in capering,
shouting crowds, singing jubilee and the end of care.
These were "Sherman's prophets."

Out on the flanks mad Kilpatrick, "the Yankee devil in
a blond beard," achieved bizarre variations on the motif
of destruction. His men mixed kerosene with the barreled
flour and left it for a mockery; poured corn-meal over the
carpets and molasses over the corn-meal, kicked holes in the
windows and slashed the mattresses with swords. Wheeler
made superhuman efforts to lay the devil by the heels. Near
Millen he almost did it, surprising Kilpatrick's headquarters
by night, but the irrepressible Yankee leaped from a window
in his nightshirt, grabbed up a saber somewhere and,
mounted on a mule, headed a charge that broke through the
Confederate line and sent Wheeler's whole commando tumbling back in wreck and despair.

Barbarity? The man Sherman had a home of his own.
Listen: from William T. Sherman, Major-General, U. S. A.,
to an old Southern lady he had known in happier days:

"Why, oh why, is this? If I know my heart, it beats as
warmly as ever toward those generous families that greeted
me with such warm hospitality in days long past, and today, were any of all our cherished circle to come to me as
of old, I believe I would strip my own children that they
might be sheltered. And yet they call me vandal, barbarian,
a monster. All I pretend to say is, on earth as in heaven, men
must submit to some arbiter. I would not subjugate the
South but I would make every citizen of the land obey the
common law—no more and no less—our equals and not our
superiors. God only knows how reluctantly we accepted the
issue, but the issue once joined the Northern races, once
aroused, are more terrible than the most inflammable of the
South. To be sure, I make war vindictively; war is war, and
you can make nothing else of it."

The army marched. One by one the links connecting
Virginia with the deep South went dead; the supply trains
ceased to come to Richmond, the Confederate Congress held

a secret session to discuss the lack of food, voting that there was not enough to supply army and people for another six months and "it must be imported through a seaport." Oh, irony! The Confederacy had two seaports left—Savannah and Charleston, with Sherman marching toward them like a fate.

The army marched. In the North there was no news, only vague rumors, a thousand times increased, distorted through the refracting medium of the Confederate press. "Sherman's men are starving. . . . The Georgians have risen and are shooting the Yankees down at every cross-road. . . . Five thousand prisoners from Sherman's army arrived here yesterday. He has barely a division left." Strange rumors, wild rumors, the product of mendacious hope and fear without foundation. For thirty-two days the land was wordless as a country of the dead. "What do you hear of Sherman?" was the first question they asked every rebel deserter along the Shenandoah or before Nashville. Anxiety gripped the North like a fever; Lincoln paced the floor at night.

The gunboat *Dandelion*, on duty off Wasaw Sound, saw a pillar of smoke ascending slowly into the red sky of evening above the rice-fields round Savannah, and heard a gun boom. She ran in; her captain made out through his glasses a group of men standing round an old mill and signaled "Who are you?" in international code. "General Sherman," came the answer. "Have you taken Savannah?" "Not yet, but we will in a minute." There was a burst of explosions, a series of flashes, bright in the gathering dimness along the line that marked the limits of the protecting forts of the city, and then a rocket rose majestically to the zenith.

"Tell President Lincoln—" said the flickering signal lanterns—"tell President Lincoln that General Sherman makes the American people a Christmas present of the city of Savannah with 150 heavy guns and 25,000 bales of cotton. Message ends."

Sherman had cut the Confederacy in two, and he had not lost 400 men. Now, General Lee—

45

UNDER THE IRON ROD

Hood's spring was short; when he crossed the Tennessee the pine-barrens lay before him, a lonely land of rising flats and scattered habitations, without means to nourish an army 55,000 strong. He had to wait for rations and build up a wagon-train, three weeks, a fatal delay, for that was the amount of time Thomas needed to put his defenses in order. The Confederacy was losing its dash; in the old days they would not have hesitated like this, whatever the cause. Or put it otherwise—the disease was endemic, the old Southern failure to keep up with paper-work; war is grand while we can make brilliant charges, let the Northern store clerks count their bales and boxes. Or another factor; young Wilson was around the flanks with clouds of Union cavalry that really knew its business; the columns could not spread along by-roads for rapid movement but must hold to the main turnpike with careful flank-guards.

Yet with the three weeks over, the army rolled up out of the southland, a thundercloud of war, the lion and his brood, grim men with set faces. They would fight with fanatic strength; let the Rock of Chickamauga look well to his arms.

Time pressed hard at Nashville; Thomas' army was piecemeal fragments. The IV and XXIII corps numbered only 22,000 men; 9,000 casuals, convalescent sick, men back from leave, and the unfit of Sherman's forces were there, but without officers or organization. Thomas put them into a "provisional division" under an engineer named Steedman

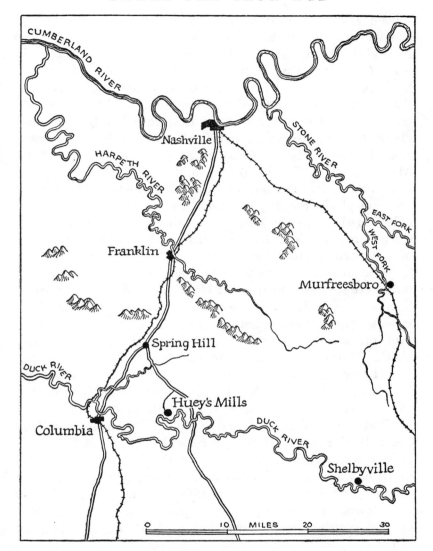

Thomas in Tennessee

and drilled them through the city streets. Young Wilson had 12,000 cavalry, but no horses for so many, nor could they be bought; he wired Stanton about it twice a day till the war secretary overrode law and protest with an order to seize every horse south of the Ohio River and let the owners sue. Wilson did no less; he took the draft-horses from the Nashville street-cars, the trick horses from the circus in town (all but one white stallion, blandished away from him by a pretty equestrienne) and the spanking team of bays that pulled the carriage of Andrew Johnson, Vice-President-elect of the United States. Johnson raised a terrific stink about it in Washington, but Lincoln referred him to Stanton and Stanton to the devil. An army corps was coming from Missouri, the XVI, 12,000 men under Andy Smith, but fall rains had melted the roads and he still was far distant when the lion of the South gathered his strength and poured his columns through the barrens, in three corps—S. D. Lee's, Cheatham's and Stewart's—with Forrest's incomparable cavalry hovering round the wings.

Wilson had mounts for less than half his men; the casuals were still unorganized. If Hood reached Nashville while things were in this state, he could lay the place under siege, smash Smith's Corps coming in or block it out forever, or even mask the town and go careering to the Ohio without a check. Thomas sent Schofield out to delay him with the XXIII Corps and most of the IV. Cox, the universal genius, had the XXIII Corps, blustering, quarrelsome Stanley the IV, and Wilson accompanied with a division of horse.

Two rivers make ditches of defense between the Tennessee border and Nashville; Schofield took post at Columbia on the southernmost, the Duck, with a strong bridgehead south of the stream and his batteries crowning a high hill on the other side. This was the 26th November; a sleet storm had slowed Hood's march to ten miles a day, but he came up that evening and at seven o'clock firing began along the skirmish lines.

The Union position was very strong but its rearward outlets few; Hood planned, and not badly, to encircle and capture their army. During the night of the 26th the Confederate artillery was brought up round Columbia and left there booming away as though to blast a hole through

Schofield's center, with Lee's Corps in support. Forrest went upstream to force a crossing; Wilson had to put his men out in small parties to keep all the fords, and on the night of the 28th the rebels got through at Huey's Mills, eight miles above Columbia. Wilson called in his detachments and made a stand, but Forrest was too heavy for him, he was driven steadily back along the northward road to Franklin, while Cheatham's and Stewart's corps crossed in Forrest's rear and headed north to cut across Schofield's retreat. Schofield, deceived by the artillery fire in his front, and willing to be deceived because of his orders to hold to the last, clung to the line of the Duck until that night, when a chit from Wilson informed him Forrest was across and the Union cavalry already far separated from the foot.

Schofield ordered a reconnaissance east; it struck infantry pickets and he realized what was going on. Stanley with the IV Corps went rearward at once to hold Spring Hill, where the roads converge; Cox, with the XXIII, stayed to make a rearguard and give the artillery and trains time to escape.

In the Confederate lines Hood was with Lee. His orders to Cheatham, who led the advance, had been vague, and that officer, instead of hurrying to Spring Hill, halted outside and went to visit some ladies he knew in the neighborhood. Stanley and the IV Corps got to Spring Hill at twilight; found Forrest in possession, but drove him through the town after a hot combat, foot and artillery against horsemen, then intrenched. Toward morning Hood himself rode up to Cheatham's men, found their commander dancing attendance on the ladies while the cut-off maneuver stood still, flew into one of his majestic Texan rages and ordered instant attack. Cleburne and Brown, with two divisions, made it. Wagner's division of the Union IV Corps bore the brunt of the shock. It happened that the retreating artillery from Columbia had just come abreast; Wagner called on them for help, and the entire artillery force of two corps swung into line, unlimbered and deluged Cleburne's advancing men with a terrible storm of fire. They reeled back, all shot to pieces; even Hood was convinced that Schofield had somehow united his army. He waited for Stewart; this gave Schofield time to call in Cox from Columbia, and when Hood struck again, just after dark, there was nothing left to strike; the Union army was safe away to Franklin and the crossings of the Harpeth River.

As the rebel officers jingled along beside their tramping columns an angry quarrel flared up. Hood, contemptuous of every man who lacked his own savage driving force, was haggard with sleeplessness and his nerves worn raw by the failure to cut the Federal column in two. He lashed out at Cheatham as a parlor-hero. Cleburne and Brown defended their commander hotly; Hood turned on them, called them a pair of mincing toe-dancers, and the matter went close to pistols, for Irish Cleburne was proud of his by-name of "the Ney of the Confederacy, the bravest of the brave." Every man in the group was pale and muttering as the army flowed through a gap of hills to the plain around Franklin in the evening, where they saw a long crescent of trench and barricade before the town, its convex side facing them.

"Attack," said Hood; without a word the irritated officers rode to their commands to start a charge that should prove their courage.

Within the town there had been a day of hurry and clamor. The Harpeth is not fordable and the bridges were gone; Schofield had sent a rider on the day before to bring a pontoon train from Nashville, but when his troops reached Franklin it had not come; his little force was caught with its back to a deep river and twice its number in front. The engineers found the piles of a burned bridge in position, sawed them off an inch or two down, where the water had quenched the flames, and laid a crude corduroy of planks; in the afternoon the artillery began to cross with water sloshing round the horses' hocks. The guns were put in battery on the northern bank; a division of the IV Corps went next to give them support, then the slow wagons in Indian file, while the XXIII and the rest of the IV threw up lines around the town.

Wagner of the XXIII had the rearguard, holding a kind of outwork on high ground south of the town, which lay at the bottom of a series of shelving terraces. At four o'clock Wagner sent back word that the Confederates were ranking; it did not take them long, and they came running forward with trailed arms, the artillery at the gallop in the intervals. There was a ragged fusillade from Wagner's line; then the whole Confederate army was in front, right, left, around, behind and over him in a tidal wave. Wagner's men were captured or swept away; mingled with the fugitives, the rebels came piling in on the main line, shrieking and yelling, the generals swinging sword and pistol as they rode with the van.

On the Union right they met rolling volleys of musketry that took the feet from under them, and though they won the outer ditch they could not get a step farther. But on the Union left, where Wagner fled, the furious attackers followed the Union men right in, up and over the parapet and into the town. The four guns that guarded the main road were taken, the Union line was broke, the men in gray began to cheer, but it was too soon, they had not won yet. Stanley had been sick in bed; at the roar of battle, he leaped up, mounted a horse and flung himself into the struggle around the road; the reserves followed him in; Cox, cursing weirdly in six languages, rallied Wagner's fugitives, a brigade came from the right, another from the left, and packed together in one mass, four men deep, the soldiers of the Union flung themselves onto the rebels. There was a savage melee for a moment; Stanley's horse, shot dead, pitched him to the ground; he rose and led the line on foot; a bullet hit in the throat; he slashed down the rebel who fired it with a stroke that split the man from head to navel, and then, as though by a magic, the Confederates were out of the trench-line again.

They would not give up; Cleburne, Brown, Cheatham,

led on another furious assault; Cleburne was shot through the head; General John Adams rode right into a volley and fell dead, horse and man over the barricade. Schofield had brought the artillery up on the other side of the river now and it was sweeping the Confederate flank with an enfilade, but they clung to the outside of the barriers, stabbing and firing through the logs as at Spottsylvania's Bloody Angle for half an hour more before they staggered back to count up the ghastly losses. Cleburne gone, Brown wounded, Cheatham wounded, no less than six other generals killed, and 6,000 men with them, and the worst of it all was that it was so needless, for Hood could have crossed the Harpeth higher up and flanked Schofield out of his position. Forrest, indeed, had tried it for himself, to reach the Union rear. But while fire and steel made a fierce twilight along the Franklin barricades, the rebel riders came up, mounted out at the stream to encounter something new in cavalry tactics—Wilson's own invention—troopers who sent their horses to the rear and fought it out on the ground from cover with those deadly repeaters. In vain the great raider tried to break through, tried to outflank; the level lines of bullets were everywhere, as Hood's main force went reeling back into that night of disaster, all but the dead were on the south bank again and Nathan Bedford Forrest had taken the first defeat of his career.

The rude check ruined Hood's pursuit; he followed on with limping step and arrived before Nashville on the 2d December, with his officers looking askance and saying very little. He laid the place under a kind of siege, with trench-lines to the south of it, Cheatham on the right of his position, Stewart on the left and Lee in the center.

Andy Smith and his XVI Corps had joined Thomas; he was strong enough to fight a battle, and the Washington people wanted him to do it at once, before the slippery rebels should get away southward or maneuver round his wings for an invasion. Thomas refused; Wilson still had not all his cavalry mounted. An argument by wire rose; Lincoln, Grant

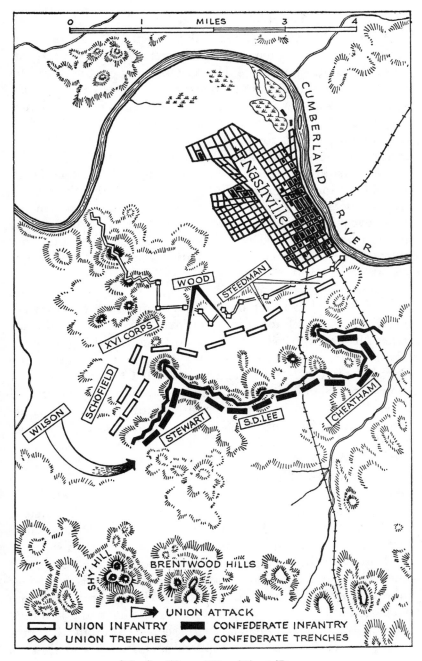

Nashville—The First Day

and Halleck telegraphed every day, a song of a single note: "Move before it is too late," but still Thomas would not. They thought that since Hood had escaped Sherman he would also get away from Thomas, but the old man understood it was a question of supply; in Alabama Hood had moved light, living on the country, here he was pinned to his wagons. Grant threatened him with removal; Thomas said he would submit to that but would not attack till ready. "The Washington authorities treat me like a schoolboy," he told Wilson, "but if they'll let me alone I'll lick them yet." The thing went on for two weeks; on the 12th wired that he was ready, but a storm of sleet blew up that night and the ground became glazed with ice on which cavalry could not move. On the 14th Grant lost patience and sent Logan out to take command.

Thomas had not heard of it; the night Logan got on the train it started to thaw and when the morning sun rose behind a curtain of fog his battalions moved out to the attack. He had worked out an arrangement nothing short of Napoleonic; Steedman with the "provisional troops" came forward on the left of the line toward Cheatham, who of course could not see what manner of men they were and must keep his position to resist an assault that never came. The IV Corps (now under Wood instead of wounded Stanley) similarly demonstrated to hold Lee fixed, center. With two-thirds of the Confederate army thus neutralized by less than one-third of his, Thomas had the XXIII and XVI Corps and Wilson's cavalry to throw against Stewart on the rebel left.

Forrest was off on a raid with most of Hood's horse, a mistake at a time when the exhausted Confederacy could not afford errors. The rest, under Chalmers, made a stand as Wilson came sweeping down on the flank of their line, but they were smothered by superior numbers; their stand was hardly a delay. Behind his left flank Hood's protective line consisted of a series of redoubts with guns in them. The men of Smith's and Schofield's corps, seeped through the gaps everywhere, drove out the supporting infantry and shot up

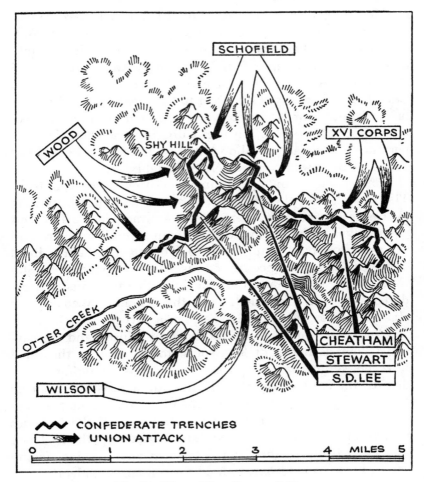

Nashville—The Second Day

the redoubts with their own artillery from three sides.
Stewart could not stand it; his whole position was being
taken, point by point. He called on Lee for help; Lee sent
a division but at that moment Thomas released Wood and
the IV Corps for a frontal attack on Lee's line, and that
broke too. The Confederate left and center were crushed
and driven in, and as twilight closed down on the day of
fighting, the rebels were flowing back by every road. They

had lost 3,000 men and 20 cannon; Thomas barely 500.

It was hopeless to make a long retreat in the face of Wilson's cavalry; the game had to be played out. Fortunately for Hood's army, night found them only two miles behind their first position on a knot of hills, the Brentwood Hills. Cheatham's Corps was switched to the weak left and strung back from Stewart's position, where he had a salient at Shy Hill; everybody spent the night digging trenches. The experience of the war had shown that such a position could not be taken by assault; Hood felt reasonably safe.

The change in Cheatham's position had countered Thomas' plan for the morning; he spent the night sliding the IV Corps behind the others to get around Hood's left, but when dawn broke, he found Cheatham in position there and the rebel line paralleling his own. There was an angle in it, however; Thomas concentrated his artillery opposite the Shy Hill salient to enfilade the line in both directions and ordered Wood in. He failed; Post, the brigadier who led the charge, was killed, and Hood's plan a success.

A success—but it failed to allow for Wilson and the cavalry. Thomas had sent him south to get around the rebel left; he submerged Chalmers and came swinging north against the flank of Cheatham's line, the irresistible troopers coming right over everything. Cheatham dug some trenches to stop them; they lapped around the ends of the trenches and through their center. Nothing could stop them; Hood took men from all three corps to form another line, facing south, backs to his front, to hold the onrushing riders.

Wilson found the going harder; rode off to seek his general. He found Thomas standing opposite Schofield's part of the line, talking calmly with that leader. "For God's sake, order an attack," cried the young cavalryman. "My men are in Hood's rear, you can see their guidons flutter beyond that hill." The old man lifted his glasses with maddening deliberation, gazed through them for a minute, then turned quietly to Schofield. "You may attack at once, general." Wilson started to gallop back to his command; before he had gone twenty paces, Schofield's, Smith's and Wood's men went forward at the run, and the Confederate line cracked like an egg-shell, everywhere at once and without a break.

They were done; the Union infantrymen swarmed through their trenches and took prisoners by the regiment. By nightfall Hood had lost 72 guns and 5,000 captured, the biggest haul since Vicksburg. That night, as Wilson led the pursuit out the southern roads, far in advance of the infantry, expecting to ride into the rebels every moment, he heard the beat of galloping hooves behind him and pulled up to see what the messenger would bring. It was not a messenger, it was Thomas himself, "Slow-trot" Thomas, ten miles ahead of his army—"Dang it to hell, Wilson," he shouted through the dark, "didn't I tell you we'd lick them? Didn't I tell you we'd lick them?"

He had done more than that. Through the night, through the next day and next night, Wilson launched his troopers on the flying army in the most devastating pursuit of American history. Hood never got a chance to rally, never a chance to set up a rearguard. Thirteen thousand of the rebels were captured, another 10,000 cut down or taken by Wilson's merciless horsemen, nearly all the rest dispersed. Of the army of 55,000 who had followed the lion of the South across the Tennessee, less than 9,000 weary and footsore fugitives gathered behind that river a week later. Hood's army had been destroyed, the only army destroyed on the battlefield in the war; "the Rock of Chickamauga was the hammer of Nashville." There was something almost incredible in it, like the fall of an oak of a thousand years; with a shock of surprise men realized that the war in the West was ended. The Confederate government had been and was not; there were policemen in blue at every post office and Jefferson Davis was President of only three states.

46

HERE THEY COME

POLITICIANS belong to two types; the ambulant, or Francis
Blair model, in the game for excitement, who will
shoulder a musket as readily as the next man; and the
static, or the armchair-Napoleon model, terrible Turks in
speech and white mice in action. The latter type predomi-
nated in the Confederate Congress during the horrible winter
of '64–'65; all the good men had gone to war. The city lay
under a blanket of intense nervous strain; there was not
enough to eat, trains came through irregularly with the
Union cavalry raiders cutting them off now and again;
every still day brought the rumble of siege-guns, and the
hammering foot-beat of Sherman's onrushing host from
the West struck like the pounding of a gong against ear-
drums stretched to sensitivity. Defeat, defeat, defeat—the
drums of Champion's Hill and Chattanooga throbbed nearer
and nearer, the wires were down across Georgia, the only
news from the West came through the grapevine telegraphs
of rumor. Postal service had ceased; people wondered vaguely
what had become of so-and-so in Mobile or New Orleans.
Vague, ill-omened bats of the twilight fluttered through the
city; an Englishman, a Northern Quaker, an emissary from
the Blairs, trying to make a negotiated peace, efforts that
broke down inevitably on President Davis' demand for independence as the one condition, President Lincoln's demand for restoration of the Union as the one essential. Men
—and women, too—went slightly mad in Richmond those
days. Mrs. Brockett knitted her husband an entire suit of

homespun wool, an absurd pocketless creation which he wore through the streets without even exciting comment, so ordinary had any strange device to supply the overwhelming needs become. Mr. Davis dismissed the Quartermaster General of the army for making remarks about Mrs. Davis' figure. Congress demanded the dismissal of Secretary of War Seddons—"a wreck of a man, a walking skeleton, industrious, facile and senile." They sat in continual session, pouring forth all human despair and aspiration in raging debates that were never reported—to what end? for there was no paper on which to print the reports. They voted grandiose measures, touched with the unreality of madness—bill to construct twenty ironclad warships (with no shipyard in which to build them and no foundry to cast the cannon); bill to purchase and arm 200,000 black slave-soldiers (with not 5,000 muskets in the Confederacy); bill to enforce more strictly the conscription act in Texas and Louisiana (from which there had not even been letters since the fall of Vicksburg 18 months before); bill, finally, to make Robert E. Lee military dictator of the Confederacy, superseding Mr. President Davis, in whom no one any longer had confidence.

This, at least, was concrete, realizable. Lee took hold. The great essential was to stop Sherman; he called Joe Johnston out of retirement to the task, and gave him Hardee and Bragg for corps commanders. In the hour of emergency the Confederacy was sinking personal feelings to bring together whatever it held of genius, hard fighters, skilled tacticians, for a last stand. Johnston reckoned up 34,000 men he could count on—the wreckage of Hood's western army, brought across Sherman's desert by a melancholy winter march, the militia of Georgia and the Carolinas, fragmentary forces from here and there.

He was not without hope of making good his defense; the country stood his aid. Sherman's army was in Savannah with the South Carolina littoral before it, a land low and swampy, furnishing no supplies, all cut criss-cross by rice-flats and broad, slow rivers bordered with swamps eight or nine miles wide. The whole is one huge morass, known as the Salkehatchie swamps; there are no roads but narrow causeways on which a hundred may hold back ten thousand. The weather had turned sour and stormy with the new year; January brought snow and drenching rains along the river sources and the lowlands were drowned. That heartened the Confederate generals; they met near Augusta to discuss whether Sherman would strike for that city or Charleston. Nobody could be certain, and though Augusta was more important in a strategic sense, Charleston was the cradle of the Confederacy, the heart and symbol of the South; it must be held to the last. Johnston compromised by splitting his force between the two, with strong outposts and cavalry thrusts forward to hold the causeways. It would take Sherman months to work through the swamps if, indeed, he could do it at all; as soon as his direction was certain the army could be concentrated on his front.

The conference was on the first February; the corps commanders went out to take hold, Hardee to Charleston, Bragg to Augusta, and Johnston established headquarters at Columbia to wait the coming of Hood's remnants there, in the center. On the morning of the 7th he heard a commotion in the street. Hood's come, he thought, and went to the window, but it was not Hood, it was a squadron of Wade Hampton's cavalry command and the news they bore left Joe Johnston, that old tired man of war, sitting at his table with his head in his hands and tears in his eyes. The last hope was gone; Sherman had forced his way through swamp and hostile armies, neither on Charleston nor Augusta, but straight between the two for Columbia and now stood outside the city with 60,000 men behind him.

How did he do it?—for the march was incredible, with twenty-five hundred wagons dragging along behind with the supplies and not a dry foot of ground in over a hundred miles. Partly through skill—these were woodsmen from the great Northwest. Partly through will; South Carolina had something coming anyway, she was the first state to secede, the state that had begun that war, the head of the rebellion. The army faced her in a grim mood. Then, two days out, the vanguard of Howard's wing found half a dozen of their skirmishers hanging from trees beside a causeway; the men had been tortured and mutilated before killing and on each breast was pinned a note—"Death to all foragers." The news ran down the marching files, touching them to incandescent anger. There was a solemn funeral service through the camp, with the tight-lipped captains for mourners; then the soldiers turned north to make the Carolinas feel the weight of their war. "The whole army is burning with an insatiable desire for vengeance on South Carolina," wrote Sherman. "I almost tremble for her fate, but I feel she deserves all that seems in store for her."

She got all she deserved. The advance-guard deployed through swamps and bottom-lands where the water stood to their shoulders, carrying cartridge-boxes around their necks and muskets overhead. They climbed tree-roots to shoot the rebel defenders down; they swam rivers naked to get in their rear; they attacked every post with the reckless and disciplined fury of a swarm of wasps. The causeway guards ran away when voices called at them out of the dark—"We're Bill Sherman's men; you better git!" Behind this surge of fighters, under the dripping skies by day, under flaring torches by night, the choppers toiled; down came the trees, their tops were woven to a lattice on which the trunks were laid to form a corduroy of wooden road, and the wagons rumbled ceaselessly behind. At Beaufort's Mills the Salkehatchie has fifteen channels; fifteen bridges were built over them in a day; the Edisto is half a mile wide; Howard's wing spanned it in four hours. The Army of the West had penetrated the wide marsh, a task as huge as a labor of Hercules, in sixteen days. Johnston could not believe it at first, then, "There has not been such an army since Julius Cæsar," he cried. "We are lost!" And whenever that pitiless army reached a town or lonely house, everything in it went; no pillage—smash, burn, destroy.

Columbia was a large city of fine wooden homes. When Hampton's rebel cavalry left, they piled long ranks of torn cotton bales down the centers of the streets, intending to burn them, but Logan's XV Corps was so hot on their heels they fled before the job was done. The wind blew up a gale, scattering puffs of cotton through the air like smoldering snow. Sherman gave orders to put the fires out, but the citizens, in a silly effort at conciliation, brought the Union soldiers whisky by the pailful. They got roaring drunk; instead of extinguishing the fires they set new ones; the resinous pine houses caught fast, and before morning the city was a torch, an inferno of flame and yells, with a mob of escaped slaves, stragglers and released convicts from the penitentiary howling among the ruins. Bitter is the wine of wrath, but remember, Carolinans—"You can have no conflict without yourselves being the aggressors. You have no oath registered in heaven to destroy this government—"

Sherman had outmaneuvered Johnston by his blow at the center. The loss of Columbia split the outlying wings of the little Confederate army; they could not be concentrated short of Raleigh in North Carolina, the railroad roots of Charleston were cut off and Hardee had to march out ingloriously without even a stand, for a long, exhausting tramp up country. He met the other corps there early in March; the same day Johnston received a letter from Lee—"If you are forced back from Raleigh and we are deprived of the supplies from eastern North Carolina I do not see how this army can be supported. The supplies in Virginia are exhausted." Sherman was rushing on inevitably; on the 9th he had taken Cheraw, where Hampton tried to surprise a Union camp by night and met a stinging defeat when wild Kilpatrick came thundering through the gray false dawn at the head of his horsemen; on the 13th Fayetteville went and with it the last arsenal in the East.

Only one way to stop Sherman—beat him in a battle, not an easy thing to do, but if anyone could, it was Joe Johnston. The country was now rolling upland, thickly wooded, not unlike the Wilderness of Virginia, hence favorable to the smaller force. At Averasboro Johnston intrenched Hardee's Corps for a delaying fight in difficult ground between river and marsh. Sherman himself was with the advance; he pinned Hardee to his trenches with artillery from the front, sent a brigade by circuit through the marsh, broke the rebel left and swept along their line; darkness alone saved Hardee.

It rained with infinite persistence, but the Union army ploughed right ahead through the muck, and worse was coming, for Schofield and the XXIII Corps, garlanded with the great victory at Nashville, were brought round by Washington and sea, and were coming up-country to join the invincible Sherman. If Johnston could not beat him before they fell in, he would never be able to do it afterward and he knew it, and every man in his army knew it, and the Confederacy knew it, and there was something like a hush of breathless dread over the lowlands as he gathered his strength for one last fierce blow at the Union columns on the roads south of Bentonville.

Last stand! Slocum had the Union left wing, with the XIV Corps in the lead; the XX Corps, delayed by rain and road-accidents, was eight miles behind. On the morning of the 13th March the rebel rearguard resistance stiffened; Union General of Division Carlin noted that the foragers sent out that morning were in the roadside ditches; they had been unable to deploy. The country was plastered with dense thicket that made for invisibility at twenty paces, and there was firing up ahead. Toward noon Carlin came to a clearing and a line of breastworks right across the road, reaching away into the unknown on either hand. There were cannon behind the breastwork and a rolling volley indicated the presence of a heavy force of infantry. Carlin deployed and joined battle; the rebels pressed him hotly with local charges among the thickets and their lines reached beyond both his flanks. Slocum rode up, saw the state of affairs, and hurried the other two divisions of the corps into line, Morgan on Carlin's right, Buell in close reserve.

Morgan stabilized things on his side, but Carlin was

still flanked from his left; Slocum had to put in his last man, making one long line without reserves. Just as Buell moved into position there came a crash of musketry from the flank, the old rebel yell went thrilling through the woods and half Johnston's army stormed out of nowhere onto his flank and rear. He was caught between two fires; regiment after regiment melted off and away; Carlin's flank was naked, the onrushing Confederates came right down the line and carried everything before them. Morgan, now caught by the double fire, was driven back to a desperate defense on the edge of a swamp, cut off from the rest and almost surrounded.

But these were not green troops to break up, however they might be caught at disadvantage. Half a mile back Buell had rallied; Williams with the vanguard of the XX Corps arrived, and the men in blue came back for a sturdy bayonet charge into the flank of the rebels who were trying to scoop up Morgan. The Confederates faced round; more and more of the XX Corps came up; Carlin rallied, Slocum extended his line, and when the rebels extended to meet the movement, he threw forward a heavy column in another bayonet charge that pierced their center. They went back; at twilight they were in their trench-line again, clinging for dear life. Last stand!

No more than Hood in similar case dared they retreat. The last stand had to be made there. At dawn Sherman rode onto the field, with a cloak of cheering round him, and the Confederates' hearts sank into their boots. Behind the Union general came Logan and the XV Corps, who had marched double-quick all night. Without a rest they came into the morning's battle; the rebels were slowly driven backward to a defensive line with its wings on swamps. At noon Blair and still another Union corps came in; Sherman sent them in a sweeping circuit around Johnston's left just as a messenger arrived to say Schofield was only half an hour distant. Blair's men threaded the swamp, opened fire on the rebel rear; the other three Union corps came rolling on in front, and the last hope of the Confederacy spun back and back, down into the black abyss of utter ruin. When Johnston collected the little force there were not 17,000 left; he had lost Raleigh and Goldsboro and was being crowded toward the coast by Sherman's 90,000, with the pillars of smoke by day and fire by night that marked the burning homesteads of the Carolinas coming nearer hour by hour.

He surrendered; and the Radicals in Congress disgraced themselves by refusing to carry out the just and generous terms that Sherman gave.

47

FINAL INTERLUDE

The High Clear Note

Aᴌᴌ along the east coast the dawn came in under ragged clouds pursued by a gale, and discharging torrents of rain. In New York they canceled the jubilee for the fall of Charleston, but the inauguration of a President is a more serious matter, and as early as eight o'clock people began to assemble in the mud beneath the platform at the east portico of the Capitol. There were pickets of cavalry at the street corners, but their purpose was as ornamental as that of the marshals who galloped up and down in parti-colored uniforms through what gradually became a drizzle, and as noon approached, clearing weather. Just before the hour the honored guests came out and began to take their places, General Hooker prominent among them with his handsome florid face, and dear old Admiral Farragut. By this time a good many crinolines had been crushed and the ladies who wore them were plentifully bedaubed with mud.

The President was prompt, looking worn and thin; he paused at the door to tell the chief marshal not to let Johnson speak outside, since the new Vice-President had just created a horrible scandal by appearing drunk in the Senate chamber and pronouncing so incoherent a harangue that Welles thought him deranged and many of the senators covered their faces. Mr. Lincoln shuffled his papers and stepped forward. There was silence.

"Fellow-countrymen:—At this second appearing to take the oath of the presidential office there is less occasion for an extended address than there was at the first. Then a statement somewhat in detail of a course to be pursued seemed fitting and proper. Now, at the expiration of four years, during which public declarations have been constantly called forth on every point and phase of the great contest which still absorbs the attention and engrosses the energies of the nation, little that is new could be presented. The progress of our arms, upon which all else chiefly depends, is as well known to the public as to myself, and it is, I trust, reasonably satisfactory and encouraging to all. With high hope for the future, no prediction in regard to it is ventured.

"On the occasion corresponding to this four years ago all our thoughts were anxiously directed to an impending civil war. All dreaded it, all sought to avert it. While the inaugural address was being delivered from this place, devoted altogether to *saving* the Union without war, insurgent agents were in the city seeking to *destroy* it without war—seeking to dissolve the Union and divide effects by negotiation. Both parties deprecated war, but one of them would *make* war rather than let the nation survive, and the other would *accept* war rather than let it perish—"

An appreciative murmur and a few handclaps came from the crowd.

"—and the war came.

"One-eighth of the whole population was colored slaves, not distributed generally over the Union, but localized in the southern part of it. These slaves constituted a peculiar and powerful interest. All knew that this interest was somehow the cause of the war. To strengthen, perpetuate, and extend this interest was the object for which the insurgents would rend the Union even by war, while the Government claimed no right to do more than to restrict the territorial enlargement of it. Neither party expected for the war the magnitude or the duration which it has already attained. Neither anticipated that the *cause* of the conflict might cease with or even before the conflict itself should cease."

The first small cheer.

"Each looked for an easier triumph, and a result less

fundamental and astounding. Both read the same Bible and pray to the same God, and each invokes His aid against the other. It may seem strange that any man should dare to ask a just God's assistance in wringing their bread from the sweat of other men's faces, but let us judge not, that we be not judged. The prayers of both could not be answered. That of neither has been answered fully."

A short burst of laughter quickly died.

"The Almighty has His own purposes. 'Woe unto the world because of offenses; for it must needs be that offenses come, but woe to that man by whom the offense cometh.' If we shall suppose that American slavery is one of those offenses which, in the providence of God, must needs come, but which, having continued through His appointed time, He now wills to remove, and that He gives to both North and South this terrible war as the woe due to those by whom the offense came, shall we discern therein any departure from those divine attributes which the believers in a living God always ascribe to Him? Fondly do we hope, fervently do we pray, that this mighty scourge of war may speedily pass away. Yet, if God wills that it continue until all the wealth piled by the bondsman's two hundred and fifty years of unrequited toil shall be sunk, and until every drop of blood drawn with the lash shall be paid by another drawn with the sword, as was said three thousand years ago, so still it must be said, 'The judgments of the Lord are true and righteous altogether.'

"With malice toward none, with charity for all, with firmness in the right as God gives us to see the right, let us strive on to finish the work we are in, to bind up the nation's wounds, to care for him who shall have borne the battle and for his widow and his orphan, to do all which may achieve and cherish a just and lasting peace among ourselves and with all nations."

There was a polite pattering of hands. The opinion of the reporters was that he had done neither well nor badly, but Mr. Sumner's face was twisted in a smile of contempt.

48

EVENING STAR

I<small>T</small> <small>WAS</small> autumn; Grant pecked viciously at the lines round Petersburg and Richmond in affairs of a single corps, quick half-arm jolts that had Lee rushing men to and fro like the collision-crew of a foundering vessel. "We loosened our laces each night in uncertainty as to where the next blow would come," said one defender—let just one blue wave come through, the whole ocean follows and down goes the ship. While Sheridan and his uproarious horsemen were blowing along the Shenandoah, Grant took Hancock and the II Corps out of line, slipped them across the James and tried a straight drive on Richmond along the northern bank. It failed; Lee got there first and threw up new works, Hancock lost 2,700 men and made no gain. Before he rejoined at Petersburg, Warren tried a sweep round Lee's right wing. He stalled in the scrub, but before he stalled got across the Weldon Railroad. Lee could not bear that; it reduced the Richmond supply roads to three. He rapidly switched his small mobile force from the north of the James to the south of Petersburg and sent A. P. Hill in on Warren for a surprise attack. Hill rolled up half Warren's line with all the old rebel dash, but the V Corps clung to the railroad by its eyebrows; Warren rallied his routed men and brought them back in a counterstroke that lamed Hill. The railroad was held; Grant brought Hancock back from the north and sent him in a wider sweep south around Warren's position. He crossed the railroad at Ream's Station. Lee's cavalry had spotted the movement, he sent Hill out

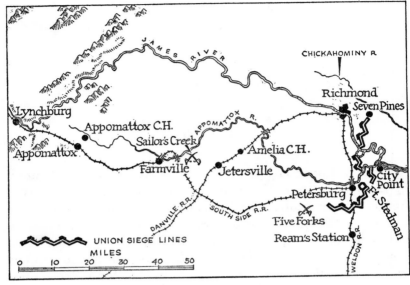

The Last Stand

again and Hill ambushed Hancock. The II Corps was driven with heavy loss.

Right—left—right; Grant kept pounding away with both hands. Ord with the XVIII and Birney with the X Corps tried next, north of the James again, a wide sweep. Ord skirted Lee's new works, hurried fast-moving columns in at break of day and carried Fort Harrison, a key-work of the main Richmond defenses, then turned to clear out the line both ways. He fell wounded; the general who succeeded got mixed on directions and the gain stopped, for this leak was so serious that Lee hurried three divisions and James Longstreet up to plug it. The same night Warren and Hancock began pounding the south end of the line again, trying to curve round for a lodgment on the South Side Railroad. They failed after a bitter, tangled struggle in the scrub; Lee extended his lines once more and threw up a whole new system of fortifications.

Left—right—left; Cavalry Gregg took his riders on a raid south along the Weldon Railroad; they broke up the wagon service Lee had organized to replace that supply-line, and the Confederates sent out Hill's Corps to suppress them. Grant had foreseen that; he had Hancock lying in wait on the flank of Hill's route. When Hill came along Hancock jumped out of the bushes onto him and there was a roaring battle in which he repaid them with interest for his check at Ream's Station. The XVIII Corps circled across the old Seven Pines battlefield and bored into the defenses north of Richmond. The outer lines were won; then Lee got his collision-crew up to plug this leak, too, new forts were built and winter came in sleet and darkness to bring a truce after six months of battle.

Lee had been magnificent, fending off twice his numbers by able engineering, quick movement and audacious riposte; now he had to spend the winter getting things to eat. His army was in a terrible state; bled white by battle-losses. Grant's hammering had done its work on their minds, too, they were deserting by dozens—what, face another such summer in hell? From Seven Pines down the front was one long fort, thirty-seven miles of fort, and less than 60,000 left to man it as spring came on, a bare garrison on the best of terms and no reserve for emergencies. To fight it out there was hopeless; he knew his Grant now, fair skies and spring weather would bring him pounding down, one-two, two-one, both flanks and in the center, the thinned lines would rupture. There was only one chance; Lee and President Davis worked it out together at a secret conference, a plan of matchless boldness—concentrate on the east side of Petersburg, hurl a fast-moving column through Grant's lines there like a cannon-shot, smash up his base at City Point. He must draw troops from both wings to restore the center there; when he did it, the Army of Northern Virginia would be loaded onto trains, ride like fire down the Danville road into Carolina, unite with Johnston and smite Sherman a knockout blow. . . . But that will mean abandoning Richmond to Grant? . . . But if we destroy Sherman it can easily be recovered; if we cannot stop Sherman nothing matters.

The assault was planned with minute care; Gordon, the

best fighter since Hood, to lead it. A corps of pioneers marched first with axes to cut through the abatis of the Federal lines; then three columns of infantry, the flower of the army, lastly the cavalry, to make the rush for City Point.

On the night of March 25 picked men, simulating deserters, belly-wobbled their way to the Union picket-line and smothered it; on the morning of the 26th, half-past four, pitch dark and a soup of fog, the attackers rose and rushed. The trench-guards were taken, the storming columns swept out two batteries and went up the parapet of a big work, Fort Stedman. The garrison woke; their guns thundered into the thick of the columns while their leaders were already within the fort. There was a long-drawn, stumbling, snarling fight among the traverses in the half-dark before the place was won. Mischance dogged Gordon; his guides had fallen at the first fire, he fumbled through the ground behind the fort with what men he had at hand, unable to find the route to the works that held the Nationals' second line. Daybreak found him there; Parke of the IX Corps, on whose men the shock had fallen, got his reserve artillery onto a hill where it fired down into Fort Stedman, Union divisions charged down the line from both sides and rewon all but the fort itself. Stedman was isolated, with a destructive mortar-fire plunging into it; retreat and advance alike were barred off by fences of bullets. Gordon's storming columns slipped through his fingers like water, trickling back in little groups to the Confederate lines, the men caught in the fort surrendered and the great assault was beaten to smash with a loss of 6,000 men.

Grant heard of it at half-past seven and the purpose of the move was not hidden from him; at half-past eight he had Ord in motion from the north of the James to the south of Petersburg, a secret march to get around the Confederates, across the railroads back from Richmond and cut Lee's retreat. Ord's men took Warren's place in the trenches; the V Corps came out to lead the march. Behind Warren moved the II Corps, now under a new commander, Humphreys, "an extremely neat man, continually washing himself and putting on paper dickeys" but full of the spirit of combat, who rode among the whistling bullets with a giggle—"A pretty little fight. He, he, he!" At the head of them all roved blazing Sheridan, with the cavalry of Cedar Creek behind him, 13,000 strong; he had charge of the whole movement as Grant's deputy, who had been urging just this move for three weeks, pacing the headquarters floor like a hound in leash—"I tell you I'm ready to strike out now and smash them up. Let me go! Let me go!"

Lee noted the signs of movement in the lines opposite, penetrated Grant's design as Grant had penetrated his. Bold and skillful to the last, he scraped up every battalion he could gather and, placing 15,000 infantry and all his horse under Pickett, the dashing red-haired captain who had commanded the charge at Gettysburg, sent them on a wide circuit to crush the Union left from Five Forks and roll up their whole line. A. P. Hill should swing into the movement from his position. Last stand!

Both armies felt toward contact through the forest; on the 30th, they began to touch; the 31st was a day of pouring rain and few movements, though Humphreys and Warren had a hard fight with the rebels on their front, stopped A. P. Hill and then drove him back to his point of departure. Sheridan's outriders were driven in by Pickett's stroke, but they impacted, dismounted, around Dinwiddie Court House, and the Confederate leader could not move them farther.

On the morning of the 1st April, Sheridan was up and united; he beat back the rebel cavalry, drove it in onto their foot soldiers and forced the latter to intrench a flat crescent around Five Forks. With one cavalry division he menaced their front, dismounted men skipping among the trees as though the skirmishers of a heavy force; with another, he circled toward their right flank, westward. Pickett was held, not daring to pivot on his left; if he tried it, those horsemen would be in his rear. But Sheridan's real attack was coming from the other wing; Warren bringing the V

Corps in on an oblique behind the rear of Pickett's line from the position he had gained in the counter against Hill.

Warren was a good man, but an engineer and a perfectionist; he first delayed, sending dispatches with a dozen different suggestions for changing routes of march, then drew his sketch-map with the orders wrong, so that two of his divisions missed Pickett's flank entirely, and the third, with which Sheridan rode, took fire into its own left from Five Forks. Under the general's eye it wheeled round, beat off the rebel blow, and then attacked, right along the line that was facing the Union horsemen, while the independent cavalry division of Mackenzie, which Grant had hurried forward, swept for Pickett's rear. Sheridan, with a cavalry guidon in one hand, leaped his big black horse over the rebel barricade; Pickett's line went all to pieces, his men fled, his force was thrown west and away, across the South Side Railroad, he lost 2,500 casualties, 4,500 prisoners, his artillery, and Lee's mobile force, the blade and point of his sword, was destroyed. Sheridan was dissatisfied with Warren's conduct; the man would argue about his orders instead of executing them; in spite of his service and renown, he was removed and Griffin succeeded to the corps.

But Five Forks was not the worst for Lee; Sheridan had sent runners to advise Grant he was heavily engaged. Grant reasoned thus—if Lee has found men to make a sortie at the end of the line, his thirty-seven miles of forts must be thinly held elsewhere. He ordered assault along the whole front. Ord, Wright, Parke, Humphreys hurled their heavy masses at the intrenchments that had defied them for a year. The men in blue went running forward, possessed by a febrile excitement; the cannon cut lanes in the ranks, but there were no slips of paper now, they rushed right in. The defenders stood to their guns with desperate valor for half the day— then a great cheer welled up from Parke's IX Corps. They had won through; Ord's men, next in line, redoubled their efforts, then they began to cheer, too, then Wright, then Humphreys, the lines were broken at every point, and Petersburg was taken, the last bulwark of the Confederacy.

April 2 was a Sunday. President Davis went to St. Paul's Church as usual. "The sound of the church bells rose into the cloudless sky and floated on the blue tide of the beautiful day." An air of elation possessed Richmond; the day before a wonderful rumor had come through that Lee had crushed Grant's whole front in a surprise night attack, the *Examiner* had commented on the glad news. Half-way through the service a man entered the church, stood a moment irresolute, oblivious of the stares he attracted, then stepped down the aisle and pressed a note into the President's hand. Those in the adjoining pews saw Mr. Davis flush; he got to his feet and left the church, followed by his wife. Half an hour later a rumble of wagons began in the streets; crowds of sharp-faced individuals, never seen by daylight, gathered round the commissary stores, summoned by some mysterious telegraphy of their own, and then the men of General Ewell's Corps began marching through the streets, heads down, ragged and dirty, faces turned west and away. Doors banged, people with misshapen bundles filled the sidewalks, hurrying toward the railroad stations. Somewhere there was an explosion and a black column of smoke ascended into the still air. As night came on there began to be yelling and riots; the mob burst into the liquor shops and the gutters ran freshets of booze at which vagabonds dipped with pails. The tobacco warehouses at the south end of the city were burning; Mayor Mayo, incoherently masticating tobacco, was trying to preside over a session of the City Council in the attic-room of the Capitol, but felt called on every five minutes to run out for a look at the fires or listen to the latest explosions. Nobody slept; under the red glare women and children camped in the parks, dressed in their best clothes in order to save them, and it was years before dawn crept in beneath the black mantle of smoke that hung over the city. And with the dawn came a tremendous shout of bugles, and then a river of men in new blue uniforms brimmed the street, with a general riding at their head and the cavalry horses waltzing as the band played "Garry Owen."

Richmond could not believe it till a black regiment passed,

teeth and sabers shining—then it knew that it was a captured town.

Last stand! Lee was trying to get away to Danville or Lynchburg and make a guerrilla fight of it among the mountains. He had ordered a train of supplies for his starving army up to Amelia Court House, where the Appomattox makes a long loop, but the Richmond politicians were stupid to the last. They changed the destination of the train to Richmond, threw the food off and loaded it with their archives. Archives! Lee's men had nothing to eat. Before he could get to Amelia Court House, for that matter, Sheridan was hot in pursuit with the cavalry and the V Corps.

On the 4th they got across Lee's line of retreat at Jetersville; the V Corps intrenched. Meade was following fast with the II and VI Corps and if Lee tried to break through the V Corps they would strike his flanks. That ended the chance of Lee's joining Johnston; there remained the possibility of reaching Lynchburg and making a mountain campaign. "Where shall I halt for the night?" Ewell asked his general. "Just across the Tennessee line," answered Lee in grim humor. Sheridan's horse were all around him, it was one continual rearguard fight. One of the Confederate corps would halt and intrench a holding position, past which the rest marched; then another corps intrenched behind the first line and the earlier rearguard passed through. It was slow work, with constant rain and bad roads. A division of Sheridan's slipped around one of the rearguards, captured the rebel wagon-train and burned Lee's papers and baggage. Most of his artillery went the same way.

Thanks to stops for holding off gadfly Sheridan, the rebel march went slow and slower; the Union infantry gained and on the 6th Humphreys and the II Corps caught up with Ewell, then in rearguard at Sailor's Creek. It was a pretty little fight, he, he, he; the Union guns fired across the stream at the height where Ewell had taken position, Humphreys' infantry began to work on his flanks. Ewell could not charge the galling guns across the marshy brook; Wright and the

VI Corps got up and thrust into the gap between him and Lee's main army; a deadly hail of bullets flicked at the hill from every direction, and General of Division R. S. Ewell, with bursting heart, put up a white flag and surrendered a whole corps of the army of Northern Virginia, what was left of a whole corps, 8,000 men.

Lee dared not stay and attempt a rescue; the ghost of the great Army of Northern Virginia staggered on with Sheridan whipping round to get across its retreat before it would reach Lynchburg and the mountain gaps. Grant was in Farmville the night of the 7th; a note came from Sheridan saying that his cavalry had worked across Lee's line at Appomattox Court House, but he might not be able to sustain the position against the full strength of the Confederates. He wanted an infantry corps to help him and another one to make an attack on Lee's rear that would delay his march for half a dozen hours, or long enough for the infantry to get up behind his riders. Ord was on the roads south; Grant sent him to Sheridan by forced marches through the night. The VI Corps had just come up from a hard day's march and were camping near Farmville; Grant ruthlessly ordered them out of bed for the attack on the rebel rear.

Did they grumble? No—a high jubilation had taken possession of the Army of the Potomac, they were all marching as though in seven-leagued boots and fighting like wildcats. "Notwithstanding their long march that day the men sprang to their feet with a spirit that made everyone marvel, and came swinging through the main street of the village with a step as elastic as on the first day of their tramp. They spied the Commander-in-Chief watching them from the piazza of the hotel with evident pride. Bonfires were lit on both sides of the street, the men seized straw and pine knots as improvised torches, the bands burst into music, arms were tossed in the air and caught again," and Wright drove in. Last stand! Lee's men beat off the attack in sad, heroic rallies.

Toward morning he disengaged and took up his *via dolorosa* once more. At Appomattox Court House the vanguard ran into Sheridan's cavalry. The Confederates opened fire, but the Union horsemen, disdaining to answer, parted left and right to reveal solid blue lines of infantry, all in position round their numerous cannon. Gordon was leading Lee's march. He went back to seek the general and told him of what he had seen. Lee threw back his head—"Then there is nothing left for me to do but to go and see General Grant, and I would rather die a thousand deaths."

They met early in the morning at the house of a Mr. McLean, a curious meeting, well arranged to be the subject of a painting. Lee was gorgeous in full dress uniform, with the gold-mounted sword given him by the state of Virginia at his side; Grant unkempt and frowzy, in an old private's jacket with the stars of his generalship attached to the shoulders. They talked a few minutes, a strained, halting conversation; then Grant wrote out the terms for the surrender of the Army of Northern Virginia. Lee read them, calm and dignified—"This will have a very happy effect on our people," he remarked when he came to the provision that allowed his men to keep their horses and his officers their sidearms. His aide wrote out an acceptance; with a little embarrassment in his voice, he asked for rations for his starving soldiers, then signed the surrender, clasped hands with Grant, stepped to the door and rode out of history.

Grant left the room a moment later, stopping on the porch to light a cigar, then turned to one of his staff:

"Ingalls," he said, "do you remember that old white mule so-and-so used to ride in the city of Mexico?"

The Civil War was over.

A CATALOG OF SELECTED
DOVER BOOKS
IN ALL FIELDS OF INTEREST

A CATALOG OF SELECTED DOVER
BOOKS IN ALL FIELDS OF INTEREST

CONCERNING THE SPIRITUAL IN ART, Wassily Kandinsky. Pioneering work by father of abstract art. Thoughts on color theory, nature of art. Analysis of earlier masters. 12 illustrations. 80pp. of text. 5⅜ x 8½. 23411-8 Pa. $3.95

ANIMALS: 1,419 Copyright-Free Illustrations of Mammals, Birds, Fish, Insects, etc., Jim Harter (ed.). Clear wood engravings present, in extremely lifelike poses, over 1,000 species of animals. One of the most extensive pictorial sourcebooks of its kind. Captions. Index. 284pp. 9 x 12. 23766-4 Pa. $12.95

CELTIC ART: The Methods of Construction, George Bain. Simple geometric techniques for making Celtic interlacements, spirals, Kells-type initials, animals, humans, etc. Over 500 illustrations. 160pp. 9 x 12. (USO) 22923-8 Pa. $9.95

AN ATLAS OF ANATOMY FOR ARTISTS, Fritz Schider. Most thorough reference work on art anatomy in the world. Hundreds of illustrations, including selections from works by Vesalius, Leonardo, Goya, Ingres, Michelangelo, others. 593 illustrations. 192pp. 7⅛ x 10¼. 20241-0 Pa. $9 95

CELTIC HAND STROKE-BY-STROKE (Irish Half-Uncial from "The Book of Kells"): An Arthur Baker Calligraphy Manual, Arthur Baker. Complete guide to creating each letter of the alphabet in distinctive Celtic manner. Covers hand position, strokes, pens, inks, paper, more. Illustrated. 48pp. 8¼ x 11. 24336-2 Pa. $3.95

EASY ORIGAMI, John Montroll. Charming collection of 32 projects (hat, cup, pelican, piano, swan, many more) specially designed for the novice origami hobbyist. Clearly illustrated easy-to-follow instructions insure that even beginning papercrafters will achieve successful results. 48pp. 8¼ x 11. 27298-2 Pa. $2.95

THE COMPLETE BOOK OF BIRDHOUSE CONSTRUCTION FOR WOOD-WORKERS, Scott D. Campbell. Detailed instructions, illustrations, tables. Also data on bird habitat and instinct patterns. Bibliography. 3 tables. 63 illustrations in 15 figures. 48pp. 5¼ x 8½. 24407-5 Pa. $2.50

BLOOMINGDALE'S ILLUSTRATED 1886 CATALOG: Fashions, Dry Goods and Housewares, Bloomingdale Brothers. Famed merchants' extremely rare catalog depicting about 1,700 products: clothing, housewares, firearms, dry goods, jewelry, more. Invaluable for dating, identifying vintage items. Also, copyright-free graphics for artists, designers. Co-published with Henry Ford Museum & Greenfield Village. 160pp. 8¼ x 11. 25780-0 Pa. $9.95

HISTORIC COSTUME IN PICTURES, Braun & Schneider. Over 1,450 costumed figures in clearly detailed engravings—from dawn of civilization to end of 19th century. Captions. Many folk costumes. 256pp. 8⅜ x 11¾. 23150-X Pa. $12.95

CATALOG OF DOVER BOOKS

STICKLEY CRAFTSMAN FURNITURE CATALOGS, Gustav Stickley and L. & J. G. Stickley. Beautiful, functional furniture in two authentic catalogs from 1910. 594 illustrations, including 277 photos, show settles, rockers, armchairs, reclining chairs, bookcases, desks, tables. 183pp. 6½ x 9¼.   23838-5 Pa. $9.95

AMERICAN LOCOMOTIVES IN HISTORIC PHOTOGRAPHS: 1858 to 1949, Ron Ziel (ed.). A rare collection of 126 meticulously detailed official photographs, called "builder portraits," of American locomotives that majestically chronicle the rise of steam locomotive power in America. Introduction. Detailed captions. xi + 129pp. 9 x 12.   27393-8 Pa. $12.95

AMERICA'S LIGHTHOUSES: An Illustrated History, Francis Ross Holland, Jr. Delightfully written, profusely illustrated fact-filled survey of over 200 American lighthouses since 1716. History, anecdotes, technological advances, more. 240pp. 8 x 10¾.   25576-X Pa. $12.95

TOWARDS A NEW ARCHITECTURE, Le Corbusier. Pioneering manifesto by founder of "International School." Technical and aesthetic theories, views of industry, economics, relation of form to function, "mass-production split" and much more. Profusely illustrated. 320pp. 6⅛ x 9¼. (USO)   25023-7 Pa. $9.95

HOW THE OTHER HALF LIVES, Jacob Riis. Famous journalistic record, exposing poverty and degradation of New York slums around 1900, by major social reformer. 100 striking and influential photographs. 233pp. 10 x 7⅞.
                    22012-5 Pa. $10.95

FRUIT KEY AND TWIG KEY TO TREES AND SHRUBS, William M. Harlow. One of the handiest and most widely used identification aids. Fruit key covers 120 deciduous and evergreen species; twig key 160 deciduous species. Easily used. Over 300 photographs. 126pp. 5⅜ x 8½.   20511-8 Pa. $3.95

COMMON BIRD SONGS, Dr. Donald J. Borror. Songs of 60 most common U.S. birds: robins, sparrows, cardinals, bluejays, finches, more—arranged in order of increasing complexity. Up to 9 variations of songs of each species.
                    Cassette and manual 99911-4 $8.95

ORCHIDS AS HOUSE PLANTS, Rebecca Tyson Northen. Grow cattleyas and many other kinds of orchids—in a window, in a case, or under artificial light. 63 illustrations. 148pp. 5⅜ x 8½.   23261-1 Pa. $4.95

MONSTER MAZES, Dave Phillips. Masterful mazes at four levels of difficulty. Avoid deadly perils and evil creatures to find magical treasures. Solutions for all 32 exciting illustrated puzzles. 48pp. 8¼ x 11.   26005-4 Pa. $2.95

MOZART'S DON GIOVANNI (DOVER OPERA LIBRETTO SERIES), Wolfgang Amadeus Mozart. Introduced and translated by Ellen H. Bleiler. Standard Italian libretto, with complete English translation. Convenient and thoroughly portable—an ideal companion for reading along with a recording or the performance itself. Introduction. List of characters. Plot summary. 121pp. 5¼ x 8½.
                    24944-1 Pa. $2.95

TECHNICAL MANUAL AND DICTIONARY OF CLASSICAL BALLET, Gail Grant. Defines, explains, comments on steps, movements, poses and concepts. 15-page pictorial section. Basic book for student, viewer. 127pp. 5⅜ x 8½.
                    21843-0 Pa. $4.95

BRASS INSTRUMENTS: Their History and Development, Anthony Baines. Authoritative, updated survey of the evolution of trumpets, trombones, bugles, cornets, French horns, tubas and other brass wind instruments. Over 140 illustrations and 48 music examples. Corrected and updated by author. New preface. Bibliography. 320pp. 5⅜ x 8½. 27574-4 Pa. $9.95

HOLLYWOOD GLAMOR PORTRAITS, John Kobal (ed.). 145 photos from 1926-49. Harlow, Gable, Bogart, Bacall; 94 stars in all. Full background on photographers, technical aspects. 160pp. 8⅜ x 11¼. 23352-9 Pa. $11.95

MAX AND MORITZ, Wilhelm Busch. Great humor classic in both German and English. Also 10 other works: "Cat and Mouse," "Plisch and Plumm," etc. 216pp. 5⅜ x 8½. 20181-3 Pa. $6.95

THE RAVEN AND OTHER FAVORITE POEMS, Edgar Allan Poe. Over 40 of the author's most memorable poems: "The Bells," "Ulalume," "Israfel," "To Helen," "The Conqueror Worm," "Eldorado," "Annabel Lee," many more. Alphabetic lists of titles and first lines. 64pp. 5³⁄₁₆ x 8¼. 26685-0 Pa. $1.00

PERSONAL MEMOIRS OF U. S. GRANT, Ulysses Simpson Grant. Intelligent, deeply moving firsthand account of Civil War campaigns, considered by many the finest military memoirs ever written. Includes letters, historic photographs, maps and more. 528pp. 6⅛ x 9¼. 28587-1 Pa. $11.95

AMULETS AND SUPERSTITIONS, E. A. Wallis Budge. Comprehensive discourse on origin, powers of amulets in many ancient cultures: Arab, Persian Babylonian, Assyrian, Egyptian, Gnostic, Hebrew, Phoenician, Syriac, etc. Covers cross, swastika, crucifix, seals, rings, stones, etc. 584pp. 5⅜ x 8½. 23573-4 Pa. $12.95

RUSSIAN STORIES/PYCCKNE PACCKA3bl: A Dual-Language Book, edited by Gleb Struve. Twelve tales by such masters as Chekhov, Tolstoy, Dostoevsky, Pushkin, others. Excellent word-for-word English translations on facing pages, plus teaching and study aids, Russian/English vocabulary, biographical/critical introductions, more. 416pp. 5⅜ x 8½. 26244-8 Pa. $8.95

PHILADELPHIA THEN AND NOW: 60 Sites Photographed in the Past and Present, Kenneth Finkel and Susan Oyama. Rare photographs of City Hall, Logan Square, Independence Hall, Betsy Ross House, other landmarks juxtaposed with contemporary views. Captures changing face of historic city. Introduction. Captions. 128pp. 8¼ x 11. 25790-8 Pa. $9.95

AIA ARCHITECTURAL GUIDE TO NASSAU AND SUFFOLK COUNTIES, LONG ISLAND, The American Institute of Architects, Long Island Chapter, and the Society for the Preservation of Long Island Antiquities. Comprehensive, well-researched and generously illustrated volume brings to life over three centuries of Long Island's great architectural heritage. More than 240 photographs with authoritative, extensively detailed captions. 176pp. 8¼ x 11. 26946-9 Pa. $14.95

NORTH AMERICAN INDIAN LIFE: Customs and Traditions of 23 Tribes, Elsie Clews Parsons (ed.). 27 fictionalized essays by noted anthropologists examine religion, customs, government, additional facets of life among the Winnebago, Crow, Zuni, Eskimo, other tribes. 480pp. 6⅛ x 9¼. 27377-6 Pa. $10.95

FRANK LLOYD WRIGHT'S HOLLYHOCK HOUSE, Donald Hoffmann. Lavishly illustrated, carefully documented study of one of Wright's most controversial residential designs. Over 120 photographs, floor plans, elevations, etc. Detailed perceptive text by noted Wright scholar. Index. 128pp. 9¼ x 10¾. 27133-1 Pa. $11.95

THE MALE AND FEMALE FIGURE IN MOTION: 60 Classic Photographic Sequences, Eadweard Muybridge. 60 true-action photographs of men and women walking, running, climbing, bending, turning, etc., reproduced from rare 19th-century masterpiece. vi + 121pp. 9 x 12. 24745-7 Pa. $10.95

1001 QUESTIONS ANSWERED ABOUT THE SEASHORE, N. J. Berrill and Jacquelyn Berrill. Queries answered about dolphins, sea snails, sponges, starfish, fishes, shore birds, many others. Covers appearance, breeding, growth, feeding, much more. 305pp. 5¼ x 8¼. 23366-9 Pa. $8.95

GUIDE TO OWL WATCHING IN NORTH AMERICA, Donald S. Heintzelman. Superb guide offers complete data and descriptions of 19 species: barn owl, screech owl, snowy owl, many more. Expert coverage of owl-watching equipment, conservation, migrations and invasions, etc. Guide to observing sites. 84 illustrations. xiii + 193pp. 5⅜ x 8½. 27344-X Pa. $8.95

MEDICINAL AND OTHER USES OF NORTH AMERICAN PLANTS: A Historical Survey with Special Reference to the Eastern Indian Tribes, Charlotte Erichsen-Brown. Chronological historical citations document 500 years of usage of plants, trees, shrubs native to eastern Canada, northeastern U.S. Also complete identifying information. 343 illustrations. 544pp. 6½ x 9¼. 25951-X Pa. $12.95

STORYBOOK MAZES, Dave Phillips. 23 stories and mazes on two-page spreads: Wizard of Oz, Treasure Island, Robin Hood, etc. Solutions. 64pp. 8¼ x 11. 23628-5 Pa. $2.95

NEGRO FOLK MUSIC, U.S.A., Harold Courlander. Noted folklorist's scholarly yet readable analysis of rich and varied musical tradition. Includes authentic versions of over 40 folk songs. Valuable bibliography and discography. xi + 324pp. 5⅜ x 8½. 27350-4 Pa. $7.95

MOVIE-STAR PORTRAITS OF THE FORTIES, John Kobal (ed.). 163 glamor, studio photos of 106 stars of the 1940s: Rita Hayworth, Ava Gardner, Marlon Brando, Clark Gable, many more. 176pp. 8⅜ x 11¼. 23546-7 Pa. $12.95

BENCHLEY LOST AND FOUND, Robert Benchley. Finest humor from early 30s, about pet peeves, child psychologists, post office and others. Mostly unavailable elsewhere. 73 illustrations by Peter Arno and others. 183pp. 5⅜ x 8½. 22410-4 Pa. $6.95

YEKL and THE IMPORTED BRIDEGROOM AND OTHER STORIES OF YIDDISH NEW YORK, Abraham Cahan. Film Hester Street based on Yekl (1896). Novel, other stories among first about Jewish immigrants on N.Y.'s East Side. 240pp. 5⅜ x 8½. 22427-9 Pa. $6.95

SELECTED POEMS, Walt Whitman. Generous sampling from *Leaves of Grass*. Twenty-four poems include "I Hear America Singing," "Song of the Open Road," "I Sing the Body Electric," "When Lilacs Last in the Dooryard Bloom'd," "O Captain! My Captain!"—all reprinted from an authoritative edition. Lists of titles and first lines. 128pp. 5³⁄₁₆ x 8¼. 26878-0 Pa. $1.00

CATALOG OF DOVER BOOKS

THE BEST TALES OF HOFFMANN, E. T. A. Hoffmann. 10 of Hoffmann's most important stories: "Nutcracker and the King of Mice," "The Golden Flowerpot," etc. 458pp. 5⅜ x 8½. 21793-0 Pa. $9.95

FROM FETISH TO GOD IN ANCIENT EGYPT, E. A. Wallis Budge. Rich detailed survey of Egyptian conception of "God" and gods, magic, cult of animals, Osiris, more. Also, superb English translations of hymns and legends. 240 illustrations. 545pp. 5⅜ x 8½. 25803-3 Pa. $11.95

FRENCH STORIES/CONTES FRANÇAIS: A Dual-Language Book, Wallace Fowlie. Ten stories by French masters, Voltaire to Camus: "Micromegas" by Voltaire; "The Atheist's Mass" by Balzac; "Minuet" by de Maupassant; "The Guest" by Camus, six more. Excellent English translations on facing pages. Also French-English vocabulary list, exercises, more. 352pp. 5⅜ x 8½. 26443-2 Pa. $8.95

CHICAGO AT THE TURN OF THE CENTURY IN PHOTOGRAPHS: 122 Historic Views from the Collections of the Chicago Historical Society, Larry A. Viskochil. Rare large-format prints offer detailed views of City Hall, State Street, the Loop, Hull House, Union Station, many other landmarks, circa 1904-1913. Introduction. Captions. Maps. 144pp. 9⅜ x 12¼. 24656-6 Pa. $12.95

OLD BROOKLYN IN EARLY PHOTOGRAPHS, 1865-1929, William Lee Younger. Luna Park, Gravesend race track, construction of Grand Army Plaza, moving of Hotel Brighton, etc. 157 previously unpublished photographs. 165pp. 8⅞ x 11¾. 23587-4 Pa. $13.95

THE MYTHS OF THE NORTH AMERICAN INDIANS, Lewis Spence. Rich anthology of the myths and legends of the Algonquins, Iroquois, Pawnees and Sioux, prefaced by an extensive historical and ethnological commentary. 36 illustrations. 480pp. 5⅜ x 8½. 25967-6 Pa. $8.95

AN ENCYCLOPEDIA OF BATTLES: Accounts of Over 1,560 Battles from 1479 B.C. to the Present, David Eggenberger. Essential details of every major battle in recorded history from the first battle of Megiddo in 1479 B.C. to Grenada in 1984. List of Battle Maps. New Appendix covering the years 1967-1984. Index. 99 illustrations. 544pp. 6½ x 9¼. 24913-1 Pa. $14.95

SAILING ALONE AROUND THE WORLD, Captain Joshua Slocum. First man to sail around the world, alone, in small boat. One of great feats of seamanship told in delightful manner. 67 illustrations. 294pp. 5⅜ x 8½. 20326-3 Pa. $5.95

ANARCHISM AND OTHER ESSAYS, Emma Goldman. Powerful, penetrating, prophetic essays on direct action, role of minorities, prison reform, puritan hypocrisy, violence, etc. 271pp. 5⅜ x 8½. 22484-8 Pa. $6.95

MYTHS OF THE HINDUS AND BUDDHISTS, Ananda K. Coomaraswamy and Sister Nivedita. Great stories of the epics; deeds of Krishna, Shiva, taken from puranas, Vedas, folk tales; etc. 32 illustrations. 400pp. 5⅜ x 8½. 21759-0 Pa. $10.95

BEYOND PSYCHOLOGY, Otto Rank. Fear of death, desire of immortality, nature of sexuality, social organization, creativity, according to Rankian system. 291pp. 5⅜ x 8½. 20485-5 Pa. $8.95

A THEOLOGICO-POLITICAL TREATISE, Benedict Spinoza. Also contains unfinished Political Treatise. Great classic on religious liberty, theory of government on common consent. R. Elwes translation. Total of 421pp. 5⅜ x 8½. 20249-6 Pa. $9.95

MY BONDAGE AND MY FREEDOM, Frederick Douglass. Born a slave, Douglass became outspoken force in antislavery movement. The best of Douglass' autobiographies. Graphic description of slave life. 464pp. 5⅜ x 8½. 22457-0 Pa. $8.95

FOLLOWING THE EQUATOR: A Journey Around the World, Mark Twain. Fascinating humorous account of 1897 voyage to Hawaii, Australia, India, New Zealand, etc. Ironic, bemused reports on peoples, customs, climate, flora and fauna, politics, much more. 197 illustrations. 720pp. 5⅜ x 8½. 26113-1 Pa. $15.95

THE PEOPLE CALLED SHAKERS, Edward D. Andrews. Definitive study of Shakers: origins, beliefs, practices, dances, social organization, furniture and crafts, etc. 33 illustrations. 351pp. 5⅜ x 8½. 21081-2 Pa. $8.95

THE MYTHS OF GREECE AND ROME, H. A. Guerber. A classic of mythology, generously illustrated, long prized for its simple, graphic, accurate retelling of the principal myths of Greece and Rome, and for its commentary on their origins and significance. With 64 illustrations by Michelangelo, Raphael, Titian, Rubens, Canova, Bernini and others. 480pp. 5⅜ x 8½. 27584-1 Pa. $9.95

PSYCHOLOGY OF MUSIC, Carl E. Seashore. Classic work discusses music as a medium from psychological viewpoint. Clear treatment of physical acoustics, auditory apparatus, sound perception, development of musical skills, nature of musical feeling, host of other topics. 88 figures. 408pp. 5⅜ x 8½. 21851-1 Pa. $10.95

THE PHILOSOPHY OF HISTORY, Georg W. Hegel. Great classic of Western thought develops concept that history is not chance but rational process, the evolution of freedom. 457pp. 5⅜ x 8½. 20112-0 Pa. $9.95

THE BOOK OF TEA, Kakuzo Okakura. Minor classic of the Orient: entertaining, charming explanation, interpretation of traditional Japanese culture in terms of tea ceremony. 94pp. 5⅜ x 8½. 20070-1 Pa. $3.95

LIFE IN ANCIENT EGYPT, Adolf Erman. Fullest, most thorough, detailed older account with much not in more recent books, domestic life, religion, magic, medicine, commerce, much more. Many illustrations reproduce tomb paintings, carvings, hieroglyphs, etc. 597pp. 5⅜ x 8½. 22632-8 Pa. $11.95

SUNDIALS, Their Theory and Construction, Albert Waugh. Far and away the best, most thorough coverage of ideas, mathematics concerned, types, construction, adjusting anywhere. Simple, nontechnical treatment allows even children to build several of these dials. Over 100 illustrations. 230pp. 5⅜ x 8½. 22947-5 Pa. $7.95

DYNAMICS OF FLUIDS IN POROUS MEDIA, Jacob Bear. For advanced students of ground water hydrology, soil mechanics and physics, drainage and irrigation engineering, and more. 335 illustrations. Exercises, with answers. 784pp. 6⅛ x 9¼. 65675-6 Pa. $19.95

SONGS OF EXPERIENCE: Facsimile Reproduction with 26 Plates in Full Color, William Blake. 26 full-color plates from a rare 1826 edition. Includes "The Tyger," "London," "Holy Thursday," and other poems. Printed text of poems. 48pp. 5¼ x 7. 24636-1 Pa. $4.95

OLD-TIME VIGNETTES IN FULL COLOR, Carol Belanger Grafton (ed.). Over 390 charming, often sentimental illustrations, selected from archives of Victorian graphics—pretty women posing, children playing, food, flowers, kittens and puppies, smiling cherubs, birds and butterflies, much more. All copyright-free. 48pp. 9¼ x 12¼. 27269-9 Pa. $5.95

PERSPECTIVE FOR ARTISTS, Rex Vicat Cole. Depth, perspective of sky and sea, shadows, much more, not usually covered. 391 diagrams, 81 reproductions of drawings and paintings. 279pp. 5⅜ x 8½. 22487-2 Pa. $6.95

DRAWING THE LIVING FIGURE, Joseph Sheppard. Innovative approach to artistic anatomy focuses on specifics of surface anatomy, rather than muscles and bones. Over 170 drawings of live models in front, back and side views, and in widely varying poses. Accompanying diagrams. 177 illustrations. Introduction. Index. 144pp. 8⅜ x11¼. 26723-7 Pa. $8.95

GOTHIC AND OLD ENGLISH ALPHABETS: 100 Complete Fonts, Dan X. Solo. Add power, elegance to posters, signs, other graphics with 100 stunning copyright-free alphabets: Blackstone, Dolbey, Germania, 97 more–including many lower-case, numerals, punctuation marks. 104pp. 8⅛ x 11. 24695-7 Pa. $8.95

HOW TO DO BEADWORK, Mary White. Fundamental book on craft from simple projects to five-bead chains and woven works. 106 illustrations. 142pp. 5⅜ x 8. 20697-1 Pa. $4.95

THE BOOK OF WOOD CARVING, Charles Marshall Sayers. Finest book for beginners discusses fundamentals and offers 34 designs. "Absolutely first rate . . . well thought out and well executed."–E. J. Tangerman. 118pp. 7¾ x 10⅝. 23654-4 Pa. $6.95

ILLUSTRATED CATALOG OF CIVIL WAR MILITARY GOODS: Union Army Weapons, Insignia, Uniform Accessories, and Other Equipment, Schuyler, Hartley, and Graham. Rare, profusely illustrated 1846 catalog includes Union Army uniform and dress regulations, arms and ammunition, coats, insignia, flags, swords, rifles, etc. 226 illustrations. 160pp. 9 x 12. 24939-5 Pa. $10.95

WOMEN'S FASHIONS OF THE EARLY 1900s: An Unabridged Republication of "New York Fashions, 1909," National Cloak & Suit Co. Rare catalog of mail-order fashions documents women's and children's clothing styles shortly after the turn of the century. Captions offer full descriptions, prices. Invaluable resource for fashion, costume historians. Approximately 725 illustrations. 128pp. 8⅜ x 11¼. 27276-1 Pa. $11.95

THE 1912 AND 1915 GUSTAV STICKLEY FURNITURE CATALOGS, Gustav Stickley. With over 200 detailed illustrations and descriptions, these two catalogs are essential reading and reference materials and identification guides for Stickley furniture. Captions cite materials, dimensions and prices. 112pp. 6½ x 9¼. 26676-1 Pa. $9.95

EARLY AMERICAN LOCOMOTIVES, John H. White, Jr. Finest locomotive engravings from early 19th century: historical (1804–74), main-line (after 1870), special, foreign, etc. 147 plates. 142pp. 11⅜ x 8¼. 22772-3 Pa. $10.95

THE TALL SHIPS OF TODAY IN PHOTOGRAPHS, Frank O. Braynard. Lavishly illustrated tribute to nearly 100 majestic contemporary sailing vessels: Amerigo Vespucci, Clearwater, Constitution, Eagle, Mayflower, Sea Cloud, Victory, many more. Authoritative captions provide statistics, background on each ship. 190 black-and-white photographs and illustrations. Introduction. 128pp. 8⅞ x 11¾. 27163-3 Pa. $13.95

EARLY NINETEENTH-CENTURY CRAFTS AND TRADES, Peter Stockham (ed.). Extremely rare 1807 volume describes to youngsters the crafts and trades of the day: brickmaker, weaver, dressmaker, bookbinder, ropemaker, saddler, many more. Quaint prose, charming illustrations for each craft. 20 black-and-white line illustrations. 192pp. 4⅝ x 6. 27293-1 Pa. $4.95

VICTORIAN FASHIONS AND COSTUMES FROM HARPER'S BAZAR, 1867–1898, Stella Blum (ed.). Day costumes, evening wear, sports clothes, shoes, hats, other accessories in over 1,000 detailed engravings. 320pp. 9⅜ x 12¼. 22990-4 Pa. $14.95

GUSTAV STICKLEY, THE CRAFTSMAN, Mary Ann Smith. Superb study surveys broad scope of Stickley's achievement, especially in architecture. Design philosophy, rise and fall of the Craftsman empire, descriptions and floor plans for many Craftsman houses, more. 86 black-and-white halftones. 31 line illustrations. Introduction 208pp. 6½ x 9¼. 27210-9 Pa. $9.95

THE LONG ISLAND RAIL ROAD IN EARLY PHOTOGRAPHS, Ron Ziel. Over 220 rare photos, informative text document origin (1844) and development of rail service on Long Island. Vintage views of early trains, locomotives, stations, passengers, crews, much more. Captions. 8⅞ x 11¾. 26301-0 Pa. $13.95

THE BOOK OF OLD SHIPS: From Egyptian Galleys to Clipper Ships, Henry B. Culver. Superb, authoritative history of sailing vessels, with 80 magnificent line illustrations. Galley, bark, caravel, longship, whaler, many more. Detailed, informative text on each vessel by noted naval historian. Introduction. 256pp. 5⅜ x 8½. 27332-6 Pa. $7.95

TEN BOOKS ON ARCHITECTURE, Vitruvius. The most important book ever written on architecture. Early Roman aesthetics, technology, classical orders, site selection, all other aspects. Morgan translation. 331pp. 5⅜ x 8½. 20645-9 Pa. $8.95

THE HUMAN FIGURE IN MOTION, Eadweard Muybridge. More than 4,500 stopped-action photos, in action series, showing undraped men, women, children jumping, lying down, throwing, sitting, wrestling, carrying, etc. 390pp. 7⅞ x 10⅝. 20204-6 Clothbd. $25.95

TREES OF THE EASTERN AND CENTRAL UNITED STATES AND CANADA, William M. Harlow. Best one-volume guide to 140 trees. Full descriptions, woodlore, range, etc. Over 600 illustrations. Handy size. 288pp. 4½ x 6⅜. 20395-6 Pa. $5.95

SONGS OF WESTERN BIRDS, Dr. Donald J. Borror. Complete song and call repertoire of 60 western species, including flycatchers, juncoes, cactus wrens, many more–includes fully illustrated booklet. Cassette and manual 99913-0 $8.95

GROWING AND USING HERBS AND SPICES, Milo Miloradovich. Versatile handbook provides all the information needed for cultivation and use of all the herbs and spices available in North America. 4 illustrations. Index. Glossary. 236pp. 5⅜ x 8½. 25058-X Pa. $6.95

BIG BOOK OF MAZES AND LABYRINTHS, Walter Shepherd. 50 mazes and labyrinths in all–classical, solid, ripple, and more–in one great volume. Perfect inexpensive puzzler for clever youngsters. Full solutions. 112pp. 8⅛ x 11. 22951-3 Pa. $4.95

PIANO TUNING, J. Cree Fischer. Clearest, best book for beginner, amateur. Simple repairs, raising dropped notes, tuning by easy method of flattened fifths. No previous skills needed. 4 illustrations. 201pp. 5⅜ x 8½.　　　23267-0 Pa. $6.95

A SOURCE BOOK IN THEATRICAL HISTORY, A. M. Nagler. Contemporary observers on acting, directing, make-up, costuming, stage props, machinery, scene design, from Ancient Greece to Chekhov. 611pp. 5⅜ x 8½.　　　20515-0 Pa. $12.95

THE COMPLETE NONSENSE OF EDWARD LEAR, Edward Lear. All nonsense limericks, zany alphabets, Owl and Pussycat, songs, nonsense botany, etc., illustrated by Lear. Total of 320pp. 5⅜ x 8½. (USO)　　　20167-8 Pa. $6.95

VICTORIAN PARLOUR POETRY: An Annotated Anthology, Michael R. Turner. 117 gems by Longfellow, Tennyson, Browning, many lesser-known poets. "The Village Blacksmith," "Curfew Must Not Ring Tonight," "Only a Baby Small," dozens more, often difficult to find elsewhere. Index of poets, titles, first lines. xxiii + 325pp. 5⅜ x 8¼.　　　27044-0 Pa. $8.95

DUBLINERS, James Joyce. Fifteen stories offer vivid, tightly focused observations of the lives of Dublin's poorer classes. At least one, "The Dead," is considered a masterpiece. Reprinted complete and unabridged from standard edition. 160pp. 5³⁄₁₆ x 8¼.　　　26870-5 Pa. $1.00

THE HAUNTED MONASTERY and THE CHINESE MAZE MURDERS, Robert van Gulik. Two full novels by van Gulik, set in 7th-century China, continue adventures of Judge Dee and his companions. An evil Taoist monastery, seemingly supernatural events; overgrown topiary maze hides strange crimes. 27 illustrations. 328pp. 5⅜ x 8½.　　　23502-5 Pa. $8.95

THE BOOK OF THE SACRED MAGIC OF ABRAMELIN THE MAGE, translated by S. MacGregor Mathers. Medieval manuscript of ceremonial magic. Basic document in Aleister Crowley, Golden Dawn groups. 268pp. 5⅜ x 8½.　　　23211-5 Pa. $8.95

NEW RUSSIAN-ENGLISH AND ENGLISH-RUSSIAN DICTIONARY, M. A. O'Brien. This is a remarkably handy Russian dictionary, containing a surprising amount of information, including over 70,000 entries. 366pp. 4½ x 6⅛.　　　20208-9 Pa. $9.95

HISTORIC HOMES OF THE AMERICAN PRESIDENTS, Second, Revised Edition, Irvin Haas. A traveler's guide to American Presidential homes, most open to the public, depicting and describing homes occupied by every American President from George Washington to George Bush. With visiting hours, admission charges, travel routes. 175 photographs. Index. 160pp. 8¼ x 11.　　　26751-2 Pa. $11.95

NEW YORK IN THE FORTIES, Andreas Feininger. 162 brilliant photographs by the well-known photographer, formerly with *Life* magazine. Commuters, shoppers, Times Square at night, much else from city at its peak. Captions by John von Hartz. 181pp. 9¼ x 10¾.　　　23585-8 Pa. $12.95

INDIAN SIGN LANGUAGE, William Tomkins. Over 525 signs developed by Sioux and other tribes. Written instructions and diagrams. Also 290 pictographs. 111pp. 6⅛ x 9¼.　　　22029-X Pa. $3.95

ANATOMY: A Complete Guide for Artists, Joseph Sheppard. A master of figure drawing shows artists how to render human anatomy convincingly. Over 460 illustrations. 224pp. 8⅜ x 11¼. 27279-6 Pa. $10.95

MEDIEVAL CALLIGRAPHY: Its History and Technique, Marc Drogin. Spirited history, comprehensive instruction manual covers 13 styles (ca. 4th century thru 15th). Excellent photographs; directions for duplicating medieval techniques with modern tools. 224pp. 8⅜ x 11¼. 26142-5 Pa. $11.95

DRIED FLOWERS: How to Prepare Them, Sarah Whitlock and Martha Rankin. Complete instructions on how to use silica gel, meal and borax, perlite aggregate, sand and borax, glycerine and water to create attractive permanent flower arrangements. 12 illustrations. 32pp. 5⅜ x 8½. 21802-3 Pa. $1.00

EASY-TO-MAKE BIRD FEEDERS FOR WOODWORKERS, Scott D. Campbell. Detailed, simple-to-use guide for designing, constructing, caring for and using feeders. Text, illustrations for 12 classic and contemporary designs. 96pp. 5⅜ x 8½. 25847-5 Pa. $2.95

SCOTTISH WONDER TALES FROM MYTH AND LEGEND, Donald A. Mackenzie. 16 lively tales tell of giants rumbling down mountainsides, of a magic wand that turns stone pillars into warriors, of gods and goddesses, evil hags, powerful forces and more. 240pp. 5⅜ x 8½. 29677-6 Pa. $6.95

THE HISTORY OF UNDERCLOTHES, C. Willett Cunnington and Phyllis Cunnington. Fascinating, well-documented survey covering six centuries of English undergarments, enhanced with over 100 illustrations: 12th-century laced-up bodice, footed long drawers (1795), 19th-century bustles, 19th-century corsets for men, Victorian "bust improvers," much more. 272pp. 5⅝ x 8¼. 27124-2 Pa. $9.95

ARTS AND CRAFTS FURNITURE: The Complete Brooks Catalog of 1912, Brooks Manufacturing Co. Photos and detailed descriptions of more than 150 now very collectible furniture designs from the Arts and Crafts movement depict davenports, settees, buffets, desks, tables, chairs, bedsteads, dressers and more, all built of solid, quarter-sawed oak. Invaluable for students and enthusiasts of antiques, Americana and the decorative arts. 80pp. 6½ x 9¼. 27471-3 Pa. $7.95

HOW WE INVENTED THE AIRPLANE: An Illustrated History, Orville Wright. Fascinating firsthand account covers early experiments, construction of planes and motors, first flights, much more. Introduction and commentary by Fred C. Kelly. 76 photographs. 96pp. 8¼ x 11. 25662-6 Pa. $8.95

THE ARTS OF THE SAILOR: Knotting, Splicing and Ropework, Hervey Garrett Smith. Indispensable shipboard reference covers tools, basic knots and useful hitches; handsewing and canvas work, more. Over 100 illustrations. Delightful reading for sea lovers. 256pp. 5⅜ x 8½. 26440-8 Pa. $7.95

FRANK LLOYD WRIGHT'S FALLINGWATER: The House and Its History, Second, Revised Edition, Donald Hoffmann. A total revision–both in text and illustrations–of the standard document on Fallingwater, the boldest, most personal architectural statement of Wright's mature years, updated with valuable new material from the recently opened Frank Lloyd Wright Archives. "Fascinating"–*The New York Times*. 116 illustrations. 128pp. 9¼ x 10¾. 27430-6 Pa. $11.95

AUTOBIOGRAPHY: The Story of My Experiments with Truth, Mohandas K. Gandhi. Boyhood, legal studies, purification, the growth of the Satyagraha (nonviolent protest) movement. Critical, inspiring work of the man responsible for the freedom of India. 480pp. 5⅜ x 8½. (USO)   24593-4 Pa. $8.95

CELTIC MYTHS AND LEGENDS, T. W. Rolleston. Masterful retelling of Irish and Welsh stories and tales. Cuchulain, King Arthur, Deirdre, the Grail, many more. First paperback edition. 58 full-page illustrations. 512pp. 5⅜ x 8½.   26507-2 Pa. $9.95

THE PRINCIPLES OF PSYCHOLOGY, William James. Famous long course complete, unabridged. Stream of thought, time perception, memory, experimental methods; great work decades ahead of its time. 94 figures. 1,391pp. 5⅜ x 8½. 2-vol. set.
Vol. I: 20381-6 Pa. $12.95
Vol. II: 20382-4 Pa. $12.95

THE WORLD AS WILL AND REPRESENTATION, Arthur Schopenhauer. Definitive English translation of Schopenhauer's life work, correcting more than 1,000 errors, omissions in earlier translations. Translated by E. F. J. Payne. Total of 1,269pp. 5⅜ x 8½. 2-vol. set.   Vol. 1: 21761-2 Pa. $11.95
Vol. 2: 21762-0 Pa. $11.95

MAGIC AND MYSTERY IN TIBET, Madame Alexandra David-Neel. Experiences among lamas, magicians, sages, sorcerers, Bonpa wizards. A true psychic discovery. 32 illustrations. 321pp. 5⅜ x 8½. (USO)   22682-4 Pa. $8.95

THE EGYPTIAN BOOK OF THE DEAD, E. A. Wallis Budge. Complete reproduction of Ani's papyrus, finest ever found. Full hieroglyphic text, interlinear transliteration, word-for-word translation, smooth translation. 533pp. 6½ x 9¼.
21866-X Pa. $10.95

MATHEMATICS FOR THE NONMATHEMATICIAN, Morris Kline. Detailed, college-level treatment of mathematics in cultural and historical context, with numerous exercises. Recommended Reading Lists. Tables. Numerous figures. 641pp. 5⅜ x 8½.
24823-2 Pa. $11.95

THEORY OF WING SECTIONS: Including a Summary of Airfoil Data, Ira H. Abbott and A. E. von Doenhoff. Concise compilation of subsonic aerodynamic characteristics of NACA wing sections, plus description of theory. 350pp. of tables. 693pp. 5⅜ x 8½.   60586-8 Pa. $14.95

THE RIME OF THE ANCIENT MARINER, Gustave Doré, S. T. Coleridge. Doré's finest work; 34 plates capture moods, subtleties of poem. Flawless full-size reproductions printed on facing pages with authoritative text of poem. "Beautiful. Simply beautiful."–*Publisher's Weekly.* 77pp. 9¼ x 12.   22305-1 Pa. $6.95

NORTH AMERICAN INDIAN DESIGNS FOR ARTISTS AND CRAFTSPEOPLE, Eva Wilson. Over 360 authentic copyright-free designs adapted from Navajo blankets, Hopi pottery, Sioux buffalo hides, more. Geometrics, symbolic figures, plant and animal motifs, etc. 128pp. 8⅜ x 11. (EUK)   25341-4 Pa. $8.95

SCULPTURE: Principles and Practice, Louis Slobodkin. Step-by-step approach to clay, plaster, metals, stone; classical and modern. 253 drawings, photos. 255pp. 8⅛ x 11.
22960-2 Pa. $10.95

CATALOG OF DOVER BOOKS

PHOTOGRAPHIC SKETCHBOOK OF THE CIVIL WAR, Alexander Gardner. 100 photos taken on field during the Civil War. Famous shots of Manassas Harper's Ferry, Lincoln, Richmond, slave pens, etc. 244pp. 10⅝ x 8¼. 22731-6 Pa. $9.95

FIVE ACRES AND INDEPENDENCE, Maurice G. Kains. Great back-to-the-land classic explains basics of self-sufficient farming. The one book to get. 95 illustrations. 397pp. 5⅜ x 8½. 20974-1 Pa. $7.95

SONGS OF EASTERN BIRDS, Dr. Donald J. Borror. Songs and calls of 60 species most common to eastern U.S.: warblers, woodpeckers, flycatchers, thrushes, larks, many more in high-quality recording. Cassette and manual 99912-2 $8.95

A MODERN HERBAL, Margaret Grieve. Much the fullest, most exact, most useful compilation of herbal material. Gigantic alphabetical encyclopedia, from aconite to zedoary, gives botanical information, medical properties, folklore, economic uses, much else. Indispensable to serious reader. 161 illustrations. 888pp. 6½ x 9¼. 2-vol. set. (USO) Vol. I: 22798-7 Pa. $9.95
Vol. II: 22799-5 Pa. $9.95

HIDDEN TREASURE MAZE BOOK, Dave Phillips. Solve 34 challenging mazes accompanied by heroic tales of adventure. Evil dragons, people-eating plants, blood-thirsty giants, many more dangerous adversaries lurk at every twist and turn. 34 mazes, stories, solutions. 48pp. 8¼ x 11. 24566-7 Pa. $2.95

LETTERS OF W. A. MOZART, Wolfgang A. Mozart. Remarkable letters show bawdy wit, humor, imagination, musical insights, contemporary musical world; includes some letters from Leopold Mozart. 276pp. 5⅜ x 8½. 22859-2 Pa. $7.95

BASIC PRINCIPLES OF CLASSICAL BALLET, Agrippina Vaganova. Great Russian theoretician, teacher explains methods for teaching classical ballet. 118 illustrations. 175pp. 5⅜ x 8½. 22036-2 Pa. $5.95

THE JUMPING FROG, Mark Twain. Revenge edition. The original story of The Celebrated Jumping Frog of Calaveras County, a hapless French translation, and Twain's hilarious "retranslation" from the French. 12 illustrations. 66pp. 5⅜ x 8½. 22686-7 Pa. $3.95

BEST REMEMBERED POEMS, Martin Gardner (ed.). The 126 poems in this superb collection of 19th- and 20th-century British and American verse range from Shelley's "To a Skylark" to the impassioned "Renascence" of Edna St. Vincent Millay and to Edward Lear's whimsical "The Owl and the Pussycat." 224pp. 5⅜ x 8½. 27165-X Pa. $4.95

COMPLETE SONNETS, William Shakespeare. Over 150 exquisite poems deal with love, friendship, the tyranny of time, beauty's evanescence, death and other themes in language of remarkable power, precision and beauty. Glossary of archaic terms. 80pp. 5 3/16 x 8¼. 26686-9 Pa. $1.00

BODIES IN A BOOKSHOP, R. T. Campbell. Challenging mystery of blackmail and murder with ingenious plot and superbly drawn characters. In the best tradition of British suspense fiction. 192pp. 5⅜ x 8½. 24720-1 Pa. $6.95

THE WIT AND HUMOR OF OSCAR WILDE, Alvin Redman (ed.). More than 1,000 ripostes, paradoxes, wisecracks: Work is the curse of the drinking classes; I can resist everything except temptation; etc. 258pp. 5⅜ x 8½. 20602-5 Pa. $5.95

SHAKESPEARE LEXICON AND QUOTATION DICTIONARY, Alexander Schmidt. Full definitions, locations, shades of meaning in every word in plays and poems. More than 50,000 exact quotations. 1,485pp. 6½ x 9¼. 2-vol. set.
Vol. 1: 22726-X Pa. $16.95
Vol. 2: 22727-8 Pa. $16.95

SELECTED POEMS, Emily Dickinson. Over 100 best-known, best-loved poems by one of America's foremost poets, reprinted from authoritative early editions. No comparable edition at this price. Index of first lines. 64pp. 5³⁄₁₆ x 8¼.
26466-1 Pa. $1.00

CELEBRATED CASES OF JUDGE DEE (DEE GOONG AN), translated by Robert van Gulik. Authentic 18th-century Chinese detective novel; Dee and associates solve three interlocked cases. Led to van Gulik's own stories with same characters. Extensive introduction. 9 illustrations. 237pp. 5⅜ x 8½. 23337-5 Pa. $6.95

THE MALLEUS MALEFICARUM OF KRAMER AND SPRENGER, translated by Montague Summers. Full text of most important witchhunter's "bible," used by both Catholics and Protestants. 278pp. 6⅝ x 10. 22802-9 Pa. $12.95

SPANISH STORIES/CUENTOS ESPAÑOLES: A Dual-Language Book, Angel Flores (ed.). Unique format offers 13 great stories in Spanish by Cervantes, Borges, others. Faithful English translations on facing pages. 352pp. 5⅜ x 8½.
25399-6 Pa. $8.95

THE CHICAGO WORLD'S FAIR OF 1893: A Photographic Record, Stanley Appelbaum (ed.). 128 rare photos show 200 buildings, Beaux-Arts architecture, Midway, original Ferris Wheel, Edison's kinetoscope, more. Architectural emphasis; full text. 116pp. 8¼ x 11. 23990-X Pa. $9.95

OLD QUEENS, N.Y., IN EARLY PHOTOGRAPHS, Vincent F. Seyfried and William Asadorian. Over 160 rare photographs of Maspeth, Jamaica, Jackson Heights, and other areas. Vintage views of DeWitt Clinton mansion, 1939 World's Fair and more. Captions. 192pp. 8⅞ x 11. 26358-4 Pa. $12.95

CAPTURED BY THE INDIANS: 15 Firsthand Accounts, 1750-1870, Frederick Drimmer. Astounding true historical accounts of grisly torture, bloody conflicts, relentless pursuits, miraculous escapes and more, by people who lived to tell the tale. 384pp. 5⅜ x 8½. 24901-8 Pa. $8.95

THE WORLD'S GREAT SPEECHES, Lewis Copeland and Lawrence W. Lamm (eds.). Vast collection of 278 speeches of Greeks to 1970. Powerful and effective models; unique look at history. 842pp. 5⅜ x 8½. 20468-5 Pa. $14.95

THE BOOK OF THE SWORD, Sir Richard F. Burton. Great Victorian scholar/adventurer's eloquent, erudite history of the "queen of weapons"–from prehistory to early Roman Empire. Evolution and development of early swords, variations (sabre, broadsword, cutlass, scimitar, etc.), much more. 336pp. 6⅛ x 9¼.
25434-8 Pa. $9.95

THE INFLUENCE OF SEA POWER UPON HISTORY, 1660–1783, A. T. Mahan. Influential classic of naval history and tactics still used as text in war colleges. First paperback edition. 4 maps. 24 battle plans. 640pp. 5⅜ x 8½. 25509-3 Pa. $12.95

THE STORY OF THE TITANIC AS TOLD BY ITS SURVIVORS, Jack Winocour (ed.). What it was really like. Panic, despair, shocking inefficiency, and a little heroism. More thrilling than any fictional account. 26 illustrations. 320pp. 5⅜ x 8½. 20610-6 Pa. $8.95

FAIRY AND FOLK TALES OF THE IRISH PEASANTRY, William Butler Yeats (ed.). Treasury of 64 tales from the twilight world of Celtic myth and legend: "The Soul Cages," "The Kildare Pooka," "King O'Toole and his Goose," many more. Introduction and Notes by W. B. Yeats. 352pp. 5⅜ x 8½. 26941-8 Pa. $8.95

BUDDHIST MAHAYANA TEXTS, E. B. Cowell and Others (eds.). Superb, accurate translations of basic documents in Mahayana Buddhism, highly important in history of religions. The Buddha-karita of Asvaghosha, Larger Sukhavativyuha, more. 448pp. 5⅜ x 8½. 25552-2 Pa. $9.95

ONE TWO THREE . . . INFINITY: Facts and Speculations of Science, George Gamow. Great physicist's fascinating, readable overview of contemporary science: number theory, relativity, fourth dimension, entropy, genes, atomic structure, much more. 128 illustrations. Index. 352pp. 5⅜ x 8½. 25664-2 Pa. $8.95

ENGINEERING IN HISTORY, Richard Shelton Kirby, et al. Broad, nontechnical survey of history's major technological advances: birth of Greek science, industrial revolution, electricity and applied science, 20th-century automation, much more. 181 illustrations. ". . . excellent . . ."–Isis. Bibliography. vii + 530pp. 5⅜ x 8¼. 26412-2 Pa. $14.95

DALÍ ON MODERN ART: The Cuckolds of Antiquated Modern Art, Salvador Dalí. Influential painter skewers modern art and its practitioners. Outrageous evaluations of Picasso, Cézanne, Turner, more. 15 renderings of paintings discussed. 44 calligraphic decorations by Dalí. 96pp. 5⅜ x 8½. (USO) 29220-7 Pa. $4.95

ANTIQUE PLAYING CARDS: A Pictorial History, Henry René D'Allemagne. Over 900 elaborate, decorative images from rare playing cards (14th–20th centuries): Bacchus, death, dancing dogs, hunting scenes, royal coats of arms, players cheating, much more. 96pp. 9¼ x 12¼. 29265-7 Pa. $11.95

MAKING FURNITURE MASTERPIECES: 30 Projects with Measured Drawings, Franklin H. Gottshall. Step-by-step instructions, illustrations for constructing handsome, useful pieces, among them a Sheraton desk, Chippendale chair, Spanish desk, Queen Anne table and a William and Mary dressing mirror. 224pp. 8⅛ x 11¼. 29338-6 Pa. $13.95

THE FOSSIL BOOK: A Record of Prehistoric Life, Patricia V. Rich et al. Profusely illustrated definitive guide covers everything from single-celled organisms and dinosaurs to birds and mammals and the interplay between climate and man. Over 1,500 illustrations. 760pp. 7½ x 10⅛. 29371-8 Pa. $29.95

Prices subject to change without notice.

Available at your book dealer or write for free catalog to Dept. GI, Dover Publications, Inc., 31 East 2nd St., Mineola, N.Y. 11501. Dover publishes more than 500 books each year on science, elementary and advanced mathematics, biology, music, art, literary history, social sciences and other areas.